Mediating the Power of Buddhas

SUNY series in Buddhist Studies
Matthew Kapstein, editor

Mediating the Power of Buddhas

Ritual in the *Mañjuśrīmūlakalpa*

Glenn Wallis

State University of New York Press

Published by
State University of New York Press, Albany

Printed in the United States of America

For information, address State University of New York Press,
90 State Street, Suite 700, Albany, NY 12207

Production by Diane Ganeles
Marketing by Fran Keneston

Library of Congress Cataloging-in-Publication Data

Wallis, Glenn.
Mediating the power of Buddhas : ritual in the Mañjuśrīmūlakalpa / Glenn Wallis.
p. cm. — (SUNY series in Buddhist studies)
Includes index.
ISBN 0-7914-5411-8 (alk. paper) — ISBN 0-7914-5412-6 (pbk. : alk. paper)
1. Tripiṭaka. Sūtrapiṭaka. Tantra. Mañjuśrīmūlakalpa—Criticism, interpretation, etc. I. Title. II. Series.

BQ2180 .M347 2002
294.3'85—dc21 2001049443

10 9 8 7 6 5 4 3 2 1

This work is for Friederike, Alexandra,
and Mia, who give it all meaning.

Contents

Preface

This book is about a text, a ritual, and a reader. It is also about an abiding concern of Buddhists—one that has persisted from the earliest days of Buddhism, among the small group of mendicants surrounding Śākyamuni in a corner of northeastern India, to the present day, throughout the world among variegated groups of Buddhists.

The text is called the *Mañjuśrīmūlakalpa*, *The Primary Ritual Ordinance of Mañjuśrī*. The *Mañjuśrīmūlakalpa* is an Indian work, written in a somewhat unconventional form of Sanskrit. It is difficult to determine when and where it was written, but a working estimate would be the eighth century in the east. This places the text in what is referred to as the Pāla era of Indian history. The Pālas controlled the areas comprising roughly Bengal and Bihār from ca. 760–1142. It was in the eighth century that texts like the *Mañjuśrīmūlakalpa* began to be composed by adherents of the major Hindu and Buddhist communities of India. These texts were manuals that recorded the ritual knowledge necessary for living in the religious worlds engendered by those communities.

The rituals recorded in the *Mañjuśrīmūlakalpa* were seen by Buddhists of later centuries as being characteristically tantric; and so even today the *Mañjuśrīmūlakalpa* is unquestioningly classed, by Tibetans, Nepalis, and Westerners alike, as an early instance of Vajrayāna literature. If we put aside such pre-interpretive ordering principles, however, a more ambiguous picture emerges. While the rituals do conform to what is generally understood as Vajrayāna, the Buddhist world of the rituals looks decisively Mahāyāna. It might be, then, that in studying the *Mañjuśrīmūlakalpa* we are glimpsing into a formative period in Buddhist history, a moment in time that lay on the cusp of what would become two major, distinctive thrusts.

Who was the reader of such a text? The *Mañjuśrīmūlakalpa* refers to its reader as a *sādhaka*, one who *practices* the rituals, and thereby *realizes* his ultimate potential (as a *buddha*). Hence, a *sādhaka* is one who aims to perfect himself by means of both the actions and the knowledge recorded in the text. On the basis of what we know about medieval Indian society and culture, it might be possible to hypothesize about the historical *sādhaka*/reader of the

Mañjuśrīmūlakalpa. When I look for this reader though, I discern only dim, shifting shadows—little worth noting, I think. I would prefer therefore to leave that project to a historian. My concern in this study is to examine the reader who is right before my eyes, as I read: the reader *in the text*. This reader remains hypothetical, yet we (readers of the text) have access to him. Because the instructions of the text are admonishment and rhetorical argumentation, they constitute strategies for forming the human dispositions deemed necessary for the text to exercise its claims on the real reader. Consequently, by attending carefully to the workings of the text itself, this internal reader—the reader as textual construct—can be discerned.

The *Mañjuśrīmūlakalpa* presents a solution to a persistent question posed by the critics of Buddhism as well as by Buddhists themselves. This question concerns the accessibility of a *buddha's* power in the world. Some Buddhists, notably philosophers and their commentators, have grappled with the very coherence of such a possibility. Viewing the question from a logical perspective, it has been necessary for such systematic thinkers to reconcile the apparent inconsistency ensuing from the two essential qualities deemed definitive of a *buddha*. A *buddha* is one who, by virtue of his awareness of the nature of reality, is completely liberated from the life-impelling force of mental defilements, and is thus beyond the scope of our world; *and* he is one who, by virtue of his profound compassion, is naturally compelled to continue engagement with beings still delusively ensnared in the world. Logically, these two qualities are at odds. Not all Buddhists, however, have sought a solution to the dilemma of accessing a *buddha's* power on the basis of logical or epistemological theory. Rather, some Buddhists have sought an imaginative-cultic solution. Relics, statues, paintings, architectural monuments, books, remembrance, meditation, and visualization have, at various times and in various places, been held to be the most effective means of rendering present the otherwise inaccessible or obscured power that accompanies a *buddha*. In this book, I trace one means that has served as such a vehicle of enlightened presence.[1]

In my exploration of the *Mañjuśrīmūlakalpa*, I have sought to sustain a perspective that is simultaneously critical and appreciative. The *Mañjuśrīmūlakalpa* posits a world; a world, moreover, which its serious readers aspire to realize, and in which they seek to act meaningfully. The conceptual bases of such worlds of religious literature, however, are too easily made to appear stunted and disfigured by the light of rationality, making the actions of believers appear foolish. The job of the student of a religion, then, is certainly not completed once he has evaluated the propositions on which those worlds and those actions are posited. Like a believer, the student is often challenged by the data itself to venture beyond the logically possible, or the empirically verifiable. But unlike the believer, the student's primary vehicle is not faith, but the critical intellect. I am using "intellect" here in the old-fashioned sense of "the understanding." An intellectual encounter is one that employs reason and critical thought, but also imagination and appreciation, to move continuously toward understanding. The first job of a student of a text like the *Mañjuśrīmūlakalpa*, or of a religion in general, is well stated with Wittgenstein's dictum: "Don't think, look!" Don't allow the customs of a discipline or the terms of a methodology to determine the limits of intelligibility. If you do, you will likely think yourself into the view that the claims, worlds, rituals, and so on, of a religion are instances of unsophisticated thought, or of bad science in need of exposure. It is better to make an effort to look, and try to see how these things function and are used in the lives of practitioners.

Because it is a study of a form of Buddhism that has, in the past twelve hundred years, spread from medieval India to Nepal, Tibet, Japan, and North America, this book should offer something of interest to scholars of religion as well as to those engaged in the practice of Buddhism. With the latter in mind, I have put most of the textual apparatus in the indices. Some sections of chapter 1, however, contain data that, although important for establishing certain claims that I am making about the date, style, genre, and so forth, of the *Mañjuśrīmūlakalpa*, can be skipped over by the nonspecialist without losing the gist of my argument. Section 1.3.3 is a good example of this: the point of the argument should be clear enough from the introductory paragraphs; so the technical lists that follow can be passed over by the nonspecialist reader.

I would like to direct two points here to Buddhist studies scholars. I have included transliterations of the Sanskrit and Tibetan passages translated in the book. I want to emphasize here that my translations of the *Mañjuśrīmūlakalpa* are based solely on the Sanskrit. The Tibetan translation often proved illuminating in those cases where the Sanskrit text was particularly difficult; and it is for this reason that I consulted the Tibetan and included a transliteration of it. A close comparison between the Sanskrit edition and the Tibetan translations—the latter of which there are in fact several—was outside the scope of this study. Such an investigation, however, is a desideratum for the study of the *Mañjuśrīmūlakalpa*. The difficulty of the Sanskrit usually lay with the fact that it is not standard, and is often inconsistent in its own peculiar grammar and morphology. This should be kept in mind by those consulting the transliterations in the index. The second point concerns the lack of "Mañjuśrī literature" treated in this study. By that I mean texts held by Tibetan Buddhist communities past and present and Western scholarly communities to comprise a "cycle" of texts that have the *bodhisattva* Mañjuśrī as a central figure. In this study, I am concerned with tracing the ritual world of a single text. I think that the best way of going about this is to attend to that single text's own allusions and direct references to other sources. Enough of these are present in the *Mañjuśrīmūlakalpa* to fashion a historically responsible and accurate reconstruction of the text's ritual world.

Acknowledgments

In matters of reading, writing, and thinking about the issues addressed in this book, I am most indebted to Charles Hallisey. If not for him, it is possible that I would have never heard of the *Mañjuśrīmūlakalpa*, probable that I would have never read it, and certain that I would not have understood a single word of it. I hope that the influence of his broad knowledge and incisive thought remains visible in this work.

It was also my good fortune to have Leonard van der Kuijp and Stephanie Jamison read through an earlier version of the book. The present work has benefited from their numerous suggestions concerning style, line of argument, and translation. Friederike Baer-Wallis, my wife, also read through drafts at every stage, offering challenges and discerning advice on matters intellectual and practical. I am grateful to Jens-Uwe Hartmann and Kidder Smith, who gave me extensive feedback on the section on *mantras*, making numerous suggestions for improvement. This section was previously published by the *Journal of the International Association of Buddhist Studies* (volume 24, number 1, 2001) under the title "The Remains of the Buddha: *mantra* in the Mañjuśrīmūlakalpa." The late Masatoshi Nagatomi prodded, provoked, and warmly guided me in the earliest stages of this work, and I am thankful to him for that. I would also like to express my gratitude to Phyllis Granoff and Ronald Grimes for stimulating "conversations" (via e-mail). My contact with these scholars precipitated crucial breakthroughs in my understanding of both the rituals of the text and of the very idea of "ritual." Kurtis Schaeffer kindly corrected the transliterated Tibetan text. Finally, I offer my gratitude to Matthew Kapstein, the editor of the SUNY Buddhist studies series, and Nancy Ellegate of SUNY Press for their encouragement and counsel in seeing this into print.

My parents, Robert Wallis and Joan Wallis, have offered me indispensable emotional and financial support along the way. For that, I convey my deep appreciation to them.

CHAPTER 1

Introduction

1.1 Aims

The aim of this study is to recover and analyze, on the basis of the *Mañjuśrīmūlakalpa*, a specific mode of practice that was available to Indian Buddhists in the early medieval period. This study seeks, furthermore, to demonstrate that the principle underlying this practice was the assumption of the persistence of the Buddha's power in the world, and that the design of the practice was to enable the practitioner to mediate that power and manipulate it toward particular ends. Because the practice is enclosed within a specific rhetorical framework, namely, a text, that text itself comprises a concurrent object of this study. The text is viewed here as an aspect of the practice in itself, its strategies for describing the rituals as intrinsic to the nature of those rituals. In other words, the *Mañjuśrīmūlakalpa* is taken to be an additional datum, and not, strictly speaking, a "window" onto or a record of the past. As a document of ritual activity, the *Mañjuśrīmūlakalpa* is similar to a doctored photograph.

The *Mañjuśrīmūlakalpa's* treatment of practice exhibits a concern with four themes in particular. These four are *darkness, disclosure, transformation,* and *totality*. The authors' reasoning concerning these can be summed up as follows. The men and women of the world are engulfed by moral and mental darkness. This darkness prevents them from perceiving the enlightened power of the Buddha at work in the universe. There are means, however, by which this power can be disclosed. The text reveals these means. In employing these means—ritual and cultic in nature—the practitioner is transformed into a being of power himself or herself. The disclosure of the text and the transformation of the practitioner represent the culmination of India's religious history.

A central contention of this study is that the *Mañjuśrīmūlakalpa* posits a world, or, as Richard Davis calls it, a "ritual universe,"[1] and that successful practice of the rituals depends on the practitioner's ability to enter fully into that world. This "ritual universe" is a particularized world, permeated by the cosmological and metaphysical assumptions operating in the text; the rituals, grounded in these assumptions, constitute the actions by which these are, in turn, realized. It is a world held by its proponents to be ontologically superior to that which is known through other, insufficient sources of knowledge—other texts, communities, teachers, and modes of apprehension. The efficacy of the practice is derived, then, from this dynamic between action and knowledge.

I am using the term "practice" in both a narrow and broad sense. Narrowly, "practice" refers to a system of formalized, prescribed, sequential, and generally repetitive activity. In this sense, "practice" is synonymous with the colloquial usage of "ritual." For instance, lighting incense, prostrating and then reciting three times the three refuges before an image of the Buddha every morning and evening is a form of practice. In a broader sense, "practice" signifies the wider range of ritualized activities surrounding such a ritual. These surrounding practices, furthermore, create the conditions that make successful practice, narrowly construed, possible. In the *Mañjuśrīmūlakalpa*, three such practices are imagining the cosmos presented in, and presupposed by, the text, creating the object of worship, and becoming an adept. Each of these practices is localized in, respectively, the assembly (*sannipātamaṇḍala*), the primary cult object (*paṭa*), and the practitioner (*sādhaka*). In this study, I analyze these three "locations" as a means of illustrating the mode of practice taught in the *Mañjuśrīmūlakalpa*.

Throughout, the *Mañjuśrīmūlakalpa* moves between these various locations, or spaces. In this sense, the *Mañjuśrīmūlakalpa's* manner of argumentation can be said to be spatial. The text does not offer logical propositions in order to substantiate its claims of power and of superiority over other forms of practice. Rather, it is concerned with defining spaces and prescribing the activity that should occur in those spaces. It is within these presentations of space and activity that power and superiority are established. In each instance, the space articulated is a purified area where power is mediated through ritualized practice and relationship. There is, for instance, the circle of the initiation *maṇḍala,* drawn on the ground, where the *sādhaka*, by means of a specific rite of consecration, forms a special relationship with his teacher and with the Buddha, enabling him to recite *mantras* of a special potency. As sonic embodiments of *buddhas* and *bodhisattvas*, even these *mantras* are presented as spaces in the *Mañjuśrīmūlakalpa:* they are forms to be filled by the presence of enlightened forces. The text, furthermore, defines the extraordinary space within any given ritually delineated area—such as a solitary field, riverbank, *caitya*, or mountaintop—where the Buddha's power manifests in a particularly concentrated manner. This space is the *paṭa*. As central as it is to the cult of the *Mañjuśrīmūlakalpa*, however, the *paṭa* is a refractive space, reflecting an even greater domain of power: the space of the Ākaniṣṭha heaven serving as the present realm of Śākyamuni and as the origin of his teaching.

Studies of practices, or rituals, whether based on anthropological fieldwork or on texts, are typically descriptive. In this study, such an approach, though not completely incompatible with the nature of my source text, would severely circumscribe our use of the text. For, although extensive, the *Mañjuśrīmūlakalpa* generally offers only formulaic descriptions of ritual per se. It might seem paradoxical that a seven-hundred page ritual ordinance would frustrate an attempt to classify and delineate the very practices that it is promulgating. The fact that this is so, however, is indicative of what the text does, how it does it, and, therefore, of how it might be fruitfully studied. In short, my study of the *Mañjuśrīmūlakalpa* proceeds under the premise that the *Mañjuśrīmūlakalpa* is a text that primarily *indicates*—simultaneously serves as a sign for and reveals—the presence of enlightened power within the ritual world of the practitioner, and that it does this by *demonstrating* the mediating function of the elements of the rituals. The text evinces a concern with broad demonstrations of power, and only secondarily with explications of ritualized actions—and practically no concern whatsoever with philosophical justifications. With this intention in mind, the authors of the text took much for granted, assuming as axiomatic basic structures, both formal and theoretical. The text they produced instead emphasizes what Friedhelm Hardy calls "the unrestrained creative exuberance and the spirit of experimentation underlying" India's ritual literature.[2] For this reason, my goal of analyzing a mode of Buddhist practice on the basis of the *Mañjuśrīmūlakalpa* is best approached through the "experiments"—the innovations brought to bear on common structures—that are worked out in the text. These statements, however, involve propositions and assumptions on my part that underlie my understanding of the *Mañjuśrīmūlakalpa* and its practices, and which, therefore, constitute the guiding ideas of this study as a whole. Therefore, I will try to clarify what I mean here. I will do so by focusing on the narrow sense of the term "practice."

The term *practice* in this study is a translation of the *Mañjuśrīmūlakalpa*'s own term, *caryā*. In the *Mañjuśrīmūlakalpa, caryā* refers to a system of formalized, prescribed, and sequential activity. In this sense, *practice* is synonymous with "ritual," or ritualized activity. The term encompasses several additional terms. These can be grouped into two orders. The first order consists of *karma* (activity), *sādhana* (effecting rituals), *puraścaraṇa* (preliminary practices), *pūrvasevā* (prerequisite worship), *dhyāna* (contemplative visualization). At this level of order, there is nothing remarkable or distinctive about the practice promulgated in the *Mañjuśrīmūlakalpa*. It is an example of the economy of forms, whereby prior modes and theoretical bases of cultic activity are preserved.[3] A description of the practice at this level illustrates that it may have conceivably occurred in virtually any period, region, social class or cultic group in India's history. It will be useful to describe the bare ritual in this regard: early in the morning, a man, who has previously received initiation and instruction by a master, carries a rolled-up cloth painting and a bag containing small lamps, bottles of camphor and sandalwood oil, incense, rice and other implements to a desolate field. There, after bathing in a nearby pond, he cleans the area and arranges the cloth on the ground. Sitting on a mound of grass in front of this cloth, he repeatedly recites a short phrase, a *mantra*. With a pleasant voice he sings hymns of praise to visualized enlightened beings and deities. Finally, he may light a small fire before the cloth and make oblations of wooden sticks or flowers.

Devoid of any description of particular features, the most basic questions concerning this practice arise: Does it describe the activity of a Vedic brahman in 1000 B.C.E. outside of a farming village, on the banks of the river Sarasvatī in the Punjab? Does it occur only occasionally, in a field outside of the modern city of Varanasi? Was the practitioner a wealthy landowner, a scholar, a monk, an ascetic, a small craftsman, peasant, woman? Did the practitioner of the rite place his or her trust in the gods of the Vedic pantheon, in Śiva, Viṣṇu, in tranquil *buddhas* and *bodhisattvas*, or in the wrathful force of Kālī or Heruka? What was intended by the action; that is, what did the rite do? Did it manipulate forces, seen or unseen? Did it bring one man or woman closer to heaven, liberation, enlightenment, cure an illness, harm an enemy; or was it intended simply to express one's love for his or her personal god? At the first level, where forms such as *pūrvasevā* and *sādhana* are economized, these questions cannot be answered.

Each first level term, however, presupposes more elemental forms of the practice; for example, *mantra* (inherently potent verbal formulas), *mudrā* ("sealing" hand gestures), *homa* (oblation), *paṭa* (painted cult image), *maṇḍala* (the animated "circle" of beings generating both the authority and power sustaining the practices, as well as a rough depiction of this assembly drawn on the ground), *abhiṣeka* (initiation, consecration). Although such elements can be seen as economized cultural forms in their own right, it is here that the *Mañjuśrīmūlakalpa* introduces particularity into these common forms. At this level, we can observe what Hardy calls "the phenomenon of uninhibited proliferation" in India's cultic life. It will be helpful to quote Hardy at length in this regard.

> [I]t is conceivable that were one to substitute musical notes for each discrete ritual item (e.g. scattering the petals of a particular flower), a musical structure might evolve. Such a structure extricated for an entire ritual event would then resemble a number of basic notes and discrete themes, and a set of increasingly complex variations on these themes. Thus on the one hand we are clearly dealing here with an aesthetic principle that underlies ritualistic proliferation. Such a 'self-authenticating' character may well explain the occurrence of ritual events in contexts that in terms of strict philosophy

> allow for no such practice (e.g., the Jain temple or the ancient Buddhist stupa). But on the other hand . . . such ritual events are not like the fixed and 'authentically performed' musical compositions of our Western classical tradition. The phenomenon of uninhibited proliferation suggests instead a comparison with the improvisatory character of the Indian musical tradition, in which each performance appears as an extempore creation that is structured merely by some formal conventions and by the *rag*.[4]

Improvisation and experimentation are observed in the variations of use and meaning brought to bear on common structures. We learn little from the fact that a ritual practitioner performs an oblation, since this is a widely shared form. But that the practitioner may burn only *aśoka* wood and not *āmla* wood in the fire teaches us a good deal about the basic orientation of the practice. This tells us, for example, that the practitioner is engaged in one of the cults directed toward pacification (of evil supernatural influences, etc.) and increase (of worldly or spiritual fortune, etc.). Conversely, we can conclude that the practitioner is not a devotee of one of the wrathful "left-handed" (*vāmācāra*) cults. When we additionally learn of the hand gestures, verbal formulas, visualized iconographic configurations, and so on, that are employed during the oblation, the specific nature of the cult—its cosmology, doctrine, and broader affiliations—begins to emerge. It is in this manner that the *Mañjuśrīmūlakalpa* creatively transforms common elements of India's religious culture into vehicles for particular forms of knowledge and power, into emblems of a unique practice. Its practices, therefore, are best approached through the "experiments" that are worked out (or, to continue Hardy's musical metaphor, jammed on) in the text.

1.2 Methods

The methods used in this study are textual. The focus of the study is on the contents of a single text, and the ritual prescriptions that comprise the content of the text are analyzed strictly on the basis of their presentation and description in textual form, as opposed to practiced form. Occasionally, the narrow scope of the single Buddhist text that is the object of this study is complemented by reference to the wider context of medieval Indian ritual literature, in particular that of the Śaiva Siddhānta and Vaiṣṇava Pañcarātra sects.

The printed text that forms the basis of this study, *Āryamañjuśrīmūlakalpa*,[5] was prepared by T. Gaṇapati Śāstrī from the single known manuscript of the work, discovered near Padmanabhapuram, in South India, in 1909. This was published in three parts in the Trivandrum Sanskrit Series: Part I = no. LXX, 1920; Part II = LXXVI, 1922; Part III = LXXXIV, 1925, Trivandrum. This was reprinted in a single volume by CBH Publications, Trivandrum, 1992, and recast with superficial changes by P. L. Vaidya, *Mahāyānasūtrasaṅgraha,* Part II, Buddhist Sanskrit Texts, no. 18, Bihar, 1964. Concerning the manuscript of the *Mmk*, Śāstrī writes in the Preface:

> It is a pretty large palm-leaf manuscript containing about 13,000 granthas. The palm-leaves are long, light and soft and the manuscript is written in Devanagarī characters with ink. Though the leaves have an appearance of being from 300 to 400 years old, the characters (except in the first and last leaf) look clear and legible as if they were just written down.

Since it was prepared from a single manuscript, the printed text should be viewed as the equivalent of a "copy," and by no means as a text-critical edition. Śāstrī writes, "as no second manuscript has been obtained, the text in this edition is adopted exactly as it is found in the original manuscript" (Preface). I have consulted an eleventh century Tibetan translation as well: Taipei Edition, volume XVIII *bka' 'gyur*, *'phags pa 'jam dpal gyi rtsa ba'i rgyud*, 540 no. 543, 25/175 (1)-96/667. I should reiterate here that my translations of the text are based solely on the Sanskrit.

Because of the length of the *Mmk*—55 chapters comprising 721 pages in the printed edition—the problem of selection and organization arises. My approach is to focus of chapters 1–11 (the contents of each *Mmk* chapter is given in Appendix A). These chapters contain the basic features that form the foundation of the practice with which I am primarily concerned: *Mmk* 1 presents the imaginal and cosmological background of the practice-world; *Mmk* 2 provides the instructions for the initiation rite and numerous *mantras* to be utilized in the practice; *Mmk* 4-7 gives the instructions for the creation of the cult object (*paṭa*), which is central to the rituals of the *Mmk*; *Mmk* 8–10 instructs on specific applications of the "superior" ritual activity (*uttamasādhana*) that is the focus of this study; and, finally, *Mmk* 11 provides the most explicit statements about the practitioner of the text. *Mmk* 1–11 contains the instructions on the activities that are imperative preconditions to successful practice; therefore, this section is sufficient for an illustration of the basic structure and specific applications of the ritual being investigated.

Subsequent chapters fall largely into one of two categories. The first consists of those that elaborate on certain features of the practice, such as *mudrās, mantras,* the fire oblation, and prognostication. It should be noted, however, that the elaborations are typically in the form of inventories and lists rather than amplifications of meaning. For example, chapters 41–46 comprise a "*mudrākośa,*" listing, and instructing briefly on the formation of, numerous *mudrās;* it does not, however, offer a "theology" of the *mudrā*. So, unlike Śaiva and Vaiṣṇava ritual texts, the *Mmk* does not alternate between ritual discourse and explanatory discourse. The second category consists of those chapters that present specific applications of the practices. Chapter 29, for instance, gives instructions on the use of a particular *mantra*; and chapters 47–49 instruct on the worship of the four *bhaginī* deities. Virtually all of the chapters from 12–55 presuppose the fulfillment of what is contained in chapters 1–11; and, additionally, many of those replicate the basic structure of chapters 8–10 and parts of 11. Therefore, chapters subsequent to *Mmk* 1–11 are referred to only secondarily.

This book is structured roughly along the thematic lines of *Mmk* 1–11. Chapter 1 gives an overview of the *uttamasādhana* ritual as it appears at *Mmk* 8–10. The purpose here is to introduce the structures and elements that comprise the basic ritual. Chapter 2 is an analysis of *Mmk* 1. *Mmk* 1 renders the cosmological setting that provides both the natural and metaphysical foundations for the ritual claims of the work. Chapter 3 draws from *Mmk* 4-7 to discuss the *paṭa*, the cult image that is painted on cloth. Chapter 4 evaluates the descriptions of the practitioner that can be found scattered throughout the text, but primarily in *Mmk* 2, 10, and 11. Finally, Chapter 5 seeks to summarize the processes and strategies at work behind the text's presentation of its ritual world, and to suggest to present-day scholars a hermeneutic for reading Buddhist literature.

1.2.1 Studying Ritual from a Text

Studying the textual record of a performed activity raises questions of relationship that complicate the initial impulse to differentiate clearly between the two. This is particularly true when the textual record is itself an integral aspect of the performance. An example of this type of text is a musical score. A musical score is a plan of procedure, containing the details of a work to be performed. It is thus both a script *for* and a record *of* musical composition. The score, however, does not stand prior to performance: the composer composes *music* to be played and heard, and not a text to be read for its own sake. Even when read for its own sake, the knowledgeable reader of a musical score will hear music as she views the notation in the text. Performance is written into the text, and the text is an inscribed form of musical performance.

The *Mmk*, too, is a programmatic text. It is employed by a community of users for two main purposes: to prescribe and authorize a performed activity, and to form the moral and mental dispositions deemed necessary for the successful performance of that activity. The text itself thus becomes an aspect of performance in two ways. First, it serves as the script for the performers of the rituals, and as a blueprint for the practical, metaphysical, and mythical knowledge required for performance. Second, it is employed as an instrument in the activities that it prescribes—it is to be consulted, meditated on, recited from, and even worshiped; it instructs, inspires, and effectuates. Like the knowledgeable reader of a musical manuscript, the informed reader of the *Mmk* (including the twenty-first century scholar) will, in the very act of reading, perform the ritual to some extent: the *mantras* will reverberate in his mind, he will envision the array of *bodhisattvas* as they are described, and so on. In studying a ritual text such as the *Mmk*, then, are we studying a text, a ritual, or both?

There can, of course, be no definitive answer to this question. Too much depends on the analogy deemed representative of the relationship between text and ritual in a given instance. I have used a script/performance analogy because I think that this best approximates the relationship between the ritual manuals and ritual performances—Buddhist and non-Buddhist—with which I am familiar. The relationship between script and performance, however, is not uniform; there are numerous versions of the script/performance analogy. For example, the scripts used in improvisitory theater provide only the rough scenarios on which the actors must spontaneously build. The relationship between script and performance in this case will be necessarily loose and vague. It will be impossible to predict a performance from a script. Conversely, a Shakespearean script, in the hands of the Stratford Festival players, will be studiously followed with an eye for what tradition has deemed proper interpretation of the script. The script and its rubrics will yield a predictable performance that changes little over time.

When studying a religious script, such as a liturgical guide or ritual manual, we have to take into account the tradition's own views on the relationship between script and performance. From the evidence of the *Mmk*, it is reasonable to conclude that looseness and improvisation on the part of the rituals' teachers and practitioners were assumed. For instance, the text provides four options for the creation of the cult object. These options reflect varying degrees of aptitude and commitment in terms of time, expense, effort, and so on, on the part of the practitioner. Often, offerings are to be made, and *mantras* and texts selected for recitation, "according to one's wishes." The text, furthermore, is not comprehensive in its prescriptions and descriptions of ritual activity. We may infer from this that the idiosyncrasies of individual teachers were permitted some latitude in their oral instructions, and that a good deal of cultural knowledge—itself inexact and indeterminate—was presupposed.

In short, the *Mmk* shows an openness to improvisation and experimentation concerning the practice of the rituals that it prescribes. Obviously, this textual variation would have been reflected in practice. The details and emphases placed on the various aspects of performance would have varied according to community and teacher.[6]

1.3 The Text: *Mañjuśrīmūlakalpa*

1.3.1 Date, Origin, Language

The *Mmk*, like many Indian religious works, is most likely what Paul Hacker describes as an "anonymous" text that has "gradually grown . . . [and has] received [its] form only through compilation, redaction, diaskeuase . . . [it] contains parts that, at one time, existed independently."[7] Yūkei Matsunaga, too, has argued that the Sanskrit text of the *Mmk* cannot be dated as a whole since portions, even single chapters, have varying dates of composition. Matsunaga writes that the *Mmk* "was not composed with a single design from beginning to end," and that it "must be seen as a gradual compilation of rituals that were themselves passing through several stages of development." Matsunaga emphasizes this point by further stating that "the text is actually a random collection of chapters that are unrelated and were neither compiled in the same way nor at the same time."[8] He goes on to show how the translation history of several of the chapters of the Chinese version of the *Mmk* support this contention. Matsunaga's results, however, are largely negative in that his intention is to emend and qualify some more positive claims made previously by Jean Przyluski.[9]

In brief, Przyluski argues that the *Mmk* contains two primary historical strata: an older one commencing with *Mmk* 4, and a more recent one consisting of *Mmk* 1–3. He bases this conclusion primarily on the following internal evidence: (1) The chapter colophons of *Mmk* 1–3 read *parivartaḥ* (chapter), while those of *Mmk* 4 and on read *paṭalavisaraḥ* (chapter). This shift in terminology "proves that the first three *parivarta* are not of the same redaction as the following *paṭalavisara*" (303), and that the former term, being more recent than the latter, points to a more recent addition. (2) Beginning with *Mmk* 4, the term *mahāyānavaipulyasūtra* or *mahāvaipulyasūtra* appears in the chapter colophons; *Mmk* 1–3, being added around the eleventh century, the period when the Tibetan translation was made, omits this designation. Przyluski holds that the reason for this omission is that *Mmk* 1–3 was written at a time when tantric elements were becoming more pronounced than the historically prior Mahāyāna *vaipulya* elements. It is for this reason that the eleventh century Tibetan translation reads *tantra* (*rgyud*) in place of *vaipulya*, which is found in the tenth century Chinese translation. (3) This latter contention, Przyluski holds, is supported by the fact that in *Mmk* 1–3, Mañjuśrī "supplants" Śākyamuni as "the central personage, the eminent speaker who instructs the Grand Assembly" (304). In other words, the fact that the *bodhisattvas* gradually come to "exercise the functions of the speaker previously reserved for the Buddha Śākyamuni" (304) is among the evidence of a later, tantric development in Buddhist literature. (4) *Mmk* 14 is identical to

Chinese texts datable to 702–705. Thus, Przyluski argues that the *Mmk* is a text in which we can observe "the transformations of beliefs and the evolution of doctrines" (306) in a period from the early eighth to the eleventh centuries (Chinese translation of *vaipulya* sections = 980–1000 [the Chinese translation of this period consists of 28 chapters, corresponding to Sanskrit 1–17 and 24–34; the Tibetan translation consists of 37 chapters, and is datable between 1034 and 1044;[10] the Tibetan *Mmk* corresponds to Sanskrit 1–17, 24–38, and 50–54]).[11]

As Matsunaga notes, Przyluski is the first scholar "who has seriously addressed himself to the problem of the date of the *MMK*" (887). A more exact dating of the *Mmk* will require further implementation of the procedure applied to the problem by Przyluski; namely, careful analysis of terminological, stylistic, and doctrinal variation, and a close comparison of the Sanskrit, Tibetan, and Chinese versions of the text. Matsunaga, utilizing these methods, has in fact been able to bring more precision to Przyluski's results, thereby emending them in certain details. Matsunaga shows, for example, that Przyluski's comparison of *Mmk* 14 with a series of Chinese translations that are datable to the early eighth century in fact produced the erroneous conclusion that *Mmk* 14, too, dates to this period. Przyluski's conclusion was based on the fact that both the Sanskrit and Chinese texts contained the same core feature: the *mūlamantra bhrīṃ*. Matsunaga, however, shows that apart from this, the texts have little in common, and that, on the whole, the Chinese texts, rather, resemble *Mmk* 9. Because such adjustments do not alter the basic time frame of the *Mmk*, they serve more as qualifications and problematizations of the concrete, though largely speculative, conclusions drawn by earlier scholars such as Przyluski.[12]

The fact that a text now known as the *Mmk* was compiled at all should give us pause to consider that, in the eyes of its custodians throughout the span of its formation, the text—or texts from which it was compiled—did in fact exhibit a thematic and stylistic consistency. The extent to which the *Mmk* can be shown to be a "random collection of chapters that are unrelated" awaits a careful linguistic and doctrinal analysis of each chapter. Such an analysis is well beyond the scope of this study. In the meantime, it may be more beneficial to entertain the possibility that the *Mmk's* apparent "randomness" is a result of our incomplete knowledge of indigenous notions of "text" and "related categories," and of the process of text formation in medieval India. For the purposes of this study, it is sufficient to note that the *Mmk* documents a form of Buddhism that was prevalent from, at the latest, the eighth century C.E. The strongest evidence for this is indirect: identical cultic patterns are recorded in Śaiva and Vaiṣṇava ritual texts. These texts are dated from the seventh to the ninth centuries with more certainty.[13] As a written document, the *Mmk* shows similar intention, function, style, and structure as these texts. (This is argued in more detail in chapter 2, below.) Dating the *Mmk* to this period is therefore based on the evidence of ascendancy of both the cultic pattern and literary genre of which it is a type. (Some suggestive data for considering the *terminus ad quem/a quo* of the *Mmk* are given in Appendix A.)

Origin

The issue of provenance parallels that of date. Portions of the text may have originated in different places, eventually to be formed into a whole—although what constituted a "whole" likely varied from place to place. However, with the exception of *Mmk* 53, the text betrays virtually nothing concerning provenance. On the contrary, whether intentionally or not, the origin or origins of the text are obscured; and in their place we find assertions of universal origin and applicability.

Ariane MacDonald, refuting Saṅkṛtyāyana's claim that the text, and the *vaipulyasūtras* in general, originated in Śriparvata and Dhanyakaṭaka in South India, cites *Mmk* 10, "a long passage on geography."[14] There, dozens of regions are mentioned as being conducive to successful *mantra* practice. She rightly concludes that these geographical passages do not give preference to any one region, and thus, do not provide any evidence for provenance. This section, in fact, appears to constitute a map of medieval Mahāyāna pilgrimage "power places" (*siddhikṣetra*), as they are called at *Mmk* 10 (this is discussed more at chapter 4, below).

Concerning *Mmk* 53, Jayaswal states:[15] it "was written in Bengal. Geographically it is to Gauḍa and Magadha that the author pays greatest attention. In fact his history from the Nāga (ca. 140 C.E.) and Gupta times (350 C.E.) to the beginning of the Pāla period (750 C.E.) is a survey from Gauḍa—written from the point of view of Gauḍa, showing an intimate concern with Gauḍa and the provinces in the proximity of Gauḍa. To him Gauḍa means the whole of Bengal and includes generally Magadha." While this assertion may be true, it applies to *Mmk* 53 only, and not to the text as a whole.

Language

The *Mmk* is written in a form of Sanskrit that deviates regularly from the norms of Pāṇini. In virtually every sentence examples of the following are found: homogeneity of nominative and accusative; use of plural subject with singular verb; mixing of passive and active forms; variant and inconsistent spellings. While many of these forms can be found in other *vaipulya* works, as is documented by Edgerton in both volumes of the *Buddhist Hybrid Sanskrit Grammar and Dictionary*, others await further analysis of internal consistency, as well as a comparison of the printed text with the manuscript, in order to determine whether they are viable local forms of written Sanskrit, editor's errors, or printer's errors.

1.3.2 Classification and Use: kalpa and mahāyānavaipulyasūtra

kalpa

The *Mmk* is a *kalpa*. The noun *kalpa* derives from the verbal root √*kḷp*, which means "to be well ordered or regulated, to arrange, fix, accomplish, perform." An early meaning of *kalpa* was a "manner of acting, proceeding, practice prescribed by the Vedas." This was, in fact, the *prathamaḥ kalpaḥ*, the primary duty regulating one's cultic life. *Kalpa* was thus employed technically to denote the "sacred precept, law, ordinance." Jan Gonda points out that the meaning of *kalpa* as used by the Vedic communities at the earliest stage encompassed neither "'texts' (books) nor special 'schools' but subjects of instruction to be studied in order to understand the Vedic texts and to perform the rites."[16] In this sense, *kalpa* was counted as one of the six *vedāṅgas* (auxiliaries to the Vedas). The subject covered by *kalpa* was ritual, or the proper performance of the rites. The texts that eventually emerged from the need to codify a school's particular understanding of a ritual procedure were called *kalpasūtras*, or "ritual texts." Gonda defines *kalpasūtra* as a comprehensive term for "the various ceremonial guides or didactic manuals on ritual practice (*kalpa*), detailed expositions of the procedures and rules for the performance of Vedic sacrifices."[17]

From the term *kalpa* we thus learn that the *Mmk* is a manual of ritual practice disclosing all of the elements of the course of practice promulgated in the text. As a Buddhist *kalpa*, the *Mmk* parallels the Vaiṣṇava *samhitās*, Śākta *tantras,* and Śaiva *āgamas*. Such ritual manuals comprised what Richard Davis calls the "new genre of liturgical texts [that] became prominent during the early medieval period."[18] The Śaiva *āgamas*, for instance, "set forth a sequence of transformative rituals—initiations and consecrations—that progressively incorporate the subject into the Śaiva community, move him toward liberation, and empower him to act as a temple priest or adept. In this respect, the *āgamas* provide liturgical compendiums for Śaiva priests (*ācārya*), for renunciatory adepts (*sādhaka*), and for committed householders worshiping at home shrines. They are the primary ritual texts of medieval Śaivism."[19] It is argued in chapter 2 and chapter 4 below that Davis's characterization of the *āgamas* applies to the *Mmk*; that is, that it was one Buddhist community's answer to the medieval concern to record, clarify, systematize, and extoll the community's ritual practices.

mahāyānavaipulyasūtra

The term *vaipulya* means "largeness, spaciousness, great extent." Edgerton notes that *vaipulya* is equivalent to *vaitulya*, which, in turn, is cognate to Pāli *vettulla/vetulya*. There is evidence that suggests that the Pāli terms referred to "a heretical sect, by some identified with Mahāyāna."[20] The commentary to the *Kathāvatthu*, for instance, states: "This view is now held by those of the Vetulakas, who are known as the Mahāsuññatāvādins."[21] The term *mahāsuññatāvādin* refers to a Buddhist who accepts the cardinal Mahāyāna Buddhist doctrine that all phenomena (*dharmas*) are conceptual constructs possessing no inherent essence. An additional doctrinal position of the Vetulakas was that the Buddha was *vipula*, immense, immeasurable, infinite.[22] A *vaipulyasūtra* is thus a copious text in which Mahāyāna metaphysical and cosmological notions are either propagated or presupposed. It is to this position, in contrast to earlier forms of Buddhism, that Etienne Lamotte refers when he writes that the *vaipulya* works shared common "sources of inspiration," and that they comprised a unitary "philosophical-mystical movement."[23]

As a technical term, *vaipulya* denotes a genre of literature contained in an early twelvefold classification scheme: *sūtra, geya, vyākaraṇa, gatha, udāna, nidāna, ityukta, jātaka, vaipulya, adbhūtadharma, avadāna,* and *upadeśa*.[24] The term was later used synonymously with the term *bodhisattvapiṭaka* ("canon of the *bodhisattvas*"). In the *Bodhisattvabhūmi*, for instance, Asanga (ca. 290–360) advises the *bodhisattva* to study "the canon (*piṭaka*) of the *bodhisattvas* . . . which is the *vaipulya* in the twelve-member scripture."[25] This connection between the two terms, *vaipulya* and *bodhisattvapiṭaka,* is expressed in most of the chapter colophons of the *Mmk*, where the text is referred to as a *bodhisattvapiṭakāvataṃsakamahāyānavaipulyasūtra*.[26] For certain communities, then, the *Mmk*, as a *vaipulya* text, both corroborated and was corroborated by, a larger group of texts espousing a particular Buddhist worldview. The *Mmk* refers indirectly to this larger group: in *Mmk* 2 and 11 liturgical rubrics call for recitation from four *vaipulya* texts: *Prajñāpāramitā, Daśabhūmika, Suvarṇaprabhāsottama,* and *Gaṇḍavyūha*.

Both terms, *vaipulya* and *kalpa,* are operative in the *Mmk*. As a *kalpa*, the *Mmk* orders, arranges and fixes the ritual prescriptions of the community; it regulates the corporate and private devotional activity of the practitioner; it specifies to him how to perform the rites of the cult, and thereby makes explicit how to accomplish the goals held by the community to be worthy or acceptable. As a *vaipulyasūtra*, the *Mmk* reveals, in often exuberant language and imagery, the cosmological basis of its cult. In this manner, as I show in detail below, the text's claims of ritual efficacy are given a metaphysical foundation.

1.3.3 Index

At the end of each chapter of the *Mmk* is a statement indicating the basic content of the chapter, its position within a larger unit, and the title and genre of the text as a whole. A typical example is the colophon of *Mmk* 9, which reads:

> Completed is the second [chapter] from the section on the rituals leading to superior success: the ninth [chapter] of the *Āryamañjuśrīmūlakalpa*, the extensive Mahāyāna text, an ornament of the canon of the *bodhisattvas*.[27]

From such chapter colophons we learn of the compilers' organizing principles and of their categories of orientation. Here, *Mmk* 9 is presented as the second in a series of chapters on a specific ritual category: *uttamasādhana*, soteriologically directed rituals, rather than those aiming at worldly results. The content of the chapter is thus given as this type of ritual practice. The text as a whole is presented as being a contributor to the loosely defined corpus of literature propagating the *bodhisattva* ideal. This also indicates the self-perception of the medieval practitioners of the *Mmk* rituals as Mahāyāna Buddhists who adhered to the general tenets propagated in the *vaipulya* texts.[28]

A more specific form of organization and categorization is found at *Mmk* 1. *Mmk* 1 contains several passages that, as a whole, can be read as an index. By index I mean both a list or table of contents, and a signpost guiding the reader to larger claims being made in the text. The index tells the reader what to expect not only from the text as a treasury (*koṣa*) of specific knowledge, but from the practice promulgated in the text as well. It thus possesses rhetorical force. As a form of argument, for example, it serves to make the *Mmk*'s claim of privilege over other methods of practice. This becomes clear when we read the lists that make up the index in light of our knowledge of the diverse forms of Buddhist and non-Buddhist practice available in the medieval period. Because of the types of claims that the index is making—authoritative, hegemonic, totalizing—it can be understood as positing a *śāstric* argument. That is, the index points to a codification of *what should be done;* and this codification is posited as being primordial, revealed, and all-encompassing. The entire design of the *Mmk* is to show that "what should be done" is to practice rituals employing *mantras* (*mantracaryā*)—the knowledge of which only it, the *Mmk*, can provide. The index points to this knowledge. The end to which the rituals and the knowledge are applied is, in practice if not theory, immaterial.

Index lists

The opening paragraph gives a succinct statement of the ritual project of the *Mmk*. Śākyamuni is announcing to the *devaputras* in the *śuddhāvāsa* heaven that he is about to give a teaching "upon which all beings depend."

> Hear, O *devaputras*, about that upon which all beings depend: the inconceivable, wondrous, miraculous transformation of the *bodhisattva*, the [use of the] [*paṭa*] for superior liberation, purity, meditative absorption, [Tibetan adds: supernatural powers: *rdzu 'phrul* < *ṛddhi*], proper conduct; [hear about] the *mantras* of that great being, the princely *bodhisattva* Mañjuśrī, which completely fulfill all beings' wishes for power, health and long life.[B1] (letter/ number notation refers to an Appendix entry)

This is a statement about the primacy of ritual as a Buddhist practice: the Buddha's teaching is a teaching about rituals. Broad categories of this teaching include the use of the *paṭa*, methods of purification, and so on. The linchpin of the entire ritual complex is mentioned here: the transformative power of the *bodhisattva*. The final clause is a general, though wide-ranging, statement about the applications and results of the rituals. Power, health, and long life include not only such mundane things as the power of clairvoyance, the ability to heal eyesores, and the avoidance of untimely death. They also include the power to proceed to the heavens of gods, unassailable health, and mortal existence for several eons.

For the sake of clarity, we can arrange the text's claims about the functions of ritual practice vertically. (Each instance should be prefaced by: "the text contains knowledge about.")

> [**List 1**: *Mmk* 1.1.6–9]
>
> - the use of the cult image for enlightenment
> - purity, meditative absorption, proper conduct
> - the *mantras* of the *bodhisattva* Mañjuśrī,
> - complete power, health, and long life
> - the operative force of the rituals: the miraculous transformation of the *bodhisattvas*

As mentioned above, this list alludes to central and prerequisite components of the *mantracaryā*, specifically, the cult object (*paṭa*), *mantras*, purification, imaginative worship, and ethical behavior. The list contains a claim of universal application, and then closes with an allusion to the foundation of the entire ritual structure. This is immediately followed by a more defined, though still relatively general, list.

> Then, with hands folded in salutation, those *devaputras* dwelling in the Pure Abode [Tibetan: exclaiming "excellent!" asked the Blessed One (about) the *bodhisattvas'* practices of superior meditative absorption], the obtaining of the superior stages [of the *bodhisattva* path], the approach to buddhahood, the turning of the wheel of the teaching for the overcoming of Māra, liberation

> of *pratyekabuddhas* and *śrāvakas*, birth as a god or human, pacification of all illness, poverty and suffering, attraction of wealth, the invincibility of all ordinary and extraordinary *mantra* rituals, the complete fulfillment of all hopes, the certain retention of the words of all *tathāgatas*. Out of compassion for us and for all beings, let the Blessed One, who is loving and benevolent, speak about that![B2]

(Here, each listing is a general claim about ritual function, and should thus be prefaced by: "the rituals are a means to.")

[**List 2**: *Mmk* 1.1.12–18]

ordinary attainment (laukika)

- the abolition of disease and poverty
- the attraction of wealth
- birth as a god or human

extraordinary attainment (lokottara)

- liberation of *pratyekabuddhas* and *śrāvakas*
- the approach to buddhahood
- obtaining the superior stages [of the *bodhisattva*]
- the certain retention of the words of all *tathāgatas*

universality

- the pacification of all suffering
- the invincibility of all ordinary and extraordinary *mantra* rituals
- the fulfillment of every hope

The means of attaining each of these is precisely the *mantracaryā* delineated in the *Mmk*. The one exception is "the turning of the wheel of the teaching for the overcoming of Māra," which is, presumably, a reference to *Mmk* 53, the chapter on Buddhist history. Otherwise, the rituals are presented as addressing concerns bearing on health, fortunate rebirth, and liberation. The references to liberation contain allusions to the three ascending orders of *śrāvaka*, *pratyekabuddha*, and *bodhisattva*. Like the first list, this list closes with rhetorical claims of absoluteness.

The first two lists are proclaimed by Śākyamuni and the *śuddhāvāsa* gods respectively. The third is spoken by the *bodhisattva* Mañjuśrī. He is explaining to Saṅkusumitarājendra—the *buddha* in whose world-realm he is living[28]—that he is going to the *sāha* world in order to serve Śākyamuni by teaching the beings there about the following:

> prescriptions for the *maṇḍala,* which (*maṇḍala*) is the means of attainment in all *mantra* rites, the prescriptions for the esoteric cult image in the ritual ordinance, the essential forms of all *tathāgatas*, the secret *mudrās*, the initiation rite, to fulfill completely every hope of every being.[B3]

[**List 3**: *Mmk* 1.2.13–15]

- the means of attainment (*sādhana*)
- the creation of the [initiatory] *maṇḍala*
- the initiation rite
- the essential forms of all *tathāgatas*
- secret *mudrās*
- the creation of the esoteric cult image (*paṭa*)
- rituals employing *mantras*
- fulfillment of all beings' every hope

List 3 contains the cardinal categories of the ritual practice prescribed in the *Mmk*. Ordered as above, the list gives the necessary, and complete, sequence of the practice. The means of attainment in the *Mmk* is, first, to have a master to prepare the initiatory space, namely, the *maṇḍala*, followed by the initiation ceremony itself. During this ceremony, the *sādhaka* is given the potent "essence" (*hṛdaya*) *mantra* and other *mantras* required for ritual practice, and he receives secret instruction on how to perform the "sealing" bodily gestures (*mudrā*) that must accompany *mantra* recitation. Once he has received this initiation, he may proceed with the final requisite of ritual practice—creation of the cult image (*paṭa*). Only then may he perform the *mantra* rituals "which lead to absolute fulfillment."

The fourth list repeats categories given previously, and introduces several new ones. Four sections in the *Mmk* are referred to: *Mmk* 11 (dwelling in a fixed place), *Mmk* 17–21 (gems and planets), *Mmk* 22–26 (proper time), and *Mmk* 53 (prophecies on the sovereignty of kings). In addition to this, two "ordinary" (*laukika*) "supernatural attainments" (*siddhi*) are mentioned—invisibility and clairvoyance—and one "extraordinary" (*lokottara*) attainment—the ascension to the stages of the *śrāvaka*, *pratyekabuddha*, *bodhisattva,* and *buddha*. In this passage, Saṅkusumitarājendra is granting Mañjuśrī permission to hear Śākyamuni teach about the following:

> the *maṇḍala* used in the *mantra* rituals, initiation into the esoteric ordinance, *mudrās*, creation of the cult image, the fire oblation, [*mantra*] recitation, discipline, complete fulfillment of every hope and complete satisfaction of all beings, knowledge of present, past, future by means of the extensive

section on gems and planets, [the section on the] prophecies on the sovereignty of kings, recitation of *mantras,* [the section on] dwelling at the borders of countries, ability to become invisible, the extensive section on the period [when the practitioner is] under the vow, everything, with nothing excluded, concerning the rituals conducive to all that is ordinary and extraordinary, the ascension to the stages of the *śrāvaka*, *pratyekabuddha*, *bodhisattva,* and *buddha.*[B4]

[**List 4**: *Mmk* 1.2.22–27]

general

- discipline
- gestures
- fire oblation
- recitation of *mantras*
- gems and planets
- prophecies on the sovereignty of kings
- wandering
- the proper time [for particular practices]

preliminary

- initiation into the esoteric ordinance
- the *maṇḍala* used in the *mantra* rituals
- creation of the cult image
- *mantra* recitation

ordinary attainment: instrumental power

- ability to become invisible
- knowledge of present, past, future

extraordinary attainment: soteriological power

- the ascension to the stages of the *śrāvaka*, *pratyekabuddha*, *bodhisattva,* and *buddha*

universality

- complete fulfillment of every wish
- complete satisfaction of all beings
- everything, with nothing excluded, concerning the rites conducive to all that is ordinary and extraordinary

In the final indexical passage, Śākyamuni is instructing Mañjuśrī to teach the *śuddhāvāsa* gods. In doing so, Śākyamuni simultaneously outlines the contents of the *Mmk* and describes the ideal "treasury of the true teaching" (*dharmakośa*), the book of rituals serving the "welfare and pleasure of numerous people." This final statement of List 5 closes the indexical section of the *Mmk* by invoking the value and authority of the text itself.

> [The ritual text, *Mañjuśrīmūlakalpa*, deals with] the rituals of the great beings, production of and establishment in enlightenment, complete attainment of all the goals of a *bodhisattva*, initiation into the ordinances for the *mantras*, *maṇḍala,* and *mudrās* for the esoteric initiation ceremony, long life, good health, power, the fulfillment of every wish, means of attainment, periodical performance of that which is known through familiarity with the *tantras*, [acquisition] of royal lands; in short, the complete fulfillment of every hope of every individual in past, present and future, attending to the *mantra* rites which awaken one's virtues, causing the sage to cause others' happiness, wander invisibly, traverse the sky; the power of attraction, the ability to enter into the underworld, maledictory incantations, the attainment of every desire, attaction of all spirits, *piśācas*, *kiṃkaras*, violent male and female *yakṣas*, causing one to remain young or advanced in years, as the case may be; in short, complete fulfillment and joy in all of one's endeavors, the performance of rites of malediction, pacification, and increase. Just as it was practiced by me, so was this extensive jewel, this great ordinance, ornament of the *bodhisattva* canon, proclaimed and authorized by me and spoken by all *buddhas*. Teach this treasury of the true teaching to all pure beings, men, and gods, for the welfare and pleasure of numerous people.[B5]

[**List 5:** *Mmk* 1.6.13–22]

general

- the rituals of the great beings (i.e., of *bodhisattvas*)
- means of attainment
- the performance of rites of malediction, pacification, and increase
- attending to the *mantra* rites (known through the *tantras*, etc.)

preliminary

- preparing the *maṇḍala* for the initiation ceremony
- initiation into esoteric *mantras* and *mudrās*

ordinary attainment

- long life
- good health
- power

- awakening virtues in oneself
- causing joy in other people
- causing sages to:
  wander about on foot
  traverse the sky
  disappear
- power of attraction
- entrance into the underworld
- attaction of all spirits, *piśācas*, *kiṃkaras*, violent male and female *yakṣas*
- cessation of aging and maintenance of youth
- [acquisition] of royal lands

extraordinary attainment

- production of and establishment in enlightenment
- complete attainment of all the goals of a *bodhisattva*

universality

- complete fulfillment and joy in all of one's endeavors
- the complete fulfillment of every wish of every individual in the past, present, and future

Although there is a good deal of overlap in these five lists, each one has a particular emphasis. List 1 is the most general, referring to the broadest features of the *mantracaryā*. In addition, it states the mechanism believed to be operating behind the *mantracaryā*: *vikurvaṇa*, the miraculous transformation of *buddhas* and *bodhisattvas*. List 2 refers to the functions of the *mantracaryā*. These can be organized under the two categories provided by the text, ordinary and extraordinary attainment. As with all of the lists, Lists 1 and 2 include claims of universal application. List 3 can be organized sequentially, laying out the step by step process of the *mantracaryā*. Otherwise, the categories presented there involve, like lists 2–5, the preliminary stages, as well as general features, of the *mantracaryā*. Lists 4 and 5 combine information about the contents of the text with claims about the function of the rituals.

Taken as a whole, these five lists represent the index to the *Mmk*. This index has a double function. It presents the contents of the text in both general and specific terms, and reports on the results of its prescribed practice. Like a *śāstra,* the index thus presents, in summary form, *what should be done* and *what may be expected*. The basis of the first of these is the authority of the Buddha, and, by extension, of all *buddhas*. This is stated at *Mmk* 1.6.13–26, above. The basis of the second is given at the outset: the *vikurvaṇa* of enlightened beings. Constituting efficacy in this manner presupposes a philosophical stance regarding the Buddha, the cosmos, and the relation of these to the lives of men and women. In this sense, the index is a form of teaching claiming to supersede all previous Buddhist and non-Buddhist modes of practice. The statements about universal application point to its intended function as a comprehensive practice interlocking monastic and lay boundaries, and soteriological and instrumental concerns.

As will be shown when we turn to the *uttamasādhana* below, the categories of the index apply to the ritual sequence as well. That is, the passages on the ritual refer to a preliminary stage when certain essential preparatory actions were fulfilled; they state the general prescriptions concerning recitation, oblations, and so forth; they reveal instrumental results and soteriological results that ensue from practice; and, finally, they make universal claims about the practice. The comprehensive index can be arranged as follows.

general

- the means of attainment (*sādhana*)
- rituals employing *mantras*
- the use of the cult image for superior liberation
- the secret essence of all *tathāgatas*
- purity, contemplation, proper conduct
- secret gestures
- the *mantras* of the *bodhisattva* Mañjuśrī
- the *maṇḍala* used in the *mantra* rituals
- creation of the cult image
- fire oblation
- discipline
- recitation of *mantras*
- methods of attainment
- the performance of rites of malediction, pacification, and increase
- maledictory incantations
- periodical performance of that which is known through familiarity with the *tantras*

- attending to the *mantra* rites
- the rituals of the great beings
- gems and planets
- prophecies on the sovereignty of kings
- dwelling in a fixed place
- the proper time [for particular practices]

preliminary

- initiation into the esoteric ordinance
- the creation of the *maṇḍala*
- the creation of the esoteric cult image (*paṭa*)
- esoteric initiation into *mantras* and *mudrās*
- preparing the *maṇḍala* for the initiation ceremony
- continuous recitation

ordinary attainment (laukika): instrumental power

- the abolition of disease
- birth as a god or human
- ability to become invisible
- knowledge of present, past, future
- complete power, health, and long life
- awakening virtues in oneself
- causing joy in other people
- causing sages to:
  wander about on foot
  traverse the sky
  disappear
- power of attraction
- entrance into the underworld
- attaction of all spirits, *piśācas*, *kiṃkaras*, violent male and female *yakṣas*
- cessation of aging
- [acquisition] of royal lands
- the certain retention of the words of all *tathāgatas*

extraordinary attainment (lokottara): soteriological power

- final emancipation of *pratyekabuddhas* and *śrāvakas*
- the approach to buddhahood
- obtaining the superior stages [of the *bodhisattva*]
- the ascension to the stages of the *śrāvaka*, *pratyekabuddha*, *bodhisattva*, and *buddha*
- production of and establishment in enlightenment
- complete attainment of all the goals of a *bodhisattva*

universality

- the destruction of all suffering
- the invincibility of all ordinary and extraordinary *mantra* rituals
- complete satisfaction of all beings
- everything, with nothing excluded, concerning the rites conducive to all that is ordinary and extraordinary
- complete fulfillment and joy in all of one's endeavors
- the complete fulfillment of every wish of every individual in the past, present, and future

the operative force of the rituals

- the miraculous transformation of the *bodhisattvas*

1.4 The Ritual

The focus of this study is the ritual sequence classified in the *Mmk* as "superior" (*uttama*). This sequence is found at *Mmk* 8–10. *Mmk* 8 opens with the Buddha's stating, "I will fully expound the section on rituals, the separate section abounding in excellent qualities, the means to success."[30] The colophon is explicit about a special section devoted to "superior" rituals. It reads in part, "the eighth [chapter]: the first chapter from the section on the rituals leading to superior success."[31] *Mmk* 9 is the "second chapter on the rituals leading to superior success."[32] The colophon of *Mmk* 10 reads somewhat unclearly, "chapter ten: the chapter on the prescriptions for the superior *paṭa*."[33] Based on the contents of the *Mmk* 10, this can be understood as referring to the employment of the large *paṭa* in rituals directed toward "superior attainment." This is what is indicated by the opening statement of the chapter: "Blessed Śākyamuni once again spoke about the superior rituals of attainment" (*karmasādhanottama*),[34] and the summary statement at the end of the chapter that the *sādhaka* "in short, should perform all the superior rituals, situated in superior places, in front of the superior *paṭa*, joyfully offering superior worship and other superior rituals."[35]

The ritual sequence in *Mmk* 8–10 is called "superior" in reference to a threefold classification. At *Mmk* 4, we read of exalted (*uttiṣṭha*), intermediate (*madhyama*), and minor (*kanyasa*) attainment (*siddhi*).[36] The *Mmk*, however, nowhere provides a clear systematization of these classes of attainment. There is constant overlap and intermixing throughout the text. Nominally, the superior rituals are said to be so by virtue of their being directed toward enlightenment. At *Mmk* 4, the chapter devoted to the largest *paṭa*, we are told that "Mañjuśrī . . . particularly declares success for those beings who are constantly proceeding towards enlightenment."[37] This would seem to indicate that the superior rituals are those with a soteriological value. As we will see in the analysis of such rituals, however, the ritual path to enlightenment entails the attainment of instrumental powers that, theoretically, belong to the two lesser classes of accomplishment. Similarly, examples of the intermediate accomplishments include the ability to disappear and the attainment of high social status,[38] while instances of the minor accomplishments are given as attaining the worldly pleasures experienced by the *devas* and *asuras*,[39] as well as various forms of pacification (*śāntika*), increase (*pauṣṭika*), and expulsion of terrific forces (*dāruṇa*).[40] Ultimately, however, even these lower forms of ritual entail soteriological results. This is made evident in the section dealing with the the *uttama, madhyama,* and *kanyasa paṭas* (*Mmk* 4–7) where, at the end of each chapter, it is emphasized that merely seeing the *paṭa*, regardless of size or specific ritual employment, produces liberating results. Concerning the smallest, and ostensibly ritually least potent, *paṭa*, the text says that "that same merit that ensues from worship of all *buddhas*, the saviors, the sage can obtain by seeing the small *paṭa*."[41] Such merit would exceed the *madhyama* and *uttama* attainments.

A further indication of a theoretical division between soteriological and instrumental ritual is found at *Mmk* 1. In several instances the text distinguishes between "ordinary" (*laukika*) and "extraordinary" (*lokottara*).[42] At *Mmk* 2, Śākyamuni refers to Mañjuśrī's "class of *mantras in toto*, ordinary and extraordinary."[43] Both types of *mantra* must always be applied within the context of a broader ritual complex, the purpose of which is the attainment of specific ends. Thus, *Mmk* 1 states that the teaching of the Buddha concerns the "invincibility of all ordinary and extraordinary *mantra* rituals,"[44] and that the rituals are directed toward "everything, both the ordinary and extraordinary" (*aśeṣalaukikalokottara*).[45] These statements yield two central facts about the ritual project of the *Mmk*. First, the purpose of the work is to expound potent *mantras*, to prescribe the rituals in which these are employed, and to indicate the results that can be expected to follow from these. Second, each case allows for *any instance* of both the ordinary/instumental and extraordinary/soteriological.

1.4.1 uttamasādhana: structure

As mentioned above, the "ritual for superior attainment" is found at *Mmk* 8–10. Although variations of the sequence are found throughout the text, it is considered "superior" at *Mmk* 8–10 because of the fact that it is performed with the "superior" cult image (*jyeṣṭapaṭa*) there. Otherwise, in both structure and content the *uttama* ritual is representative of *Mmk* ritual as a whole. What differences there are lie mainly in the intention of the practitioner, and in the manner in which each specific presentation of the ritual is framed.

This latter point applies to *Mmk* 8–10 as well. Each chapter uniquely frames the ritual, although the sequence itself is commonly structured throughout. *Mmk* 8 begins with an introduction to the section as a whole, employing common Buddhist literary features. For instance, the scene opens with Śākyamuni's proclaiming to Mañjuśrī his intention of expounding "the section on rituals" (*karmavibhāga*).[46] He then smiles, emitting brilliant, colorful, and cosmically cataclysmic rays of light from his mouth. The *bodhisattva* Vajrapāṇi, perplexed about the significance of this display, asks the Buddha to explain. Śākyamuni answers that the reason for his smile is that people will appear in the world who will practice and honor the *Mmk*.

> [There will be] those who will perform, uphold, have proclaimed, have confidence in this supreme lord among *sūtras*, the *Mañjuśrīmūlakalpa,* which has come forth from, and results in complete penetration into, the cloud of teaching establishing the means of ritual success for the performance of the practice of spells. They will have it written down in a book and worship it with garlands of sandalwood powder, unguents, incense and flower garlands, with umbrellas, flags and various kinds of musical instruments. They will even obtain a mental disposition of sympathetic joy, horripulate with excitement, and become joyous upon hearing about the power and might of the spells, and they will obtain the practice. I predict that, having attained unsurpassed, perfect enlightenment, they will all become blessed *buddhas.* It is for this reason that the victorious ones smile, and for no other.[C1]

This opening statement of the "ritual section" underscores the totality of both the rituals and the text in which they are recorded. It also refers to the wider conceptual world operating in the *Mmk*. Specifically, it points to the idea that enlightened beings are actively engaged in the world on behalf of devotees. The rituals, and the book of rituals, are the means by which the power of these beings are made to manifest. This idea, in turn, points to both the physical and metaphysical vision of the cosmos underlying the *Mmk*. More is said about this below. Here, it is important for our understanding of the ritual to note that the *uttamasādhana* is prefaced, in its first instance, by a rhetorical claim to absolute authority and efficacy.

Mmk 9 prefaces the ritual with a discussion of the *mantra kḷlhīṃ*. This is followed by medical and protective applications, presumably requiring the invocation of *kḷlhīṃ*. *Mmk* 10 opens with descriptions of the *uttamasādhana* being performed on a boat in the Ganges and on a ship crossing a sea. There follows a long verse section naming the optimal geographical places for the *mantracaryā*. It then closes the section on the *uttamasādhana* with an elaborate version of the ritual performed on the ground.

Each of these presentations of the *uttamasādhana* is similarly structured. In what follows, I will analyze this structure. Because of its relative clarity and concision, I am using the presentation of the *uttamasādhana* from *Mmk* 8 as the basis of my discussion, although I will refer to other chapters of the *Mmk* as well.[47]

> First, he who has observed the vow, fulfilled the preliminary practices (*puraścaraṇa*), received the initiation, taken the essential (*hṛdaya*), basic *mantra* from this best of ordinances (*kalpa*), or the *upahṛdaya*[48] or some other *mantra*, or having received a single syllable [*mantra*] or another one—according to one's wishes—and who, having gone to a great forest, eats leaves and roots, who subsists on fruits and water, should recite [the *mantra*] three million times. He becomes one who has completed the preliminary practice. Then, having climbed to the top of a mountain and set up the superior cult image facing to the west, he faces east himself, seated on a mound of *kuśa* grass. He should offer one lac of white lotuses and oiled white saffron at the base of the *paṭa* to the blessed Śākyamuni and to all the noble disciples, solitary *buddhas*, *bodhisattvas*, and *buddhas*. And he should burn as much camphor and incense as he can afford. He should worship the *nāgas* and gods with as many lotuses as he can procure. Then, at midnight, during the equinox, when the moon is bright and extraordinarily full, after having created an area for the fire at the base of the *paṭa*, and having lit the lotus-shaped fire with sticks of white sandalwood, combining saffron and camphor he should then make one thousand and eight oblations—creating as much protection as possible. Thereupon, rays of light proceed from the blessed Śākyamuni, and the entire *paṭa* blazes forth as a single shining [object]. Then, when the *sādhaka* has made three quick circumambulations around the *paṭa*, and has paid homage to all *buddhas, bodhisattvas*, solitary *buddhas* and noble disciples, the *paṭa* is to be taken hold of. Just as he grasps the edge of the previously drawn *paṭa*, the *sādhaka* flies up. He proceeds instantly to the Brahmaloka. He stays in the world-realm Kusumāvātī, where the *tathāgata* Saṅkusumitarājendra dwells, exists, abides

> and teaches the *dharma*. He beholds Mañjuśrī directly. He hears the true teaching (*dharma*). He also sees several thousand *bodhisattvas*, and worships them. He becomes one who playfully enjoys non-aging and immortality for a thousand great eons. The *paṭa* is also there. He is empowered by all *buddhas* and *bodhisattvas*, and he declares to them his firm resolution [to attain enlightenment] and proceeds to their hundred thousand paradises. [Their] hundred thousand bodies are revealed to him. He becomes possessed of numerous powers and supernatural abilities. The noble Mañjuśrī becomes his virtuous friend. He becomes one for whom the goal of enlightenment is certain.[C2]

The ritual consists of two main stages. Both of these consist in turn of several constituents. The first stage precedes ritual practice itself. The text refers to this as the stage of "preliminary practice" (*puraścaraṇa*). Each of the several practices that constitutes *puraścaraṇa* is lengthy and exacting. This fact is significant: a fairly brief ritualized act, in order to succeed, must be preceded by a long period of preparatory training. This training includes instruction on specific ritual procedures, philosophical tenets, and ethical comportment.[49]

The *uttama* ritual passage above, too, alludes to these aspects of the preliminary stage: taking the vow of the *bodhisattva* (to act on behalf of all beings, etc.), initiation into the particular teachings of the *Mmk*, reception of a personal *mantra*, going to a secret place for prolonged recitation of the *mantra* before the cult image, and maintenance of a purificatory diet.[50] The practitioner is introduced "by degrees" to each of these aspects of the practice. As we will see in chapters 3 and 4, each aspect of the *puraścaraṇa* is a complex set of ritualized activity in itself. The initiation rite, for instance, incorporates several subcategories of rituals to be performed over a three-day period. Each aspect, furthermore, presupposes fulfillment of the previous set of ritual activities. In this sense, the "preliminary practice" is not only a global term for what is prerequisite to *sādhana*, but consists itself of sets of preparatory practices.

The text lays great stress on preparation. This is a central feature of medieval *mantracaryā*. Summarizing the treatment of Vaiṣṇava Pañcarātra *mantraśāstras* on the topic, Sanjukta Gupta writes:[51]

> After his initiation, the novice has learned the nature and function of his mantra and the rites connected with it. He retires to some holy and quiet place and starts his daily religious practice, the *upāsanā* [i.e., the intent engagement] of his mantra, which always culminates in a long meditation on the mantra. He withdraws his senses from external phenomena and contemplates the mantra by mentally repeating it (*japa*) a great many times. He determines the number of recitations in advance. With acts of worship and

> with meditation, he fulfills the two basic requirements of a Pañcarātrin. He intensifies his passionate devotion for and trust in god with his worship (*pūjā/yāga*); he sharpens his awareness to a razor's edge and finally achieves gnosis. When that happens his experience of his mantra's true nature becomes real and the identity with it which he imagined during the practice is realized. He becomes the possessor of the power (*śakti*) of his mantra. All his religious practice prior to this is technically known as *puraścaraṇa* (acts performed previously), i.e., before acquiring the mantra's power.

The clarity, firmness, and power on the part of the practitioner that is required for "seeing the Buddha," and so on, during *uttamasādhana* ritual practice derive from the fulfillment of these preliminary practices. Indeed, the very term *sādhaka*—adept, accomplished—evokes a practitioner who has already advanced through several demanding stages of practice. The last of the *puraścaraṇa,* the *pūrvasevā*, gives some indication of the effort involved in preparing for ritual practice. The *uttamasādhana* passage above refers to one who has "gone to a great forest, eats leaves and roots, who subsists on fruits and water, recit[ing] [the *mantra*] three million times." The period prior to the ability to perform *sādhana* is marked by ascetic diet and practice. As the Pañcarātra *saṃhitas* make clear, it is the *pūrvasevā* which finally opens up the possibility of ritual success. *Mmk* 10 is explicit about this: "[w]ith devotion and faith, he should thoroughly practice the *pūrvasevā* rituals, which are the means to the ritual of superior attainment."[52]

The concern of the *puraścaraṇa* is then gradual, though intensive, preparation of the practitioner for ritual practice. The preparation begins with "intentness" toward the practice. This necessarily precedes acceptance by a qualified master. Once accepted, the practitioner must take the *bodhisattva*'s vow, and prove himself worthy through his comportment and ethical behavior. Only once he has indicated this degree of ability and seriousness may he be conferred initiation and granted permission to practice rituals. It is during the initiation ceremony that the practitioner receives practical and philosophical instruction required for practice. When he has acquired the knowledge necessary for practice, the practitioner may have the cult image fashioned. Only then is he a fully qualified *sādhaka*—one who is capable of effecting desired ends through goal-specific application of the ritual.

The second part of the ritual is called the effecting ritual (*sādhana).* In the above *uttamasādhana* passage, the sentence beginning "[t]hen, having climbed to the top of a mountain," marks the commencement of the *sādhana.* The term *sādhana* is not as restrictive in the *Mmk* as it is in other, explicitly tantric, texts. That is, it does not denote the meditational ritual of identifying with the enlightened entity, although it may include imaginative generation and worship of this being. In the *Mmk*, *sādhana* means, literally, *effecting* a result. The *sādhana* as ritual complex is *the means to attainment*, which is another sense of the term *sādhana*. As with the *puraścaraṇa*, the *sādhana* encompasses various ritual actions, such as recitation of the *mantra*, fire oblations, visualization, and worship of enlightened beings.

Although there is variation concerning the details of the practice and the ends sought, the pattern throughout the text is consistent with the above example. First, the practitioner, who has previously completed a prolonged period of intensive recitation (*puraścaraṇa*), goes to a place removed from human beings. In this private place, he unrolls the *paṭa* and places it on the ground before him. He then commences "extensive worship" (*mahatī pūjā*) of the image. Worship consists of *mantra* recitation and offerings to the cult image. *Mmk* 10 states this explicitly: "First, he offers the extensive worship to the superior *paṭa*; burning camphor incense . . . he recites [the *mantra* until dawn]."[53]

Precisely what is encompassed by this term *mahatī pūjā* is not stated, unless, of course, we take the text at face value. In the context of Buddhism, the term itself suggests some variation of the widespread medieval form of worship known as *anuttarapūja*. The *Gaṇḍavyūha*, a text extolled in the *Mmk*, contains an early version of this "sevenfold" sequence of practice;[54] and Śāntideva's (ca. 685–763) *Bodhicaryāvatāra* contains what may have been a widespread medieval form of the liturgy.[55]

There is at least one instance in the *Mmk* that seems to indicate that something more than material offerings and *mantras*—something akin to the "sevenfold worship"—is involved in *pūjā*. A section at *Mmk* 11 gives instructions for daily worship. It says there that, after making ablutions, the practitioner should worship as follows. (Note that at one point he is instructed to perform a "confession of faults" [*pāpadeśanā*] before the *buddhas* depicted on the cult image.[56] This is one of the features of the classical sevenfold practice.)

> He should salute the protector.
>
> Having offered such praise,
> he joyfully worships
> the master of the world,
> praising him repeatedly
> with offerings of various hymns of praise.
>
> Let him praise thus
> with fragrant flowers,
> offering half a measure of [*mantra*] recitation.
> Lowering his head in obeisance to the *buddhas*,
> he then becomes [their] disciple.
>
> [Let him] confess his faults before those masters of the world.

> [*Mmk* 11.99.7-12]
> From that time, when the edge of the sun is in the sky,
> he should abandon *mantra* recitation;
> doing so, the observer of the vow offered
> something of value.[C3]

Even if some form of conventional *anuttarapūjā* is implied here, the emphasis is clearly on *mantra* recitation. This suggests another connection with the term *anuttarapūjā*: the *uttamasādhana* becomes, for the *Mmk* cult, the *proper* method of *anuttarapūjā*. Remnants of the old form are preserved in the recitation of hymns of praise, and so forth, but these become secondary to *mantra* recitation. In other words, the text's descriptions of *mahatī pūjā* can be taken at face value. The *uttamasādhana* passage states only that the practitioner should make an abundant offering of certain materials and *mantra* recitation. The passage reads: "He should offer one lac of white lotuses and oiled white saffron at the base of the *paṭa* to the blessed Śākyamuni and to all the noble disciples, solitary *buddhas*, *bodhisattvas*, and *buddhas*, and he should burn as much camphor and incense as he can afford; he should worship the *nāgas* and gods with as many lotuses as he can procure." The statement at *Mmk* 10 in the previous paragraph might be understood as a gloss: *mahatī pūjā* is a material offering in conjuction with (or, including) lengthy *mantra* recitation. As indicated by a passage at *Mmk* 9, the material offering can be quite extensive: "lamps made of silver and gold, of copper and clay, filled with frankincense and seseme oil, or with lamps filled with cow's ghee, with pieces of new cloth, with cloth that has been rolled up."[57] As in the *pūjā* segment of the classical *anuttarapūjā*, offering comprises yet another form of preparation in the *Mmk uttamasādhana*.

1.4.2 mantras

In the *Mmk*, a *mantra* is presented as a linguistic space that is occupied by the force of some enlightened being, such as a *buddha* or a *bodhisattva*. It is thus analogous to a relic or an icon. Like its close relative, the *dhāraṇi,* a *mantra* is a vessel that bears, holds, preserves, and contains. A *mantra* is spoken, so it is a form of speech. Like ordinary speech, it must be learned. Learning it means knowing how to use it, and in which contexts. But the sense of a *mantra* relies on a "grammar" completely different from ordinary speech. That is, the system of rules implicit in *mantric* language does not concern linguistic features, but social, doctrinal, and ritual ones. A *mantra*, like an ordinary word, is effective only when spoken under the proper conditions; and the proper conditions exist only once numerous social, doctrinal, and ritual rules have been strictly followed. These conditions are discussed below.

The discussions at 1.3.3 on the ritual catalog and 1.4.1 on the structure of the *uttamasādhana* attest to the centrality of the *mantra* to the practice of the *Mmk.* Indeed, the very term for the mode of practice propagated in the text is called *mantracaryā.* In the *Mmk*, the "word of the Buddha," the *buddhavacana*, consists not of his discourses, but of the *mantras* that he, and "all *buddhas*," have spoken throughout time.

The *Mmk* begins and ends with *mantra.* The text is preceded by a phrase that commonly marks the appearance of either a *sūtra* or a *mantra*: *namaḥ sarvabuddhabodhisattvebhyaḥ* ("Homage to all *buddhas* and *bodhisattvas*").[58] And it ends, 721 pages later, with the statement: *samāsena sarvamantraṃ sādhayati* ("in short, every *mantra* causes success").[59] The former phrase intimates that every word that follows is to be regarded as *mantra*, as a form occupied by the power of an enlightened being. The fact that the book itself, as a repository of such forms, is to be treated as a potent object of veneration supports this. The position of the latter statement, too, tells us something about the nature of the *mantra*; namely, that its success is dependent on a considerable infrastucture. In the text that lies between the two phrases are found the social, doctrinal, and ritual foundations on which the success of the *mantra* rests.

The *Mmk* does not say what a *mantra* is. Rather, it shows what it is. In other words, the nature of the *mantra* in the *Mmk* can only be understood from the images of *mantric* use presented in the text; it is not known from explicit statements. As I said at 1.1, this is characteristc of the *Mmk* as a whole. Certainly, there is nothing approaching the sort of "theological" discussions concerning the *mantra* found in the *jñānapada* sections of Vaiṣṇava and Śaiva ritual texts.[60]

The *Mmk* community's reticence to make explicit statements about the *mantra* should not be passed over too quickly. As authors and practitioners of a ritual *vaipulyasūtra/kalpa,* those who embraced the text would have been well aware of the exegetical and apologetic traditions governing ritual discourse. All the major groups—Vedic, Śaiva, Vaiṣṇava, Śākta, Buddhist—in their numerous varieties have developed such traditions. So why is the *Mmk* silent on philosophical justification?

As I noted in chapter 1, it is not that the text is devoid of rhetorical justification; rather, what is significant is the form that the justification takes. The *Mmk* shows what other texts say. It presents images and teaches the reader how to make those images his own, in reality. In this sense, the *Mmk* reflects an extra-intellectualist and extra-theoretical tradition. Here, philosophical propositions are considered instruments of a logic that applies only to the most limited aspects of the world. The authors of the *Mmk* avoid philosophical modes of discourse because they—this tradition—see it as ineffectual in the pursuit of enlightened power. This attitude evokes the ancient image of the Buddha as one who speaks only about that which is conducive to the end of suffering and to enlightenment—or, more to the point, as one who *shows* the direct way. To this way of thinking, language represents the limits of the world. Transcending the possibilities of the immediate world—which occurs at the *highest* level of practice, the *uttamasādhana*—can therefore not be spoken about, but only shown. This is not to say that the *Mmk* is beyond criticism concerning its "pictoral" propositions. That is, the text is still making claims that can be tested for their coherency. But if a skeptic argued in terms of foundations and justifications, the practitioner of the *Mmk* would respond by showing him an image—imaginative or actual—and teaching him how to realize it as his own. This is the spirit behind the text: a theory about *mantra* has nothing to do with *mantra*; a theory is a mere calculus, a lifeless symbolic notation; this sort of thing is of no use soteriologically, or even practically to a *sādhaka*—for he is one who *practices*.

The text, thus, shows the *mantra*. It does this by ascribing it authority, describing its use, and demonstrating its effect. *Ascription of authority, description of use, and demonstration of effect* are the means by which the several dimensions of the *mantra* in the *Mmk* are revealed. Therefore, I will attempt a presentation of the *mantra* in the *Mmk* along these lines.

Ascription of authority

The *Mmk* shows that its *mantras* are inscribed with the authority of *buddhas*. The following passage is the first presentation of *mantras* in the text. Mañjuśrī is abiding in the "*buddha*-field" known as the Land of Flowers (*kusumāvatī*), presided over by the *buddha* Saṅkusumitarājendra. Saṅkusumitarājendra is enjoining the *bodhisattva* to go "stand in the presence" of Śākyamuni in order to receive the instructions that comprise the *mantracaryā* of the *Mmk*. The vehicle for attaining this "presence," in spite of the Buddha's location in a distant *buddha*-field, is invocation of a *mantra*.

> The blessed *tathāgata* Saṅkusumitarājendra further said to the princely Mañjuśrī: "Moreover, O prince, your *mantra* practice . . . has been pronounced, and will be pronounced, by one hundred thousand *tathāgatas*, perfected ones, perfectly enlightened ones, equaling the sands of the Ganges river . . . Now consented to by me as well, you must go, O princely Mañjuśrī, if you think the time is fit, and stand in the presence of Śākyamuni. You will listen to this discourse on the doctrine, and then you, too, will proclaim that. The *mantra* [for this purpose] is: *namaḥ sarvatathāgatānām acintyāpratihataśāsanānāṃ oṁ ra ra smara / apratihataśāsanakumārarūpadhāriṇa hūm hūm phaṭ phaṭ svāhā* (Homage to the inconceivable, unobstructed teachings of the *tathāgatas*: *Oṁ ra ra*

> *remember O unobstructed teaching O bearer of the princely form hūm hūm phaṭ phaṭ hail!*) This, O princely Mañjusrī, is the basic *mantra,* the essence of all *buddhas*. It has been, and will be, uttered by all *buddhas*. Now, you, too, will utter it. When you have arrived in the Sahā world, [utter] each all-accomplishing [*mantra*] in turn. The [*mantra* of] supreme essence has been authorized by the *tathāgata* Śākyamuni. It is: *Oṃ vākye da namaḥ*; and the *upahṛdaya* is: *vākye hūm.* [D1]

Mañjuśrī then enters into a deep meditation. The four directions are filled with *buddhas*. He is praised for achieving this deep meditation. Saṅkusumitarājendra then reveals the "utmost essential, utmost secretive" *mantra* (*paramahṛdayaṃ paramaguhyaṃ*). Saṅkusumitarājendra suddenly becomes quiet. Entering into meditation, he brings forth the *mantra* with his benevolent mind (*maitrātmakena cetasā*):] *namaḥ sarvabuddhānām* (homage to all *buddhas*). This *mantra*, the text states, "is Mañjuśrī, the utmost essence, the panacea" (*mantraḥ eṣa mañjuśrīḥ paramahṛdayaḥ sarvakarmakaraḥ*).[61]

When the text ascribes authority to *mantra* utterance, it is doing several things at once. It is, first of all, making a claim about "mythic" origin. The *mantras* were originally uttered by not only Śākyamuni Buddha, but by all *buddhas* throughout space and time. The fact that Saṅkusumitarājendra accesses the *mantra* by entering into a contemplative state suggests that this is where *mantras* originate: in the minds of the *buddhas*, which are infused with benevolence. Similarly, that Mañjuśrī receives the *mantra* only after he has entered into a deep meditation suggests that it is in the deeper layers of consciousness that such *mantras* are held to resonate fully. We read, for instance, that *dhāraṇīs*, a type of *mantra*, "arise from the penetrative mind, which ensues naturally from meditative absorption," and that *vidyārājñīs*, the bearers of *mantras* called *vidyās*, "issue forth from the meditative absorption on the body of Avalokiteśvara."[62] The "inconceivable, unobstructed teaching of the *tathāgatas,*" furthermore, is the *ur*-transmission of the *mantras* and accompanying practices that have constituted the practice of all *buddhas*. This is a picture of both a lineage and a particular relationship. The teaching on *mantra* practice is given to the *bodhisattva* Mañjuśrī by the *buddha* Saṅkusumitarājendra. Once he has received it, Mañjuśrī must then teach it to beings in the world, where it will be inscribed into the text. The reader of the text is thus placed within the lineage, into direct relation to all *buddhas*.

The presentation of mythic origin leads easily into a claim about the means of knowledge (called *pramāṇa* in Indian epistemology): the validity of the knowledge about *mantras* contained in the passage is established precisely on the fact that both text and *mantras* were spoken by *buddhas*. To a nonadherent, this is a weak form of *pramāṇa*. The logical dubiousness of this claim, however, is overcome by a further dimension of the ascription of authority, since this aspect lays the theoretical foundation for efficacy and, thus, for "direct perception," the strongest form of *pramāṇa.* As we saw in the index lists, the theoretical basis for the *mantra* is "the inconceivable, wondrous, miraculous transformation of the *bodhisattva,*" or *vikurvaṇa.* This process is alluded to above in the statement, "this *mantra* is Mañjuśrī, the utmost essence, the *panacea*" (*mantraḥ eṣa mañjuśrīḥ paramahṛdayaḥ sarvakarmakaraḥ*). The *vikurvaṇa* of the *bodhisattva* is a wide-ranging concept. We will see below (2.3) how this concept serves as the mechanism of embodiment, *avatāra,* in general. Here, I would like to consider its bearing on the text's claims about *mantra.*

The statement, "that upon which all beings depend: the miraculous transformation of the *bodhisattva* (*bodhisattvavikurvaṇa*)," refers to a foundational axiom in the *Mmk* concerning both the method of the Buddha's activity in the world and the constitution of ritual efficacy. The mode of practice recorded in the *Mmk* has no basis—as *Buddhist* practice—removed from this foundation. It might even be argued that it is primarily the framework supported by the concept of *vikurvaṇa,* "miraculous transformation," that distinguishes the Buddhist ritual of the *Mmk* from other forms of medieval Indian cultic activity.

The term *vikurvaṇa* has several layers of meaning. Combining the root √*kṛ* (to make), with the affix *vi* (apart, asunder, different directions), it means "to make different, change, transform." As the Pāli equivalent *vikubbana* indicates, however, Buddhists employed the term technically from an early date to denote a transformation effected by potent mental forces (*iddhivikubbana*).[63] Being on the same scale as a *bodhisattva*—albeit at a lower point—the practitioner of the *Mmk* develops such psychic powers, enabling him to perform several supernatural transformations, or "miracles," such as becoming invisible, walking on water, flying through the air, ascending to the highest heavens.

The implications of the term *bodhisattvavikurvaṇa* in the *Mmk,* however, exceed even these technical meanings. As one of the ten powers of the *bodhisattva* (*bodhisattvabala*),[64] the power of miraculous transformation (*vikurvaṇabala*) is, for the Buddhist engaged in the *Mmk,* the mechanism generating the *mantra.* Mañjuśrī, by means of his powers of transformation, "becomes the *mantra.*" The *mantra* is an effective instrument by virtue of its being nothing less than a form assumed by the *bodhisattva* Mañjuśrī. As the various categories of *mantras* mentioned above indicate—*hṛdaya, upahṛdaya, paramahṛdaya*—the *mantras* are the very essence, the heart (*hṛdaya*) of the *bodhisattva.* The *paramahṛdayamantra* is "Mañjuśrī himself" (*svayam eva mañjuśrīḥ*), existing (*upasthitaḥ*) through the form of the *mantra (mantrarūpena*).[65] One indication of the force believed to pervade the *mantra* is the power attributed to it: "when merely remembered, it [the *paramahṛdaya mantra*] cleanses [the practitioner] of the five acts entailing immediate retribution."[66]

Since the *bodhisattva* and the "form of the *mantra*" are, in essence, one, and because the text is not explicit about its claims, an analysis of one of these forms should reveal a clearer picture of the relationship between the *mantra* and the *bodhisattva* in the *Mmk*.

> [The *mantra* is preceded by the liturgical formula:] Homage to all *buddhas* and *bodhisattvas*, whose conduct follows from unobstructed intelligence. Homage to the king of emperors, to him who completely purifies and calms all suffering—to the *tathāgata*, the perfected one, the perfectly enlightened one. Here [is the *mantra* to be recited]: *Oṁ* purify purify! O destroyer of all obstacles O you of great compassion O bearer of youthful form! perform a miraculous transformation perform a miraculous transformation! remember your vow! be present be present! *hūm hūm phaṭ phaṭ svāhā*![D2]

In the opening scene of the *Mmk*, Mañjuśrī was "impelled" (*codaṇa*)[67] by the radiating force of Śākyamuni's omniscience to perform his obligation as a tenth-stage *bodhisattva*. His "being" the *mantra* is one mode through which that obligation is fulfilled. The power that enables this equivalency, in turn, involves two additional doctrinal stances operating in the *mantra*. The first, as we have seen, is indicated by the imperative to "perform a miraculous transformation" (*vikurva*); the second, in the imperative "remember your vow" (*samayam anusmara*). The power of *vikurvaṇa* is one of the ten supernatural powers of the *bodhisattva* (*bodhisattvabala*). Based, in turn, on the doctrinal axiom of "the ontological equivalence or ultimate convertibility of phenomena and absolute,"[68] *vikurvaṇa* is, in Luis Gómez's words, "the capacity to effect, by sheer psychic power, the transformation, displacement or multiplication of the human body."[69] The *bodhisattva* is a being situated in the world. Because, however, the *bodhisattva* is an enlightened being, he or she realizes the illusory nature of the world and thereby gains the ability to move unimpededly through the world, manipulating its forms at will. The world of the *bodhisattva* becomes the *dharmadhātu*, the world seen as a composition of ultimately nonsubstantial components subject—precisely because of their lack of real substance—to manipulation. The *Samādhirājā*, also referred to in the *Mmk*,[70] likens the freedom of movement that ensues from this understanding of reality to "wind blow[ing] swiftly through space" or the unbounded flight of birds in the sky.

> As birds do not leave a path in space, thus do Bodhisattvas awaken to the true nature of Awakening. The sky is said to be ungraspable, in it there is nothing to grasp. This is the true nature of *dharmas*, ungraspable like the sky.[71]

The invocation of the *bodhisattva* by means of the purificatory *mantra* impells him to inhabit, and thus become identical with, in this case, certain ritual implements. The means generating this result is alluded to in the plea that the *bodhisattva* remember his vow, and in the invoking of his universal compassion. Another text referred to in the *Mmk*, the *Gaṇḍavyūha*,[72] contains an elaborate version on the *bodhisattva* vow (called *samaya* in the *Mmk*, and *pranidhāṇa* in the *Gaṇḍavyūha*).[73] In the following extract, allusions are made to the several points of doctrine mentioned above.

> By the power of supernatural abilities,
> swiftly abounding everywhere,
> by the power of universally eminent knowledge,
> by the power of perfectly virtuous conduct,
> by the power of universal love,
> by the power of perfectly pure merit;
> by the power of unobstructed knowledge,
> by the power of wisdom, means, and contemplation,
> acquiring the power of enlightenment,
> completely purifying the power of retributive actions (*karma*),
> completely grinding the power of afflictions,
> rendering powerless the power of death and time (*māra*)—
> may I fufill all the powers of good conduct.
>
> Having completely fulfilled all of those [vows],
> may I act for the happiness of beings
> as long as [they remain] in the world.[74]

The above *mantra* is thus inscribed with the authority of the *bodhisattva*. The *bodhisattva's* original vow to attain enlightenment for the benefit of all beings eventually produces the being capable of traversing the world, and of playfully entering and transforming linguistic "shells," or spaces.

Description of use

From the angle of the ascription of authority, we learned that the *mantra* is a sound, word, or series of words that was spoken by enlightened beings in the past and, through the mechanism of *vikurvaṇa*, embodied by their force in the present and future. A *mantra* is therefore presented as a sonic embodiment or crystallization of a particular type of power. When we consider the *mantra* from the angle of the text's descriptions of its use, these sounds, words, and series of words begin to separate out into subtly different types of utterance stemming from distinct aspects of that power.

Essence (hṛdaya) mantras

At the beginning of *Mmk* 2, there is reference to Mañjuśrī's "class of *mantras*."[75] This is followed by a compendium of the *mantras* used in the *Mmk* rituals. The first group comprises *hṛdaya mantras*. Examples of these were given above (at *Mmk* 1.2.20–22, 27–3.9): the *hṛdaya, paramahṛdaya* and *upahṛdaya mantras*. There, it was said that the *hṛdaya mantra* accomplishes the task of leading Mañjuśrī into the presence of Śākyamuni, while the other two are called "all-accomplishing," or "*panaceaic*" (*sarvakarmakara*)—*mantras* to be employed for any purpose. These *mantras* are "all-accomplishing" because they are the "utmost essence" (*paramahṛdaya*) of compassionate, enlightened power, which is unlimited. These were the same *mantras* suggested for use in the preparation phase of the practice. The *uttamasādhana* passage at 1.4.1 read:

> First, he who has observed the vow, fulfilled the preliminary practices, received the initiation, taken the essential (*hṛdaya*), basic *mantra* from this best of ordinances, or the *upahṛdaya* or some other *mantra*, or having received a single syllable [*mantra*] or another one—according to one's wishes—and who, having gone to a great forest, eats leaves and roots, who subsists on fruits and water, should recite [the *mantra*] three million times. He becomes one who has completed the preliminary practice.[C2]

Here, by means of the mental purity attained through prolonged recitation, the *sādhaka* is able to "come into the presence" of the Buddha. The image presented at *Mmk* 2 of the power inhering in these *mantras* emphasizes the purifying, protective, and "all accomplishing" nature of these *mantras*. Mañjuśrī addresses the section to Vajrapāṇi. Vajrapāṇi appears in the *Mmk* as the "lord of *yakṣas*, the master of *guhyakas*."[76] By mastering these destructive divinities, Vajrapāṇi converts them into powers serving the aims of the practitioner. Thus, the *mantras* presented here are of this nature. They destroy, purify, and convert energy of various forms of embodiment, including mental, supernatural, and physical.

The first *mantra* presented is that of Yamāntaka, the "sovereign of wrath" (*krodharāja*),[77] who, in later tantric theory, though not here, is identified as an emanation of Mañjuśrī himself. For the reader of the *Mmk*, as for the practitioner of its rituals, the first step toward acquiring essential knowledge is protection and the destruction of obstacles.

> Then Mañjuśrī [bestowed] the preeminently heroic, all achieving essence (*hṛdaya*) of the sovereign of wrath, Yamāntaka . . . *oṃ āḥ hūṁ*. This is the essence (*hṛdaya*) of him whose wrath is great; it is all accomplishing; it is taught by the great being Mañjughoṣa for [use in] all *maṇḍala* and *mantra* rituals; it destroys all obstacles.
>
> Then Mañjuśrī lifted his right hand and placed it on the head of Krodha, and spoke thus: "Obeisance to all *buddhas*! May the blessed *buddhas* pay heed! May the *bodhisattvas*, who are dwelling in whatever world of the ten directions, and who possess unlimited, infinite, supernatural power (*maharddhika*), be

> firm in their vow!" Saying that, he circled [T. his hand] around the king of wrath, and dismissed him. The instant that the great king of wrath was dispatched to the entire world-realm, beings possessing great supernatural powers immediately restrained all evil-minded beings. He made them enter the Śuddhāvāsa, the great assembly. Making them remain there, becoming the family of those who are engulfed in flaming garlands, he stood at the head, among the evil-beings.[D3]

The *mantra oṃ āḥ hūṁ* embodies the "essence" of Yamāntaka; it is therefore used in any ritual for the purpose of destroying malevolent obstacles. Here, the text presents an image of the violent, prelinguistic archetype operating behind the use of this *mantra*. Placing his hand on the head of Yamāntaka, Mañjuśrī invokes the authorizing presence of all *buddhas*. Yamāntaka becomes an agent of the *bodhisattva*, who, in turn is an agent of all *buddhas*. So empowered, Yamāntaka gains mastery over all evil forces within the world. In subduing "all evil-minded beings," Yamāntaka converts them into agents of his own aggressively purifying, protective force. When the practitioner recites the sounds *oṃ āḥ hūṁ*, this image, capturing the essential (*hṛdaya*) function and activity of Yamāntaka, is effected. That is, hindering forces are dispelled from the ritual space; protection is achieved, and the area where a given ritual is performed is thereby consecrated.

Additional "essence *mantras*" given at *Mmk* 2 are presented as belonging to the *bodhisattva* Vajrapāṇi, although the references within the *mantras* point to, respectively, Yamāntaka or Mañjuśrī. Perhaps the ambiguity is intentional. The protective function of Mañjuśrī is effected by Vajrapāṇi and Yamāntaka; the forms of each are ultimately undifferentiated. In any case, the *mantras* of this class are presented as serving as "rulers of great wrath that destroy all obstacles."

> Then the youthful Mañjuśrī spoke to the *bodhisattva* Vajrapāṇi: "O master of *guhyakas*, these *mantras* are esoteric and supremely secretive [. . .]
>
> Homage to all *buddhas* and *bodhisattvas*, whose teachings are indestructible. *uṃ kara kara kuru kuru mama kāryam bhañja bhañja sarvavighnāṃ daha daha sarva vajravināyakam mūrdhaṭakajīvitāntakara mahāvikṛtarūpiṇe paca paca sarvaduṣṭāṃ mahāgaṇapatijīvitāntakara bandha bandha sarvagrahāṃ ṣaṇmukha ṣaḍbhuja ṣaṭcaraṇa rudramānaya viṣṇumānaya brahmādyāṃ devānānaya mā vilamba mā vilamba iyal iyal maṇḍalamadhye praveśaya samayam anusmara hūṁ hūṁ hūṁ hūṁ hūṁ hūṁ phaṭ phaṭ svāhā* (*O maker O maker do do for me what should be done shatter shatter all obstacles burn burn all adamantine impediments O killer of Mūrdhaṭaka O you of extraordinary appearance cook cook all evil O killer of great Gaṇapati bind bind all demons O six-faced one O six-armed one O six-legged one subdue Rudra subdue Viṣṇu subdue the gods, beginning with Brahman do not delay do not delay become silent become silent enter into*

> *the maṇḍala remember your vow! hail!*)
>
> O supreme master of *guhyakas*, this [*mantra*] is the supreme mystery, the great hero, Mañjuśrī; it is called "six-faced one," and is the ruler of the great wrath, which destroys all obstacles. By merely reciting that, *bodhisattvas* who are established in the ten stages are dispersed, let alone evil obstructions. By merely reciting that, great protection is created. There is also a sealing gesture (*mudrā*) known as "the great spike," the destroyer of all obstacles.[D4]

This *mantra*, equated with both Mañjuśrī ("this is . . . Mañjuśrī") and Yamāntaka (the "six-faced one"), begins with an interjection of anger and pacification (*uṃ*). Among the powers that it serves to shatter and subdue are those connected to other cults: Viṣṇu, Śiva (Rudra), Gaṇapati, Mūrdhaṭaka, and Brahma. The *mantra* counteracts the power of these deities that has been set in motion by their adherents, and subjects that power—these deities—to the ends of the *Mmk* practitioner. This point is made explicit several pages later when the *mantras* of these cultic deities are presented as having been taught by Śākyamuni. Like an antibody, this *mantra* repels not only alien forms of power encroaching on the ritual space of the practitioner, but even the most advanced, allied *bodhisattvas* (tenth-stage ones). This indicates a degree of power bordering on the noxious. It is a small step from incapacitating the *effected* powers of rival deities to incapacitating those who effect such power. Indeed, the next *mantra* given justifies the destruction of "all enemies," presumably human as well as impersonal forces.

> This is the essence (*hṛdaya*) of the ruler of wrath [Yamāntaka]: *oṁ hrīḥ jñīḥ vikṛtānana hum / sarvaśatrūṃ nāśaya stambhaya phaṭ phaṭ svāhā* (*shame! destroy all enemies incapacitate! hail!*) By means of this *mantra*, all enemies are seized by the great spike disease or by the fever that arises every four days. With a hundred recitations, or as many as desired, benevolence is not practiced. Then, he obtains a compassionate mind. May there not be liberation at the end of the recitation. Those offending the three jewels, saying, "he dies," should not be treated entirely as those of gentle mind. The sealing gesture (*mudrā*) called "the great spike," should be used. In this instance, the secondary essence [*mantra*] (*upahṛdaya*) is this: *oṁ hṛīṁḥ kālarūpa hūṃ khaṃ svāhā* (*shame O you with the appearance of a crow! hail!*) The sealing gesture to be used is also "the great spike." Whatever evil he desires, that he accomplishes. The *paramahṛdaya* [*mantra*] is indeed the single syllable empowered by all *buddhas*: *hūṁ*. This accomplishes all deeds. The sealing gesture to be used is also "the great spike." It hinders all misfortunes. In short, O ruler of wrath, this [*mantra*] is to be employed in every ritual for the subjugation of all demons.[D5]

Additional *hṛdaya mantras* are given at *Mmk* 2. These are equated directly with the Buddha and Mañjuśrī.

> Homage to all *buddhas*. *Oṁ ra ra smara apratihataśāsanakumāra-rūpadhāriṇa hūṁ hūṁ phaṭ phaṭ svāhā* (*remember O indestructible teaching bearer of the form of a prince hail!*) That, O honorable men, is the root (*mūla*) *mantra* of me who is called the noble Mañjuśrī. The [corresponding] *mudrā* is known as "the five-crested great *mudrā*." Making that [sealing gesture] when the root *mantra* [is being recited], it becomes all-accomplishing and quintessential. The Buddha is all-accomplishing and auspicious.
>
> *Oṁ dhānyada namaḥ* (*O giver of grain, homage!*) Here the *mudrā*, is known as "three-crested." It is an increaser of all kinds of wealth. And here is the secondary essence [*mantra*] *upahṛdaya*: *bāhye hūṁ*. The *mudrā* in this case is known as "three-crested," and is that which attracts all beings.
>
> Here is the *paramahṛdaya*: *muṃ*. In this case the *mudrā* is known as "the seat of the peacock;" it is the subjugator of all beings. It is the essence of all *buddhas*. It, too, is unsurpassed, possessing great potency indeed; it has eight syllables, is the foremost among the eminent, is greatly purifying, cuts off what belongs to the way of the three realms of existence, hinders all evil destinies, causes universal tranquility, is all-accomplishing, leads to peace, to *nirvāṇa*, is approached, seen, and encountered as if it were the Buddha.
>
> This *bodhisattva* Mañjuśrī himself is approached through the form of this *mantra*, the supreme essence [*mantra*] (*paramahṛdaya*), for the sake of all beings, fulfilling every wish. When merely remembered it cleanses [the practitioner] of the five acts that entail immediate retribution. What speech, once more, should be produced? Which is that? *Oṁ āḥ dhīra hūṁ svacara*! (*O firm one O self-moving one!*) O you honorable men, I am this potent eight syllabled supremely secret *hṛdaya [mantra]*, abiding visibly as the state of enlightenment. In short [T. = in all rituals, the boundless qualities of that utterance is not exceeded by even myriad millions of eons]. The *mudrā* in this instance is known as "possessing great potency," and is that which filfills all wishes.[D6]

The mention of the *mudrā* in each of the *mantra* passages points to a significant aspect of the *mantra* as it is used in the *Mmk*. The hand gesture is an indispensable aspect of the type of ritual promulgated in the Vaiṣṇava Pañcarātra *saṃhitas*, Śaiva Siddhānta *āgamas,* as well as in the *Mmk.* By the early medieval era, the *mudrā* becomes an increasingly widespread element of the type of worship known as *mantracaryā* or *tantra*.[78] The importance of the *mudrā* for the practitioners of the Buddhist form of *mantracaryā* is evident from the fact that ten of the fifty-five chapters of the *Mmk* are devoted to it. At *Mmk* 34 we read of a *mudrākośa*, a treasury of ritual hand gestures.[79] *Mmk* 34–37 and 41–46 is an extensive compendium, a "text on hand gestures" (*mudrātantra*).[80] In the *Mmk*, these gestures invariably accompany verbal actions. The two, *mudrās* and *mantras*, are in fact so closely bound that they can be said to form a single instrumental act:[81] "The *mudrās* are the seals of the *mantras*; and with the *mantras* they are well-sealed. There is no *mantra* without a *mudrā*; devoid of the *mudrā*, there is no seal."[82] In many instances, the *mudrās* seem to be bodily presentations of the object either invoked or offered by means of the *mantra* (e.g., the "three-headed" and "five-headed" gestures imitating the head dress of Mañjuśrī; "the spike," and the "seat of the peacock"). Stephan Beyer calls these types of *mudrās*, "*mimetic representations* of the objects being offered—simulacra that control the transmission of worship to the god, just as the mantras of offering enjoin its acceptance and response."[83] Beyer also mentions a "stereotyped gesture," that is, a ritualized use of a common gesture for threat. Such *mudrās* correspond to *mantras* such as *phaṭ*—that is, the ritual use of sounds that are employed in everyday expression. Examples of this type of *mudrā* are gestures of "reverence, threat, welcome, or farewell."[84] (No such gestures are prescribed at *Mmk* 2.) In sum, the *mudrā*, when employed by a serious initiate[85] in conjunction with the proper *mantra*, creates quick and infallible results.[86]

So far, I have discussed *hṛdaya mantras*. The text describes several uses of these *mantras*. Those related directly to the Buddha/all *buddhas* and to Mañjuśrī are "all-accomplishing"; that is, their application is manifold, ranging from the fulfillment of personal wishes, good health, and fortunate rebirth, to enlightenment. Those attached specifically to the "fierce" aspect of Mañjuśrī—in the form of Vajrapāṇi and Yamāntaka—are used to purify and protect the mental and physical space of the practitioner.

Invocation (āhvānana) mantras

After the presentation of the "powerful eight-syllabled" *hṛdaya mantra* (*Mmk* 2.26.13–27.3), *Mmk* 2 presents what it calls *āhvānana mantras*. As the term indicates, these are to be used specifically for the invocation (*āhvānana*) of both enlightened forces and worldly forces and spirits.

> Here are the *mantras* for invocation: *Oṁ he he kumārarūpisvarūpiṇe sarvabālabhāṣitaprabodhane āyāhi bhagavaṃ āyāhi kumārakrīḍotpaladhāriṇe maṇḍalamadhye tiṣṭha tiṣṭha samayam anusmara apratihataśasana hūṁ mā vilamba ru ru phaṭ svāhā* (*O you whose own form is the form of a prince O awakening spoken by all youth approach O blessed one approach O you who bear the lotus playing as a prince abide abide in the middle of the maṇḍala! remember the vow! O indestructible teaching hūṁ! do not delay! hail!*) This is the *mantra* for invoking the blessed Mañjuśrī, and [for invoking] all beings, all *bodhisattvas*, all solitary *buddhas*, noble

> hearers, gods, *nāgas, yakṣas, gandharvas, garuḍas, kinnaras, mahoragas, piśācas, rākṣasas, bhūtas.*[D7]

Several of the *mantras* presented so far have referred to the *maṇḍala.* The fact that this section on *mantras* precedes the prescriptions for the *abhiṣeka* ritual indicates that the *mantras* are to be applied specifically during that ritual. The initiation is performed within a *maṇḍala.* This point will be elaborated on at 4.1, below. The act of invoking auspicious, protective, and converted threatening forces is a standard feature of the *Mmk* ritual practice. One example should suffice to show this. The raw cotton used for making the cult image must be consecrated (*abhimantraṇa*) before it is woven into a canvas. This is achieved by invoking the force of "all *buddhas*" in the form of Mañjuśrī.

> [The *mantra* is preceded by a liturgical formula:] Homage to all *buddhas* and *bodhisattvas*, whose conduct follows from unobstructed intelligence. Homage to the king of emperors, to him who completely purifies and calms all suffering—to the *tathāgata*, the perfected one, the perfectly enlightened one. Here [is the *mantra* to be recited]: *oṁ śodhaya śodhaya sarvavighnaghātaka mahākāruṇika kumārarūpadhāriṇe vikurva vikurva samayam anusmara tiṣṭha tiṣṭha hūṃ hūṃ phaṭ phaṭ svāhā (purify purify! O destroyer of all obstacles O you of great compassion O bearer of youthful form! perform a miraculous transformation perform a miraculous transformation! remember your vow! be present be present! hūṃ hūṃ phaṭ phaṭ hail!)*[D2]

Similarly, the *āhvānana mantras* consecrate the object into which some force is being drawn, or, in the language of the text, is being implored to approach (*āyāhi*) the object and abide (*tiṣṭha*) within it. While the *mantra* is always specific in that its terms refer directly to the effected object, and its corresponding *mudrā* often "mimicks" the object, the pattern of invocation is consistently generalized throughout the *Mmk.*

Offering mantras

From the *mantra* used to summon powers to the *maṇḍala* or to any other place where rituals are performed, the text moves to the forces to whom the offerings are directed. Since the goal of these offerings is to make present the invoked force, these *mantras* may be considered a subcategory of *āhvānana mantras.* The following example shows the sensual nature of the language of these passages.

> Having prepared the sandalwood water, consecrated seven times, he should scatter it everywhere: in all four directions, upwards, downwards, horizontally. All *buddhas* and *bodhisattvas*, the retinue of Mañjuśrī himself, all *mantras*,

> ordinary and extraordinary, all classes of creatures, and all beings must appear. Homage to all *buddhas*, whose teachings are indestructible! *Oṁ dhu dhura dhura dhūpavāsini dhūpārciṣi hūṁ tiṣṭha samayam anusmara svāhā* (*O you dwelling in the incense O luster of the incense abide remember your vow hail!*) [This is the] "incense *mantra*." Then, having prepared the saffron, camphor, and sandalwood, [the incense *mantra*] should be bestowed on the incense. All *tathāgatas* and *bodhisattvas* come, and they are drawn out of the heart of the gratified incense. The *mudrā* of this [*mantra*] is known as "the garland," and is auspicious, attracting all beings. These *mantras* of invocation and their *mudrās* are beautiful garlands of lotuses. They should be offered to all the *buddhas, bodhisattvas* and other beings who come. After stirring water with camphor, sandalwood, and saffron, and preparing a mixture of two draughts of crushed *bakula* flowers, white lotuses grown in the rainy season and fresh garlands of jasmine with some other fragrant flower that is in season, an offering should be made along with the *mantra*. Homage to all *buddhas*, whose teachings are indestructible! The *mantra* is: *he he mahākāruṇika viśvarūpadhāriṇi arghyaṃ pratīcchad pratīcchāpaya samayam anusmara tiṣṭha tiṣṭha maṇḍalamadhye praveśaya praviśa sarvabhūtānukampaka gṛhṇa gṛhṇa hūṁ ambaravicāriṇe svāhā* (*hey hey you of great compassion, bearer of manifold forms regard this offering receive this offering remember your vow! abide abide in the center of the maṇḍala! lead into it enter into it! O you who possess compassion for all beings seize seize O you who traverse the sky!hail!*) The *mudrā* for this is known as "abundance," and it is followed by all *buddhas*.[D8]

The equivalency of the *mantra*, *mudrā,* object of consecration, and possessing force is explicit in these offering *mantras*. These are called variously incense *mantras* (*dhūpamantra*), fragrance *mantras* (*gandhamantra*), oblative *mantras* (*balimantra*), lamp or illumination *mantras* (*pradīpamantra*), and fire *mantras* (*agnimantra*).

> And here are the perpetually fragrant *mantras* (*gandhamantra*). Homage to all *buddhas*! Homage to the *tathāgata*, whose glory, brilliance and fragrance are universal! The *mantra* is: *gandhe gandhe gandhāḍhye gandhamanorame pratīcche pratīcchemaṃ gandham samantānusāriṇe svāhā!* (*O fragrant one O fragrant one O you abounding in fragrance O joy within the fragrance attend attend to me O you who entirely penetrate this fragrance! hail!*) The sealing gesture in this case is called "the bud that completely fulfills all desires." And here are the flower *mantras* (*puṣpamantra*). Homage to all *buddhas*, whose teachings are indestructible! Homage to the *tathāgata*, the ruler of those who have fully blossomed! The *mantra* is this: *kusume kusume kusumāḍhye kusumapuravāsini kusumāvati svāhā* (*O blossoming O blossoming O you abounding in blossoms O you dwelling in the city of blossoms O land of blossoms! hail!*) He should thus fumigate with the incense *mantra* (*dhūpamantra*), mentioned above, [and] with incense.
>
> Making obeisance to the *buddhas*,

> who possess inconceivably wondrous forms,
> I will proclaim this oblative *mantra* (*balimantra*),
> which has been spoken by the perfectly enlightened *buddhas*.
>
> Homage to all *buddhas* and *bodhisattvas*, whose teachings are indestructible! The *mantra* is this: *he he bhagavaṃ mahāsattva buddhāvalokita mā vilamba idaṃ baliṃ gṛhṇāpaya gṛhna hūṁ hūṁ sarvaviśva ra ra ṭa ṭa phaṭ svāhā* (*hey hey blessed one! O great being! do not delay take this offering take! O all and everything! hail!*) Along with [reciting] this, he should present the offering and the oblation to all sentient beings. The *mudrā* has the power to ward off all evil. Homage to the indestructible teachings of all *buddhas* and *bodhisattvas*, which completely destroys the darkness of delusions! Homage to the *tathāgata*, whose glory, resplendence and fragrance shines universally! The [illumination *mantra* (*pradīpamantra*: 28.15)] is: *he he bhagavaṃ jyotiraśmiśatasahasrapratimaṇḍitaśarīra virkurva vikurva mahābodhisattvasamantajvālodyotitamūrti khurda khurda avalokaya avalokaya sarvasattvānāṃ svāhā* (*O you whose body is adorned with a hundred thousand rays of light transform transform O manifestation who shines replendently and universally on the great bodhisattvas play play behold behold all beings! hail!*) These are the illumination *mantras*. Together with this, the lamp (*pradīpa*) should be offered. The *mudrā* is called "the beam of light that beholds all beings." Homage to all *buddhas* and *bodhisattvas*, whose teachings are indestructible! The [*mantra*] is: *jvala jvala jvālaya jvālaya hūṁ vibodhaka harikṛṣṇapiṅgala svāhā* (*blaze blaze illuminate illuminate O awakening O reddish-brown dark green one! hail!*)
>
> These are the fire *mantras*. The *mudrā*, called "the covered box" (*saṃpuṭa*), is famous throughout the world. Shining brilliantly on all beings, it was previously proclaimed by those best of *munis* for the wise *bodhisattva*.[D9]

The verse highlights the fact that a *mantra* must be preceded by a liturgical formula. As with the *uttamasādhana*, preparation is a central feature of any form of *mantra* recitation. In every instance, preparation involves mentally focusing on the authority that stands behind the power being made manifest by means of the *mantra*.

Dismissal (visarjana) mantras

Following the *āhvānana mantras*, the text gives the "dismissal *mantra*" (*visarjana mantra*). This is used for withdrawing the power of the *mantra* after it has "effected" the goal of the practitioner.

> The dismissal *mantras*. Homage to all *buddhas*, whose teachings are indestructible. [The *mantra*] is: *jaya jaya sujaya mahākāruṇika viśvarūpiṇe gaccha gaccha svabhavanam sarvabuddhāṃś ca visarjaya saparivārāṃ svabhavanaṃ cānupraveśaya samayam anusmara sarvārthāś ca me*

siddhyantu mantrapadāḥ manorathaṃ ca me paripūraya svāhā (conquer conquer completely conquer O you of great compassion who appears in various forms go go to your own abode and dismiss all buddhas enter your own abode along with your retinue remember your vow may the mantra words effect all of my goals and my heart's desire completely fulfill! hail!) This dismissal *mantra* should be employed in all rituals. The sealing gesture is known as "the throne of good" (*bhadrapīṭha*). Together with this, a seat should be offered. The *mantra* adept (*mantrasiddhi*) should employ the *visarjana* together with seven [silent] mental recitations for all ordinary and extraordinary [rituals], *maṇḍala* [rituals] and *mantra* [rituals], and when under occasional vows—during *jāpa* recitation [i.e., during the *pūraścaraṇa*].[D10]

vidyā mantras

Following this is a long section on a class of *mantras* called *vidyā*, taught by Mañjuśrī to the assembly gathered in the Śuddhāvāsa palace. As with the above classes of *mantras*, the *Mmk* does not offer explicit explanations of the *vidyā*, but presents images and descriptions of use. The main image of the *vidyā* is of a "female companion" (*anucarī*) of Mañjuśrī—all *vidyās* are given in the feminine gender. The *vidyās* are "possessed of beautiful hair" (*keśinī, upakeśinī*), "star-like" (*tārāvatī*), "possessed of brilliant, glorious beauty" (*śvetaśrīvapu*), "of great loveliness" (*mahālakṣmī*).[87] As with all other *mantras*, *mudrās*—usually "mimetic"—invariably accompany *vidyās*. And, as the following examples illustrate, *vidyās* are applied for various purposes.

Homage to all *buddhas*, whose teachings are indestructible: *oṁ riṭi svāhā!* This is the *vidyā* that does everything; it is called "lovely hair," [and is] the female companion of Mañjuśrī. During all rituals requiring an attendant the great sealing gesture, "five-crests," is used. Homage to the universal *buddhas*, whose teachings are indestructible: *oṁ niṭi*. This *vidyā*, called *upakeśinī*, is *panaceaic*. [This] should be used with the sealing gesture "blooming" in all rituals of seizure.

Homage to the universal *buddhas*,
who possess inconceivably wondrous forms.
Oṁ nu re [T. = *tāre*] *svāhā*
This *vidyā*, called "star-like" (*tārāvatī*)
is commended for all rituals.
Performed together with the sealing gesture
"staff of force,"
[this *vidyā*] is a destroyer of obstacles.

Homage to the universal *buddhas*,
who proceed on an unobstructed course.
[The *vidyā* is] *oṁ śrīḥ*
This spell, "she of great loveliness,"

> was taught by the protectors of the world.
> Practiced with the sealing gesture
> "bowl-shaped,"
> she grants the rank of "emperor."[D11]

The *vidyās* refer to feminine deities that were appropriated by Buddhists. As such, they are classed as belonging not to the family of *buddhas* (*tathāgatakula*), but to that of the "lotus" (*abjakula*). *Mmk* 1 mentions numerous *vidyārājñīs* "proceeding from the *samādhi* of the manifest Lokeśvara"; the *vidhārājñīs* "proceed from the *mantras* and penetrate the vow of the lotus family."[88]

Non-Buddhist mantras

In this vein, the section on *mantras* at *Mmk* 2 ends with an appropriation of the *mantras* of major non-Buddhist deities. This subsection is prefaced by a polemical "revisionist" history of the *mantras* that are then presented. The central contention of the history is that all previous *mantras*—those of Brahma, Śiva, Viṣṇu, and so on—were originally spoken by the Buddhist *bodhisattva* Mañjuśrī, though in the form of Brahma, Śiva, and so forth. Mañjuśrī merely took the form of these Hindu deities as an *upāya*—in this case, as a means of conversion. Specifically, the preface identifies Mañjuśrī with Kārttikeya (also called Skanda), the six-headed son of Śiva in Purāṇic mythology. In this manner, the *Mmk* presents its own Purāṇa fragment of sorts, rewriting the history of Kārttikeya, revealing essential facts about his life that had been excluded from the Śaiva account. In the *Mmk* version, Kārttikeya's name is combined with Mañjuśrī's: Kārttikeyamañjuśrī. This synthetic name gives a clear picture of the authors' intention to co-opt Śaiva claims and subordinate these to those of the *Mmk*. Although there are allusions to Kārttikeya/Skanda's role as the leader of the demons who cause illness in children, here that role is reversed: Kārttikeyamañjuśrī declares a *mantra* that "completely frees from illness during the period of youth." Finally, Kārttikeya is assigned the roll of attendant (*anucara*) to the *bodhisattva*.

> This was spoken by the *bodhisattva* Mañjughoṣa,
> the protector, whose six[-faced] transformation
> shook the entire world.
>
> To hinder evil beings
> for the sake of all beings' welfare,
> the terrible son of Maheśvara (= of Śiva)
> came here in order to convert others.
>
> Well marked by the emblems of demons
> and with charcoal,
> he who speaks sweetly
> spoke to Skanda with a mind engrossed

in compassion.

This the great-souled *bodhisattva*,
for creating welfare for children,
proclaimed wherever beings wandered
throughout the world.

Combined with the sealing gesture of the great-souled one,
[called] "staff of force,"
he leads one to Brahma, and to all the other gods,
let alone to human results.

Kārttikeyamañjuśrī declared this *mantra*,
in brief, so that one may be
completely free from illness during
the period of youth.

Desirous of conferring benefits on beings,
the *bodhisattva* came here
to proclaim the three-syllabled essence
of his *mantra*.

He attends closely to attracting fortune
for the welfare of all beings,
and, fixed with the sealing gesture "staff of force,"
accomplishes all deeds.

oṁ hūṁ jaḥ
This *mantra* would achieve human results fully.

Homage to all *buddhas*, whose embodiments manifest universally.
oṁ vikṛtagraha hūṃ phaṭ svāhā (*O mutilated demon! hail!*)
And the employment of its *upahṛdaya*
together with the force of the sealing gesture,
averts *bhūtas*, *grahas*, and *mātaras*.

Fixing it with sealing gestures
that seal all,
it would be fruitful.
It causes terror to *bhūtas*,
releasing those intent on evil.

This is the youthful, all-achieving attendant of Mañjuśrīkumārabhūta, named Kārttikeyamañjuśrī. Through mere repetition [of the *mantra*], he accomplishes all deeds, terrifies all *bhūtas*, attracts, subjugates, hurts, kills, or whatever is desired by the practitioner of spells—all of that is effected.[D12]

The *mantras* given here reflect the synthetic nature of the section as a whole. The one *mantra*, *oṁ hūṁ jaḥ,* has both the formal and functional elements of the *buddha/bodhisattva hṛdayamantras*, while the other, *oṁ vikṛtagraha hūṃ phaṭ svāhā,* has those of the *abjakula* protective forces. This double function of the *mantras* is apparent when the text turns to those of Brahma, Śiva, and Viṣṇu.

> Homage to the universal *buddhas*,
> whose teachings are indestructible.
> [The *mantra* is]: *oṁ brahma subrahma bramavarcase śāntiṃ kuru svāhā* (*O Brahma perfect Brahma O divine splendor make peace! hail!*)
>
> This *mantra*, "great Brahmā,"
> was spoken by the *bodhisattva*.
> Beings attained peace;
> from this moment on they are gentle.
>
> Employed with the five-crested sealing gesture,
> he would quickly make auspicious progress.
> It is mentioned in the *Atharva Veda*
> for all of the rites of malediction.
> In short, this is taught in the abridged [version]
> of that ordinance.
>
> Homage to the universal *buddhas*,
> whose teachings are indestructible.
> [The *mantra* is]: *oṁ garūḍavāhana cakrapāṇi caturbhuja hūṁ hūṁ samayam anusmara / bodhisattvo jñāpayati svāhā* (*O you who ride upon Garūḍa O you who hold the discus in your hand O four-armed one! hūṁ hūṁ remember your vow! the bodhisattva has revealed this—hail!*)
>
> Authorized by Mañjughoṣa,
> [this *mantra*] accomplishes all matters quickly
> and is auspicious.
> With the form of Viṣṇu as a body,
> as a body for the people,
> it causes demons to be put to flight.
>
> Employed with the "three-crested" sealing gesture
> it is steadfast, accomplishing all matters quickly.
> Those extensive ordinances that were proclaimed
> in the Vaiṣṇava *tantra*
> were spoken by Mañjughoṣa
> as but a means for converting people.[D13]

After making identical claims about the *mantras* used in the cults of Śiva and Garūḍa,[89] the *Mmk* ends this section on *mantras* with an image showing the relationship between these cults and the *bodhisattva* Mañjuśrī. According to this image, those who employ non-Buddhist—that is, non-*Mmk*—*mantras*, do so foolishly, like playing children who wander dangerously far from their mother. But these non-Buddhist practitioners are ultimately saved from their transgression since the forms that they worship, and the *mantras* that they recite, are really aspects of the *bodhisattva*, gently prodding them into the family of the *buddhas*.

> Just as a mother watchfully plays
> with her children in various ways,
> I (Mañjuśrī) wander among those
> of childlike intelligence in the form of the *mantra*.
>
> Previously proclaimed by *buddhas*,
> and now uttered by me—the resplendant prince—
> is the meaning of all *mantra* texts.
>
> Those [*mantras*] which were sung by the greatest of victors,
> those [*mantras*] which were sung by the sons of the *buddhas*—
> those were sung by him whose voice is pleasant [that is, by Mañjuśrī
> in the aspect of miraculous, inconceivable forms.[D14]

The image of the mother (*dhātrī*) playing (*lālati*) with her children evokes the mythological image of the cosmic play (*līlā*) of the creator (*dhātṛ*) with his creation, and of the *bodhisattva* playfully entering and transforming material forms. It also calls to mind the *uttamasādhana*, where the *sādhaka* "becomes one who playfully (*līlin*) enjoys immortality" and other results of *mantra* practice. The metaphor of play is apt for a ritual text like the *Mmk*. In a sense, it can be argued that the very purpose of such a text is to provide the rules for playing. The game being played is of course the game of *mantric* utterance. Like a mother protecting her children by setting limits, the *Mmk* protects its aspiring *sādhakas* by laying down the rules for what its community holds to be real achievement, namely the achievement of the *uttamasādhana*, demonstrated in the *uttamasādhana* passage. The *Mmk* protects by laying down the rules for the efficacious use of the *mantra* and all of the benefits that that entails.

Demonstration of effect

By "demonstration of effect," I mean the *Mmk's* presentation of a passage describing the results of *mantra* practice. An example—from the *uttamasādhana*, which is the object of this study—is as follows.

> [The *sādhaka*] proceeds instantly to the Brahmaloka. He stays in the world-realm Kusumāvātī, where the *tathāgata* Saṅkusumitarājendra dwells, exists, abides and teaches the *dharma*. He beholds Mañjuśrī directly. He hears the true teaching. He also sees several thousand *bodhisattvas*, and worships them. He becomes one who playfully enjoys non-aging and immortality for a thousand great eons. The *paṭa* is also there. He is empowered by all *buddhas* and *bodhisattvas*, and he declares to them his firm resolution [to

> attain enlightenment] and proceeds to their hundred thousand paradises. [Their] hundred thousand bodies are revealed to him. He becomes possessed of numerous powers and supernatural abilities. The noble Mañjuśrī becomes his virtuous friend. He becomes one for whom the goal of enlightenment is certain.[C2]

When the *Mmk* presents a passage demonstrating the effect of the *mantra*, it is showing the end of its own form of *mantracaryā—end*, in several senses: purpose, consummation, extent, realization. But the ablity to effect the power of the *mantra* represents more than the culmination of a religious practice; it represents the ends of both Buddhism as a whole and of the culture from which this practice emerges. If, as is the view of religious practitioners, such practices lead to levels of meaning and satisfaction not attainable through nonreligious means, then demonstrations of effects are eschatological, in the most literal sense of the word: they are discourses (*logos*) on what lies furthest (*eschatos*)—furthest from the cultural norms of which they are the culmination. A community that cultivates a Christian worldview will present as "last things" such issues as the end of history, redemption, final judgment, heaven, and hell. Such concerns follow from the temporal and spatial notions embedded in, and generating, Christian cosmology. Christian liturgy, worship, prayer, and so on, are, then, believed to be the keys for unlocking that cosmic structure. A group that cultivates Buddhist views will offer a different set or sets of final things, such as *nirvāṇa*, salvific knowledge, liberation, cessation of suffering and of *saṃsāra*, and it will mold the keys, produced by its culture, to fit its specific cosmology. So, when the *Mmk* demonstrates the effect of its *mantra* practice, it is revealing what its community held to be the most valuable ends grounded in, though transcending, the social world that gives that practice life and meaning.

At the beginning of this section, I noted that a *mantra* is a form of speech, and that, like ordinary speech, it must be learned, and then used in specific contexts, if it is to be effective. I mentioned too that the system of rules implicit in *mantric* language is not dependent on linguistic features. The first two subsections then considered some of the ritual and doctrinal features of *mantric* "grammar." This subsection will look at the social dimension of *mantric* utterance.

"The social dimension of *mantric* utterance" is a phrase used by Harvey Alper to emphasize the fact that the acceptance of the ideas revolving around the Indian *mantra* is "not itself discursive, it is social."[90] Alper has drawn his inspiration from categories developed by Wittgenstein—particularly in his *Philosophical Investigations*—and attempted to apply "Wittgensteinian concepts to the study of mantras." I want to limit my observations to three points made by Alper that find correspondence in the *Mmk*. These points are as follows (in Alper's words): (1) uttering a *mantra* is a thing done, and hence, a learned activity; (2) uttering a *mantra* is both a context- and a rule-dependent activity; (3) the activity of uttering a *mantra* may be compared profitably to a move in a game.

Before turning to a discussion of these points, it will be helpful to give as background the general sense of what is meant by "the social dimension of *mantric* utterance." Alper offers a clear statement in this regard.

> In the Hindu tradition . . . there is an explicit awareness that achieving religious consummation involves the mastery of specifiable techniques. Ironically, this situation obscures the fact that the mastery of specifiable techniques itself presupposes a prior mastery of skills that resist specification. The successful use of an "instrument" such as mantric utterance presupposes that one has already acquired the proper attitudes, demeanor, and expectations—that is the proper frame of mind—by having been successfully socialized in the society that recognizes mantric utterance as an "authorized" technique that makes possible one of the kinds of transcendence it is deemed acceptable to experience.
>
> The confident, routine use of mantras surely presupposes a specific, identifiable set of convictions concerning the human condition, the ideal social order, and the purpose of existence. Acceptance of these convictions is a tacit ground without which Mantraśāstra would neither have been invented nor have remained vital. Whatever reasons might be adduced to defend these convictions, their acceptance is not itself discursive, it is social. As lived, they are part of the forms of life, "the formal conditions, the patterns in the weave of our lives," that give meaning to the language-game of uttering mantras.
>
> . . . Self-evidently, the language-game of uttering mantras is situated within a social cosmos organized according to the principles of caste hierarchy, culminating in and yet transcended by institutional renunciation (*saṃnyāsa*), which, as such, recognizes the authority of an elite of "perfect spiritual masters" (gurus) and which experiences the cosmos as a fabric interwoven of various "powers," as *śāktic*. These are, in general, the "situation and facts" that are invariably concomitant with mantric utterance. They are the preconditions that make it possible and lend it meaning.

1. "Uttering a *mantra* is a thing done, and hence, a learned activity."

The *Mmk sādhaka* must learn how to employ a *mantra*. The force of a *mantra* can be harnessed only through acquired technique, the possibility and infrastructure of which was embedded in medieval religious culture. The efficacy of the *mantra* is thus equally dependent on both the power of enlightened force, as shown above, *and* proper training within a socially authorized structure. As great as it is, the force of *buddhas* alone does not ensure the success of the *mantra*; rather, the activation of this force is dependent on the presence of further, social, conditions.

The clue to the social nature of effective *mantric* utterance is given at the beginning of each *uttamasādhana* passage.

> First, he who has observed the vow, fulfilled the preliminary practices (*puraścaraṇa*), received the initiation, taken the essential (*hṛdaya*), basic *mantra* from this best of ordinances, or the *upahṛdaya*[91] or some other *mantra*, or having received a single syllable [*mantra*] or another one—according to one's wishes—and who, having gone to a great forest, eats leaves and roots, who subsists on fruits and water, should recite [the *mantra*] three million times. He becomes one who has completed the preliminary practice.[C2]

As I noted above, even the briefest ritualized act, in order to succeed, must be preceded by a long period of preparatory training (*puraścaraṇa*). For our purposes here, we could translate *puraścaraṇa* as *inculturation.* "Preparation" entails an infusion into the practitioner of everything his culture might bring to bear on his quest for enlightenment, liberation, power, and so forth. Hidden behind the description here is the agent of that infusion: the *guru.* The *guru* is the person who "socializes" the *sādhaka,* guiding him through the process that will enable him to use *mantric* speech appropiately and effectively. Another passage, at *Mmk* 11, brings the *guru,* and his socializing role, more into the open.

> First, one must take upon oneself intentness towards knowledge, the vow, and moral conduct. First of all, one must obey the precepts and instructions of the *maṇḍala* master [i.e., the *guru* presiding over the initiation].
>
> The *sādhaka* . . . should make a request to the *maṇḍala* master in this manner: "I desire to enter into, through the agency of the master, the vow (*samaya*) of the great *bodhisattva,* the princely, noble Mañjuśrī." This having been said, [he says, "may] the master [become] compassionate, his mind impelled by sympathy for us!" Then, having been carefully examined by the *maṇḍala* master, by whom instruction, in accordance with the ordinance, was previously given, as previously described [at *Mmk* 2] the student is introduced [to the practice]. Having conferred the initiation, as previously mentioned [at *Mmk* 2], [the *guru*] should bestow the *mantra.* Duly, by degrees, he should reveal the vow. And, having considered very carefully that the time has arrived, and knowing the mental disposition [of the *sādhaka*] he should reveal the esoteric *mudrās* from the text (*tantra*) as well as the subsequent rituals . . . Then, the *maṇḍala* master has to bring about the notion "son" (*putraka*). He [the *sādhaka*] should behave like a son, who says "the benefits (*bhoga*) are to be offered to my mother."[D15]

We saw in the previous subsection that Mañjuśrī "wander[s] among those of childlike intelligence in the form of the *mantra,*" and that he does so "just as a mother watchfully plays with her children in various ways."[92] The child-parent relationship is made explicit here, too. The practitioner is "the son, the child of *dharma*, [and must] be protected always, with continued effort."[93] The ultimate form of protection that the *Mmk guru* can extend to his disciple is that afforded by effective *mantric* utterance. As an embodiment of his culture's highest spiritual ideals, the *guru* is thus extending that culture's ultimate form of protection, too. The full implications of these equivalencies are explored in chapter 4. Here, I want to bring out the fact that *mantric* speech is both meaningful and effective only when properly learned and applied. This fact is significant because it challenges the explanation of *mantras* as "magical speech" that is commonly found in scholarly studies on the subject.[94] On the contrary, it is like ordinary speech. Someone who utters incoherent sounds will fail in social life; even someone who speaks with poor grammar or a "low class" accent will be limited through his language. Assuming, for the sake of argument, the desirability of attaining the upper levels of a culture's material structure—status, wealth, and so forth—then social protection involves teaching a child the appropriate forms of language. This analogy can be applied to *mantric* speech. Though the interface of this type of speech is not limited to social reality, it is a form of speech whose efficacy depends on the user's ability as a speaker of *mantras* (*mantravādin*), or, as the text often puts it, as a "mantra-er" (*mantrin*). Like ordinary speech, *mantras* can fail to serve as instruments serving the speaker's goals. That point is made explicit throughout the *Mmk*, as in the inverse of the following statement.

> The disciple who honors that teacher (*guru*)
> obtains an excellent destiny.
> His *mantras* are successful
> because he has been thoroughly shown
> the path of the ordinances.[D16]

2. "Uttering a *mantra* is both a context- and a rule-dependent activity."
As that last statement shows, there is a direct correlation between being socialized into *mantric* speech, and the adherence to rules: like regular speech, the rules are what make it social (Wittgenstein: "one person alone cannot follow a rule").

The *Mmk* is nothing if it is not a text of rules. It is a sort of etiquette for *sādhakas*. It records the community's prescriptions for all of the forms of behavior expected of the *sādhaka*. From gathering the wood for prayer beads (*Mmk* 12), sleeping, eating, and begging alms (*Mmk* 11), to constructing the oblation pit (*Mmk* 13), the text binds its practitioner to a strictly delineated mode of acting in the world. The promise behind its prescribed limits is that real power and freedom, both social (*laukika*) and "spiritual" (*lokottara*), will follow from observing the rules. The reason that this is so is that the rule-dependent activities of the *sādhaka* produce the conditions—the necessary context—for effective *mantric* utterance:

> "When the *mantras* are applied according to the ordinances,
> then one rapidly succeeds."[95]

3. "The activity of uttering a *mantra* may be compared profitably to a move in a game."

The metaphor of *mantric* utterance as a move in a game follows easily from the previous two assertions. Games are clear instances of learned, and context- and rule-dependent activities. The movement of a piece of wood on a checkered board or the kicking of a leather ball on a gridded field must be interpreted within the larger framework within which they take place—the games of chess and soccer (Wittgenstein's favorite examples); otherwise, they appear to be senseless activities. Efficacy, furthermore, follows from sense—these moves are effective within the strictures provided by the rules, and the rules orient the player toward the accepted notion of success, or victory. Uttering a *mantra* is like this. Saying *oṁ āh hūṃ* only makes sense within the larger game-matrix of *mantracaryā*. The meaningfulness of *mantracaryā*, in turn, is founded on what Alper calls an "epistemological event" (the *sādhaka* sees the *buddha*, attains enlightenment) and an "ontological fact" (the existence of the beings and forces that are embodied in the *mantras*)—*mantracaryā* notions of victory.

The *Mmk* is the book of rules for the game of *mantracaryā*. Recitation of *mantras* comprises the moves in the game, leading the player, the *sādhaka*, to victory. It is profitable to compare the activity of uttering a *mantra* to a move in a game because this brings out points that the text is emphatic about. These are: *mantras* are effective (1) because of the presupposed cosmological situation (the "unlocking" of which constitutes winning the game), (2) when socially learned, (3) when the rules of their utterance are adhered to (playing by the rules), (4) when engaged in (playing). This appreciably clarifies the context for such seemingly trivial statements pervading the text, such as "those *well-recited mantras* are majestic, extremely powerful," "the majestic *mantras* succeed for *those of faith*, and for *no others*," "the success of the *mantra* is *not impelled* by an ascetic of bad morals."[96] A *mantra* is effective by virtue of its being a "key that unlocks the *śaktic* structure of the cosmos," as Alper says. But the ability to employ a *mantra* effectively requires that the practitioner properly negotiate the complex game of *mantracaryā*. To the extent that he does this, recitation of a *mantra* becomes the linguistic game-piece, which, like a wooden chessman, is indispensable to the game.

CHAPTER 2

The Source of Power: The Assembly *(sannipāta)*

In the same manner that successful use of language requires that the speaker be integrated into a social world of shared linguistic meaning, effective application of the *mantras* and other ritual performances depends on the practitioner's ability to enter into a ritual world of shared conceptual meaning. A basic assumption of the *Mañjuśrīmūlakalpa* is that the power of its rituals is limited by the practitioner's mental darkness concerning this understanding. It is thus one of the functions of the text to disclose to the practitioner the required knowledge. Only when this knowledge is acquired can the elements of cultic practice successfully mediate enlightened power, and thereby transform the practitioner into a being of power himself.

"Cultic practice," then, clearly includes within its scope a wide range of activities not normally contained in that term. In the *Mañjuśrīmūlakalpa*, an essential practice that presupposes cultic performance per se is that of properly conceptualizing the space that serves as the matrix of the *mantracaryā*. Significantly, the *Mmk* discloses this space at the very outset, at *Mmk* 1. In so doing, the text is arguing, in its own spatial manner, that the very foundation of its ritual course is the structure of the cosmos itself. This is the meaning of the lexically complex term *dharma*. The *dharma* (teaching) is the *dharma* (truth) because of the *dharma* (the way things are). The *Mmk*'s teaching is what it is because the cosmos—transfigured, as we will see, by the light of the *buddhas*—is integral to each of its elements. *Mmk* 1 evokes for the reader the proper vision of the cosmos. In this chapter, I look at the manner by which the reader is emotionally, imaginatively, and conceptually guided by the text to an understanding of the structure and forces of the cosmos behind, and within, the rituals.

Since we, too, are "readers of the text," it will be useful to call before us, before proceeding to an analysis, the initial image presented by the text to the reader.

> Homage to all *buddhas* and *bodhisattvas*! Thus have I heard. At one time the Blessed One was dwelling in the vault of sky above the Śuddhāvāsa heaven, in the pavilion of the assembly of inconceivably, miraculously, wondrously distributed *bodhisattvas*. There, the Blessed One spoke to the

> *devaputras*, the inhabitants of the Śuddhāvāsa: "Hear, O *devaputras*, about that upon which all beings depend: the inconceivable, wondrous, miraculous transformation of the *bodhisattva*, the [use of the] *maṇḍala* for superior liberation, purity, contemplation, proper conduct; [hear about] the *mantras* of that great being, the princely *bodhisattva* Mañjuśrī, which completely fulfill one's wishes for power, health and long life. Listen to that and bear it well in mind. I will speak to you."
>
> Then, with hands folded in salutation, those *devaputras* dwelling in the Śuddhāvāsa heaven [requested to be taught]: "Out of compassion for us and for all beings, may the Blessed One, whose mind is benevolent and well-disposed, speak about that."
>
> Then, the blessed Śākyamuni, looking down upon the entire dwelling of the Śuddhāvāsa, entered into a state of concentration called *destroying through the dispersion of light into the purified sphere of activity*. Immediately upon entering into this state, the Blessed One [issued forth] a ray of light called impelling the *bodhisattva* in Saṅkusumita. Seeing the brilliant white light, and smiling slightly, he spoke to the group of *bodhisattvas*: "This, O sons of the conqueror, is my impelling of the light. Come here. Prepare yourselves."[E3]

The opening passage of the *Mañjuśrīmūlakalpa* heralds the dispersion of an enlightening power into the world. The emergence of this power is signified by the ray of light emanating from the Buddha. This light is a sign from the Buddha to particular celestial and earthly beings that he is going to teach about "that upon which all beings depend" for their worldly happiness and ultimate liberation. It is also an impelling force causing this host of beings to assemble in his presence. Once they have heard the teaching, this assembly will disperse again to the earthly and celestial regions of the world to serve that teaching—it is for this that they must "prepare" themselves. The ray of light, and the Buddha's smile, is thus a sign that the Buddha has turned his thoughts to our world, "out of compassion for all beings," and will now act to lay the groundwork of a universally applicable teaching: the *mantracaryā* of the *Mañjuśrīmūlakalpa*.

This passage, and the first chapter of the *Mañjuśrīmūlakalpa* as a whole, presents the place where the teaching of the *Mmk* originates and unfolds. This place, the "vault of sky above the Śuddhāvāsa (Pure Abode), in the pavilion of the assembly," exists in a space between our empirical world of name and form and the realm of formless nonconceptuality that is perceived by enlightened beings only. The *Mmk* is thus positing the related notions of a Buddha-field (*buddhakṣetra*) and the "body of communal enjoyment" (*sambhogakāya*).[1] A Buddha-field is the purified sphere of activity referred to in the passage that comprises the range of a Buddha's responsibility; it is an area within the universe that he has vowed to purify of suffering. A Buddha may manifest in his field in the form of a common, though extraordinary, body of a man (*nirmāṇakāya*), as Śākyamuni did for eighty years, or as a glorified, resplendent body (*sambhogakāya*) directly accessible only in advanced states of meditative absorption (*samādhi*), as is Śākyamuni now.

In this manner, *Mmk* 1 sets the stage for the ritual practices that comprise the teaching of the text and its community. As I stated above, effective practice depends on a wide range of ritualized activities that surround a given ritual. One of these surrounding practices is imagining the cosmos presented in the text. By beginning "at the beginning," *Mmk* 1 emphasizes that the cosmic drama unfolding in the pavilion of the assembly is embedded in each subsequently prescribed ritual action, ensuring its efficacy. The successful utterance of a single *mantra* requires the cooperation of an entire universe. The very presence of *Mmk* 1 imparts to the reader the notion that the ritual possibilities posited by a given community must follow from the cosmos envisioned by that community. This, in turn, points to a corollary. A universe, too, to have effect, to be real, requires the cooperation of an agent; its "existence" is dependent on its being imaginatively apprehended/fashioned by the practitioner. The *Mmk* insists, then, on the interaction of the reader to construct knowledgeably the cosmos that its *mantracaryā* requires. That is, it is not merely seeking an affective response to the picture that it presents. Rather, by encountering primordial cosmic patterns at the outset, the reader is guided to an understanding of the structure of the previously hidden world behind (and within) the rituals and, therefore, of the implications and possibilities entailed by this structure.

The dual premise of a constructed *and* imagined universe points in two directions. First, it points to a public world of shared conceptions and meaning. With little alteration, the opening passage of the *Mmk* could be rewritten in accordance with, for instance, Śaiva or Vaiṣṇava convictions. The passage invokes images that have widespread intersectarian meaning. With even fewer changes, the passage could appear in virtually any Mahāyāna text, even those prescribing forms of practice significantly different from that of the *Mmk*. The premise of a constructed universe thus points to a larger, public world of ideas, beliefs, and concepts that are, in the case of the *Mmk*, largely presupposed and thus *behind* the text. One approach to *Mmk* 1 is therefore through a consideration of implicit doctrine.

Second, the premise of a cognitively conceived universe points to a private world of imagination. The universe presented in the *Mmk* is a literary creation. Although it is accorded ontological status, it is through the conventions of written language that the reader-practitioner encounters that image of the universe. *Mmk* 1 stimulates and molds the imaginative powers of the reader to this end. As we saw in the previous section, the strategy of the *Mmk* is to argue by means of images rather than propositions. This fact may throw some light onto the relationship between implicit doctrine and a narrative vision of the universe. As Luis Gómez points out, "[t]he fantastic is unreal only for the *literal* mind; the *literary* mind, on the other hand, allows for a certain re-creation of the real that is best expressed as poetry, not dogma."[2] The reality of the pavilion of the assembly and of all that transpires there is crafted from a "metaphysics of the vision and the dream," as Stephan Beyer puts it.[3] Like much of the *vaipulyasūtra* literature, the *Mmk* employes visionary language as a tool "to dismantle the hard categories we impose on reality, to reveal the eternal flowing possibility in which the Bodhisattva lives."[4] Dogmatic language is seen here as being a form of "hard category" itself, and, therefore, as antithetical to the fluidly envisioned revelation required by the *Mmk.* The fact that doctrine remains largely behind the text may be ascribable to literary strategy: the possibility of meaning arises *in front of* the text, in the space between the reader and the words. Accordingly, the language of *Mmk* 1 is indeterminate. There remains a gap in the public knowledge that can be filled only by the creativity of the reader. It is out of this dynamic that a private vision arises. Wolfgang Iser, who has attempted to define more precisely the phenomenology of reading, writes:[5]

> What is missing from the apparently trivial scenes, the gaps arising out of the dialogue—this is what stimulates the reader into filling the blanks with projections. He is drawn into the events and made to supply what is meant from what is not said. What is said only appears to take on significance as a reference to what is not said; it is the implication and not the statements that give shape and weight to the meaning. But as the unsaid comes to life in the reader's imagination, so the said "expands" to take on greater significance than might have been supposed: even trivial scenes can seem surprisingly profound.

Mmk 1 is a trivial scene. At first glance it strikes the twenty-first century reader of Buddhist literature as a dull cliché. Its presence is too easily explained away as serving to legitimate Mahāyāna literature, or as being evidence of the extravagance that supposedly accompanies the decline of a tradition. Other instances of such a scene have been seen by various scholars as "rubbish," "fantastic speculation," "Mahāyāna supernaturalism," "flamboyant Mahāyānaism," and "Mahāyāna space fiction."[6] As Randy Kloetzli, the author of the *only* European-language book on Buddhist cosmology, summarizes, "the references to cosmological speculation found in the Buddhist texts are consequently judged to be devoid of religious significance; meaningless accretions at best derivative in their import."[7] By looking for the forces at work behind and in front of the text, this chapter attempts to trace the profundity within the trivial.

2.1 Cosmology

The *Encyclopaedia Britannica* gives the following definition of the term *cosmology*.[8]

> [Cosmology] is that branch of learning which treats of the universe as an ordered system. The name is derived from the Greek *cosmos* ("order," "harmony," "the world"), plus *logos* ("word," "discourse"). Cosmology is that framework of concepts and relations which man erects, in satisfaction of some emotional or intellectual drive, for the purpose of bringing descriptive order into the world as a whole, including himself as one of its elements.

This definition goes on to state that observation plays a central role in cosmology: "[cosmology] is confined to a *description* of the salient features of the observed universe." It is, however, not necessary to restrict the definition to the sense employed in the natural sciences. Considering cosmology from the perspective of philosophy, Milton Munitz extends its meaning as follows.[9]

> At best, the universe is "given" through the medium of a conceptual construction—through *understanding* a cosmological model. The latter is not the product of an exercise of any one or a combination of sensory organs. It is the outcome of employing man's creative intellectual powers. It is these intellectual faculties that help to conceive what cannot be identified primarily by observational means. The concept of the universe as a whole is a theoretical concept.

A cosmology is simultaneously a focal point for metaphysical and "mythical" postulates, and the setting of ritual activity. As such, it comprises what Richard Davis calls the *ritual universe* of the practitioner. As I understand this term, "ritual universe" refers to a particularized world that is permeated by tradition-specific cosmological and philosophical propositions. From a different quarter, Stanley Tambiah calls this a "cosmological perspective," and writes that such a perspective "implies that ritual acts cannot be fully comprehended except as part of a larger frame of cultural presuppositions and beliefs which provide the phenomenological and subjective basis for engaging in the ritual in question."[10] The ritual practice of the *Mmk* is grounded in the postulates that flow from the cosmology presented in the above passage. The two are inseparable and mutually fulfilling: the rituals, supported by cosmological/philosophical postulates, constitute the actions by means of which these postulates are realized. Successful practice of the Buddhist rituals recorded in the *Mañjuśrimūlakalpa* thus depends on the practitioner's ability to dwell within the text's postulated cosmological setting.

Buddhist literature, whatever the genre, presupposes such a creative cosmology. These have ranged from the single-world system (*cakravāla*) of ancient Buddhism to the modern Buddhists' "metagalaxy."[11] Western scholars of Buddhism have, however, historically chosen to look to explicit philosophical statements for an understanding of the conceptual world of Buddhists, and to disregard the potentially rich store of meaning contained in cosmological metaphor and image. More recent work, however, gives attention to the literary features of Buddhist works—including the rhetorical nature of philosophical propositions. Pointing out the overarching simile in the eighteenth-century Pāli text called *The Advice to the Layman Tuṇḍila*, Charles Hallisey, for instance, writes that the "metaphor of the city of perfect peace is a helpful device for listing and linking a variety of doctrinal items and practices."[12] The wall of the city of perfect peace is like the perfection of patience, the door is like the perfection of generosity, the watchtower is like concentration, the lamps lighting the city are like lamps of knowledge. The spatiality of the city widens the function of the metaphor beyond its most common uses, such as extension of "meaning from something that is known well to something relatively unknown" and persuasion (303). The city is "a delightful shelter" (312) it is a "place without fear, permanent, without old age, without death, secure" (313). This place of the great city of perfect peace, moreover, is situated somewhere, presumably far beyond the heaven of Sakra, which, by contrast, is impermanent and unstable (311). It is this explicit placing of the city within a cosmological scheme—in this case within the "single world system," or *cakravāla* (*cakkavāḷa*) scheme—that sheds light on the most crucial function of cosmology. The city becomes a place located on a map. This place, moreover, can be reached by following a prescribed path; namely, by means of merit making behavior—generosity, morality, guarding the senses, renunciation of the householder's life. Though it may be true that the cosmological scheme underlying *The Advice to the Layman Tuṇḍila* is "a metaphor taken literally, the reification of a way of looking at spiritual progress," as Richard Gombrich has written about the *cakravāla* in general,[13] the distinction between mythic, metaphoric, and literal geographies—as between the real and the imagined—loses meaning: both the forces of merit making and the place of perfect peace are realizable within the practitioner's universe. Gómez notes that the "interpretation [of Buddha-fields] as metaphors coexist [in Buddhist literature] with belief in a real, spatial location."[14] For this reason, questions concerning the ontological status of the postulated universe are possibly "of no heuristic value."[15]

As Hallisey's example shows, cosmology is simultaneously a functional metaphor (a spatial organization of a particular conceptualization of Buddhist doctrine and practice) and a map of reality. The "drama of salvation"[16] summarized in a conceptual scheme of the cosmos is played out by the practitioner within the cosmos described in that scheme. It is in fact the very structure of the cosmos that makes salvation possible. The Theravādin practitioner reading of the city of perfect peace understood that he or she could reach that city because it was in fact *there*, "at the pinnacle of a cosmological hierarchy."[17] Likewise, the practitioner who embraced the *Mmk* lived in a universe inhabited by compassionate, powerful, and active *buddhas* and *bodhisattvas*. The *Mmk* presupposes a practitioner who accepts the *reality* of the universe that it depicts; and it prescribes the ritual means for the practitioner to gain entry into that reality.

2.2 *Mmk* 1: vision and cult

In her pioneering work *Le Maṇḍala du Mañjuśrīmūlakalpa*, Ariane MacDonald argues that the first three chapters of the *Mmk* attest the desire of its editors for some "doctrinal coherence" in the face of the text's inconsistencies.[18] She gives as a contributing factor to this "isolation" of the first three chapters the fact that, of the fifty-five chapters, Mañjuśrī delivers the first three only, as well as "the fact that Mañjuśrī pronounces the two initial chapters on the *maṇḍala*, in conformity to that which is announced in the chapter on the Assembly."[19] Since it can be shown that Śākyamuni, Saṅkusumitarājendra and Yamāntaka figure as predominantly as Mañjuśrī in *Mmk* 1, and that the contents of *many* subsequent chapters are "announced" in *Mmk* 1, I do not wholly agree with MacDonald. However, her point that these chapters make apparent the seams of the text resulting from editorial work has several noteworthy implications. For example, it forces us to keep sight of the fact the *Mmk* was likely compiled over many years. Relatedly, it alerts us to the possibility that medieval Indians' notion of a "book" was different from ours: "chapters" circulated as independent works, sometimes being conjoined by a community into a single book. Even more basically, the presence of disjointed sections jolts us into realizing that *they are there* at all. This challenges us to consider the reason for their presence. While MacDonald, following the philological leads of Jean Przyluski,[20] discussed this reason in terms of origins and dates,[21] I would like to consider the presence of *Mmk* 1 from the angle of literary function. To use the metaphors from the preceding paragraphs, MacDonald and Przyluski were interested in what lay behind the text (the mechanics of formation) while I am looking at what lies in front of the text (the mechanics of reading). My basic contention is that one of the reasons that *Mmk* 1 is there at all is to coalesce the two different genres of religious literature discussed at section 1.3.2, namely, the sectarian ritual manual (*kalpa*) and the expansive visionary text (*mahāyānavaipulyasūtra*).

As a ritual manual the *Mmk* played to the expectations of an audience versed in the "new genre of liturgical texts"[22] that arose around the eighth century. As Richard Davis writes, "[t]his genre comprises the Vaiṣṇava *saṃhitās*, the Śaiva *āgamas*, and somewhat later, the Śākta *tantras* centered on the Goddess."[23] We may add to these the medieval *purāṇas* and *upapurāṇas* being produced by the more orthodox oriented groups. And the *Mmk* is evidence that Buddhists, too, were recording their ritual practices at this time. This is, of course, indicated by the term *kalpa* in the title of the *Mmk*.

The *Mmk*, however, invokes the designation *sūtra* to the same degree as it does *kalpa*. As a ritual manual it was involved in innovation. As a *sūtra*, on the other hand, it was engaged in an ancient, convention-bound tradition. It was therefore incumbent on the authors/compilers of the *Mmk* to convince the intersectarian Buddhist community of its value and validity in relation to these established lines of tradition. This was accomplished by retaining literary strategies that were familiar to its Buddhist readers and hearers. *Mmk* 1, in short, aims to accomplish these different ends by providing a distinctly Buddhist framework for what was becoming a form of practice—literary and ritual—indistinguishable from other, non-Buddhist groups.

The initial concern of the medieval ritual compendium is to establish the authority on which the text's prescribed cult is based and to outline broadly the features of that cult. The manner in which this authority is established then provides the framework for the text as a whole, and indicates the basic worldview underlying the cult. The opening chapter of a Pañcarātra *saṃhita*—often titled "transmission of the teaching" (*śāstrāvatāra*)[24]—for instance, typically contains the following elements. A sage, or group of sages, approaches the mountain hermitage of an adept knowledgeable in the means of emancipation. Before imparting the teaching, the adept explains that his knowledge derives from an exalted lineage of teachers extending back to Viṣṇu himself. (In some cases, this knowledge is a direct revelation from Viṣṇu to either the seeking sage or the teaching adept.) The adept explains that, due to the diminished capacity of beings at the present time, the teachings that follow are a simplified, though no less effective, version of the original teachings. The rest of the text then deals with the various aspects of the cult as revealed by Viṣṇu. These different aspects are ideally contained in one of four divisions (*pādas*) discussing essential metaphysical knowledge (*jñānapāda*), ritual prescriptions (*kriyāpāda*), rules of proper comportment (*caryāpāda*) and methods of contemplation (*yogapāda*). As Richard Davis writes, "[t]ogether, these four parts constitute everything worth knowing from a spiritual point of view; the section on knowledge reveals how the cosmos is organized, and the other three sections fully instruct one who adheres to that view of the world in how to act in it."[25]

The *Mmk* opens with a scene that would have been familiar to a medieval reader of a Vaiṣṇava or Śaiva ritual work. The Śuddhāvāsa gods ask Śākyamuni—who is situated not on a mountain but in the sky above the gods—to speak on various matters pertaining to enlightenment. There is no need to make claims about the exalted origins of the teachings as in a Pañcarātra text since the reader himself is being allowed direct access to the original transmission from the Buddha to the gods; like Mañjuśrī, he goes "in the presence of Śākyamuni." Nonetheless, it is announced that the teachings that follow had been pronounced in the past by "one-hundred thousand *tathāgatas,* perfected ones, perfectly enlightened ones equaling the sands of the Ganges." Although it is stated that the teaching is "extensive" (*vaipulya*), subsequent treatment of certain rituals makes it known that the system of the *Mmk,* too, has been truncated because of the corrupt times.[26] The assembly, revelation, and original "impelling of the light" that opens the *Mmk* is formulaically recalled at the beginning of most subsequent chapters, thus creating a unifying frame for the text.[27]

Strictly speaking, however, the *Mmk* as a whole does not conform to the structure of these other medieval ritual works. There is no mention in the *Mmk* of any of the *pādas* found in the Śaiva and Vaiṣṇava ritual literature. Yet, the work does display an almost exclusive concern with these four categories of knowledge and action. The only category that would require some modification is that of the *jñānapāda.* Several chapters and sections are concerned with prognostic, medical or historical knowledge: knowledge of the *world*, including the heavens, is deemed essential to the accurate performance of the rituals, while knowledge of the universe and its origins is left implicit. The colophon to *Mmk* 1, however, is a succinct, if somewhat opaque, statement of the work's essential conformity to the genre of the ritual compendium. The text reads:

> The first chapter: the assembly; from the section of the fundamental ritual ordinance on the miraculous transformation of the *bodhisattva*, the youthful Mañjuśrī, from the extensive ritual ordinance giving instructions on the Mahāyāna *mantra* rites.[E1]

The colophon first of all evokes the place of the "transmission of the teaching": the assembly in the palace of the Śuddhāvāsa heaven. It also expresses the purpose of the work as a whole: to prescribe and explain a system of Mahāyāna ritual activity. This activity includes ritual acts per se, such as formalized bathing, fire oblations, recitation of *mantras*, worship of the icon (i.e., all *kriyāpāda* matters), as well as ethical or proper comportment when walking, talking, sleeping, begging, eating, and so on (*caryāpāda*) and contemplative practices (*yogapāda*). Furthermore, the colophon alludes to the metaphysical axioms supporting its prescriptions. These are bound up in the postulate of "miraculous transformation" (*vikurvaṇa*). It is argued below that this concept—and related ones such as *trisāhasramahāsāhasralokadhātu* and *buddhādhiṣṭhāna*—serves the same purpose as the *jñānapāda* sections of Śaiva and Vaiṣṇava ritual texts; namely, to situate the "truth" of the prescribed way of acting in the world within the structure of the cosmos.

It should be emphasized, however, that the *Mmk*'s conformity to certain conventions of the genre of the medieval ritual compendium is not evident from its form. In terms of the "ideal" ritual compendium, that is, that following the fourfold *pāda* structure, the *Mmk* deviates from these works. However, by placing the *Mmk* beside such non-Buddhist ritual texts of the period the view of the *Mmk* as a participant in this particular type of literary performance appears plausible. As the double self-designation of the *Mmk* as *mahāyānavaipulyasūtra* and *kalpa* suggests, the work challenges the form of the ritual text genre (blocking our view to that particular aspect of the work), while upholding the genre's intent (suggesting the possibility of this perspective). Hans Robert Jauss offers a helpful definition in this regard.

> The relationship between the individual text and the series of texts formative of a genre . . . [is defined] as a process of the continual founding and altering of horizons. The new text evokes for the reader (listener) the horizon of expectations and "rules of the game" familiar to him from earlier texts, which as such can then be varied, extended, corrected, but also transformed, crossed out, or simply reproduced. Variation, extension and connection determine the latitude of a generic structure; a break with the conventions on the one hand and mere reproduction on the other determines its boundaries.[28]

For the *Mmk,* the horizons of expectations and the familiar rules of the game can not always be reconciled within a single form; they are not conducive to a uniform approach. The demands placed on a *kalpa* are different from those placed on a *mahāyānavaipulyasūtra.* A *kalpa* is succinct and practical, it is stylistically and functionally utilitarian. A *mahāyānāvataṃsakavaipulyasūtra* is vast, exuberant and visionary. It means to overwhelm its readers with hyperbolic language and imagery. The reader of a *kalpa* expects to receive *instruction* on how to employ the elements of a specific cult. The reader of a *vaipulyasūtra* expects to encounter a *vision* of a higher order of reality unfolded by means of parables, stories, hymns, and revelatory language and images. As both a *mahāyānavaipulyasūtra* and a *kalpa*, it is incumbent on the *Mmk* to harmonize multiple expectations. *Mmk* 1 attempts to do this by invoking a vision of the reality supporting the cult. In this way, too, it constitutes the "knowledge" required of a *jñānapāda* section of a ritual text. As we will see in chapter 3, this fusion of vision and cult is perfected in the *paṭa*, the cult object of painted cloth that graphically presents the revelation of *Mmk* 1 for specific ritual purposes.

By presenting the universe through the devices of visionary language—description, allusion, metaphor, and imagery—*Mmk* 1 serves to make the reader present there; that is, to make this universe his own. This has implications for three further functions of *Mmk* 1. Like the *mantras* that it prescribes, *Mmk* 1 is deemed to have significance prior to the reader's understanding of its referential meaning. The following passage, describing Mañjuśrī's advent in the Śuddhāvāsa heaven, is a good example of this.

> Arriving there, he establishes himself in the great [palace] of precious jewels, in the vault of heaven, among the gods living in the Śuddhāvāsa heaven. When Mañjuśrī falls into a state of meditative absorption called *illumination with ornaments of brilliant jewels*, the entire palace of the Śuddhāvāsa heaven becomes illuminated by a great ray of light. In this instant, there rains down [the following] upon the measureless, blessed Śākyamuni, worshipping him as he observes this miraculous transformation of the *bodhisattva*: garlands smeared and scented with aromatic powders, the divine presence of the *bodhisattvas* metamorphized into sweet sounds, strings of bells and jewels, full of garlands, flags banners and heavenly flowers beautifully arranged, masses of lovely silk bunting spread over hundreds of thousands of miles, jeweled parasols with row upon row of jewels on top. The *devaputras* of the Śuddhāvāsa, seeing the trembling palace, horripulate and are pierced in their hearts with heat. They think, "why are we being deprived of our wealth?" Their bodies quickening, they begin to shriek loudly, "save us Blessed One! save us Śākyamuni!"[E2]

This ray of light, terrifying in its brilliance and disruptive force, is designed to overwhelm the reader and transport him or her to the glorified form of the Buddha. In that moment, the ideal reader, like the *devaputras* in the text, is pierced in his heart with heat and cries out, "Save me Blessed One! Save me Śākyamuni!" The words vouchsafe a perspective on the intermediary world of the Buddha normally accessible only through meditative absorption. Erudition concerning the history of the connotations of light imagery in Mahāyāna literature would lessen, not deepen, the initial affect of the reader. Familiarity often breeds a certain insensitivity. In this regard, the text here "means" what it does: it places the reader emotionally and imaginatively at the origin of the cult.

By gathering members of the assembly through affective participation, the *Mmk*, furthermore, constitutes its own community. The community can be roughly defined as consisting of those who respond with devotion to the vision displayed in the text. This community includes the assembly of various enlightened, divine, human and "supernatural" beings—including those of Vedic, Vaiṣṇava and Śaiva sects, as was shown in chapter 1—and natural forces, such as stars, planets, rivers, seas and trees that come from all points of the "three thousand fold-many thousand fold world system" (*trisāhasramahāsāhasralokadhātu*) to assemble around the Buddha when he teaches. In the broadest sense, then, the community consists of all living forms present in both the seen and unseen universe reconstituted as strictly *Buddhist* forces by the impelling light of the Buddha. Included in this community are the practitioners, who become present in the assembly through an affective reading/hearing of the text.

Most important in this regard is the practitioners' daily engagement with the vision encountered in the text. This is accomplished through sustained practice to the *paṭa*, the object of worship extolled in the *Mmk*. The *paṭa* is a presentation of the world as it is constituted in *Mmk* 1. The power of the *paṭa* is the result of the *paṭa's* nonmediated fusion with the Buddha's cataclysmic, "inconceivable, miraculous, wondrous" display, which causes world systems to tremble and hells to burst open. The mere sight of the *paṭa* is claimed to dissolve the force of even the most serious misdeeds, create the conditions for a long, healthy life, and ensure future buddhahood. *Mmk* 1 reveals the source of the central cult object, and provides a full description of what the *paṭa*, in its limited size, manifests only refractorily.

The rhetorical aspect of the affective and powerful language of *Mmk* 1 must also be mentioned. As I have pointed out in several contexts, *Mmk* 1, unlike philosophical works, does not attempt to guide the reader through stages of an argument to a conclusion. It rather seeks to transform its readers by means of dramatic imagery and apocalyptic language. At the bottom of this language and imagery are, typically, claims of authority and superiority: the teachings of the *Mmk* have been practiced by all *buddhas* throughout all time. They were even practiced by Śiva, Viṣṇu and Brahma. Now, in a time of degeneration, they are being revealed to the assembly so that, in the present and future, all beings will know how to achieve security and success. Behind the evocative and hyperbolic images and language of *Mmk* 1, we may begin to sense something of the social context of the work—one in which various groups were vying to win adherents and patrons. Particularly the Buddhist literature of this period and later (that is, from the eighth to the thirteenth centuries), whose content and style increasingly converged with that of the non-Buddhist sects, might be suspected of having originated in a threatening competitive environment. This rhetorical function of *Mmk* 1, moreover, helps to explain its position as the first chapter of the work. *Mmk* 1 situates the rituals, prognostications, histories, and so forth, of *Mmk* 2–55 on a foundation—or, to use the image provided by the text itself, within a circle—of legitimacy and power.

2.3 The text as cult image

As I mentioned in chapter 1, the *Mmk* is concerned with the definition of specific types of spaces and the prescription of specific types of action within those spaces. The spaces articulated by the *Mmk* are always exceptional. They are special by virtue of the *image* that occupies them. By "image" I mean a depiction that is worshiped as a cult object possessing the presence of a deity or enlightened being. In various places in the *Mmk*, the image is painted on cloth, drawn on the ground, created sonically, imaginatively visualized, or, in the case of the text itself, depicted with words. In each case, the image is a representation of either the Buddha's historical body (*nirmāṇakāya*), emanated body (*sambhogakāya*), extended body (ray of light, assembly, *sarvabuddha*), attributes, or activity. As a place where the image is created by, and thus present in, the words, the physical book of the *Mmk* is imbued with the power of the Buddha. The worship of the book in one's home or monastic cell, for example, ensures "great protection, great wealth, a long and healthy life, constant increase in fortune." [29] Such a claim indicates that the book was viewed not as the mere repository of words, that is, as something to be read only, but as the place of an *image* to be worshiped, encountered, and activated in one's life.

Mmk 1 is an image in the sense that its words are not intended to propose, narrate, or communicate concepts; they are employed to effect a response to a particular picture. The words are like the paint on the *paṭa* or the sound of the *mantra*. They do not refer to something else, but are, in the first instance, themselves a form of immediate experience. An analysis of the particular arrangement of paint, words, and sounds will lead the student of these forms toward underlying concepts; but this symbolic function is not primary for the reader. Their primary function is to move the powers of an otherwise hidden reality into the possession of the practitioner.

The words of *Mmk* 1 fashion an image enshrining an event. In its barest form, the event contains the following elements: the emergence of Śākyamuni to teach the *mantracaryā*; his emission of light to attract the assembly of beings; the arrival of numerous classes of beings to hear the teaching and vow to support the practitioner of the teaching. Like much else in the *Mmk*, this is quite unremarkable on the surface. It is common to virtually all Mahāyāna *sūtra* literature, and as we have seen, to the non-Buddhist literature of the medieval period as well. Yet, although the form is commonplace, the particular features are not. *Mmk*-specific elements arise out of this: the *paṭa* (the painted presentation of what transpires here), the *mantras* (sonic embodiment of the powers assembled here), the *mudrās* (gestural re-creation of the bodies assembled), and the initiatory *maṇḍala* (drawn replication through which the *sādhaka* officially enters here). The reader encounters here the generative event behind the *Mmk* cult. *Mmk* 1 is thus revelatory. It presents an otherwise hidden event that is rooted in the past in a manner that enables this event to unfold before the committed practitioner at any given present. In this manner it synchronizes an invisible, ideal, and "mythic" past with the visible, real, present.

2.4 Revelation and transmission

The medieval ritual manuals produced by the Vaiṣṇava Pañcarātrins commonly begin with an introductory chapter titled *śāstrāvatāra*. The two terms of this title are rich in historical allusion. The first, *śāstra*, denotes "rule" or "teaching." A sense of authority and divine inspiration accompanies the term. This connotation can be gathered from the fact that *śāstra* applies to the *Vedas* as well as to later venerated works. The second term, *avatāra*, when found in the title of a text or chapter, can mean simply "descent into," in the sense of "introduction." It is also used technically to refer to the movement of a deity from transcendence to immanence. In a Vaiṣṇava work, an even deeper allusion is, of course, to the ten earthly incarnations of Viṣṇu. The conceptual sense of the term *śāstrāvatāra*, then, ranges from "introduction to the teaching," "transmission of the authoritative teaching," to "descent of the divine teaching," or even "incarnation of the deity by means of the teaching." Perhaps even more important than its conceptual meaning is the image conveyed by the term. For the committed reader, who would be familiar with a cluster of Vaiṣṇava myths, histories, and doctrines, *śāstrāvatāra* stimulates a picture of an extraordinary revelation of transmission, thereby preparing him for reception of the specific teaching that follows. Toward this end, an additional feature of the introductory chapter is a "table of contents" or "index" embedded in the discourse.[30]

In choosing the term *sannipāta*, the authors of the *Mmk* were similarly engaged in historical allusion. The picture that emerges from this term is of an assembly of listeners gathered in a circle around the Buddha while he teaches. The motif and elements of the retinue are common to virtually all Buddhist *sūtra* literature. The use of this convention has, however, varied according to the cosmology of the school. In the earliest texts, the audience ranges from one person to five-hundred monks, and the location is a terrestrial environment that the historical Śākyamuni would have actually visited. In the Mahāyāna *sūtras*, the initial retinue is often five-hundred monks together with thousands of *bodhisattvas* and various earthly rulers and supernatural spirits. A stereotyped feature of Mahāyāna literature is the radical expansion of place and audience. The Buddha, before issuing his teaching, enters into a state of concentration, causing a ray of light to extend from his forehead into the deepest recesses of the cosmos. This ray impels countless distant *buddhas, bodhisattvas,* and gods to join the asembly. Concomitant with this revelation of an infinitely vast cosmos is the transformation of the Buddha's earthly location into some type of marvelous diamondlike edifice to hold the audience.

The basic picture of the Buddhist *sannipāta* is thus of a circular gathering of extraordinary beings. The form of a circle is often made explicit in the *Mmk* by the synonym *parṣanmaṇḍala* (circularly arrayed assembly) or simply *maṇḍala* (circle).[31] In its Buddhist usage, the term *maṇḍala* thus becomes associated with an extraordinary space delineated by a series of concentric circles and squares. David Snellgrove points out the architectural allusion of this form.[32]

> The "square," which is regularly described as having a door on each of its four sides, the main one being toward the East, and all adorned with an elaborate portal . . . represents the normal Indian four-sided temple . . . Since a temple is primarily conceived as the domain of a particular divinity, the significance of the maṇḍala as a stylized two-dimensional pattern with identical intention becomes quite explicit.
>
> The center of the enclosure is its most sacred spot while the outer ring borders on the profane world. Thus a set of concentric circles can represent various stages of accommodation to the not so sacred. There is an exact analogy with the gradations of chief ministers, lesser ministers, serving staff and messengers, with which a great king seated in state might be supposed to be surrounded. . . [T]he significance of the maṇḍala as enclosing the radiating power of the central divinity remains constant.

The possibilities of this spatial image are limitless. The *maṇḍala* as temple or palace is an ideal space for graphing extremely nuanced expressions of divine or extraordinary power. Originally empty, the palace can be filled with any conceivable iconographic configuration. This configuration may be displayed graphically with paint on cloth, (silk, paper, or a wall as in *Mmk* 3–7; discussed in chapter 3), with colored sand, powder, paste, or cords on the earth or some other surface (*Mmk* 2; discussed in chapter 4), as sculpture, as a mentally generated image, inward picture, or, relatedly, with words, as in *Mmk* 1. The end result is always a specific representation of the state of things, particularly of the various forms of power operative in the cosmos and of the practitioner's relationship to these powers. Peter Gaeffke's definition of *maṇḍalas* as "geometric designs with cosmological implications . . . used in [rituals] in order to involve the whole cosmos in the ritual act" is therefore apt.[33]

The *sannipātamaṇḍala* is the image employed in the *Mmk* to frame the revelation and transmission of the *mantracaryā*. The mythical/historical allusions of the term prepares the reader to be imaginatively transported; it prepares him to be cognitively transformed by the light of the Buddha's compassion. The *Mmk* begins:

> Homage to all *buddhas* and *bodhisattvas*! Thus have I heard. At one time the Blessed One was dwelling in the vault of sky above the Śuddhāvāsa heaven, in the pavilion of the assembly of inconceivably, miraculously, wondrously distributed *bodhisattvas*. There, the Blessed One spoke to the *devaputras*, the inhabitants of the Śuddhāvāsa: Hear, O *devaputras*, about that upon which all beings depend: the inconceivable, wondrous, miraculous transformation of the *bodhisattva*, the [use of the] [*paṭa*] for superior liberation, purity, meditative absorption, proper conduct; [hear about] the *mantras* of that great being, the princely *bodhisattva* Mañjuśrī, which completely fulfill all beings' wishes for power, health and long life. Listen to that and bear it well in mind. I will speak to you.
>
> Then, with hands folded in salutation, those *devaputras* dwelling in the Śuddhāvāsa [T: exclaiming "excellent!" asked the Blessed One (about) the *bodhisattvas'* practices of superior meditative absorption], the obtaining of the superior stages [of the *bodhisattva* path], the approach to buddhahood, the turning of the wheel of the teaching for the overcoming of Māra, liberation of *pratyekabuddhas* and *śrāvakas*, birth as a god or human, pacification of all illness, poverty and suffering, attraction of wealth, the invincibility of all ordinary and extraordinary *mantra* rituals, the complete fulfillment of all hopes, the certain retainment of the words of all *tathāgatas*. Out of compassion for us and for all beings, let the Blessed One, who is loving and benevolent, speak about that!
>
> Then, the blessed Śākyamuni, looking down upon the entire dwelling of the Śuddhāvāsa, entered into a state of concentration called *destroying through the dispersion of light into the purified sphere of activity*. Immediately upon entering into this state, the Blessed One [issued forth] a ray of light [T. from his forehead] called *impelling the bodhisattva in Saṅkusumita*. [T. Billions of rays of light circumambulate the Blessed One three times, and proceed to the realms of the three thousand fold-many thousand fold world system. (The light) passes beyond worlds in the east and north, (as numerous as the sands) of hundreds of thousands of Ganges rivers, and enters into the realm of Kusumāvatī, where it enters into the *tathāgata* Saṅkusumitarājendra. There, it enters into the forehead of the princely Mañjuśrī, who dwells together with those who are engaged, by means of the consecrated path, in the career of the great beings, the *bodhisattvas*. Upon Mañjuśrī's] seeing the brilliant light, the Buddha, smiling slightly, spoke to that assembly of *bodhisattvas*: "This, O sons of the conqueror, is my impelling of the light. Come here. Prepare yourselves."[E3]

Using a circular cosmological image, the *Mmk* begins not at the beginning, but at the center. The Buddha is sitting in the middle of the jeweled palace above the Śuddhāvāsa heaven. This heaven is situated on the boundaries of space and time, just within the range of the the *śuddhāvāsika* gods' ability to conceptualize and apprehend him. From an even more central point—the concentrated, compassionate mind of the Buddha—a light emerges. This light simultaneously serves several purposes and functions at several levels: narratively (in the story), historically (in actuality), and affectively/imaginatively (in the emotions and mind of the reader). It illuminates the scene otherwise obscured by the ignorance of unenlightened beings (the reader presumably included); it signals the advent of a Buddha's teaching; it purifies the Buddha's field of activity (including the mind of the reader) by destroying inauspicious forces, thereby cataclysmically transfiguring the field (mind); it arouses certain beings, and impels them to assemble around the teaching Buddha.

The opening image of the *Mmk* discloses that the internal structure of both the cosmos and the rituals is identical. The vivifying core of each is the Buddha's power, revealed by his ray of light. The ritual possibilities posited by the *Mmk* community are thus interwoven with the cosmic structure posited by that community. An example from another quarter might help to illustrate this point. The daily ritual practice of a medieval Śaiva Siddhāntin, as Richard Davis demonstrates, "echoes the rhythm" of the universe as it is conceived by that community. For the Śaiva Siddhāntins, a fundamental feature of the universe is that it, and thus all the constituents of reality, oscillates perpetually between emission from, and reabsorption into, the undifferentiated source of creation. Ultimately, of course, it is Śiva who governs this process. Within the ritual domain, however, the practitioner, mirroring the actions of Śiva, "repeats these fundamental principles of the cosmos in accord with their own purposes." The cosmos itself is thus "embedded as an organizing logic in the pattering of worship."[34]

The "organizing logic" of the *Mmk* is indicated at the outset of the passage. It is alluded to generally in the Buddha's emission of light. This single act points toward the buddhalogical[35] doctrine implicit in the text. An important corollary to this is made more explicit with the statement "that upon which all beings depend: the miraculous transformation of the *bodhisattva*" (*bodhisattvavikurvaṇa*). This is the argument for "divine" embodiment and power (*avatāra, śākti*) that constitutes the "logic" of the *uttamasādhana*.

The role of the Buddha as presented in the *Mmk* is unambiguous, as the following verses spoken by the Śākyamuni show.

> I have dwelled for a long time in the impenetrable wilderness
> that is *saṃsāra*. Whenever there are beings to be converted, I act.
> Just as there are [such] beings, I bestow beneficial rituals.

In this manner, I act for their welfare,
[bestowing] rituals that are refuges of auspiciousness.

. . .

Thus do I act for them, arising in various forms.
I am he who would assume an appearance
of various bodies for insiders or for outsiders.
As an abode of welfare for beings, I produce various forms.
Maheśvara, Śakra, Brahma, and so on,
Viṣṇu, the bestower of wealth,
and the demon Nairṛtā, the unjust one —
the forms of disruptive demons, too, I produce[d] in former times.

. . .

I am at peace, imperishable, tranquil, blissful, pure, auspicious.
I have attained complete emancipation and tranquility.
I am released form the bonds of birth.
Now the wheel [of this teaching] is turned,
the refuge for billions of beings.
This is revealed in the ordinance,
in the extensive discourse on *mantras*.[E4]

The point here is that the Buddha solidifies his *sambhoga* body in various forms in order to remain active within the ritual domain, even though he is beyond "the bonds of birth," or *saṃsāra*. The simplicity of this message is possible only because of the *Mmk*'s manner of representing the Buddha. The *Mmk* does not present a systematic buddhalogy. In this regard, it stands apart from the tightly structured medieval digests (*śāstras*) composed by authors whom Paul Griffiths refers to as "virtuoso monastic intellectuals."[36] This is not to say that the *Mmk* community was necessarily hostile to doctrinal texts. In one passage, in fact, we read that the various meanings of the rituals are "described in the *śāstras.*"[37] It is not surprising that there is no mention of which *śāstras* are meant. The *Mmk* is a ritual text. Its logic is therefore a logic of practice: when the conditions of success are fulfilled, the incongruities between the metaphysical and soteriological claims about the ontological status of the Buddha—a major theme in the Buddhist *śāstra* literature—are resolved in an act of ritual application. The solution offered by the *Mmk* is practical rather than speculative. If pressed into propositions, its buddhalogy would probably be quite unconvincing, even naive, but no less so than the propositional buddhalogy of a philosopher when pressed into practice, as Griffiths has shown.[38]

In place of a propositional buddhalogy the *Mmk* presents scattered images of the Buddha interacting with the elements of the cult. In the above passage the Buddha is presented as the teacher of the practices prescribed in the text, the authority ensuring the validity and legitimacy of the practices as Buddhist, the usurper of non-Buddhist traditions through identical forms of practice, the force generating the efficacy of the practices, and as that which embodies the numerous ritual devices, such as the *mantra* and *paṭa*.

The foremost characteristic of the Buddha in the *Mmk* is his being present in the world. The image at *Mmk* 1.1 (presented above) is clear. Śākyamuni is residing in a palace situated in the heaven above the highest realm of material existence (*rūpadhātu*). Space and consciousness are closely related in Buddhist cosmology. In both spatial and mental terms, this realm, known as the *akaniṣṭha*, is the final state before one enters into formlessness, nothingness, and infinity (*ārūpadhātu*). This image suggests that "complete emancipation" (*nirvṛti*) does not entail complete absence. Although situated on the boundaries of space and time, the Buddha remains within the perceptual range of both the purest, most subtle *saṃsāric* beings' (*śuddhāvāsika* gods) and the most adept *yogins*. In the subtle form of the *sambhogakāya*, however, Śākyamuni is beyond the range of ordinary humans. It is only " through the form of the *mantra*" (*mantrarūpena*) and through the support of the *paṭa* that he ruptures their field of perception. This conceptualization of the Buddha is expressed in a hymn of praise at *Mmk* 1. The hymn expresses what the reader of the *Mmk* should expect as the primary function of the Buddha; namely, to be actively engaged in preventing unwanted situations and in ensuring auspicious ones, and to do this through the medium of the *mantracaryā*.

> Homage to the liberated one, O noble one.
> Homage, O superior one among men.
> Homage, O best of men, O you who effect the goals of all *mantra* practices.
> Homage, O lion among men, O defender against all misfortunes.
> May there be homage O great hero, O destroyer of all unfortunate rebirths.
> Homage, O lotus flower among men, O you who possess boundless fragrance.
> Homage, O lotus among men, O purifier of the mire of the triple world.
> Homage to the liberated one, O releaser from all sufferings.
> Homage to the peaceful one, O perfect tamer of all the untamed.
> Homage to the perfected one, O perfecter of the goals of all *mantra* practices.
> Homage to the auspicious one, O auspicious one among all that is auspicious.
> Homage to the awakened one, O you who are completely
> awakened to all teachings.
> Homage to him who has gone thus [beyond suffering], O you who have
> gone thus for the sake of the teachings—
> O teacher who has entered completely into unmanifest form!
> Homage to the omniscient one, to you who knows all that is to be known—
> things compounded and uncompounded—you who are established in, and who
> establishes [others] on the path to, *nirvāṇa* by means of the three vehicles.[E5]

Coupling the image of the emission of light at the beginning of *Mmk* 1 with those of the fully emancipated Buddha (peaceful, imperishable, tranquil, blissful, pure, auspicious, and so on) and the "impenetrable wilderness" that is the human realm, points to a cosmogonic movement from origination to subtle and increasingly dense form. This movement is not unlike that ascribed to Viṣṇu and Śiva in the ritual texts devoted to those "creator" deities. In the *śaivāgamas*, for instance, Śiva acts as pure consciousness from the cosmic realm called the "pure domain" (*śuddhādhvan*), echoing the Buddha's position in the "Pure Abode" (*śuddhāvāsa*) as an immaterial *sambhogakāya*. Like the "unmanifest" Buddha, Śiva, too, is characterized as being liberated (*mukti*), peaceful (*śānta*), imperishable, tranquil, blissful (*ānanda*), pure (*vimala*), auspicious (*śiva*), and eternal. This is an image of an absent deity. He is, however, simultaneously pervasive (*vyāpti*) and all accomplishing (*sarvakartṛ*), by means of "mediating powers and beings."[39]

To the "virtuoso intellectuals" who composed the Vaiṣṇava, Śaiva, and Buddhist doctrinal digests, these characteristics presented problems. To say that the deity is simultaneously "unmanifest" and "all-accomplishing" is logically inconsistent. On the one hand are necessarily atemporal metaphysical claims. On the other are soteriological claims requiring temporality.[40] The attempt to reconcile this intellectual problem generated countless sectarian attempts to work out the details of received tradition. Griffiths calls these attempts "secondary doctrines."[41]

> [Secondary doctrines are] sentences expressive of doctrine for some community, but the object of these sentences is neither the setting nor the conduct of human life, but rather other doctrine-expressing sentences of that community. Such doctrines are generally intended to state rules governing how the community's primary doctrines are to be ordered, derived, recognized, interpreted, and used. [They are prompted by] internal crises, divisions, or disagreements, or by contact with alien communities.

Secondary doctrines are conceived when a community recognizes that its primary texts require elaboration. This elaboration takes the form of a shift in the mode of discourse. One way of viewing *Mmk* 1 is as an instance of such a shift in the mode of discourse. Normally this shift is from narrative to philosophy.[42] In the *Mmk* it is from injunction *to* narrative. Perhaps it is because the emphasis remains on "the conduct of human life" that *Mmk* 1 presents a narrative cosmological frame, rather than doctrinal rules, in order to govern "how the community's [rituals] are to be ordered, derived, recognized, interpreted, and used" in the face of contact with outside communities, and so on.

Like all *vaipulyasūtra* literature, the representation of the Buddha in the *Mmk* presupposes a particular conception of the universe, already mentioned above, called the *trisāhasramahāsāhasralokadhātu* (three-thousand-fold, many thousand fold world system.)[43] This conception was distinct form the *cakravāla* world system postulated by other Buddhist sects. The term *cakravāla* refers to the circle of iron mountains enclosing a finite space. The *trisāhasramahāsāhasralokadhātu*, on the other hand, evokes an infinite realm of space. The notion of finitude was challenged by the early Mahāyāna critique of the *cakravāla* model of the universe. A well-known example of this critique is found in chapter 16 of the *Saddharmapuṇḍarīka*, or the Lotus Sūtra. The verse section summarizes this as follows. The Buddha is speaking.

> Since I attained buddhahood,
> The kalpas through which I have passed
> Are infinite thousands of myriads
> Of koṭis of [incalculable] years.
> Ceaselessly preached I the law and taught
> Countless koṭis of creatures
> To enter the way of the Buddha:
> Since then are unmeasured kalpas . . .
> Truly I am not extinct
> But forever here preaching the Law . . .
> [If] in other regions there are beings
> Reverent and with faith aspiring,
> Again I am in their midst
> To preach the supreme Law. [44]

This statement of the Buddha is in response to confusion among his listeners, who were having difficulty grasping the significance of certain earlier events. The source of their confusion lay in the statement's conflict with the conventional view of the Buddha. The *Saddharmapuṇḍarīka* is of course challenging the limitations placed by more conservative groups on the uniqueness, life, and location of the Buddha. For these groups, the place of the Buddha, whether the single-world system or the billion-world system, was limited. Since the Buddha attained complete *nirvāṇa* on his earthly death at age eighty—thereby transcending even the uppermost, formless extent of the universe—his life, too, was seen as limited. For these groups, the question of the Buddha's accessibility became moot. According to this cosmology, the possibility of the living presence of a Buddha in the world of humans would not be realized again until the advent of Maitreya.

The critique of this limited view by the early followers of Mahāyāna took the form of a reconceptualization of the Buddha: the Buddha never enters complete *nirvāṇa*, he is eternally present, appearing in countless emanations. Two important consequences followed from this latter point. First, the sense of the term "Buddha" was expanded from the singular historical Buddha to an infinite number of *buddhas*, each occupying his own field of activity (*buddhakṣetra*) within the universe. Like Śākyamuni in our world—the southern *buddhakṣetra* called *sāha*—each of these *buddhas* is defined paradigmatically in the *Suvarṇaprabhāsottamasūtra*, a text referred to in the *Mmk*, as follows.[45]

> [A *buddha* is] one who has arrived at ineffable truth, one who is perfected, a completely enlightened one [who] is situated, exists and lives [in his respective field of influence] and teaches the *buddhas'* doctrine for the welfare and happiness of multitudes of people, out of compassion for the world, for the advantage of great masses of people, for the welfare and happiness of gods and humans.

Stereotyped attributes accompany each *buddha*. In the *Mmk*, for instance, a *buddha* is one "who possesses the ten powers" (*daśabala*) and the five "supernormal knowledges" (*pañcābhijñā*), whose "mind is pervaded by vast compassion" (*mahākaruṇāviṣṭamanasa*).[46] In many instances any one of these attributes is enough to explain the Buddha's ability to achieve that which is expressed in the hymn of praise at *Mmk* 1. The *abhijñā* called "power" (*ṛddhi*),[47] for instance, enables a *buddha* to perform numerous wonders: he can create an illusory body, multiplying himself at will; he can transmute elements, changing, for example, form into sound; he can rise to the *akaniṣṭha* heaven and converse with the gods there; he can emit rays of purifying light throughout the cosmos; he can create an illusory voice in order to teach the doctrine. Virtually all of the properties assigned to a *buddha* are common *yogic* stock.[48] They are, in a sense, culturally economized "secondary doctrines." This blatant lack of originality might support Griffith's contention that the primary concern of Buddhists, like that of every other religious group, was to place at the center of its cult a "maximally salvifically efficacious" being.

> Buddhalogical doctrine rests upon a single formal or procedural intuition: the intuition that Buddha is maximally great, that whatever great-making properties there are, Buddha has them maximally.[49]

Establishing the primary entity as maximally great is, so to speak, the first order of business for a cult. Otherwise the cult would have no *ultimate* ground for its basis. In fact, one of the stereotyped powers of a *yoga* master—which Indian deities, *buddhas*, *bodhisattvas*, and so forth uniformally are—is the ability to "control and surpass the *ṛddhi* of others."[50]

The reader of the *Mmk* should thus visualize the following. The Buddha is dwelling as a resplendent subtle body in a palace of inconceivable beauty situated within the (spatial and mental) universe of form. He announces to the gods inhabiting that sphere that he will teach. Immediately on saying this, he emits a ray of light called *impelling the bodhisattvas in the world-realm Saṅkusumita*, announcing to that group of *bodhisattvas*: "This, O sons of the conqueror, is my impelling of the light. Come here, prepare yourselves."[51] The reader knows that the Buddha, as a perfectly enlightened ("maximally great") being (*samyaksambuddha*), possesses the power (*ṛddhi*) to cause other beings to appear before him, to create a voice and solid body with which to teach the *dharma* (and ultimately to cause this to be written in a book), and to transmute himself into terrestrial sound (*mantra*) and image (*paṭa*).

In each of the passages that has been cited in this chapter, the reader was exposed to a thematic pattern. This pattern has four points. First, Śākyamuni became "the best among men," "the world's teacher," the "spiritual guide," and "the world's master."[52] Second, he becomes a *buddha,* unmanifest, liberated from the bonds of birth and death, at rest. Third, compelled by compassion, he acts "in the impenetrable wilderness that is *saṃsāra*." Fourth, he "arises in various forms." chapter 2 of *Suvarṇaprabhāsottamasūtra* sums this pattern up as follows:

> The Buddha does not enter complete *nirvāṇa*,
> the teaching is not completely lost.
> He appears to enter complete *nirvāṇa* in order to bring
> beings to complete maturity.
> Inconceivable is the blessed Buddha,
> eternal is the body of the *tathāgata*.
> He exhibits various manifestations
> because of his beneficence towards beings. [53]

The "various manifestations" of the Buddha become, for the reader of the *Mmk,* the present mode of Śākyamuni's being "accomplished in virtuous conduct and salvific knowledge" (*vidyācaraṇasampanna*).[54] Revealing this mode, *Mmk* 1 continues.

> Then, the princely Mañjuśrī, the *bodhisattva* and great being, his eyes wide open and unblinking, approached the light of the ray. Shining with great brilliance upon the world-realm Kusumāvatī, and making three circumambulations around the blessed *tathāgata* Saṅkusumitarājendra, the impelling ray of light disappeared into the head of the great being, the *bodhisattva* Mañjuśrī. Rising from his seat, the princely Mañjuśrī made three circumambulations around the blessed *tathāgata* Saṅkusumitarājendra, bowed his head, kneeled on the ground, and spoke to the blessed Saṅkusumitarājendra: "We have been addressed by the blessed Śākyamuni, the *tathāgata*, the perfected one, the completely enlightened one. I will go to the Sahā world-realm, O Blessed One, to see, honor and serve the blessed

> Śākyamuni, to teach about [the initiation rite, the secret *mudrās*, etc.]." [*Mmk* 1.2.16-3.3] When he finished speaking, the blessed *tathāgata* Saṅkusumitarājendra responded to the princely Mañjuśrī: "you must go, O princely Mañjuśrī, if you think fit. Moreover, Śākyamuni should be asked on my behalf about [his being in a] state of little or no illness, relative freedom from disease, good health, and about his practice of renunciation. The blessed *tathāgata* Saṅkusumitarājendra further said to the princely Mañjuśrī: "Moreover, O prince, [Śākyamuni] has pronounced, and will pronounce, your *mantracaryā*, which has been fixed by one hundred thousand *tathāgatas*, perfected ones, perfectly enlightened ones, equaling the sands of the Ganges river. . . . Now consented to by me as well, you must go, O princely Mañjuśrī, if you think fit, and stand in the presence of Śākyamuni. You will listen to the discourse on the doctrine, and then you, too, will proclaim that.[E6]

Mmk 1 as a whole is framed by two statements. The first is in the opening sentence concerning the "miraculous transformation of the *bodhisattva*," and the second is the chapter colophon:

> The first chapter: the assembly; from the section of the fundamental ritual ordinance on the miraculous transformation of the *bodhisattva*, the princely Mañjuśrī, from the extensive ritual ordinance giving instructions on the Mahāyāna *mantra* rites.[55]

The image above of Mañjuśrī's being incited by the ray of light emitting from Śākyamuni's forehead indicates that the *bodhisattva* is under the authority of the Buddha, and serves as a mediator of Śākyamuni's power. However, though incited by Śākyamuni, Mañjuśrī goes to the Śuddhāvāsa only after being ordered to do so by the *buddha* Saṅkusumitarājendra, in whose *buddhakṣetra* Mañjuśrī is dwelling. Such images introduce an ambiguity that recurs throughout the *Mmk*: precisely whose activity is producing and transmitting the teaching contained in the text? Whenever Śākyamuni attaches agency to the teaching, he refers to it simultaneously as Mañjuśrī's (*tvadīya*), and as that which is "authorized by me and spoken by all *buddhas*."[56] When Mañjuśrī ascribes agency, it is likewise "Śākyamuni's" or "all *buddhas*'" (*sarvabuddha*). The text, furthermore, is called "the original ordinance of Mañjuśrī," yet in forty-three of the fifty-five chapters Śākyamuni delivers the teaching himself. In only the first three chapters does Mañjuśrī appear as a narrator. Another instance of ambiguity is the *maṇḍala* described in *Mmk* 2 where Mañjuśrī occupies the center of the circle together with Śākyamuni.[57] The *Mmk* offers solutions to this problem of agency at several levels. The quick solution is to claim that the answer is "inconceivable, miraculous, and wondrous" (*acintyāścaryādbhuta*),[58] and therefore closed to sensible discussion. Another solution is that the question of agency is accounted for by the *abhijñā* of a *buddha*, in particular his ability to create and transmute form, and to multiply himself indefinitely. This solution is apparent in the content of *mantras* in the *Mmk*, as the analysis at 1.4.2 showed. Paul Mus held that the dispersion of light pointed to the solution presented by the *trikāya* theory. He writes, "that conception of the Law penetrating the entire universe and being present at each point [of space]—that is the concept of the Dharmakāya. It is known that this is also the meaning of the cosmic light that emits from the ūrṇa of the transcendental tathāgatas making apparent buddhas and bodhisattvas in the act of teaching, that is to say, the omnipresent Law."[59] MacDonald, too, saw the *trikāya* theory at work in the *Mmk*, whereby Saṅkusumitarājendra represents the *dharmakāya,* Śākyamuni, the *sambhogakāya*, and Mañjuśrī, the *nirmāṇakāya*.[60]

To varying degrees of explicitness, each of the above solutions is present in the *Mmk*. At *Mmk* 1, however, the stress is clearly on what can be called the nondifferentiated mediation of the Buddha's power. Śākyamuni may be the "lotus among men" who fills the entire garden with his delightful fragrance,[61] but there are many flowers in the "mire" of the world.[62] All beings who are securely on the path to enlightenment share in the power and knowledge of the Buddha to some extent. In the *uttamasādhana*, for example, even the practitioner "is empowered by all *buddhas* and *bodhisattvas,*" and "becomes possessed of numerous powers and supernatural abilities." This image reflects the "path" metaphor at work in the *Mmk*, *mantramārga*,[63] whereby a *buddha* is essentially indistinguishable from the beings who assemble around him, including the practitioner, since they are on the path that leads to the Buddha's seat of enlightenment.

The vehicle for this solution to the problem of agency is the "transformation of the *bodhisattva*" (*bodhisattvavikurvaṇa*). At 1.2.4, I considered the bearing that this concept has on the text's claims about *mantra*. There, it serves as a mechanism for crystalizing power and compassion into the earthly, "fleshless relic" that is *mantric* sound. At *Mmk* 1 it is shown to be the means by which movement occurs in the cosmic/mental sphere of the *akaniṣṭha*. A *buddha's* or *bodhisattva's* transformation originates in very specific states of mental concentration, and extends outward. *Mmk* 1 begins with Śākyamuni's entering into a *samādhi* called *destroying through the dispersion of light into the purified sphere of activity*. A cosmic ray of light, called *impelling the bodhisattva in Saṅkusumita*, proceeds from this as a display of the Buddha's power of transformation. In the *lokadhātu* called *kusumāvatī*, the light makes three circumambulations around the *buddha* of that realm, Saṅkusumitarājendra, before entering into the head of Mañjuśrī. Immediately, Mañjuśrī knows that he is to go to the *sahā* world and listen to Śākyamuni's teaching on the *mantracaryā*. Granting him permission to do so, Saṅkusumitarājendra then enters into a *samādhi* called *attaining to the circle of enlightenment, which ensues naturally from the conduct of the bodhisattva.* From this state he pronounces a *mantra*: *namaḥ sarvabuddhānām* (*homage to all buddhas*). This pronouncement causes Mañjuśrī himself to enter into a *samādhi* called *the transformation for the excellent samādhi of those who have attained enlightenment.* He arrives instantaneously in the great jeweled palace of the *śuddhāvāsa* gods, in the presence of Śākyamini. Situated in this manner, he enters into another *samādhi* in order to display his transformation to the *śuddhāvāsa* gods. This meditative absorption, called *illumination with ornaments of brilliant jewels,* causes the entire palace of the *śuddhāvāsa* heaven to become illuminated by a great ray of light, and numerous ritual offerings, such as garlands smeared and scented with aromatic powders, to rain down on Śākyamuni, "worshipping him as he observes this miraculous transformation of the *bodhisattva*."[64]

The light of the Buddha at the opening of *Mmk* 1 is the first display of the *buddha/bodhisattvavikurvaṇa*. This light produces a ripple effect that forms the ritual universe, and ritual "family," of the *Mmk*. This culminates, at the end of *Mmk* 1, in the text and the practitioner. The text is structured to reveal the course of this movement. Following is a summary intended to give the effect of the whole.

[*Mmk* 1.6.27–1.7.6] Mañjuśrī enters into a *bodhisattvasamādhi* called *impelling the ornamentation for the marvelous display, by means of rays of light, of the transformative power of all buddhas* (*sarvabuddhādhiṣṭhānajyotiraśmivyūhālaṅkārasañcodanī*). Immediately, all the beings in the great hell *avīci* have their sufferings appeased. This ray of light incites to action the beings mentioned below, then disappears again into Mañjuśrī's forehead.

[*Mmk* 1.7.7–1.9.9] The *buddhas* living in the eastern *buddhakṣetra* are impelled by the production of light. These *buddhas* are named along with their accompanying *bodhisattvas*. They all come to Śākyamuni, his entourage, and Mañjuśrī. So do the *buddhas*, and so on from the south, west, and north; the zenith, nadir, intermediate area and *buddha* fields are illuminated; death is obscured. All of these assemble to receive "the chapter on the meaning of *mantras*, and instructions on the way of the *bodhisattva*"; they "are desirous of being taught about exalted *bodhisattvas* being transformed into *buddhas*, are desirous of having revealed to them the indestructible teaching of the *tathāgatas* contained in the excellent, extensive chapters on contemplation and the execution of the *mantracaryā*." These and others illuminate the Śuddhāvāsa, where Śākyamuni dwells, and take their places on lotus seats. These are named.

[*Mmk* 1.9.9–1.11.5] These are followed by *bodhisattvas* "bearing the form of women, disguised as medicinal herbs, and inconceivable magical words (*vidyāpadas*), *dhāraṇīs,* and *mantras,* in order to establish followers securely on the path, to be refuges for living beings, for completely accomplishing in the world the goals of the boundless rituals; who attend to the rituals performed by beings, pervading innumerable beings and nonbeings, such as gems, *mantras*, jewels, *rākṣasas, yakṣas,* manifold flocks of birds; who are leaders of beings, altering form in accordance with one's wishes." These are named and described. Then come others of the *vidyārājñī* class. These are accompanied by *bodhisattvas* bearing names beginning with *tathāgata*. Then come *vidyārājas* of the lotus family (*abjakula*). Then innumerable *vidyārājñīs* "proceeding from the *samādhi* of Lokeśvara." These are named; the first mentioned is Tārā. All are female. These are accompanied by various other beings, male and female: *kiṃkaras, yakṣas, rākṣasas, piśācas*. The *vidhārāñjīs* "proceed from the *mantras* and penetrate the vow of the lotus family (*abjakula*)." All of the above come to the Śuddhāvāsa and zealously worship Śākyamuni.

[*Mmk* 1.11.6–1.12.3] Vajrapāṇi summons his own *vidyāgaṇa*. These are named and described. With these *vidyārājas* and *mahākrodhas* are others who are "destroyers of death, destruction, epidemics, ruin, and tamers of all beings without exception; bestowers upon the faithful; discharged for the practitioners of rituals of malediction, increase, and pacification." Each takes his or her proper place in the *maṇḍala*.

[*Mmk* 1.12.3–1.13.4] Other great messengers of Vajrapāṇi, accompanying numerous thousands of *vidyārājñīs*, come. These are named; all are feminine. They take their places in the assembly. *Dhāraṇīs*, "produced by the penetrative mind that ensues naturally from contemplation, punishers of evil beings," take their places in the assembly.

[*Mmk* 1.13.4–22] Next come "blessed *pratyekabuddhas*, who are excluded from *buddha* fields, who resemble the rhinoceras's horn [in their solitariness] (*khaṅgaviṣāṇakalpa*), forest wanderers, who have accomplished the goal of all beings, who have manifested the eye of the law, consenting silently, who are subject to *saṃsāra*, who are perpetually depressed, being continuously devoid of compassion, whose thoughts have previously conceived of producing the mind of enlightenment (*bodhicitta*), but have not conceived of dwelling in this mind entirely, whose minds are turned away from one, two, three, up to eight *bodhisattvabhūmis*, whose thoughts are depressed, fearful of the terror of *saṃsāra*." These *pratyekabuddhas* take their places in the great assembly.

[*Mmk* 1.13.22–1.15.10] Then come numerous *mahāśrāvakas*. They are characterized as follows: they know the taste of liberation, have, through the vehicle of the teaching, attained what was to be done, namely, the goal of the triple vehicle, which is to escape from *saṃsāra*; they are absorbed in the meditation of threefold, fourfold, many-fold abidings, are extremely intent, properly ordained as monks, and so forth. They immediately attain the ten stages of the *bodhisattva*. All of these gathered, desirous of having the meaning of the *mantracaryā* clairified.

(*Yamāntaka and his acolytes*)
[*Mmk* 1.15.11–17] Śākyamuni asks Mañjuśrī to teach the assembly verses on liberation, pacification, the law of fruition, and the Buddhist teaching. Śākyamuni then causes Mañjuśrī to enter into a meditative absorption (*bodhisattvasamādhi*) called *production of the ritual ordinance, which is equal to the establishment of certainty and to the ten powers of the tathāgatas, and which possesses universal power, destroying the power of death.*

[*Mmk* 1.15.18–1.16.6] Upon doing so, thousands of world systems (*trisāhasramahāsāhasralokadhātu*) tremble, and are filled with light. Mañjuśrī relates his own *mantras*. But first, he pays homage to all *buddhas*, *pratyekabuddhas*, *śrāvakas*, and *bodhisattvas* who have mastered the ten stages of a *bodhisattva*. The *mantra* invokes Yamāntaka: *Oṃ kha kha khāhi khāhi duṣṭasattvadamaka asimusalaparaśupāśahasta caturbhuja ṣaṭcaraṇa gaccha gaccha mahāvighnaghātaka vikṛtānana sarvabhūtabhayaṅkara aṭṭahāsanādine vyāghracarmanivasana kuru kuru sarvakarmāṃ / chinda chinda sarvamantrān / bhinda bhinda paramudrām / ākarṣaya ākarṣaya sarvamudrām / nirmatha nirmata sarvaduṣṭān / praveśaya praveśaya maṇḍalamadhye / vaivasvatāntakara kuru kuru mama kāryam / daha daha paca paca mā vilamba mā vilamba samayam anusmara hūṁ hūṁ phaṭ phaṭ / sphoṭaya sphoṭaya sarvāśāpāripūraka he he bhagavan kiṃ cirāyasi mama sarvārthān sādhaya svāhā //* (*O tamer of evil beings! O you with noose, axe, club, and sword in the hand, four-armed, four-faced, six-legged one, go, go destroyer of great obstacles, ugly one, creator of fear in all demons, you who bellows with loud laughter, wearer of tiger skins execute execute all rituals, pierce pierce all mantras, bind bind the superior seal, attract attract the seal of all! crush crush all evil ones! enter enter into the center of the maṇḍala! O destroyer of the sun, make make of me what is feasible! burn burn cook cook do not tarry do not tarry remember your vow! hūṁ hūṁ phaṭ phaṭ! crush crush O fulfiller of all desires! hey hey O Blessed One, why do you delay?! accomplish all things for me! hail!*)

[*Mmk* 1.16.7–12] Yamāntaka, the great king of wrath (*mahākrodarāja*), then says: For the blessed Mañjuśrī, this one, the destroyer of death, called

Yamāntaka, the great king of wrath, leads and kills even the rulers of death, let alone another being. Instantly, everyone approaches the Blessed One, their hearts filled with fear, minds perturbed, disturbed, jolted with arrows of terror. They cry out, "there is no other refuge, there is no other protection, there is no other resort if the blessed Buddha and the youthful Mañjuśrī are abandoned!"

[*Mmk* 1.16.13–29] Countless beings of earth, water, air, self-produced, mobile, stationary, and so on, abiding in the world realms, are in an instant led by Yamāntaka to the zenith, nadir, and intermediate regions.

[*Mmk* 1.17.1–25] Through the power (*bodhisattvādhiṣṭhāna, ṛddhibala*) of Yamāntaka numerous others spirits, supernatural beings, natural forces, and human beings who have mastered supernatural powers come to the *maṇḍala* to hear the teaching: magical serpents (*nāga, mahānāga* [*mahā*° repeated for most of following]), genii (*yakṣa*), imps (*rakṣasa*), goblins (*piśācas*), celestial musicians (*kiṃkaras*), *pūtana* and *graha* demons, accomplished human masters of supernatural feats, such as *siddhas, yogins,* and *ṛṣis,* heavenly musicians (*gandharvas*), heavenly beings (*devas*), great humans, men, oceans, rivers, mountains, seas, earths, trees, birds, kings, the forms of Vedic, Vaiṣṇava and Śaiva deities, such as Śakrā, Yama, Brahmā, Lokendra, Harihārīti. All of these take their places in the great assembly in Śuddhāvāsa in order to hear the teaching.

[*Mmk* 1.17.26–1.21.23] Several of these groups are then repeated, naming members of the respective group. For example, kings of the *mahārākṣasas* are named, *mahāpiśācas*, kings of the *mahānāgas*, *ṛṣis*, kings of the *garuḍas*. Planets and lunar mansions entering the assembly are named. The thirty-six signs of the zodiac are named; these, too, enter the assembly. *Mahāyakṣinīs, mahāpiśācas*, the divine mothers arrive, and are named. Hells burst open. There is no strife whatsoever between the living beings in the assembly. Through the power of the Buddha (*buddhādhiṣṭhāna*) and the ornament of the community of *bodhisattvas* (*bodhisattvasaṅghālaṅkāra*), all beings behold the Blessed One and Mañjuśrī standing at the summit.

[*Mmk* 1.21.24–27] Śākyamuni, gazes down on the world realm with his *buddha* eye, and speaks to Mañjuśrī: "Speak, speak, O pure being, this section on meditative absorption, on the certainty of attaining the goal of the *mantracaryā*, this canon of the *bodhisattvas*, if you think the proper time has arrived."

(*Yamāntaka's vow of protection*)
[*Mmk* 1.22.1–13] Thus authorized by Śākyamuni, Mañjuśrī enters into a meditative absorption called *adorning the marvelous array by spreading it*

out like cloth and compacting it like a diamond. Immediately, the Śuddhāvāsa extends over several hundred thousand miles and becomes adamantine (*vajramaya*). Then, the *yakṣas, rākṣasas*, and so forth, "through the supernatural power of the *bodhisattvas* in all the realms of beings, are established unhurt in the diamond-like divine palace." Noticing this, Mañjuśrī speaks, in *mantric*-like utterance, to Yamāntaka: *bho bho mahākrodarāja sarvabuddhabodhisattvanirghātaḥ evaṃ mahāparṣatsannipātamaṇḍalaṃ sarvasattvānāṃ ca rakṣa rakṣa vaśamānaya / duṣṭān dama / saumyān bodhaya / aprasannāṃ prasādaya / yāvadahaṃ svamantracaryānuvarttanaṃ bodhisattvapiṭakaṃ vaipulyamantracaryāmaṇḍalavidhānaṃ bhāṣiṣye / tāvad etāṃ bahir gatvā rakṣaya* (*friend, friend, O king of great wrath, subdue, protect, protect all the beings encircled in the great assembly, protect from destruction all the buddhas and bodhisattvas! tame the evil! awaken the gentle! cause the anxious to become tranquil! For as long as I proclaim the practice of my mantra rites, the bodhisattva canon, the instruction of the maṇḍala and the extensive mantra rites, so long must you, having gone outside, protect!*)

[*Mmk* 1.22.14–20] Upon receiving this command, Yamāntaka, surrounded by several thousand wrathful beings, stood firmly and released a terrifying roar toward the four directions. And those gentle, cheerful beings who had gathered did not violate that command. They heard this sound: *He who would transgress this vow has his head split open like the bud of the ajaka flower. This is the resolution (adhiṣṭhāna) of the bodhisattvas!*

(There follows a long section [*Mmk* 1.22.21–24.8] on the qualities required of a *bodhisattva* practitioner. This will be discussed at chapter 4.)

(*results of worship*)
[*Mmk* 1.24.9–23] "Then, the entire assembly, comprised of *buddhas, bodhisattvas*, *pratekyabuddhas*, and *śrāvakas*, were roused to declare: 'Excellent, excellent, O good son of the Victorious One, is this well-formulated instruction on the religious discourse devoted to the entrance into the wisdom of the teaching concerning rituals for the purpose of the wonderful *mantracaryā*, for the sake of all sentient beings. O princely Mañjuśrī, well-spoken is this agreeable *mantracaryā*, in obeyance with the teaching on the wonderful *dharma*! Whatever great king declares in the future this chapter on the assembly, preserves it, learns it by heart, will, having mounted an elephant beforehand, prevail in battle; if he offers worship by anointing [it] with various flowers, incense and fragrances, we will subject (his) enemies, (his) adversaries, we will cause the destruction of (his) enemy's armies. Or, if having written it down in a book, it is maintained in one's own home, we will cause increase in fortune, a healthy life, a long life, great wealth, and

great protection to a laywoman or layman, a monk or nun, a king or queen, or the son or daughter of a good family." Saying this, the entire assembly becomes silent.

This linear, narrative presentation of the text parallels the circular image of the visualized cosmic *maṇḍala*, the square image of the initiatory earth *maṇḍala*, and the rectangular image of the larger *paṭas*. The movement of the whole begins at a point of undifferentiated abstraction: in the mind of Śākyamuni pervaded by compassion (*mahākaruṇāviṣṭamanasa*). This becomes light; the light impels a distant *buddha*; this *buddha* impels the *bodhisattva*. Although the technical center of each is the materialized locus of the light, Śākyamuni, the "triple body" forms the underpinning. The practitioner is represented in each scheme as the culmination of the dispersion of light and the ultimate object of the *vikurvaṇa*—"wherever there are beings to be converted, I act." The following scheme depicts this.

(narrative *maṇḍala*)

Light>Saṅkusumitarājendra>Mañjuśrī >*buddhas, bodhisattvas, pratyekabuddhas, śrāvakas*>Yamāntaka>supernatural beings, gods, nature, etc.>*sādhaka* and book.

(initiatory *maṇḍala*)
Saṅkusumitarājendra
o
Śākyamuni
o
Mañjuśrī
o \
\
\ *maṇḍalaka*

(large *paṭa*)
°Saṅkusumitarājendra
|
|
|
|
°Mañjuśrī
/ \
°Śākyamuni \
(center) \
\ *sādhaka*

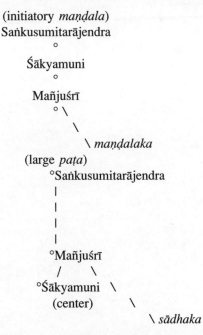

The "practice of *mantras*," *mantracaryā*, is "the course of *mantras*" from the imperceptible mind of the Buddha, throughout his cosmic field, through numerous enlightened and protective beings, through the spirits and elements of the earth, through the text, and finally to the intonation of the practitioner within the ritual field. The "path of *mantras,*" *mantramārga*, then reverses itself, leading the practitioner back again to the *sannipāta*, the source of the *mantracaryā* and the seat of enlightenment.

CHAPTER 3

The Refraction of Power: The Cult Image *(paṭa)*

From the assembly of beings arrayed through the compelling power of the Buddha's cosmic light, the *Mañjuśrīmūlakalpa* takes the reader to the space that is the cult image. The cult image (*paṭa*) is presented as the area where the Buddha's power manifests in concentrated form. The cult image is held to be a refractive space, reflecting the original domain of enlightened power. This domain is ever-present. The darkness of human ignorance, however, obscures this presence. The text remedies this by revealing to the practitioner the means by which the Buddha's cosmic assembly may be literally woven into a lively image of tremendous force. As with the recitation of *mantras* and the imagining of the assembly, as we have seen, effective fashioning of the cult image depends on the successful practice of a wide range of ritualized activities. This chapter explores the text's presentation of the cult image and the practices surrounding its creation and use.

3.1 The paṭa as image and animated object

A seventh century narrative of King Harṣa (*Harṣacarita*) tells of a storyteller called a *yamapaṭika*. In public marketplaces, this storyteller would unroll a *yamapaṭa*, a cloth painting (*paṭa*) of various scenes revealing the tortures inflicted on recently deceased humans by Yama, the god of death. The storyteller would recite commentary on the scenes displayed on the cloth while pointing to the features being emphasized.[1] We can imagine the effect that the *yamapaṭa* would have had on the observers standing in that marketplace, enraptured by the storyteller's performance. As the narrator describes the torments of hell, he thrusts his hand, and with it all eyes, toward his painted cloth illustration. Simultaneously, his audience is thrust into the very hell-realm being manifested through his words, voice and image. Sensing—hearing, seeing, feeling—the terrors that await sinners, they leave the marketplace resolved on deeper piety. This ability of a painting to make present an otherwise concealed reality is subtly alluded to in a Sanskrit literary simile called "the painted cloth simile" (*citrapaṭanyāya*). This simile goes: "just like a canvas rolled open reveals its figures, so does the Supreme One make manifest the whole world concealed in him by the karma of the souls."[2]

This illustration of the *yamapaṭa* can be used to explore the ways in which the *paṭa* functions in the *Mmk*. Most basically, the *paṭa* is a catalyst of response. As the term implies, *response* ensues from the interaction of image and observer. The example of the marketplace audience indicates the complex nature of response. Response requires the presence of emotional and conceptual factors on the side of the observer, and liveliness and efficacy on that of the image. For the *yamapaṭika's* vision of hell to have such an emotional effect on the audience, some knowledge and acceptance of the ideas surrounding that vision must be present. Although such knowledge is acquired culturally, the *yamapaṭika*, the storyteller, serves to stimulate it and fashion it toward a specific end. In other words, a specific response is elicited by an indicator of meaning. Similarly, the *paṭa* in the *Mmk* was imputed meaning by a cultural community (an audience) that knew and accepted the ideas underlying it. Like the *yamapaṭika*, the text itself functioned to elicit—to indicate, stimulate, and mold—a range of responses.

The *Mmk* organizes its presentation of the cult image in terms of three stages undergone by the *paṭa*. These three stages point to the basic senses of the term as well: canvas, painted image, and animated cult object. In my discussion of this presentation that follows, I attempt to trace the processes behind the creation of the *paṭa*, and to discern something of the manner in which both those processes and that creation served the particular form of Buddhist practice examined in this study. Here, I would like to make a few brief points about some of the implications of these three stages of the *paṭa*.

As the verb √*paṭ* ("to string together, wrap") implies, the *paṭa* is first of all a piece of cloth formed from raw cotton. The noun *paṭa* thus generally denotes a type of woven cloth used for things such as clothing, screens, and as in the *Mmk*, canvases for painting. It is difficult to imagine that the *yamapaṭika* above would have imbued his *paṭa* with very much meaning at this stage. It would, after all, be difficult to evoke the terrors of hell while pointing to an empty canvas. By contrast, as we will see, the practitioner of the *Mmk* is enjoined to suffuse even this emptiness with meaning. While this is in part indicative of the end served by the canvas, namely, cult object, it also serves as a further example of the "unrestrained creative exuberance and the spirit of experimentation"[3] of Indian cultic life in general. Onto a raw, empty canvas, that is, even prior to the painting of the image, the practitioner creatively deposits innovative and unique clusters of meaning.

Discussing the historical, iconoclastic notion of "icon" (which I am calling "cult image" and "cult object" as more specific terms) as "idol," that is, as an inherently ineffectual artifact composed of "base matter," Matthew Kapstein offers a helpful insight into this creative process. Kapstein's comments are particularly pertinent here since they are made in regard to what he calls the "world-constructing enterprise" of *paṭa* creation specifically in the *Mmk*. The value of this article for the present study will be discussed in more detail below. Kapstein writes:

> In consideration of what is yet unformed, and thus in a crucial sense empty, the construction of value emphatically appears as a matter of intentional practice by human agents within human communities. The art of esoteric Buddhism is appropriate subject matter for our reflections about this, for esoteric Buddhism . . . seems always to accentuate the constructedness of human values, with particular attentiveness to the unformed character of the stuff from which those values are constructed, and to the requirement that they be reconstituted continuously in a world of ongoing change.[4]

Long before any image is depicted on the blank canvas, the *paṭa* is a repository of a complex vision of the world. As the initial space to be fashioned and imprinted with the emblems of the specific value system propagated through the *Mmk*, the raw cotton *paṭa* is the first step in what Kapstein aptly calls "world-building, in its physical, symbolic, and conceptual dimensions."[5]

The second stage of the *paṭa* involves the painting of an image on the canvas. The common usage of the term *paṭa* is, in fact, to denote a picture painted on canvas. This applies as well to its cultural and etymological varieties, such as Hindi *pat*, Nepali *paubhā*, Bengali *paṭua*, Tibetan *thangka*, Chinese and Japanese hanging scrolls (Chinese, *zi-thang*), and Korean *tangwa*. As the English equivalent to these terms, "painting," might seem to warrant, the *paṭa* is thus typically discussed within the purview of "painting" or "sacred art." The example of the *Mmk*, however, does not warrant the equation of *paṭa* with "painting." The text does not distinguish between painted image (painting, sacred art) and cult object (icon, relic) categorically. The text is emphatic on this point: what obtains for the whole applies to each minute part. Kapstein alludes to this fact when he mentions the necessity of continuous, repetitive value creation within a single process. In the *Mmk,* a speck of raw cotton, a brilliant image, and a consecrated object are but overlapping moments in a unitary field. The Western idea of "painting," of a work of art, does not allow for this unity.

In his *Bild und Kult* Hans Belting notes the historical shift that gave rise to the notion of "art."

> A history of the image is something other than a history of art. But what does this mean? In its general usage, the term "image" encompasses everything and nothing, as does the term "art." Therefore, let it be said at the outset that by the term "image" . . . is to be understood primarily the figurative depiction, the *imago*. The *imago* presents a person, and, therefore, is treated as a person. In this sense, the *imago* became the preferred object of religious practice. In this regard it was honored as a cult object, and distinguished

from the narrative image, or *historia*, which placed before the observer—who simultaneously read a corresponding text—the sacred history.

"Art" . . . presupposes the crises of the ancient image and its new valorization as art work in the Renaissance. . . . While the old type of images were destroyed during the phase of iconoclasm, images of the new type were appearing in art collections. From that point on, it becomes possible to speak of an *epoch of art* [in distinction to the previous "*epoch of the image*"].[6]

Although *paṭas*, *thangkas*, hanging scrolls, and so on, now appear in art collections around the world, their intended use and function (past and present) are best perceived when they are viewed as images, in the sense of *imago*—animated presentations. Following Belting, therefore, I use the term *cult image* to refer to this unity of form and function.

Bearing in mind the cohesion of the painted depiction and the animated object in the *Mmk*, it will nonetheless be informative to separate them briefly and consider some general implications of each in turn. Again, my comments here are intended as an introduction to the section that follows.

As a visual presentation, the *paṭa* of the *Mmk* serves several purposes. By its specific use of color and figurative expression and form it communicates to the practitioner the attitude required of him toward both the parts and the whole. In the largest *paṭa*, for example, Mañjuśrī is painted a soft, muted orange, his expression gentle; Yamāntaka is dark and ferocious-looking; the whole is backgrounded by a calming, deep blue sky with soft, billowing white clouds. These features instill an attitude of reverence; and they are instructive of the appropriateness of that attitude. In fact, the practitioner himself is depicted in the *paṭa* reverentially making an offering to the assembly, stressing this didactic feature. The ordered presentation points to an additional function of the *paṭa* as visual product. By presenting various classes of beings in relation to one another, a hierarchical scheme emerges. The scheme is an indicator, and agent, of social relations. It is a way of incorporating and ordering the diverse elements, both Buddhist and non-Buddhist, that bore on the structure of the *Mmk* cult. Selecting elemental parts from autonomous systems and reordering these into a new whole is always ideological, and, as we will see, occasionally polemic.

This process of selection and ordering leads to an additional purpose of the visual form. Belting mentions the *historia*, the narrative image of the "sacred history," and distinguishes this from the *imago*, the image as cult object. In the *Mmk*, the presentation of the "sacred history" is an aspect indistinguishable from the cult object per se. As *historia*, the *paṭa* presents a vital moment in the *Mmk's* history. It does this in both senses of the term *present*. As an image it makes present to the imagination of the practitioner the scene of a primordial event in both the history of the Buddha's teaching and the history of salvation. In this way, it serves as a catalyst to an imaginative remembrance of that pivotal moment. As an image, then, the cult object is a refractive space. But what it reflects is a *real* domain of power, one that is conceived as being fluid, unbound by time and space, and thus unfolding continuously. In this way, the cult object transforms the imagination "into a spiritual organ of making present."[7] While it is itself a form of imaginative experience, it is one whose primary function is to make present an otherwise obscured reality.

The image, then, does not serve merely as an instrument of communal memory. The scene presented on the *paṭa* is of the continuous unfolding in the present of a past event. We might consider this past as having occurred in "mythic" space and time, or as being "sacred history," if these terms are meant to refer to the fact that all traditions creatively interpret and use "history," statically conceived. In any case, the image on the *paṭa* merges this past with the present. The *sādhaka*, as mentioned above, is to be painted in a gesture of worship on the *paṭa* itself, thereby situating him within the history of revelation. Furthermore, external to the painting, in a bodily act of devotion or ritualized coercion, he contemplates the image of revealed power presented by means of the *paṭa*. This points to both a highly synchronic conception of past and present, and to the immediacy of mundane and transcendent space.

With this idea of the merging of past and present events by means of the image, the notion of the *paṭa* as an instrument of liveliness and efficacy is introduced. The interpretive translation of the term *paṭa* as "animated cult image" is useful in this respect. Through correct ritualized production, the *paṭa* becomes permeated by the power of the Buddha. As such, the *paṭa* was believed to possess miracle-producing properties often associated with *buddhas*. For example, proper ritual employment of the *paṭa* enabled the adept to traverse great distances of space rapidly, overcome the force of time, heal sickness, produce food during a famine, and converse with gods and enlightened beings. Most important perhaps, it assured the practitioner of the attainment of buddhahood. Throughout the history of Buddhist cultic life, other objects have played this role. Relics, statues, architectural monuments, books, remembrance, and visualization have, at various times and in various places, been believed to render present the otherwise inaccessible power that accompanies a living Buddha.

3.2 Creation of the cult object *(paṭavidhāna)*

3.2.1 Previous scholarship

The creation of the *paṭa* has been dealt with previously by Marcelle Lalou, in *Iconographie des étoffes peintes (paṭa) dans le Mañjuśrīmūlakalpa* (Lalou 1930 in bibliography), and Matthew Kapstein, in "Weaving the World: The Ritual Art of the *Paṭa* in Pāla Buddhism and Its Legacy in Tibet" (Kapstein

1995). Although brief and limited in scope, these two studies provide a foundation for further study of the *paṭa* in the *Mmk*.

Marcelle Lalou's work consists mainly of translations of the sections that describe *paṭas*. She translates the pertinent sections of *Mmk* 4–7, dealing with, respectively, the large, intermediate, small, and simplified *paṭas*. In seven appendices, she brings together the remaining sections where iconographic instructions are given in the *Mmk*, namely, *Mmk* 14, 26, 27, 28, and 39. Lalou's introduction to her translations is brief, noting only several general facts about the *paṭa*. By contrast, the notes to her translations provide clarification, emendation, and elaboration on the Sanskrit text. One of the merits of Lalou's work is that she has consulted the Tibetan and Chinese translations of the Sanskrit text, and mentions these wherever they offer clearer readings. An additional merit is the seven plates in which the *Mmk's* eleven *paṭas* are schematized. Like her footnotes, Lalou's plates lend order and clarity to the text's often diffuse and unclear presentation of its iconography. In short, *Iconographie des étoffes peintes (paṭa) dans le Mañjuśrīmūlakalpa* is a pioneering work that reflects the philological concerns of an earlier generation of Buddhist scholars to edit and translate Buddhist literature. As the series title "Buddhica: documents et travaux pour l'étude du bouddhisme" indicates, this work was meant to precede and complement any subsequent interpretive or comparative work. Lalou's valuable contribution in this regard is recognized in my own translations below.

Matthew Kapstein intends his contribution to the study of the *paṭa* to be both corrective and analytical. Because his work is supportive of a central proposition of my thesis, Kapstein's article is discussed in some depth here.

I stated in the introduction that the rituals of the *Mmk* were best understood within the broader context of "practice." Practice, in this expanded sense, signifies the wider range of ritualized activities surrounding elemental ritual practices, such as oblations or *mantra* recitation. Since these surrounding practices constitute the conditions that make successful ritual possible, they should not be sharply differentiated from the ritual per se. One of the surrounding practices that I am considering is the process of creating the *paṭa*.

Kapstein's overall concern is to "make sense out of the relationship between Indian and Tibetan artistic practice and religious practice."[8] To this end, he seeks to show that "the creation of Buddhist icons in the esoteric traditions of Pāla Buddhism, as well as in their Tibetan offshoots, was itself preeminently understood as an integral aspect of a collective virtuoso religious practice, contributing to a holistic world-constructing enterprise" (245). Two dominant views in Buddhist studies regarding this relationship, however, obscure the nature of this collaborative relationship as it is reflected in the *Mmk*. The first of these views sees the artist as a *yogin*, or practitioner of contemplative exercises. Reproducing on canvas the forms visualized during meditation, the artist-*yogin* is bound by the "unalterable adherence" to an iconography detailed by the "cultural system in which he acts" (244). Kapstein objects to this view on both counts. The *Mmk* provides evidence that the artist and *yogin* were distinct characters. (As Kapstein himself notes, the text does allow for the practitioner to paint his own cult image [251];[9] this fact, however, does not detract from Kapstein's objection to the "caricature" [244] of the artist-*yogin* often encountered in Buddhist studies.) If, according to Kapstein, the Tibetan use of the *Mmk* is any indication, we must view the iconographical norms of a text as but "options" (257) for the receiving community. That is, the idea that the artist-*yogin* reproduces fixed forms is not borne out by the evidence of practical conventions. I would add to this the fact that even within the text itself room for flexibility is allowed for. The *paṭas* in *Mmk* 4–7, for instance, are represented in a seemingly contradictory manner. On the one hand, they occupy four distinct positions in a hierarchy. On the other, they are equally potent and efficacious. Because of their varying sizes, moreover, they depict varying iconographic configurations. Nonetheless, the moment in the "sacred history" of the teachings revealed on each is identical. We might, therefore, see the four *paṭas* as "options" reflecting the kinds of social differences and degrees of religious commitment found in the real world.

This view of the artist as *yogin* has been countered by "an alternative caricature" in the literature on Indo-Tibetan Buddhist art (244). It is this "mistaken hypercorrection" that Kapstein aims to correct (258). He writes that the assumption behind this view was that "there was in principle a very great gulf separating the artist from the virtuoso practitioner of the religion, the former manufacturing objects of cultic activity on behalf of the latter. This account requires that artisans and clerics occupy two parallel, occasionally interactive, but nonetheless essentially separate domains" (244). The evidence of the *Mmk* presents a contrary situation. For the duration of the process of creating the image, artisans and practitioners inhabit the same ritual world. The precise meaning of this is discussed below. What is important here is that fulfillment of the text's prescriptions speaks against separate domains of activity.

Kapstein is, of course, well aware of the normative nature of texts. His approach, therefore, is to compare "data gleaned from living traditions that were markedly influenced by Pāla religious and artistic practices" as a way of determining the relationship between norm and practice (257). Kapstein concludes that "a relatively consistent ethos governed the production of Indian and Tibetan Buddhist ritual art" and that "the paradigms governing the production of Tibetan religious art appear to accord very well with those that may be derived from the *MMK*" (257).

Kapstein's conclusions and correctives have implications for the present study. In showing its relevance for a single living tradition, the *Mmk* is placed on a continuum extending to the present. This raises the stature of the *Mmk* as a valuable text for our understanding of not only medieval ritual practice, but modern as well. What Kapstein shows about the *manner* in which the *Mmk* bears on these modern practices is equally significant. In his consideration of the relationship between norm and practice, Kapstein provides insight into the workings of the economy of forms historically. The play of options, of improvisation and experimentation within fixed structures, is shown to be endemic to the transcultural movement of a tradition. Finally, the view of the artisan suggested by Kapstein further points to the necessity of considering the ritual of the *Mmk* within the expanded context of "practice" that I outlined in the introduction. What Kapstein calls "a complete world-constructing project" encompasses the numerous surrounding practices that presuppose specific ritual acts. And, as the term *construction* denotes, the ritual project of the *Mmk* requires considerable labor, both physical and imaginative.

I mentioned above that what applies to the whole of the *paṭa* applies to each minute part. A speck of cotton is imputed the same potency as the completed cult object; and each individual cult object manifests the power of its cosmic archetype. This further supports the extended notion of practice in the *Mmk*, where ritual encompasses activities normally considered distinct from it, such as weaving, craftsmanship, and painting. As Kapstein writes, "esoteric Buddhist practice is a way of ordering the entire world" (249). This idea of continuous value creation within a single ritualized process also suggests a consistency within that process. With this, we come to the second contribution of Kapstein's groundbreaking article.

In order to establish the holistic nature of ritual in the *Mmk*, Kapstein analyzes the "compositional principle" underlying the process of *paṭa* creation (253). In addition to revealing the pattern of this process, Kapstein's scheme provides a clear overview of the stages that I analyze in more depth below. The three basic principles of the process identified by Kapstein are as follows:

1. gathering the necessary elements (abbreviated as G);
2. arranging those into a particular order (A); and
3. consecrating or protecting what has been arranged (C or P).

Thus, the shorthand "(GAP)thread" means that the thread has been gathered from some prescribed place, arranged in the prescribed manner, and protected with prescribed incantations. The entire process whereby the *paṭa* is fashioned can then be rendered as follows (the brackets represent minor changes made to Kapstein's terminology based on the distinction that I suggested above between sacred art and cult object; also, I alter the form of the scheme to show the sequence and relationships more clearly):

(GAP)cotton wool + (GAP)virgin spinner > (GAP)thread

|

(GAP)thread + (GAP)weaver> (GAP)*paṭa* [canvas]

|

(GAP)*paṭa* [canvas] + (GAP)artist>(GAC)painting [cult object: *paṭa*]

I would suggest that this pattern is discernible at several levels within the *Mmk*. The chapters on the *paṭa* (*Mmk* 4–7), for example, are structured similarly:

amassing of the universal forces supporting the rituals (G)

|

prescriptions for the arrangement of these forces into the *paṭa* (A)

|

expression of the transformation of the *paṭa* into the locus of the *buddhas'* power (C)

Within each ritual act in the *Mmk*, furthermore, the same structure is apparent.

accumulation of preliminary trainings (G)

|

concentration of those trainings into a specific order of ritual action (A)

|

transformation resulting from the ritual action (C)

The consistency of this basic structure in the *Mmk* indicates a major concern of those engaged in the text's practices. They apparently saw as imperative to their security and enlightenment the *interminable* fashioning of the universe, realized specifically in the fulfillment of the prescriptions recorded in the text. Whether that composition was realized through imagined, performed, or material forms, its purpose was to mediate the Buddha's/*buddhas'* power. This applied to each component of the composition as well. Whether a speck of cotton, a *mantra*, an elaborate cosmic *maṇḍala*, or a painted cult object, each element of the ritually fashioned universe served as a refraction of the Buddha's power within the world of the practitioner.

3.2.2 Ritual use of the paṭa

The *paṭa* is the central cult object in the practice of the *Mmk*. Although there is minor variation in the rituals employing it, the ritual use of the *paṭa* always conforms to the pattern below; and it invariably functions as the catalyst of transformation. The following example from *Mmk* 8 will serve to keep both this role and the nature of the transformation in mind when we turn to the comparatively prosaic enterprise of creating the cult object.

> First, he who has observed the vow, fulfilled the preliminary practices (*puraścaraṇa*), received the initiation, taken the essential (*hṛdaya*), basic *mantra* from this best of ordinances, or the *upahṛdaya*[10] or some other *mantra*, or having received a single syllable [*mantra*] or another one—according to one's wishes—and who, having gone to a great forest, eats leaves and roots, who subsists on fruits and water, should recite [the *mantra*] three million times. He becomes one who has completed the preliminary practice. Then, having climbed to the top of a mountain and set up the superior cult image facing to the west, he faces east himself, seated on a mound of *kuśa* grass. He should offer one lac of white lotuses and oiled white saffron at the base of the *paṭa* to the blessed Śākyamuni and to all the noble disciples, solitary *buddhas*, *bodhisattvas*, and *buddhas*. And he should burn as much camphor and incense as he can afford. He should worship the *nāgas* and gods with as many lotuses as he can procure. Then, at midnight, during the equinox, when the moon is bright and extraordinarily full, after having created an area for the fire at the base of the *paṭa*, and having lit the lotus-shaped fire with sticks of white sandalwood, combining saffron and camphor he should then make 1,008 oblations, creating as much protection as possible [*Mmk* 8.79.22–25]. Thereupon, rays of light proceed from the blessed Śākyamuni, and the entire *paṭa* blazes forth as a single shining [object]. Then, when the *sādhaka* has made three quick circumambulations around the *paṭa*, and has paid homage to all *buddhas, bodhisattvas*, solitary *buddhas* and noble disciples, the *paṭa* is to be taken hold of. Just as he grasps the edge of the previously drawn *paṭa*, the *sādhaka* flies up. He proceeds instantly to the Brahmaloka. He stays in the world-realm Kusumāvātī, where the *tathāgata* Saṅkusumitarājendra dwells, exists, abides, and teaches the *dharma*. He beholds Mañjuśrī directly. He hears the true teaching (*dharma*). He also sees several thousand *bodhisattvas*, and worships them. He becomes one who playfully enjoys non-aging and immortality for a thousand great eons. The *paṭa* is also there. He is empowered by all *buddhas* and *bodhisattvas*, and he declares to them his firm resolution (*adhiṣṭāna*) [to attain enlightenment] and proceeds to their hundred thousand paradises. [Their] hundred thousand bodies are revealed to him. He becomes possessed of numerous powers and supernatural abilities. He becomes the virtuous friend (*kalyāṇamitra*) of the noble Mañjuśrī. He becomes one for whom the goal of enlightenment is certain.[F1]

The aim of the process described in this chapter is, then, to fashion an object of enormous power. In order to understand more fully the implications of this process, it will be necessary to consider the nature of the claims being made about the cult image and the ritual in which it plays such a central role.

How are we to understand what is happening in the above passage? Śākyamuni's presence is said to manifest through an image painted on cloth and effect miraculous results. Efficacy within the ritual field is dependent on the proper performance of specific actions at specific times. The steady intermixing of the several elements of the ritual (e.g., scented powders, bodily gestures, camphor incense, astrologically potent time, varying spatial positioning, liturgy of the *pūjā*, repetition of the *mantra*) results in a transformation of status and ability on the part of the practitioner: he becomes a luminous entity capable of controlling at will powerful supernatural beings; Mañjuśrī and other enlightened beings enter into his range of perception to converse with him and offer guidance leading to buddhahood. But the elements of the ritual are not in themselves producing this effect; this is the function of the *paṭa*. The goal of the ritual is achieved by means of successfully effecting the inherent power of the *paṭa*. On the face of it, then, it seems as if the text is making a claim about magical coercion. That is, the passage could be read as a literal description of a simple causal sequence. This might be the sort of claim that Guisseppe Tucci had in mind when he wrote that the *Mmk* resembled many ritual texts which "remain nothing more than formularies of magic, collections of recipes, tending to promote the devotee's prosperity . . . having nothing in common with the subtleties of gnosis or with soteriological practices. Such, for instance, is largely the MMK, in which the Buddha descends to the level of a witch-doctor, revealing *vidyā* by which any miracle, and even crime, can be performed."[11] If a simple descriptive statement is being made the claim would be subject to a test of verification, and it would fail. The ritual would not accomplish what it claims. If this is the case, however, we are faced with the problem of accounting for the fact that Buddhists have persisted for over a thousand years in believing what is false. Granting Buddhist practitioners the same degree of rationality that we claim for ourselves, we might, rather, understand the passage to be expressive rather than descriptive. In this reading, it could be interpreted as a conveyance, which, though an end-in-itself, like music, art, or theater, refers metaphorically to something else, such as posited sociopolitical, metaphysical, or psychological realities. There are, however, at least two difficulties with this reading. First, the expression is self-referential. That is, it is limited to the ritual field, having no effective relationship to the outside world. It follows from this that, second, power itself is relational, lacking ontological significance. This notion of ritual is expressed by Jonathon Z. Smith when he asserts that "[r]itual is a relationship of difference between 'nows'—the now of everyday life and the now of ritual place; the simultaneity, but not the coexistence, of 'here' and 'there,' " and that ritual, like the number zero, "is neither an ontological nor a substantive category; it is a linguistic one . . . [i]t signals signification without contributing signification."[12] What makes this reading problematic is that the text resists it at every turn by insisting that *real* presence and *abiding* power are encountered in, and made to exceed, the ritual domain. A central aim of the practice of the *Mmk* is to move the "here" into the "there," the "now of ritual place" into the "now of everyday life."

As this suggests, I understand the claim of the passage to be one of neither "bad science" nor "mere" rhetorical metaphor. The passage is meant as a literal description of a real occurrence. But like all truth claims, its validity as a meaningful statement is dependent on the context in which it is made. The context of the ritual in the *Mmk* is the comprehensive "world" that the text posits. This world is known intellectually through the *vaipulyasūtras* referred to in the *Mmk*—and among which it counts itself a member—such as the *Prajñāpāramitā, Daśabhūmaka, Gaṇḍavyūha,* and *Suvarṇaprabhāsottamasūtra.* It is a world where compassion and power abide and unfold. As we will see in fuller detail below, what makes this possible is the very structure of the physical cosmos, the relationship of this cosmos to the lives of men and women, and the metaphysical import imputed to this cosmos. The structure of the above passage, too, points to the necessity of prior intellectual training. Long before he may engage in ritual practice, the *sādhaka,* must be slowly inducted by a master into the broader context—the conceptual universe of the *Mmk*—of the rituals he will practice. That is, he is taught not only the methods of practice, but the philosophical bases of those practices as well. This lays the groundwork for the intensive period of "preliminary practice" that follows initiation. Just as the reception of propositional knowledge creates for the practitioner the conceptual context of ritual practice, the preliminary practice inaugurates the reception of a higher form of knowledge and a deepening participation in the ritual world. This participation is achieved through ritual knowledge, and culminates in a visionary encounter with what are held to be real forces. A major assumption operating in the passage is that ritual knowledge, and not intellectual knowledge, is the superior episteme. Philosophical discourse provides a rough guide to the deep structure of the world, but ritual activity effects a transformative involvement with that structure. This is, in fact, a position shared by the medieval communities that were producing ritual manuals such as the *Mmk.* We read in the *Śivapurāṇa* (1.31.98–100), for instance:

> Knowledge is said to be of two types, indirect (*parokṣa,* literally "beyond one's own sight") and direct. Indirect knowledge is unstable, they say, while direct knowledge is very firm. Knowledge acquired through reasoning and instruction is considered indirect knowledge; direct knowledge will arise through the most excellent practice of ritual. Deciding that you cannot obtain *mokṣa* without direct knowledge, you should exert yourselves assiduously to master this excellent practice.[13]

The context for understanding the passage, the cult image, and the *mantracaryā* of the *Mmk*, then, is the specific world known both indirectly and directly by the practitioner of the *Mmk.* We can examine that world in more detail by considering what is perhaps the most banal statement in the passage: the practitioner is instructed to perform the ritual "on a night during the equinox, when the moon is extraordinarily bright and full." If we venture behind this statement we will come out onto the image of the physical cosmos enclosing the ritual space of the practitioner. By then peeling back some of the layers of this image, we can move increasingly back into the ritual field, into the metaphysical assumptions held by the practitioner, and then to the center of the field—the cult image itself.

For a practitioner of ritual, knowledge of "proper time" is essential. Particular moments, days, and months are considered powerful and propitious to varying degrees. The juncture of, say, Saturn and Virgo at midnight on the fifth day of the third month, is a particularly powerful moment for effecting maledictory rituals. This is because of the type of forces active at this moment. Like wind or water, these forces can be harnessed with the aid of the proper technology—in this case, ritual technology—and directed toward a specified end. Because of their particularly inauspicious nature, these forces will subvert positive types of ritual activity, such as rituals of pacification and healing. The moment described in our text—the juncture of the equinox during the waxing phase of the moon—is considered a moment of extreme auspicious power, reserved for "rituals of superior attainment"—that is, rituals that lead the practitioner toward ultimate liberation. We learn from this brief statement about the time of the ritual, then, that the practitioner is involved in an activity that moves him toward enlightenment; in other words, the ritual, contrary to what Tucci says, does in fact have something in common with soteriological practices. We learn too that the practitioner subscribes to, and applies, the particular knowledge provided by India's astrological sciences; that, for instance, auspiciousness and inauspiciousness are part of the natural flow of the cosmos, and that this rhythm is perceivable through the movement of nature.

As this latter point about the natural flow of the cosmos indicates, the notion of ritually proper time points to an even more basic assumption about the world at work in the ritual. This is the idea that the universe undergoes an eternal cycle of emergence, evolution, and destruction, oscillating perpetually between expansion and contraction, activity and calm. There is a structure or pattern (*dharma*) inherent in this universal flux; one that, moreover, is intimately related to the lives of men and women. When a person harmonizes him- or herself with this structural law, goodness naturally ensues; when not, suffering results. In the ritual, the practitioner is taught the *dharma* by the Buddha. I translated this as "the true teaching" because of the multiple meanings inherent in the term. That is, the Buddhist teaching is the *dharma* because practicing it enables one to harmonize with what is true, with the *dharma* as structure. By applying the *dharma* (the teaching), the practitioner of the ritual moves more deeply into the structure of the *dharma* (the law)—

he encounters enlightened beings, and receives instruction on how to enter even more deeply into this structure.

The possibility of this deepening participation in the *dharma* follows from the general notion of an eternally fluctuating cosmos. One further assumption about this is that it is possible to move away from the world of multiplicity that we live in—that is, the world of extreme expansion and activity—toward ever-increasing realms of contraction and calm, eventually arriving at the original, undifferentiated point of creation. The movement in this direction is always from impurity to purity, disintegration to integration, from the gross to the subtle, from ignorance to wisdom, and from dissatisfaction to bliss. It involves stilling the fluctuations of consciousness until a one-pointed concentration is achieved. The inner quietude that arises from this leads to insight (termed *vipaśyana* in Buddhist meditational literature) into the fundamental order of things. As the term *vipaśyana* implies, quieting the mind produces an inner-directed vision. The movement from differentiation and disintegration to unity and integration is an internal movement through increasingly subtle layers of awareness. Precisely how this is achieved is worked out in different ways by the different communities that operate out of these general premises about the universe. The important point here is that the ritual is presented as a means of moving the practitioner through these subtle states of mind into places not accessible to everyday consciousness. Continuous recitation of the *mantra* compresses the practitioner's mind into a single point while he fixes his sight on the image in front of him. Light suddenly emits from the image, and he contemplates this. Then, the movement occurs: he traverses the world of the gods, and proceeds to the heavenly paradise of the *buddha* Śākyamuni. The ritual, then, creates the conditions for a direct vision into a higher order of reality—a subtle reality outside of our normal, restricted viewpoint—but one that is nonetheless knowable to the ritual practitioner.

The conclusion that the ritual is claiming *real* presence and encounter as a result of this movement becomes inescapable when we look at the central ritual act: recitation of the *mantra* in front of the cult image. The text states that the practitioner "carries a rolled up cloth painting to a desolate field. . . clears an area and arranges the image on the ground. Sitting on a mound of grass in front of this image, he recites a short phrase, a *mantra*, 1008 times."

Looking at the import that the *sādhaka* affixes to the physical cosmos just described should throw some light onto this action. The text provides a clear signal for us in this regard. Elsewhere, the practitioner is told to conclude his recitation by reading passages from texts such as the *Daśabhūmaka, Gaṇḍavyūha, Suvarṇaprabhāsottamasūtra,* and particularly the *Prajñāpāramitā.*[14] This fact provides us with some basis for reconstructing the *madhyamaka/vaipulyasūtra* view of reality that renders rational the practitioner's activity within the larger cosmos.

Whereas the cosmos outlined above was physical—it said something about the universe as a thing—a text such as the *Prajñāpāramitā* addresses itself to the metaphysical universe, that is, to the nature of reality that lies "behind" or "beyond" natural things. This is of course one connotation of the Sanskrit term *prajñāpāramitā*. A thick, interpretive translation would be *going beyond the world of things to an awareness of things as they really are*. This evokes a common Buddhist trope: our experiential world is on the shore of a vast ocean of interminable dissatisfaction. Real happiness is possible; but it requires that we cross over from the world of conceptualization to "the other shore" of wisdom. As this suggests, wisdom is understood as a state of consciousness that arises out of rigorous analysis of what we call reality. The type of analysis that the *vaipulyasūtras* have in mind is not an intellectual one that results in knowledge *that* something is the case. Rather, the analysis is more akin to a meditative absorption whereby the practitioner transcends the erroneous imaginings of conceptual consciousness and enters into direct vision of reality as it is. Analysis dissolves, leaving the mind fixed one-pointedly on the result of the analysis. When one has arrived at this state, he or she is said to be "perfected in wisdom," and thus to have crossed over to the other shore. "Perfection," of course, arises out of the result of this analysis, which is, namely, that all phenomena comprising our world of experience are empty of inherent existence. That is, everything that we can name, point to, or think about is constructed out of parts or aspects which themselves are dependent on other parts and aspects. Each of these parts, furthermore, arises in relation to causes and conditions. The same holds for the constituents of these parts, and so on. There is no essential defining point that gives a thing the kind of stability that we ascribe to real existence. In short, our notion of reality is based on how things appear, namely, solid and essentially existent from their own side, rather than on how they are—conventional designations only (i.e., their reality is imputed on them from our side, from the side of mind and culture), but devoid of innate, essential being.

What does all of this have to do with the practitioner's reciting a *mantra* in front of the cult image? According to those who subscribe to this "soft" view of reality, which claims that all entities are pure appearance, a second premise follows naturally from it. This is the proposition that beings who have fully grasped the nature of reality are able to manipulate the phenomenal realm at will. Two major cultural axioms are implicit in this proposition. The first is that intense ascetic practices, such as the ones undergone by the historical Buddha, automatically yield what we would call supernatural powers. For most Indian traditions, these powers are considered "supernatural" only if by this we mean that they lie outside of the reach of our habituated everyday awareness, though not of consciousness per se. In most traditions of *yoga*, acquisition of these powers is considered as an indication that progress is being made on the path. Numerous traditions, including Buddhist ones, draw from a common store of powers including, knowledge of the past and future, knowledge of other people's thoughts, the ability to generate body heat at will, the ability to have visions of perfected beings, and the power to transform, displace, or multiply oneself. This latter ability points to the second axiom that we have to understand here; namely, that divine or perfected beings, by virtue of their profound compassion, remain within the range of conscious apprehension. This means that they remain within the universe, though in realms so pure and subtle that they are visible only to the awareness of advanced practitioners, that is, to those who have attained the ability to have visions of perfected beings. As in the ritual that we are looking at, these beings often appear first as a blazing light before forming into the kind of image on the cult object, depicting the Buddha giving instruction in his "heavenly paradise."

The two primary ways in which enlightened beings manipulate matter in order to manifest in the world of our *everyday* awareness, then, are sonically, that is, by means of the *mantra*, and iconographically, through the cult object. The *Mmk* states this explicitly. Concerning the sonic crystallization of the Buddha's power, it says:

> This [*mantra*] is the blessed omniscient one, who compassionately exists, with [all] *buddhas*, through the form of the *mantra*. Exalted, they wandered among those of various embodiments.
>
> Uniting for the sake of compassion, that one exists as this syllable [i.e., as the *mantra bhrūm*, the subject of *Mmk* 25].
>
> Having gone to the realm of reality (*dharmadhātu*), this one exists as that, appearing in various forms. As the bodies of *buddhas*, relics (*dhātu*) are engaged in the world.
>
> Remains of flesh (*sāmiṣa*) are to be honored in the world—above all, are those without flesh (*nirāmiṣa*) [to be honored].
>
> The true relics of the *dharma* are proclaimed to be fleshless remains, for the sake of the world.
>
> Remains of flesh signifying the body are proclaimed to be the supernatural power of the victorious masters. Various relics are proclaimed as being the faultless moon of sages [i.e., Śākyamuni].
>
> Both, remains of flesh and those without flesh, proceed forth on behalf of the world. Intermixed in the realm of reality, out of compassion for beings,
>
> the lord of the world, the maker of light remains through the form of the *mantra*. The omniscient one, possessing all forms, appears on the surface of the earth.[F2]

Because the world of appearance is just like empty space, enlightened beings are able to traverse it "just as the wind blows swiftly through space, [or like] birds gliding through the sky."[15] The Buddha's gross body is no longer present in the world, and his subtle body is visible only to advanced adepts; so, he transmutes his compassionate power into sonic vibrations, manifesting as sound.

By the same reasoning, the cult object becomes an instrument of liveliness and efficacy. The compassion of the Buddha and other enlightened beings is an immense force pervading the universe. Only those practitioners who have achieved the ability to access the deepest layers of consciousness can perceive this fact directly. Those who move through a "hard" world, with an awareness that arises out of only the grossest layers of conceptualizing consciousness, require tools in order to realize this power. In the ritual that we are seeking to understand, the cult object is the primary tool. It is held to be the fullest form, the highest scale, in which compassionate power discloses itself.

3.2.3 Mmk 4 and Mmk 7

Marcelle Lalou raises a provocative question in the introduction to *Iconographie des étoffes peintes (paṭa) dans le Mañjuśrīmūlakalpa*. Her question concerns the difference between the elaborately executed *paṭas* of *Mmk* 4–6, and the "simplified" *paṭa* of *Mmk* 7. She asks whether "the simplified *paṭas* are the reflection of popular painting prior to the code elaborated in the initial chapters [on the *paṭa*] of the *Mañjuśrīmūlakalpa*. Or, on the contrary, are they degenerated elements of those chapters"?[16] She offers the following answer.

> It would undoubtedly be imprudent to affirm that the simplified *paṭa*s are degenerated elements, since, in practice, common (*vulgaire*) ritual images exist parallel to refined magic paintings. It is possible that the *Mañjuśrīmūlakalpa* had initially exposed the subtle code of magic imagery about which we read in the beginning [i.e., in the chapters preceding chapter seven], and then, growing without cease until it became the voluminous compilation that has come down to us in Sanskrit, framed and legitimized popular customs.[17]

On the one hand, at present, the chronology entertained by Lalou—from earlier/refined to later/popular—cannot be determined. On the other hand, it is readily evident that roughly fashioned cultic objects exist, in practice, parallel to finely executed ones. If there is anything clear and consistent about the *Mmk*, it is that it upsets the balance between the rough/popular and fine/elite dichotomy. It is a medieval text (elite) that promotes practices to increase, among other things, worldly fortune (ostensibly popular). It prescribes an intricate and time-consuming *maṇḍala* for those desiring to "approach the seat of enlightenment" (*Mmk* 2); yet it also gives the instructions for a crude *maṇḍala* for those who wish to cure an illness or attract a wife (*Mmk* 3). I suggest that a combination of caution and common sense permits the following interpretation of such textual evidence. The *Mmk* does not demonstrate a split between elite and popular, but rather recognizes at all levels a multiplicity of concerns, as well as means to satisfy those concerns. Something like an elite-popular division might ensue from this. The basis of this hierarchy, however, is not necessarily social. A *śudra* who pursues the seat of enlightenment is higher on this scale than a *brāhmaṇa* who uses the practices as a means to acquire wealth. Nonetheless, only a relatively wealthy person would have had the means to produce the large *paṭa* described in *Mmk* 4, whereas a poor person could have produced the small *paṭa* of *Mmk* 7. The large *paṭa* is said to ensure superior success (enlightenment), while practice to the small *paṭa* results in minor success (worldly joy, fortunate rebirth) only. This socially based hierarchy would seem here to cancel out the former, intention-based one. The *Mmk* offers a simple solution to this: seeing the image of the *paṭa* equalizes all distinctions. The act of reciting a *mantra* with firm faith before the image of the *paṭa* ensures not only the fulfillment of all desires whatsoever, but of buddhahood as well. Ultimately, this occurs regardless of the size of the *paṭa* or degree of commitment on the side of the practitioner.

Even if all distinctions are finally reconciled before the image of the Buddha, the presence of four, progressively less complicated, *paṭas* in the *Mmk* nonetheless serves to highlight those distinctions. The distinction might be between the ideal and the real, between norm and practice, or it may point to the flexibility required of a tradition to accommodate a variety of concerns, preferences, and means. Whatever the case, the presence in the *Mmk* of alternative practices for creating the cult object affords us with the opportunity to decrease the gap between normative descriptions and conventional practices, and to explore a wider range of options. For this reason, my approach here is to juxtapose the superior *paṭa* of *Mmk* 4 and the simplified *paṭa* of *Mmk* 7.

Mmk 4 begins by evoking the animated *maṇḍala* revealed in *Mmk* 1.

> Mañjuśrī then looked down upon the entire residence of the *śuddhāvāsa* gods. Beholding once again the circle (*maṇḍala*) of the great assembly, he fell to the feet of Śākyamuni. With a cheerful countenance, he spoke thus to the Blessed One: "Wonderful, O Blessed One, out of compassion for all beings, is the section concerning the production of results according to one's wishes, raining forth from the cloud of the Law, gushing diffusely, securing the success of the *mantra* rites; [wonderful is] the regulation for the *paṭa*, which generates unsurpassed merit, originates the seed of complete enlight-

enment, originates perfect knowledge, omniscience; which, in short, fulfills all of one's desires, completely accomplishes the result of all *mantras*, realizes that which is effected beneficially and fruitfully, fulfills the career of all *bodhisattvas*, is fastened as armor to the great *bodhisattvas*, causing the flight and defeat of Māra's army. Speak of that, O Blessed One, out of love for us and for all beings.[F3]

Evoking the animated *maṇḍala* serves several purposes. The *maṇḍala* is the array of enlightened forces securing the efficacy of the rituals. As was discussed in detail in chapter 2, this opening passage, like that of all *vaipulyasūtra* literature, presupposes a standardized conception of the universe. This is the *trisāhasramahāsāhasralokadhātu*, the "three-thousandfold, many thousandfold world system."[18] As was mentioned above, this term connotes an infinite realm of space populated by wise, benevolent beings who, in the remote past, vowed to exert their extraordinary powers—to the point of miracle and cataclysm—on behalf of the practitioner. We also saw in chapter 2 that from throughout the universe, numerous classes of beings and natural elements have come to gather around the Buddha. This assembly presents a model of the world as it should be viewed by the practitioner. According to this model, *buddhas* and *bodhisattvas*, trees, rivers and birds, are primed to respond to the ritual manipulation of the *sādhaka*. The opening sentences of the above passage also call to mind the fact that this *maṇḍala* is the place where the teachings originated. Prior to being committed to aiding the *sādhaka*, the assembly must listen to the Buddha's teaching on the *mantra* rites. Confidence is instilled in the reader by reestablishing the authority of the teachings as those of the Buddha's. Most important, the opening of *Mmk* 4 elicits the re-creation of the *maṇḍala*. The place of the Buddha's teaching and power is created anew through the imagination of the practitioner, synchronizing his life with that of the Buddha and his retinue in their present residence. The opening sentences create a mental image of the Buddhist cosmos, known in detail from *Mmk* 1, within which the rituals are practiced and rendered effective. The specific teaching of *Mmk* 4 and 7 involves the transference of this image onto the *paṭa*. The actual cosmological setting, the written evocation of this, the apprehension of it imaginatively, and its embodiment as cult object therefore comprise a continuous whole.

Several general claims about the *paṭa* are being made by Mañjuśrī in this passage. The teaching that serves the creation of the cult object is said to originate in the love of the Buddha for all beings. Then, by means of the text ("this section"), the teaching pours down on the world to become available to all. The uses of the teaching, and, by extension, of the *paṭa*, are unrestricted. It may be applied "according to one's wishes" as a means of general fulfillment. This passage indicates that the *paṭa* is an indispensable element of the rituals. The success of the *mantra* rites is "secured" by use of the *paṭa*. That is, the *paṭa* is an infallible instrument. Practice to the *paṭa*, furthermore, reduplicates aspects of Śākyamuni's own earthly practice. It produces the seed of omniscience and enlightenment, while serving as the *bodhisattva's* protective armor against the hindering forces stemming from time, death, and illusion.

The Buddha's response to Mañjuśrī emphasizes the centrality of compassion, authority, and power to the teaching on the *paṭa*.

> Good, O Mañjuśrī! Good is it that you think to ask the *tathāgata* about this matter, acting [as you are] for the welfare of numerous beings, [and] out of sympathy towards the world. Listen well, and bear it firmly in mind. I will speak to you about the realization of all the *mantra* rites by means of your section on the creation of the *paṭa*. I will now introduce in succession that which has been previously taught by all *tathāgatas*.[F4]

The step-by-step teaching on the *paṭa* is thus presented as the pivotal component of the *buddhas'* universal teaching. *Mmk* 4 arrives at this specific process via an image of Mañjuśrī's "cheerful countenance" and reassuring assertions of authority and power. *Mmk* 7, too, places the instructions on the cult object within the broader frame of the *buddhas'* teaching as a whole, and that of the assembled *maṇḍala* in particular. However, before turning to the actual process of fashioning the cult object, *Mmk* 7 offers elaboration on the conditions that necessitate the particular teaching on the *paṭa*. Mañjuśrī describes to Śākyamuni "a time of great terror, when . . . beings whose merit is meager will come into existence." Because the people alive at this time will be incapable of carrying out the extensive rites required in *Mmk* 4–6, the simplified process of *Mmk* 7 is prescribed.

> In the future, when the teacher of the world passes away, when the sun lineage of the *tathāgata* disappears, when every Buddha-field is abandoned by all *bodhisattvas*, noble hearers and solitary *buddhas*; when the receptacle of the world becomes darkened; when the path of the noble ones is severed; when all jewels, gems, *mantras*, medicines and knowledge are lost. When, devoid of good people, beings in the world are deprived of light, they will become lazy, desirous of destruction, faithless, divided, surrounded by bad friends, deceitful, deluded, of fraudulent conduct. Hearing this discourse on the teaching, these will be seized by fear. Those who delight in sloth and indolence will not have faith; those seeking pleasure, rejoicing in false doctrines, will not exert themselves. These will produce much non-virtue, those who discard the true teaching, who descend to the *avīci* hell, go from terror to greater terror. For the sake of those who are afflicted, subjugating the unsubjugated, in order to give safety to the meek, by means of complete skillfulness in means, O Blessed One, speak about the rules for the painted cult image and *mantras*, if you think the time is right.[F5]

This passage can be interpreted in several ways. First, the language of the passage is apocalyptic. The images employed are dramatic, conveying a sense of imminent devastation. It is tempting to claim that something of the social context of the *Mmk* is coming through here. Such language suggests an environment in which a community's established social patterns are being threatened. Chaos and loss might be detected in the first half of the passage in particular. Less drastically, the passage could point to a competitive environment, in which various groups are vying to win adherents and patrons. The apparent fact that the content and style of the Buddhist literature of this period (i.e., from the eighth to the thirteenth centuries) increasingly converged with that of the non-Buddhist sects, such as the Vaiṣṇava Pañcarātrins, might corroborate this suggestion. Unfortunately, too little is known about the date and provenance of the various portions of the *Mmk* to warrant decisive claims about the social conditions surrounding the work. We can more cautiously consider the rhetorical value of this passage. The form of Buddhist practice prescribed in the *Mmk* is not dependent on the monastic communities. The *sādhaka* is a solitary practitioner, whether monk or layman. As an *ācārya*, he may teach certain rituals to individual laypeople. Other than the initiation rite, there is no indication of communal practice in the *Mmk*. The ability to access the power of the Buddha requires secretive, extramonastic forms of training and induction. Thus, as opposed to institutional forms of Buddhism, the practice of the *Mmk* is private, lay, and esoteric. In light of this, we might interpret the "[severed] path of the noble ones" as referring not to encroaching Hindu sects, but to the erroneous systems of the Buddhist monastic establishment. It is the monks who have become "lazy, desirous of destruction, faithless, divided, surrounded by bad friends, deceitful, deluded, of fraudulent conduct . . . engaged in sloth and indolence . . . seeking pleasure, rejoicing in false doctrines." Resisting the innovations of the *Mmk*, the establishment monks "produce much non-virtue [and] discard the true teaching." Whether "the true teaching" of the *Mmk* is being contrasted to non-Buddhist or Buddhist practices, the text is proclaiming the advent of an extraordinary era when traditional practices will have lost their potency. The simplified *mantracaryā* of the *Mmk* as a whole refines and restructures the universal teaching of the *buddhas* in the same manner that *Mmk* 7 does for the specific teaching on the cult object. The above passage can thus be read as pointing to the *Mmk's* tendency toward innovative synthesis. Matthew Kapstein sees in such a tendency a central feature of esoteric Buddhism. He writes of an "apparently paradoxical dimension of esoteric Buddhist doctrine"

> which always claims that, as the world-age steadily degenerates, ever more efficacious means are revealed in the tantras. Though this no doubt served as a rationale for the introduction and gradual acceptance of new tantras and tantric techniques, it may without much interpretive violence be taken to

> mean that as [the] world becomes a messier place, so that the large-scale order of the Buddhist monastic community can no longer be well maintained, the local, ephemeral and often personal order engendered by high-powered techniques of ritual and yoga perforce become the primary points at which enlightened activity may enter the world.[19]

Throughout the *Mmk* we read of the degenerate world-age described in the *Mmk* 7 passage above. And, as in *Mmk* 7, these declarations of the "future" arrival of this age are invariably accompanied by potent *mantras. Mmk* 25, for instance, typifies this concern of the *Mmk*. It prescribes a special *mantra* to be employed by all beings during the coming dark world-age. This *mantra, bhrūm,* will ensure the success of all rituals "at the time of the disappearance of the teaching."[20] Similarly, *Mmk* 7 moves from the proclamation of an age in which new forms of practices are required to the prescription of a specific, infallible practice.

> Then, the blessed Śākyamuni applauded the princely Mañjuśrī: "Good, Mañjuśrī, good is it that you think fit to ask the *tathāgata* the meaning of this. It is, O Mañjuśrī, your supreme, most secretive, extensive section on the prescriptions for the cult image, the practice and austere observance of incantations (*vidyā*), the greatest, most excellent, esoteric meaning of the supreme essence—[it is this section] whose meaning is vast [and] which is the treasury of all *mantras*.[21] These most secret six syllables lead infallibly, in this lifetime, to success. In order to tame those beings, in order to lead [them], with *mantras*, fully into the array of skillful means, for the sake of [their] attaining enlightenment with certainty, I myself will now proclaim that which has been previously proclaimed by seven hundred and sixty million *buddhas*. For the sake of those people who have yet to be born, listen well and bear this in mind. I will proclaim this to you.[22] And what is this?"
>
> Then the blessed Śākyamuni recited the *mantra*: "*oṁ vākyārthe jaya oṁ vākyaśeṣe sva oṁ vākyeyanayaḥ oṁ vākyaniṣṭeyaḥ oṁ vākyeyanamaḥ oṁ vākyedanamaḥ.* O Mañjuśrī, these six-syllabled *mantras* of yours possess equally great power and vigor, are supremely secret and effective. Like the Buddha, they have arisen for the sake of all beings, been proclaimed by all *buddhas* as the culmination of the vow; they set [all] in motion, accomplish all deeds, and indicate the path to enlightenment. They are the most excellent *mantras* in the family of the *tathāgata*, employed three-fold for the superior, intermediate, and minor [attainments], bestowing the ripened fruit of pure actions. [These six *mantras*] will effect success at the fulfillment of the time when the teaching disappears. They are that which will effect success, that whose purpose is to protect the eye of the true law. By means of their basic practice, they will effect great fortune, sovereignty, and power. Those [who pronounce these *mantras*] will quickly, in this lifetime, at the

> right time, attain success. Finally, even by reason of [merely] desiring to be known, these supreme essence [*mantras*] lead to success. In short, just as these supreme essence [*mantras*] are practiced, in that manner do they lead to success in due time. Therefore, there is the precept on the cult image. At this time, in this period of great terror when there exist the five impurities, beings of meager merit will come into existence. Of low origin, short lifespan, poor and weak, they will not be able to undertake the creation of the cult image, and so on, which is quite extensive. For the sake of these I will speak most concisely.[F6]

When the Buddha is no longer visibly in the world, *mantras* will arise, just as the *buddha* Śākyamuni had, for the sake of the world. Here, it is specifically the six-syllable *mantra* that will perform tasks of the Buddha, such as setting in motion the teaching, and indicating the path to enlightenment. It is by virtue of their being the supreme essence (*paramahṛdaya*) of enlightened power that use of the *mantras* lead to certain success. Paradoxically, as Kapstein points out, at precisely the most ominous moment in history, "treasuries" of these potent *mantras* appear. The most impure, corrupted, and incapable beings have the most direct access to the essence of the *buddhas'* power. The culmination of the *buddhas'* teaching occurs at the juncture of Mahābhairava, a time of terror and grave impurity. The beings of meager merit who are born at this time cause, through their very weakness, the appearance of condensed, simplified forms of Buddhist practice. A final paradoxical point in this passage is the fact that precisely such apathetic beings acquire the means to attain enlightenment undoubtedly and quickly in this lifetime.

Both the elaborate and simplified sections on the creation of the cult object begin, then, with the evocation of the special worlds framing the respective rituals that follow. Each then turns to the labor of transforming an ordinary piece of cloth into a potent cult image. The newly initiated practitioner (detailed in chapter 4, below) now sets out to create his own *pata*.

> Having first gathered unspun cotton at a pure place, free of dirt, it is to be cleansed by people who are engaged in the vow [*samayapraviṣṭa;* that is, those who have taken on the commitments required for practicing the rituals; the vow is taken during the initiation ceremony]. Cleansed, it should be consecrated with eight hundred recitations of the *mantra* by the initiating master (*maṇḍalācārya*).[F7]

The practitioner's first step is to buy the raw cotton (*picu*) on which will eventually be painted the prescribed imagery. This he procures in a "pure place, free of dust." The establishment of purity is an essential component of all ritualized activity in the *Mmk.* The creation of the *paṭa,* too, is pervaded by a heightened concern for purity. Several terms are used in the *Mmk* to denote purity: *rajovigata* (free of dirt), *śuci* (radiant, holy, pure, undefiled), *śukla* (bright, pure, unsullied), *śubha* (splendid, beautiful, bright, auspicious), *saṃśodhana* (completely purifying, thoroughly purged physically), *suśobhana* (magnificent, propitious).[23] As these terms indicate, the idea of purity in the *Mmk* is multidimensional. Cleanliness is one inherent property of purity. A place is clean if it is "without rocks, gravel, ash, coal, grain, skulls, or bones."[24] The notion of purity, however, extends beyond the mere absence of dust, dirt, or physical impediments. The terms *śuci* and *śuddha*, for instance, denote both cleanliness per se and lack of defilement. Defilement stems from both physical and moral debasement. Thus, a clean place is defiled by the presence of inherently impure objects, such as a menstruating woman or a dog. For this reason, the practitioner, too, must be undefiled. The *puraścaraṇa* for instance, is essentially a cleansing practice. By eating only leaves, roots, fruits, and water, while reciting the *mantra* hundreds of thousands of times, the *sādhaka* prepares the pure mental and physical bases needed for success to be possible. The practitioner's day during the *puraścaraṇa* begins with a thorough cleansing of his residence (sweeping, etc.), body (bathing, hygiene), speech (recitation of texts and *mantras*), and mind (worship, meditation).[25] Before being granted initiation into such practices, moreover, the practitioner must have proven himself to be morally pure. The description of the practitioner in *Mmk* 11, in fact, begins with this concern: "First [that is, prior to being initiated], one must take upon oneself intentness towards the rules, vow, and moral conduct. First, one must obey the precepts and instructions of the *maṇḍala* master."[26] The *Mmk* states repeatedly that morally impure people will fail at the rituals. We read, for instance, that "there is not even a little success if the practitioner is of bad morals."[27] This points to an additional dimension of purity in the *Mmk*. Purity coincides with auspiciousness. In the *Mmk*, auspiciousness means that the power of the *buddhas* is able to manifest through the purified ritual world, consisting of the entirety of the agents and objects engaged in the ritual.[28]

The "pure place" mentioned in the above passage, thus, must meet several conditions. It must be cleansed of dirt, removed from polluting influences, and occupied by purified objects and subjects. In this sense, every space where some aspect of the ritual unfolds is treated in the same manner as each of the objects that occupies those spaces. In order to create the auspiciousness that ensures successful practice, each element must itself be attended by beneficial properties. As we will repeatedly see below, establishing the conditions for auspiciousness often requires forcefully altering the status of a ritual element.

The raw, unspun cotton, having been gathered in a pure place by a pure person, is immediately taken to initiated members of the community to be thoroughly cleansed in preparation for consecration. Consecration (*abhimantraṇa*) is a rite that establishes the purity of an object and, concomitantly, the unobstructed flow of power. As the Sanskrit term connotes, this is accomplished by reciting a *mantra* or a series of *mantras* over the object to be consecrated. The person who initiated the practitioner into the cult, the *maṇḍalācārya*, takes the leading role in this process. The language of the *mantra* conveys the charged atmosphere that accompanies such rituals of transformation:

> [The *mantra* is preceded by a liturgical formula:] Homage to all *buddhas* and *bodhisattvas*, whose conduct follows from unobstructed intelligence. Homage to the king of kings, to him who completely purifies and calms all suffering—to the *tathāgata*, the perfected one, the perfectly enlightened one. Here [is the *mantra* to be recited]: *oṁ śodhaya śodhaya sarvavighnaghātaka mahākāruṇika kumārarūpadhāriṇe vikurva vikurva samayam anusmara tiṣṭha tiṣṭha hūm hūm phaṭ phaṭ svāhā* (*purify purify! O destroyer of all obstacles! O you of great compassion! O bearer of youthful form! perform a miraculous transformation perform a miraculous transformation! remember your vow! be present be present! hūm hūm phaṭ phaṭ hail!*)[F8]

This *mantra*, along with its preceding formula, is supported by several interrelated doctrinal positions common to the *vaipulyasūtras*. The first is the idea that Śākyamuni was (and is) but the most immediate instance of a specific type of being, a *buddha*. As we saw above, this expansion from the singular, historical *buddha* in non-Mahāyāna forms of Buddhism to an infinite plurality of universal *buddhas*, is an example of what Gregory Schopen calls "the process of generalization." He defines this as the "process where individual cases—whether figures or situations—become only examples of a larger category, or where specificity of function is denied by assigning the same function to an ever increasing number of individuals."[29] We saw, too, that the *Mmk* exhibits throughout a certain ambiguity of agency and authority. Whenever Śākyamuni attaches agency to the teaching, he refers to it simultaneously as Mañjuśrī's (*tvadīya*), and as that which is "authorized by me and spoken by all *buddhas*."[30] When Mañjuśrī ascribes agency, it is likewise "Śākyamuni's" or "all *buddhas*'." The purificatory *mantra* here assumes this unified notion of *buddha*. It first invokes "all *buddhas* and *bodhisattvas*" generally, then the specific *buddha* of this world-realm, Śākyamuni, and, finally, though in a more indirect manner, the specific agency of the *bodhisattva* Mañjuśrī. Mañjuśrī is a "tenth-stage *bodhisattva*." The *Daśabhūmika*, a text alluded to in the *Mmk*,[31] defines these *bodhisattvas* as,

> those who have entered into the very powers of the Victors, [now] being nurtured by the all pervading impelling force of All-knowledge, who are unattached and unimpeded in [all] the approaches to [all] levels of the *Dharmadhātu*.[32]

The untranslatable elements of the *mantra* indicate that in addition to invocation of a positive, enlightened force, consecration involves the dispelling of potentially negative forces. We are told that *hūṁ* and *phaṭ*, when used together, produce *mantras* that are "formidable, intensely powerful, and majestic."[33] The sounds *hūṁ* and *phaṭ* thus have the power to avert what is unwanted. The *mantra* is framed by two auspicious-making exclamations, *oṁ* and *svāhā*. The *Mmk* says of *oṁ* that "*mantras* adorned with *oṁ* would become firm."[34]

The officiant recites the purifying formula one hundred and eight times. The cotton, still unspun, has so far undergone an examination by members of the community, been deemed fitting, and infused with the presence of the *buddhas'* power. In this ritualized manner the raw cotton is prepared for the several subsequent stages of its transformation into a responsive, potent cult object. At *Mmk* 7, however, there is no need to gather the cotton from a pure, or any other, place, or to subject it to the approval of the community.[35] The practitioner may simply buy whatever measurement of cloth he needs. It must be fringed and oblique, and have been woven by a weaver. At *Mmk* 4, the weaving of the raw cotton is more involved. First of all, before it can be woven, it must be spun. This phase in the *paṭa's* creation, like every event so far discussed, requires assistance from a member of the practitioner's religious community. For the spinning procedure, the assistant must be a young girl. She must not only exhibit a strong commitment to the practice of the cult, aspiring even to the *bodhisattva* ideal, but must also conform to particular standards of character and beauty.

> [She must be] a young virgin girl who does not know the [immoral] ways of village life, who is born in either a *brāhmaṇa, kṣatriya*, or *vaiṣya* family. Excluded is a girl whose family and race have too dark skin. She may not be deformed; all of her limbs are beautiful; she has received permission from her mother and father. She observes the *upoṣadha* vows, has produced the thought of enlightenment, is compassionate, has a white complexion, and no other color [T. those of other colors are turned down]. In short, [she must possess] the most praiseworthy characteristics and features of a woman.[F9]

This description exhibits standard emblems of purity and auspiciousness: prepubescence, virginity, fairness of skin, beauty, fasting. The ritual potency of premenstruous virgin girls has as a corollary the converse idea that a menstruating woman, because of the extreme degree of her impurity, causes a complete loss of power in the ritual field. Impotency, furthermore, not only prevents successful ritual practice, but invites chaos and disaster.

This passage gives some indication of the status quo position of the *Mmk* community: the girl must come from the upper levels of society. The Tibetan text emphasizes this point when it adds that "all poor families are to be turned down,"[36] that is, their offer to hire out their daughters is not to be accepted. On the one hand, exclusion of the dark-skinned, non-Āryan *śūdras* as inauspicious is unquestioned in the ritual structure underlying the *Mmk.* However, the fact that the *Mmk* practitioner may himself or herself be a *śūdra*[37] requires an alternative explanation of the prohibition here. One solution to this problem is to consider the exclusion of *śūdras* as a symbolic marker. The physical and moral nature of the female assistant required in a given cult can be seen as emblematic of the broader conceptual boundaries of that community. For example, the innocent *kumārī* of the *Mmk* contrasts significantly to each of the four types of female assistants required in the rites of antinomian Buddhist communities. The *Samvarodayatantra,* for instance, describes two such assistants, the *śaṅkhinī* (conchlike) and the *citriṇī* (colorful), as follows.

> A *śaṅkhinī* smells like a donkey and is rough to the touch like the tongue of the crow; she has the voice of a crow . . . Her [the *citriṇī's*] body is very short, but her breasts are beautiful. Her breasts are the shape of *sriphalas* [i.e., coconuts]. She has abandoned shame and is very wrathful; she always takes pleasure in quarreling. Her shanks are crippled, and she lies on her back. She has a hanging under-lip and the voice of a turtle-dove. A *citriṇī* . . . smells of meat and has her arms spread out.[38]

The text goes on to describe the degree of passion that these assistants must possess, and to give instructions on how the male practitioner should treat them sexually. Both the descriptions and language of these contrasting passages are instructive. It might even be possible to create a typology of the emerging tantric forms of medieval Buddhism on the basis of such descriptions of acceptable ritual assistants. The *Mmk* assistant conforms to what Friedhelm Hardy calls a "middle-class mentality. . . [to] the value-system of the higher castes." He adds,

> these [higher castes] were alienated and cut off from the rural scene, not necessarily by being urbanized but by virtue of the mental boundaries that separated them from the lower castes. A total commitment to their own value-system (which did not allow for alcohol, meat, fish, supposed aphrodisiacs, and non-marital, low-caste intercourse [all of which apply to the rites of the *Samvarodayatantra*] was, in fact, one of the strongest factors in the maintenance of such boundaries. From this angle, those activities were vulgar, reprehensible, and thus 'forbidden.'[39]

The term *grāmya,* in the statement that the *Mmk* assistant be "one who does not know the [immoral] ways of village life" brings this status into further relief. Similar to an early English usage of "rustic" to signify a crude and unsophisticated person, *grāmya* ("that which relates to village life") is synonymous with "low," "vulgar," and "indecent." Elements of village ritual, such as the ingestion of alcohol, were incorporated into the type of Buddhist practice documented by works like the *Samvarodayatantra,* or those composed by the even more antinomian *mahāsiddhas.* There, the feminine symbol of wisdom and enlightenment shifts from the elegant images of the goddesses Prajñāpāramitā (perfected in wisdom) and Nairātmyā (selfless one), found in orthodox, monastic literature, to the depraved Ḍombī (the washerwoman) and Caṇḍālī (the low-caste) of more autochthonous forms of practice.[40] As Hardy writes, such images point to distinct social environments. The *kumārī* points to a higher caste, cosmopolitan scene; the *ḍombī,* to a lower caste, village one.

The description of the female assistant in the *Mmk* can, thus, be seen as a boundary marker between a cult that conforms to a certain status quo, and those that intentionally position themselves outside of that mainstream value-system. Bound up with the establishment value-system is the belief in the destructive polluting influences of menstruating women, and, conversely, the security and potency that a prepubescent virgin girl brings to the ritual domain.

Having made the arrangements for an assistant, the practitioner next carefully observes the movement of the stars and planets. When he perceives that they are in an auspicious position, on an auspicious day without smoke, fog, or rain, during the moon's waxing phase, he continues the rite for the production of the *paṭa.*[41] As noted above, knowledge of "proper time" is essential for a practitioner of ritual. The calendar in medieval India was based on the lunar month. There where two halves to each month, a dark one and a bright one. The lunar month consisted of approximately thirty days. Each day was divided into thirty periods of approximately forty-five minutes each.[42] The *Mmk* is specific about the proper time to practice *mantra* recitation. It should be done "at dusk, everyday, just at the meridian between the end of the night and sunrise."[43] Again, in this emphasis on the importance of specific junctures of time we are encountering a basic assumption about the world. Auspiciousness and misfortune, namely, are part of the natural flow of the cosmos. Furthermore, the rhythm of the cosmos is perceivable through the movement of nature. As Ronald Inden writes,[44]

> The natural world of ancient and medieval India was person-based, constructed by a Cosmic Overlord out of himself. . . . This was a world greater than the human world but continuous with it. In that world all events, whether natural or human, were actions. They were, as Collingwood puts it, events that had both an inside, thought, and an outside, observable behavior. The laws of nature here were orders or commands which could be obeyed or disobeyed. Natural events occurred in India because the gods in charge of the various departments of nature thought they should happen and made

> them happen. . . . That a science of natural events as auspicious and inauspicious signs should emerge in this world not only makes sense. It was a necessity.

Medieval Buddhists rejected, of course, the existence of a "Cosmic Overlord" who determined the visible flow of the universe. The importance of astrologically "proper time" throughout the *Mmk* shows that they nonetheless left unquestioned the basic beliefs about the cosmos and time that accompanied the systems of thought that did accept such entities.[45] It is because of this belief about the relationship between cosmic flow and auspiciousness that the *Mmk* practitioner waits for an "auspicious day during the bright half of the month" in order to have the cotton spun.

Once such a day has arrived, the *sādhaka* goes with the young girl whom he has hired to a pure place.[46] There, she will spin the mass of raw cotton that he has bought. Before she begins her task, however, she must be ceremoniously purified and protected.

> Having the young virgin girl bathe in a pure place—which place was previously described—[the *sādhaka*] has her dress in fresh clothing. He creates protection by reciting the *mantra*[47] while making the great sealing gesture. Mixing together white sandalwood, saffron, and water devoid of living creatures, he sprinkles the girl and the cotton while reciting the purificatory *mantra*.[48] He should then asperse the sandalwood, saffron, and water mixture to the four directions, above, below, and to the intermediate points. Combining camphor, saffron, and white sandalwood, he, his preceptor, or someone else, should offer it in the eastern direction. Then, these words are to be spoken three times: "may the *buddhas*, the blessed ones, and those who are established on the ten grounds [of the *bodhisattva* path], the great *bodhisattvas*, inhabit this cotton thread!" In this manner, the blessed *buddhas* and the great *bodhisattvas* pay heed.[F10]

Structurally, this ritual is identical to those performed for the enclosed space and the raw cotton. First, the object is acquired (located, hired, etc.). Then, it is cleansed of dirt, purified and protected from malevolent influences. Finally, by invoking the *buddhas* and *bodhisattvas*, it is consecrated.

The purifying procedures and substances used here are identical throughout the *Mmk*. The verb √*snā* behind *snāpayitvā* ("having caused to bathe") suggests complete aspersion. The act of ritualized bathing, or ablution, as with the notion of cleanliness in general, serves more than the obvious function. That is, it frees its object from both dirt and evil influences. The practitioner has the girl dress in fresh garments, and then sprinkles both her and the earth with fragrant water. These ritualized actions are intended to create auspiciousness and seal out malevolency. The hand gesture (*mudrā*) that the *sādhaka* executes while reciting the protective *mantra* is likewise a seal, as is denoted by the term *mudrā*.[49]

The next phase of *paṭa* production requires close scrutiny to visible and audible phenomena. After the young girl makes the ablutions, and the cotton, girl, and earth have been consecrated, the adept lights incense, then watches and listens. If any of several auspicious birds, such as a peacock, curlew, crane, or *cakra* bird flies overhead or coos pleasantly or auspiciously, the practitioner takes this as a sign that the consecration and protection ritual has borne fruit.[50]

> The practitioner knows: My ritual has borne fruit! My cotton thread is inhabited by the blessed *buddhas* and the great *bodhisattvas*! It is completely animated, here in my life! The effect of my *mantra* will not be unfruitful![F11]

The ideal adept, described at *Mmk* 11, is "knowledgeable of the import of gestures," "skilled in discrimination," and "knowledgeable of the world."[51] The ability to understand the significance of physical signs, or omens, is one form of discriminative "worldly" knowledge. The *Mmk* favors two methods of divination: augury (*nimittajñāna*) and astrology (*jyotiṣajñāna*).[52] Augury proper is the ability to discern the meaning of the flight of birds. Its usage can be extended to include knowledge of the meaning of celestial phenomena, such as thunder, lightning, and meteors, as well as knowledge of sounds.[53] Astrology is the means of gaining knowledge about the human world through the observation of stars and planets. As the term indicates, auguries are auspices, omens. As we saw above, omens are consulted in order to determine, among other things, whether the proper time is at hand for a ritual act. If the omens are favorable the act will have the desired effect; if the signs are inauspicious, it will fail.

Knowledge of visible and audible signs has played a significant role in the lives of Indian religious practitioners since Vedic times. In language similar to the *Mmk* passage above, the *Yajñavalkyasmṛti* states that, in Gonda's paraphrase, "[j]ust like the behaviour of birds and the conjunction of planets omina 'bear fruit.' "[54] As with every other element of the *paṭa* ritual so far considered, the ability to understand omens is seen to be a continuing concern of medieval *mantracaryā* as well. A Vaiṣṇava Pañcarātra *saṃhita*, for instance, typically includes several chapters on various aspects of omens.[55] Like these ritual manuals, the *Mmk* contains a section (*Mmk* 17–25)[56] on, as the colophon of *Mmk* 24 concisely puts it, "astrology and the knowledge of omens."

The term *nimitta* denotes *cause, reason, sign,* and *mark,* as well as *omen*. As this indicates, causal power is imputed to the augury. The *sādhaka* knows with certainty that his ritual acts will produce the desired results because natural events have informed him that this is so.[57] As Ronald Inden was quoted as saying above, the two realms, human and natural, were seen in medieval India as a continuous whole. The two were, therefore, "never in an accidental or chance relationship to one another."[58] The *Mmk* alludes to the causal and natural aspects of the omen in a section on "ascertaining one's own *karma*:" "just as a grain is manifested through a sprout of rice, success is manifested through a sign of wealth; just as caste purity can be determined by the occupation [that a person is engaged in], the wealth [of the person] is fixed by the junctions of the planets."[59]

The adept, then, listens carefully. Evidence of auspiciousness may manifest in the form of sounds. He listens for a sound issuing from a war drum, kettle drum, tabor, conches, lute, flute, cymbal, or from a mouth. He hopes, too, that someone[60] should speak any of the following words: victory, success, accomplished, granted, given, grasped, excellent, productive, powerful, great, or any other auspicious sounds, such as the ringing of a bell or shouts of joy. If any of these sounds are heard, the practitioner knows that his ritual will succeed.[61]

Such signs of success, however, are not always forthcoming. After performing the rite of consecration and protection, the practitioner may instead hear people utter words such as: overcome, ruin, devour, destroy, annihilate, hurt, remote, very remote, not to be. The unpleasant sounds of certain vile animals also indicate failure: the monkey, ox, jackal, donkey, or cat. If any of these sounds are heard, the practitioner knows, "there will be no success for me."[62]

In the event of such inauspicious omens, the practitioner must repeat the rite just as before. If, after the seventh attempt, he still has not received an auspicious omen, he is nonetheless assured of success. The text leaves no room for doubting that even failed efforts eventually produce success: "even a person who has committed the five evil acts that result in immediate retribution"[63] is assured that his ritual was effectual.[64]

Now that the auguries of success have confirmed that the thread has been consecrated, that is, that the power of *buddhas* and *bodhisattvas* has entered into it, and that the girl has been shielded from malevolent forces, the adept may continue the process of *paṭa* production. He seats his assistant on a mound of *kuśa* grass, facing either east or north. A pile of *kuśa* grass was commonly considered particularly effective for apotropaic and protective rituals since it retained purity and was resistant to malevolency.[65] Seating himself, the *sādhaka* prepares for his assistant a meal good enough to be a divine oblation. After the assistant has eaten the ceremonial meal, the *sādhaka* has her spin the cotton. When she has finished, she gathers together the smooth, well-spun thread according to the adept's previous instructions, and carefully measures out the proper amount needed for the *paṭa*. With this, the spinning of the cotton is complete.

The labor of *paṭa* production so far has, in a sense, been of a tedious and mundane type of activity not normally associated with religious practice. Yet each step has required a ritualization of this activity. The process of gathering, arranging, and protecting/consecrating the cotton, for instance, was strictly circumscribed by the text's prescriptions. Many features contributed to transforming common procedures of material production into a solemn rite. At every step, special language and bodily gestures were employed, and numerous substances were used, in order to create and maintain the highest level of purity. The junction of the planets was observed; nature manifested signs. In this way, the entire immediate world was incorporated into the ritual domain. As Kapstein writes, "It is clear that the gathering of cotton and the spinning of thread are not to be understood solely as utilitarian acts in the service of ritual practice with which they enjoy no inherent relationship; there is no distance here between craft and ritual—we are engaged at all times in the weaving of a world."[66] The particular world being woven is known from the specific forms employed to ritualize practical activity. As we have seen, much of the ritualized activity points to widespread cultural axioms concerning, for example, the potency of purity and the impotency derived from impurity, or the interpenetration of world and cosmos. Although such ideas permeate the world being fashioned by means of the rituals, they constitute only one aspect of that world. It is through the conceptions behind the particular forms—*mantras*, *mudrās,* type of assistant, types of substances, and so on—that a unique world is being woven by the *Mmk.*

At this point, the text reminds the practitioner of the seriousness of every phase of the rite, no matter how seemingly trivial: "the knower of *mantras* expends his greatest power in all the rituals, [even] in the minor rituals that are to be mastered."[67] This statement underlines the unity of craft and ritual, and of practical and religious activity, in the *Mmk.* To impress on the practitioner the absoluteness of this unity, the text demonstrates the power of the material just produced.

> Whatever negative *karma* had been previously accumulated is destroyed from the moment [that the cotton is spun]. [This is] on account of the thread, [and is] not [dependent] on being willed.[F12]

The force of the thread is, of course, derived from its being infused by the presence of dynamic, compassionate entities—*buddhas* and *bodhisattvas* generally, and Mañjuśrī specifically. The conditions that enabled this presence resulted, in turn, from painstaking and lengthy rituals. It should be recalled in this regard that the simplified rite of *Mmk* 7 omits every phase of production so far prescribed by *Mmk* 4. The practitioner in *Mmk* 7 has thus far simply bought the required quantity of cotton and had it woven into a canvas by a weaver. By contrast, the process of weaving in *Mmk* 4 is highly ritualized.

Mmk 4 points out the power of the thread. It is so potent that absolute purity ensues from its very production. That is, the potentially negative *karma* of the practitioner, resulting from countless lifetimes of activity, is negated in an instant. Because of this potency, the material must be treated with extreme caution. The text prescribes the following procedure towards this end.

> Gathering together the thread, he should place it in a clean vessel. Having deposited it there, he should fumigate it with camphor and incense,
>
> or else with products devoid of animal parts, such as saffron, sandalwood, and the like. It [should be] honored with fragrant flowers, such as jasmine, yellow *campaka*, and the like.
>
> Kept in a clean place, it is ensconced with protection.
>
> He who is knowledgeable of *mantras*, who is versed in all the rituals, recites [the protective *mantra*] as before, fully concentrated.[68F13]

The thread remains in the vessel, protected and honored as a sacred object, until the practitioner is able to hire an acceptable weaver. The weaver must exhibit the physical emblems of respectability and auspiciousness. Not only must he not be maimed in any way, he must even be of pleasant appearance. Like the practitioner's preceptor, the weaver may not be too old, and must exhibit perfect health.[69] And, like the young girl who assisted the adept in the spinning of the cloth, the weaver must be from a respectable family of Buddhists.

> All of his limbs are intact, he is not impaired;
> he delights always in the pure teaching.
>
> He is free from sickness, affliction and old-age;
> he is free from coughing and asthma.
> He does not have gray hair, is not a eunuch, and is of proper birth.
>
> He is irreproachable; and is neither hump-backed nor lamed.
> He is possessed of all the auspicious characteristics, and is pleasant to behold.
>
> He is intelligent and handsome; his conduct is virtuous, his behavior adheres to customary ways.
> If, then, one is desirous of success, he should solicit him to weave the large *paṭa*.

> He is laudable, of a virtuous caste, is intelligent and capable.
> For this reason, [it should be woven] by the best, the most excellent, the most superior weaver of cloth.[F14]

When the practitioner finds such a weaver, he should not bargain, as is customary. The weaver quotes his price, and the adept accepts it without hesitation with the words "excellent price."[70] The reason that the business should be transacted hastily and without complication is that it concerns an object of extreme importance. In enjoining the practitioner not to bargain, the text is differentiating the *paṭa* from all other valuable objects.

> The excellent, unsurpassable *paṭa,* which creates success rapidly in all rituals, which is to be worshipped, which [bestows] divine and human happiness—proclaimed by the fully enlightened *buddhas*, it is the most excellent [object] for all beings.[F15]

The production of the *paṭa* continues once the weaver is hired. Like the assistant who spun the cotton, the weaver must undergo a ritualized preparation before he can commence his work. His own Buddhist practice is intensified by his committing to observe special precepts (*poṣadha*)[71] while he works. The precise time for his initial preparation is carefully calculated for efficacy.

> Considering whether the day falls when the moon is on the threshold of waxing, or when a very auspicious planet or star [is visible]; or else whether it is the bright half of the month or in the season of spring, abounding in flowers and trees flush with the flowering of fragrant mango blossoms. At that time, when the sun has risen in the morning . . .[F16]

On an astrologically favorable morning, the weaver is thoroughly purified and consecrated. Both the structure and elements employed in this process are nearly identical to those in the purification ritual for the young female assistant. First, the weaver is given a meal of great dignity (*haviṣyāhāra*). As the term *haviṣya* suggests, this meal is both the mark and the cause of a solemn occasion. After eating, he bathes thoroughly, puts his hair in a bun, and puts on fresh clothing. He next completely anoints his limbs with white sandalwood and saffron, and scents his mouth with camphor. Finally, allaying whatever hunger and thirst he may have, his mind is filled with joy.[72] In this manner, the weaver becomes an agent exuding auspiciousness.

The weaver then proceeds to purify his utensils in a similar fashion. First, he washes his vessel, thread and tools with the five purifying products of the cow (i.e., milk, coagulated milk, butter, urine, and feces). When these have been thoroughly cleansed, he rinses them with water, then sprinkles them with white sandalwood and saffron.

Transformed in this manner from a common, if exceptional, weaver, to a purified creator, the weaver is prepared for the full consecration that will enable him to complete the next stage of *paṭa* creation. That his task requires a special effort beyond the usual labor involved in weaving a cloth from cotton thread can be deduced from the prescribed location of the work. It is the type of place prescribed for the practice of the most solemn rites.

> In a pure place, remote, devoid of noise and the footsteps of men, in a lonely habitation, tranquil, hidden, resplendent with flowers.[F17]

Removing to such a place, the practitioner then ritually purifies and protects the space. He does this by reciting a purificatory *mantra* one hundred and eight times. To protect the purified object from the influx of negative forces, he disperses white mustard seeds to the four cardinal points, up in the air, down to the ground, and to the intermediate points, and then vigorously strikes the weaver with mustard seeds and "binds" his head with the great "five-crested" seal of Mañjuśrī. In this manner, the weaver, stamped with the insignia of the *bodhisattva*, is protected from any malevolent forces that might threaten the success of his activity. Only now may he commence the weaving.[73]

At this point in the text, the measurements of the three types of *paṭa* are given, and the relative power of each is stated. The large cult object (*jyeṣṭa paṭa*) measures 6 feet by 12 feet (4 by 8 *hasta*, or cubits[74]), a medium painting (*madhyama*) of 2 by 5 cubits, and a small painting (*kanyasa*) measuring approximately 3 by 9 inches (*angustha*[75]). The benefits derived from employing each of these in practice is said to be proportionate to their size. The large *paṭa* is for the superior attainment, enlightenment;[76] the medium one is for the acquisition of certain supernatural powers or the attainment of high social status; the small *paṭa* is for achieving the worldly pleasures experienced by the *devas* and *asuras*.[77] As discussed in chapter 1, this division into superior, intermediate, and inferior (*nīca*, *adha,* and *adhama* are used synonymously with *kanyasa* for "minor" or "small") is a common organizing principle in the *Mmk.* There are, for instance, three grades of person corresponding to the three humors of the body: (the order is always descending) *vāta* (wind), *śleṣma* (phlegm), and *pitta* (bile).[78] The three basic types of ritual, *śāntika* (pacification), *pauṣṭika* (increase), and *ābhicārika* (maledictory or terrific), are classified in this manner.[79] Both of these groups correspond to the three basic "clans" (*kula*) of the *Mmk*: *tathāgatakula* (also *jinakula* and *buddhakula*), *padmakula* (lotus clan; also *abjakula*), and *vajrakula* (thunderbolt clan; also called *kuliśakula*).[80] Further threefold hierarchies are *buddha/pratyekabuddha/śrāvaka* (these also refer to their corresponding levels of enlightenment),[81] *lokottara/śīla/laukika, buddha/deva/human.*[82] In each case, a statement is being made about the relative value of various possibilities. Rather than rejecting alternatives, this type of hierarchical classification includes and subordinates them under a preferred orientation. From the *tathāgatakula/padmakula/vajrakula* hierarchy, for instance, we can discern this process as follows. The *tathāgata*, the conventional Mahāyānist Buddha/*buddhas* known from texts referred to by the *Mmk*, such as the *Prajñāpāramitā, Suvarṇaprabhāsottamasūtra,* and the *Gaṇḍavyūhasūtra*, remains the central object of devotion. At *Mmk* 2, numerous *buddhas* are named, such as Bhaiṣajyaguru, Amitāyus, Ratnaketu, Amitābha, to mention just a few of the more familiar ones. Although each of these *buddhas* was the center of his own cult, here they are converging on the Śuddhāvāsa *maṇḍala* to hear Śākyamuni teach. While these *buddhas* and their cultic communities are considered viable—they remain within the "fold" of the Buddha Śākyamuni—both are nonetheless subordinated to Śākyamuni and the groups devoted to him. The *padmakula* members, too, were the objects of individual non-Buddhist cults in medieval India. The *Mmk* appropriates, for example, Tārā, Lakṣmī, and Lokeśvara (= Śiva), as well as nonhuman spirits such as male and female *kiṃkaras, yakṣas, rākṣasas* and *piśācas,* and places them in a supportive role.[83] The *vajrakula* deities, too, are uprooted from their cultic contexts and given specific supportive functions in the *Mmk.* Beings with names such as Vajrakrodha, Maheśvarāntaścara, Sughora and Raktāṅga appear "as destroyers of death, destruction, epidemics, ruin, and tamers of all beings without exception; bestowers upon the faithful; discharged for the practitioners of rituals of malediction, increase, and pacification."[84] Thus, the *vajrakula* class included wrathful emanations of deities and supernatural forces that, in the *Mmk*, were given a place as protectors of the law (*vidyārāja* [= a class], *mahākrodharāja* [= Yamāntaka]).[85]

Such a classification is, of course, a means of taking into account opposition and historical complexity in relation to a preferred position. We might thus understand the statements about the three *paṭas* as an ordering of values within the *Mmk.* The most highly valued goal of practice is enlightenment; others, such as worldly success and supernatural abilities, however, are considered justified. Like the originally pre-Buddhist and non-Buddhist *padmakula* and *vajrakula* entities, the *madhyama* and *kanyasa* goals are legitimized through relationship to the Buddha. The *vajrakula* deity Yamāntaka, for instance, becomes an emanation of Mañjuśrī, who, in turn, is a "son of the Buddha." Yamāntaka's originally wrathful and purely destructive power in this way becomes bound up with enlightened power, and is thus transformed into an enlightened, and enlightening, force. Seeking worldly gain by means of the *mantracaryā* taught in the *Mmk* likewise becomes transformed into an ultimately enlightening pursuit. By virtue of seeing the *paṭa*—the locus of the Buddha's image and power—the practitioner attains the state of buddhahood regardless of his immediate orientation. We learn of this not through the explicit statements about the *paṭas*' relative size and power, but through the text's demonstrations of that power. Concerning the smallest *paṭa* we read that "it is called small because it is the *paṭa* that is excellent for the minor rituals."[86] At *Mmk* 6, called "the chapter on the creation of the small *paṭa,*" the minor accomplishments are generalized as those involving the pacification of hindrances (*śāntika*), the increase of wealth, health, happiness, and so forth (*pauṣtika*), and the expulsion of terrific forces (*dāruṇa*).[87] Yet, the demonstration of even this smallest *paṭa's* power reveals the ambiguity of the text's explicit statements about the nature of the small *paṭa*.

> [He who] commits or causes to be committed an evil, extremely terrible act is freed for millions of eons upon seeing the *paṭa*.
>
> Indeed, merely seeing the *paṭa*,
> he is freed instantaneously.
> He who mentally honors millions of *buddhas*
> does not acquire even one-sixteenth [of the merit
> of one who has] seen the small *paṭa*.
>
> That same merit that ensues from worship of all *buddhas*, the saviors, the sage can obtain by seeing the small *paṭa*.
> If, in this regard, he uses—for good reason, in pure rituals —
>
> any of the *mantras* spoken by Brahma, Indra, or the *ṛṣis*, or [those] proclaimed by Vainateya [= Garuḍa], Varuṇa,
> Āditya, Kubera
>
> the *rakṣasas*, lords of treasures, the *mahoragas*, masters of the *dānavas,* and those spoken by Soma, Vāyu, Yāma, Viṣṇu, Śiva, and so on—all of those *mantras*, employed in front of the *paṭa*, succeed.[F18]

This passage is indicative of the ritual project of the *Mmk* as a whole. In short, the *Mmk* is a totalizing text. Its ritual claims rest on a summation of India's religious culture from the archaic Vedic sacrifice to medieval *bhakti* worship. Here, it incorporates high culture and pan-Indian deities alongside spirits and forces associated with low-caste village cults. It acknowledges the power of non-Buddhist *mantras*, synthesizes these into an undifferentiated whole, and then merges them into the path of the *buddhas*.[88] All previous and presently competing Buddhist paths, too, are rendered obsolete in face of the absolute power of the *paṭa*. All competing forms of worship are perfected only when correctly performed before the *paṭa*. What constitutes proper performance, in turn, is known solely through the prescriptions of the *Mmk*.

> Incomplete rituals do not succeed, even [those] of Śakra, lord of Śaci.
>
> But those who conform to the prescriptions—even of a lowly person—succeed quickly and effortlessly in all rituals.[F19]

To see the *paṭa* is to see the culmination of India's religious history. The *paṭa* absorbs and perfects this history. The *Mmk* reveals this history, instructs in its envisioning, and, via the specific path of *mantra* recitation (*mantramārga*)[89] that it teaches, enables its realization.

After this demonstration of historical and practical ultimacy, the text returns to an instructive mode. The artisan must complete his work within sixteen days in order to coincide with the waxing moon.[90] The practitioner, however, is informed that to complete it in a single day and night is particularly advantageous.[91]

Because the artisan is fashioning an object of tremendous force and priceless value, his actions are constricted; this, furthermore, ensures that the potency of the material he has been entrusted with is not compromised. His maintenance of a state of heightened internal and external purity creates the temporary ritual identity necessary for the activity of weaving.

> After he has gone [back] to his distant dwelling the artisan, who is continually established in perfectly pure conduct, should defecate and urinate. He then makes ablutions and dresses in different clothing.
>
> Wearing white apparel and garlands, he asperses them repeatedly. Pouring white sandalwood onto his hands, the artisan anoints his limbs.
>
> With great effort he weaves a single, smooth piece [of cloth].[F20]

When the weaver has finished his work, the adept "bids him well and pays him an abundant amount of money."[92] He then takes the woven cloth home and places it in a "pure place that has been made brilliant with fragrant flowers."[93] To ensure the purity of both himself and the cloth, the practitioner recites the *mantra* of protection repeatedly. Here, the text shifts back into a demonstrative mode. The practitioner is reminded again of the absolute power of the *mantra* he is reciting, of its profound vigor and vitality, and that it is nothing other than the force of the *bodhisattva* embodied in sonic form.

> [The practitioner recites, or reflects on, the first verse] Mañjuśrī, the heroic one, has been spoken through the form of the *mantra* by many past *buddhas*; and now I, too, [do so] repeatedly.
>
> He whose form is the *mantra* proceeds from all *mantras*—the heroic one, the one of great majesty, who effects the goal of all *mantras*.
>
> He creates myriad forms for the purpose of saving the numerous sentient beings who wander stupidly in the world.
>
> Perverse people of no faith, those whose behavior is wrong and destructive, never succeed in their objectives with [use of] the *mantra*.

> It is for this reason that they wander about aimlessly in the darkness of *saṃsāra*. He whose mind is pure, however, has constant faith in the auspiciousness of the ceremonies.
>
> Constantly enthusiastic toward all *mantras*—in those taken [from a text] and those memorized—those [practitioners] who desire success, those great ones of tremendous vigor and vitality,
>
> achieve success easily with the *mantras* spoken by the *buddhas*. But for people without faith, the bright *dharma* does not shine.
>
> Just like a piece of salt thrown [into the earth, or] a sprout without fruit, the root of faith lies always in the *dharma*.[94] This has been spoken by those who reveal the sense of all [the teachings]. It is said that there is success in the [employment of] *mantras* by those who practice the spirit of the teachings.[F21]

While these instructions of *Mmk* 4 have a didactic tone, those for the simplified rite of *Mmk* 7 are prescriptive. It should be recalled that the practitioner in *Mmk* 7 simply bought a quantity of cotton and had it woven into a canvas by a weaver. Taking this woven canvas home, he prepared a fragrant mixture of sandalwood, camphor, saffron, and pure water in a new vase. The woven cloth was placed in the vase, tightly covered, and allowed to soak for three days.[95] The tedious stages of purifying and protecting the elements of the emerging *paṭa* taught in *Mmk* 4 are then reduced to the following two-part process in *Mmk* 7. When the moon is waxing, the *sādhaka* goes outside and performs the protective rite on the space and on himself.[96] He then sits on a mound of *kuśa* grass facing the east, where he has positioned the vessel containing the *paṭa*.[97] Sitting in this manner, he recites these *mantra* verses:

> *Oṁ*
>
> Hey hey! O Blessed One! O you who bear numerous forms! O you with the divine eye! Look down, look down upon me! Remember your vow! O you who bear the form of a youthful prince! O great *bodhisattva*! Why do you tarry?! *hūṁ hūṁ phaṭ phaṭ hail!*[F22]

This *mantra,* invoking Mañjuśrī to enter the *paṭa*, is recited one hundred and eight times.[98] The text then instructs the *sādhaka* to go to sleep in that same location; there, during sleep, it will be revealed to him whether his invocation has succeeded or not.[99] If the *sādhaka* sees a favorable omen (*siddhinimitta*), he may, on waking, commence the painting of the image on the *paṭa*. If unfavorable signs were seen in sleep, he must take the cloth out of the vessel, dry it completely in the sun, and place it in a new vessel. Then, he must once again perform the protective ritual.[100] In either case, the *paṭa* is now prepared for the final consecration before painting. This is effected by reciting one hundred thousand times the "extremely potent six six-syllabled *mantras*" given at the beginning of *Mmk* 7: *oṁ vākyārthe jaya / oṁ vākyaśeṣe sva / oṁ vākyeyanayaḥ / oṁ vākyaniṣṭheyaḥ / oṁ vākyeyanamaḥ / oṁ vākyedanamaḥ*.[101] Immediately on completion of the recitation, the *paṭa* becomes an efficacious object ready to be imprinted with the image.[102]

According to *Mmk* 4, the image may be painted on the consecrated cloth by an artisan (*śilpin*), a painter (*citrakara*), or the practitioner himself. The character of the painter, as well as the ritualized preparations for painting, are identical to those required of the weaver.[103] When these are completed—when the place has been secured, the painter protected, given a meal, his utensils purified, and so on—the paints are perfumed with camphor, saffron, and sandalwood. Incense is then lit. While it burns, a *mantra* is recited one hundred and eight times, and the cloth is covered with flowers. The painting commences only when the painter is concentrated and focused.

> Sitting on a mound of *kuśa* grass facing east, his mind at ease, thoughts directed towards all *buddhas* and *bodhisattvas*, he takes a fine brush in his hand and, his thoughts relaxed, should paint the *paṭa*.[F23]

The image rendered by the painter at this point may be one of several possibilities presented in the *Mmk*. These vary from the "simplified" *paṭa* described in *Mmk* 7 to the elaborate *paṭas* of *Mmk* 4 and elsewhere. What these *paṭas* have in common, based on the textual descriptions in the *Mmk*, is a likeness to the Nepali *paubhās* and Tibetan *thangkas* found in modern-day Nepal. Like the medieval *paṭa* described in the *Mmk*, these are paintings on fabric depicting a central figure, typically a *buddha, bodhisattva*, or *guru*, around whom are arrayed various configurations of supportive entities of enlightened power, such as *arhats, ḍākinīs, yakṣas, gandharvas*, and so forth. Lalou has thoroughly documented, described, and translated the sections of the *Mmk* that deal with such configurations. So, I refer the interested reader to her.[104] My purpose in this chapter was to show the manner by which the *Mmk* discloses to the reader/practitioner the methods of effective *paṭa* production. Efficacy is, first of all, dependent on adequate fulfillment of the threefold process described by Kapstein as gathering, arranging, and consecrating. As we saw, this process is accomplished at each step on the way to crafting a cult object. The procedure presented in the text amounted to numerous acts of concentrated, highly ritualized labor, the purpose of which was to "reconstitute continuously in a world of ongoing change"[105] the values and promise of the text's community. The labor of construction, however, was not merely material; for the source of power that is inscribed, step by step, on the materials that eventually comprise the cult image, requires that the reader/practitioner continually and thoroughly imprint on his mind the assembly arrayed in the domain of the Buddha—arrayed in text, cosmos, and, now, cult image.

CHAPTER 4

The Empowered Practitioner *(sādhaka)*

4.1 The practitioner in the text

The *sādhaka* is the final "location" considered in this study as a means of illustrating the mode of practice taught in the *Mmk*. As we have seen in the analysis of the practitioner's apprehension of the cosmic assembly and creation of the cult object, the simple ritual act described in the *uttamasādhana* passage at section 1.4.1 presupposes a wide range of ritualized activities. Similarly, the success of that ritual rests on the practitioner's ability to become the type of person defined by the text.

The text was a tool for the *Mmk* community of users to form the moral and mental dispositions necessary for successful practice. As a *kalpa*, the *Mmk* prescribes and authorizes not only what must be done, but by whom this may be done. As a *vaipulyasūtra*, it not only inspires a vision of reality that must be imagined if progress is to be made, but a vision of a new person who must be actualized. The text, of course, would have been supplemented by training within a community of practitioners. As an initiate, for instance, the *sādhaka* was primarily formed by his human exemplar, the preceptor and initiating master (called *guru, ācārya,* or *maṇḍalācārya* in the *Mmk*). This teacher determined the practitioner's capacity for serious practice and accordingly instructed him on the metaphysical, moral, and practical knowledge required for undertaking the career of the cult. But the text itself played a role in the practitioner's development by serving as an abbreviated record of that training and knowledge. It was a handbook to be consulted, meditated on, recited from, and even worshiped. Thus, just as the practitioner is the "location" for re-forming a person into a Buddhist *sādhaka*, the text is the space for mediating the actual and the ideal. Like the medieval reader himself, what we encounter in the *Mmk* is, of course, not an actual historical figure, but a normative image of the ideal practitioner. In this sense, the *sādhaka*—as we encounter him—may be seen as a rhetorical figure who does not stand apart from the text itself. The text's strategies for describing the *sādhaka* must therefore be seen as intrinsic to the nature of that practitioner as he appears to the reader. The aim of this chapter is to clarify those strategies.

4.2 The *sādhaka*

The practitioner of the *Mmk* embodies the design of the *Mmk* community to fashion a particular form or type from a general cultural pattern. We catch reflections of this practitioner throughout the present-day Buddhist world. Some examples of these reflections will serve here as a rough sketch of the type of Buddhist that this medieval practitioner was. We see remnants of him in the Theravādin "wizards" (*weikza*) of Burma, who serve the laity with their mastery of occult powers and of the healing arts; in the Japanese Shingon "morning star" practitioner, who temporarily lives as a recluse in a solitary hut in order to devote himself exclusively to recitation of his *mantra*; in the Nepalese *vajrācārya*, the nonmonastic tantric priest who may function socially as an artisan as well as religiously as a realized master of esoteric rituals; in the advanced Tibetan tantric initiate, who, before he may "effectuate" the *mantra* and apply it to a specific end, must undergo an intense period of mental and physical purification and *mantra* recitation; and finally, in the lay or ordained practitioner who has as his primary practice the recitation of a *mantra*, such as the Taiwanese and Japanese Pure Land *nianfo/nembutso*, or the Japanese Nichiren *daimoku*.[1]

We may view the practitioner from the other direction, from his own past. Here we can perform the above operation in reverse, and sketch the practitioner as a piecemeal ideal fashioned out of diverse historical strands. The *Mmk* practitioner is formed in part from the ancient tradition of the itinerant Brahmanical ascetic, and thus abides by the prescriptions for daily oblations, begging, ablutions, eating, and wandering as codified in the medieval ritual manuals. The fusion of this ancient *śramaṇa* with the early Mahāyāna *bodhisattva* produced a nonmonastic forest renunciant ideal, a *yogi-bodhisattva* who devoted himself fully to the "perfection of wisdom" and the acquisition of supernormal powers and knowledge (*ṛddhi* and *abhijñā*) for the purpose of benefiting the world.[2] The *Mmk* practitioner is molded to a certain extent by the ideal of the *bodhisattva* as it is expressed in the *Prajñāpāramitā* texts; but his way to power and perfection is not by means of the path of meditation and the six perfections, as is prescribed in those texts. Rather, the *Mmk* practitioner utilizes a combination of methods derived from different epochs of India's religious culture. Some, for instance, evoke the archaic, perhaps pre-Aryan, practices recorded in the *Atharvaveda*, such as the manipulation of reality and the healing of disease by means of the *maṇḍala*, incantation, and herbs. Some are clear adaptations of Aryan Vedic ritual, in particular the fire oblation. Others are derived from the *bhakti* cults, such as worship of the "base" of enlightened embodiment by means of the *paṭa*.

This sketch begins to give form to a complex, composite figure known, by the early middle ages, as the *sādhaka*. Deriving from √*sādh* (to accomplish, complete, succeed), a *sādhaka* is one who, by performing prescribed rituals, is fulfilling and completing the career codified by a given cult. Viewed from the distance, the *Mmk sādhaka*, like both the text itself and the rituals that it prescribes, is indistinguishable from the practitioners of numerous other groups who were similarly designated as *sādhakas*. Whether Vaiṣṇava, Śaiva, or Buddhist, the ideal that the medieval *sādhaka* represented, and the practices that were prescribed for him, were created out of common elements. The *sādhaka* is thus a culturally economized form, an innovative figure crafted out of traditional, normative ideals and theoretical bases, such as those just mentioned.

The term *sādhaka* can be misleading, however, since it is used today as a broad generic term signifying any religious practitioner. It will be argued below that the medieval *sādhaka* was an initiatory type, and that the term therefore had a narrow technical meaning. My approach to this definition of the *Mmk* practitioner is primarily through an analysis of attributive expressions that are ascribed to the practitioner, such as nouns, adjectives, and phrases. Often these epithets are conjoined with particular spaces within which the practitioner may move. For example, the practitioner as *puraścarin* is invariably placed "in a desolate place, clean, secluded, removed from the ways of village life."[3] Only in such a place can a person carry out the prescribed ritual actions that constitute "one who has completed the preliminary practice," a *puraścarin*. In such instances, epithet and space are indistinguishable aspects.

4.3 Epithets and space

The *Mmk* does not treat the practitioner systematically. There is, for example, no section describing the various stages of training in the practitioner's career. The text nonetheless provides material for learning about the practitioner and for reconstructing the basic features of both his career and characteristic qualities. I have organized this data under the three main epithets used in the text to designate the initiated practitioner. Each of these three, *śiṣya, samayin,* and *ācārya,* is accompanied by additional synonymous terms. The *samayin*, for instance is also a *puraścarin*, one who fulfills the preliminary practice of intensive *mantra* recitation, and a *bhikṣāhāra*, a beggar of alms. As descriptive adjectives and phrases, these epithets present us with an image of the status and activity of the practitioner. These attributive expressions are, furthermore, often accompanied by either descriptions of or allusions to the particular space occupied by the practitioner. In such cases, these spaces become part of the definition of a given epithet. It is therefore through epithets and descriptions of space that we learn about the practitioner as he is envisioned by the community.

The "compositional principle" underlying the process of *paṭa* creation suggested by Matthew Kapstein can be fruitfully applied to the epithets as well. We saw in chapter 3 that this principle involves a threefold process. As Kapstein shows, the *paṭa* ritual, both as a whole and in each of its parts, requires: (1) gathering the necessary elements, (2) arranging those into a particular order, and (3) consecrating or protecting what has been arranged. This pattern allows us to arrange the text's material on the practitioner as follows. (1) Accumulation of preliminary trainings under a *guru,* culminating in the initiation. The primary epithet concerning this stage is *śiṣya.* (2) Concentration of those trainings into a specific order of ritual action. An important epithet in this category is *mantrin,* since this term is the overall designation of the type of Buddhist practitioner presented in the *Mmk.* There are numerous additional epithets for this stage that describe specific attributes and activities of the *sādhaka* as *mantrin,* such as *samayin, puraścarin,* and *tricelaparivartin.* When he has achieved the highest level of this practice, the *sādhaka* may seek to become an *ācārya,* a master and teacher in his own right. (3) Transformation resulting from the ritual action. The *sādhaka* is consecrated as a *samayin* by the *guru* in an initiation ritual. Through this act, he is transformed into a being of special status who has access to the most secretive and potent aspects of the *mantracaryā.* The *samayin's* practice culminates when he is consecrated by the *bodhisattvas* and *buddhas* whom he encounters during the *uttamasādhana.* He is thereby transformed into a *vidyādhāra, bodhisattva,* and *buddha.* (Each of these terms is elaborated on below.)

Every phase of this process is defined by the places within which it unfolds. In each instance, the practitioner initially acquires his status on the ground specially prepared for the initiation ritual. That is, it is through a special act of aspersion with water (*abhiṣeka*) that a person becomes a *śiṣya, samayin, ācārya, bodhisattva,* and, eventually, *buddha.* This aspersion, however, represents only the initial entrance into the various phases of the *mantracaryā.* As the *Mmk* itself states, the historical paradigm for its initiation ritual is the "royal consecration rite" (*rājyābhiṣeka*).[4] Like the *rājyābhiṣeka,* the aspersion by the initiating master (*maṇḍalācārya*) alters the status of the initiate by empowering him to carry out activities that had previously lain outside his scope. In the case of the *Mmk,* these activities are those which constitute the *mantracaryā.* As I will discuss in more detail below, the various areas within which these activities are fulfilled are additional defining spaces of the *sādhaka.* For instance, the *śiṣya,* as we may speculate on analogy to other medieval *mantra* cults, completes his course of practice in the home or *aśrama* of the *guru*; the *samayin* or *puraścarin,* in some outdoor "field of realization" (*siddhikṣetra*);[5] the *bodhisattva* and *buddha* in the physical and mental ground of the *uttamasādhana.* But first, it will be necessary to discuss the space of, and activity within, the *maṇḍala.*

4.3.1 The initiation maṇḍala

The initiation ground is a consecrated area, called a *maṇḍala,* drawn on the earth with colored powder. The importance of this ground to the form of practice recorded in the *Mmk* is highlighted by the fact that an entire chapter, *Mmk* 2, is devoted to its construction.[6] Ariane MacDonald has treated the main portion of this chapter in an annotated translation.[7] It will nonetheless be necessary, for the sake of my argument concerning the *sādhaka*, to summarize the main features of both the construction and form of the initiation *maṇḍala* and the ritual that occurs therein.

This initiation *maṇḍala* represents the world that is to be mastered and, thereby, manipulated by the initiate. It reveals the same cosmic structure as the *paṭa* and the cosmic assembly. Being a simulation of the actual Buddhist cosmos, it becomes, like the other simulations that we have considered in this study—the cult object, the mentally apprehended assembly, the *mantras*, and the book within which all of these are made present—a realm pervaded by the enlightened power of the Buddha/*buddhas*. For this reason, its construction is methodically executed.

The construction of the *maṇḍala*, and the manner in which this is presented in the text, is similar to the section on the creation of the *paṭa*: practical instructions concerning time, place, materials, and execution are punctuated by both descriptions of the participants' dispositions and demonstrations of the *maṇḍala's* inherent power. And like the prescriptions for *paṭa* creation, the *maṇḍalavidhāna* allow for considerable variation.

The construction of the initiation *maṇḍala* commences on an astrologically optimal day, that is on a day when the forces of nature are in the most positive phase of their cycle. Any actions performed on this day will be imbued with the cleansing, auspicious energy being emitted by the forces of nature. The peak of this favorable moment is described here as follows: "when the moon is extraordinarily full, in the spring months of Caitra (March–April) or Vaiśākha (April–May), during the bright half of the month, on a fast day ruled by a favorable planet, accompanied by an auspicious star."[8] Less than ideal moments are allowed as well: "on the first day of the waxing moon, or when the moon is full, or at any other time except in a rainy-season month."[9]

Early in the morning of such a day, the initiating master, called the *maṇḍalācārya*, is to seek out a suitable area and establish himself there. The text allows for several possibilities. The master may station himself in a large city,[10] wherever he might already be, at a river flowing toward the ocean, near the shore of the ocean, or neither too close nor too far to the northeast of a large city. The references to the large city are of particular interest. Although a rhetoric of secrecy and esotericism pervades the *Mmk*, the symbolic and "legal" entrance into its cult appears in many ways to be a public event. In a text that constantly admonishes its readers to ensure that they are acting in privacy, the sudden appearance of the term "large city" (*mahānagara*) presents a picture of the initiation ritual as a public display. A distinction is made, then, between the esoteric content of the *mantracaryā* and the exoteric reception of permission to engage in the *mantracaryā*.

Having selected the area for the *maṇḍala*, the master makes a hut of leaves, and dwells there in isolation for seven days.[11] During this period, the master clears the area of rocks, coal, and so on, and then purifies it of any malevolent forces. This is accomplished by assuming the body, words, and actions of Mañjuśrī. The master consecrates a mixture of water, camphor, sandal paste, and saffron with the five-crested sealing hand gesture together with one thousand and eight recitations of the *mantra* of Yamāntaka, and then "asperses this mixture in that area of earth, towards the four directions, above, below, horizontally, to the intermediary points, everywhere."[12]

The next phase of the *maṇḍala* construction then begins. This involves drawing its external form. On the authority of the "omniscient ones," the *buddhas* throughout time and space, the text allows for a threefold variation in size of the *maṇḍala*.[13] Depending, presumably, either on the expense that the initiates are willing to incur or the type of initiation to be performed, the outer square of the *maṇḍala* may measure either 16, 12, or 8 *hastas* (i.e., about 24, 18, and 12 feet outer squares respectively). The largest *maṇḍala* is for those "desirous of sovereignty," the intermediate one for the "increase of fortune," and the small one for the "vow only." But, as with the threefold distinction of the *paṭa*, even the smallest *maṇḍala* "achieves all deeds, is beneficent." Even a square measuring only two cubits (thirty-six square inches) may be drawn, if so desired.[14]

After drawing the square outer form of the *maṇḍala*, the master should drive in posts of *khadira* wood at each of the four directions.[15] These are then consecrated with seven recitations of Yamāntaka's *mantra*. He surrounds the outer *maṇḍala* on all four sides with the five-colored thread, which has been consecrated seven times with the *hṛdaya mantra* of Yamāntaka. Similarly, he outlines the middle and interior squares.

The *mantras* for concentrating these spaces are given in the "compendium" preceding the *maṇḍalavidhāna* section. We read there of the "preeminently heroic, all achieving essence of the sovereign of wrath, Yamāntaka . . . *oṃ āḥ hūṁ*." This *mantra* is the *hṛdaya*, "the essence of him whose wrath is great; it is all accomplishing; it is taught by the great being Mañjughoṣa for [use in] all *maṇḍala* and *mantra* rituals; it destroys all obstacles."[16] Following the *hṛdaya mantra* is another liturgical *mantra* used to create the protection necessary for ensuring the efficacy of the initiation *maṇḍala*:

> Then the youthful Mañjuśrī spoke to the *bodhisattva* Vajrapāṇi: "O master of secrets, these *mantras* are esoteric and supremely secret [. . .]
>
> Homage to all *buddhas* and *bodhisattvas*, whose teachings are indestructible. *uṃ kara kara kuru kuru mama kāryam bhañja bhañja sarvavighnāṃ daha daha sarva vajravināyakam mūrdhaṭakajīvitāntakara mahāvikṛtarūpiṇe paca paca sarvaduṣṭāṃ mahāgaṇapatijīvitāntakara bandha bandha sarvagrahāṃ ṣaṇmukha ṣaḍbhuja ṣaṭcaraṇa rudramānaya viṣṇumānaya brahmādyāṃ devānānaya mā vilamba mā vilamba iyal iyal maṇḍalamadhye praveśaya samayam anusmara hūṁ hūṁ hūṁ hūṁ hūṁ hūṁ phaṭ phaṭ svāhā* (*O maker O maker do do for me what should be done shatter shatter all obstacles burn burn all adamantine impediments O killer of Mūrdhaṭaka O you of extraordinary appearance cook cook all evil O killer of great Gaṇapati bind bind all demons O six-faced one O six-armed one O six-legged one subdue Rudra subdue Viṣṇu subdue the gods, beginning with Brahman do not delay do not delay become silent become silent enter into the maṇḍala remember your vow! hūṁ hūṁ hūṁ hūṁ hūṁ hūṁ phaṭ phaṭ hail!*)
>
> O supreme master of secrets, this [*mantra*] is the supreme secret, the great hero, Mañjuśrī; it is called "six-faced one," and is the ruler of the great wrath which destroys all obstacles. By merely reciting that, *bodhisattvas* who are established in the ten stages (*daśabhūmi*) are dispersed, let alone evil obstructions. By merely reciting that, great protection is created. The sealing gesture is known as "the spike," the destroyer of all obstacles.[G1]

The four key points of the outer *maṇḍala* are in this manner sealed off and protected from negative influences. Such influences arise from, for example, natural forces (e.g., the energies from stars and planets), supernatural beings, such as *yakṣas* and *bhūtas*, and human beings. By manifesting Yamāntaka's power through the utterance of his "sound-essence," the *hṛdaya mantra*, the master transforms the square formation into an animated replica of the cosmic assembly. As we saw in chapter 2, Yamāntaka's vow, referred to in the *mantras* above, was the result of his being admonished by Mañjuśrī to "protect all the beings encircled in the great assembly" from the outside.[17] With these actions of the *maṇḍalācārya*, that assembly now extends to the initiating *maṇḍala*.

Having constructed the basic form of the *maṇḍala*, the officiating master ensures his own and his assistant's protection by performing the sealing gesture and reciting his personal *mantra* (*mūlamantra*) one thousand and eight times while standing in the intermediate section of the *maṇḍala*. After this recitation, he departs from this position, circumambulates the *maṇḍala* three times, and sits down on a bundle of *kuśa* grass, facing east. The master brings to mind the *buddhas* and *bodhisattvas*, and spends one night outside of the *maṇḍala* together with his assistant.[18]

The text marks the break in narrative time by characterizing briefly the *maṇḍalācārya*, the person whose actions are being described. He is one who has fulfilled the extensive preliminary ritual (*puraścaraṇa*), he is skilled in the *mantras* of his own lineage, he is fervently devoted to the Mahāyāna as a means of aiding people in their quest for happiness.

When he awakes, the master consecrates the finely ground, well-prepared, brilliant five-colored powders and puts it in the center of the *maṇḍala*. Then he begins adorning the exterior of the *maṇḍala* with four walkways, in each portal of which there are banners and raised flags, and with hanging balls laden with fruit on pillars of bananas driven into the ground; together with his assistant he should make the area resonate with the sounds of strings, conch shells, small drums, great kettle drums.[19]

With the colored powders piled up in the center ready to be applied, and the exterior of the *maṇḍala* ceremoniously decorated to create, we may imagine, a three-dimensional likeness of the palace of the Śuddhāvāsa heaven, the master recites to the four directions from Mahāyāna books. Turning to the south, he recites from the *Bhagavatī Prajñāparāmitā;* to the west, from the *Candapradīpasamādhi*; to the north, from the *Gaṇḍavyūha*; and, finally, to the east, from the *Suvarṇaprabhāsottamasūtra*. If the master does not possess these books, he may hire a professional reciter (*dharmabhānaka*) who has studied the four texts. The master stands up, recites his *mūlamantra* over fragrant white flowers scented with a mixture of sandalwood paste, camphor, and saffron, and then disperses these throughout the *maṇḍala*. Finally, he exits from the interior of the *maṇḍala*.[20]

The next phase involves filling in the square sections of the *maṇḍala* with images formed from the colored powder. This is executed by "two or three" artists (*citrakara*). These artists are presented as being both very skilful artisans and serious Buddhist practitioners—the *bodhicitta* has arisen in them, they participate in the *upoṣadha*, and so on. The master fastens turbans on their heads, and consecrates them. The five-colored powder, white, yellow, red, black, and green,[21] is then taken up to begin the next phase of the *maṇḍala* construction. The text reminds the reader here of the potency with which he is dealing: if a pious, fortunate, wealthy person is commissioning the *maṇḍala*, his goal of enlightenment will be certainly attained. As with the *paṭa*, the mere sight of the *maṇḍala* assures this, let alone the actual practice of the *mantracaryā* which follows the initiation. Finally, both the *maṇḍala's* and the *Mmk's* origination in the compassion of the *buddhas* is evoked: "the resplendent Mañjuśrī, beholding the poverty of beings, proclaims the abbreviated prescriptions, the summary of the *maṇḍala*."[22]

The drawing of the figures with powder is preceded by a ceremonious offering of substances to various beings. Outside of the *maṇḍala*, to the southwest, the master creates a fire pit[23] and arranges small sticks of wood into the shape of a lotus flower. Lighting these sticks, he offers oblations into the pit, and invokes *mantras* directed toward specific ends, such as creating auspiciousness and dispelling obstacles. For example, the combined offerings of *bilva* wood, sweet milk, ghee and butter, the six-syllable essence *mantra*, and the corresponding sealing gesture of making his hand into a fist[24] invokes the presence of Mañjuśrī; offerings of white mustard seeds and the *mūlamantra* of Yamāntaka invokes that *krodharāja* and his retinue, who have vowed to destroy the power of demons, and so forth, for those engaged in the *mantracaryā*.[25]

The *maṇḍala* that is described from *Mmk* 2.39.10-44.28 is an example of the most elaborate option available. At the end of this lengthy description, however, is a brief section (*Mmk* 44.28–46.22) stating what must be "necessarily drawn." While there is, then, virtually no limit on the upper end of the range of artistic possibilities, on the lower end there is such a limit. In short, what must be depicted are representatives from the same categories of beings as presented in both the cosmic assembly and the *paṭas* (the Buddha Śākyamuni, *bodhisattvas*, gods, supernatural spirits, natural forces, etc.). The only differences lie in the geometric form and the materials used to organize and hierarchize the assembly. As in the other depictions of the assembly, the initiation *maṇḍala* is a reconstitution of the cosmos as it was established by the power of the Buddha's ray of light. As we saw in chapter 2, that ray of light itself served as the means to reconstitute the world into its most enlightened aspect, that is, where all natural and supernatural forces are redirected through the coercion of the Buddha's compassionate power.

The initiation *maṇḍala* thus represents a further instance of what Kapstein calls "world-building, in its physical, symbolic, and conceptual dimensions."[26] The physical *maṇḍala* discloses the otherwise imperceptible world arrayed in support of the *mantracaryā*. Through this symbolic means, it condenses and delineates the particularized world, the ritual universe, of the practitioner. Even more crucially in this regard, the *maṇḍala* serves as the support through which certain metaphysical conceptions, such as *vikurvaṇa*, *ṛddhi*, *abhijñā*, are brought to bear on the ritual life of the practitioner, ensuring the efficacy of the *mantracaryā*. This efficacy is created through a series of consecrations. It is through the act of consecration that "world-building" is achieved. We saw above that the preparation of the initiation *maṇḍala* involves the invocation of various forces into the physical form created by the master and his assistants. The language of the instructions there, however, does not convey the fervor of this act.[27] For this, we have to look at the liturgical language of the early portion of *Mmk* 2. One example will suffice to express the sense of animation and completeness involved in consecrating even the most basic elements of the ritual world.

> Having prepared the sandalwood water, consecrated seven times, he should scatter it everywhere: in all four directions, upwards, downwards, horizontally. All *buddhas* and *bodhisattvas*, the retinue of Mañjuśrī himself, all

> *mantras*, ordinary and extraordinary, all classes of creatures, and all beings must appear. Homage to all *buddhas*, whose teachings are indestructible! *Oṁ dhu dhura dhura dhūpavāsini dhūpārciṣi hūṁ tiṣṭha samayam anusmara svāhā* (*O you dwelling in the incense O luster of the incense abide remember your vow hail!*) [This is the] "incense *mantra*." Then, having prepared the saffron, camphor, and sandalwood, [the incense *mantra*] should be bestowed on the incense. All *tathāgatas* and *bodhisattvas* come, and they are drawn out of the heart of the gratified incense [T. = Rejoicing in satisfaction at the incense, the *tathāgata*, all *bodhisattvas*, and all beings dwell (therein)]. The *mudrā* of this [*mantra*] is known as "the garland," and is auspicious, attracting all beings. These *mantras* of invocation and their *mudrās* are beautiful garlands of lotuses. They should be offered to all the *buddhas, bodhisattvas,* and other beings who come. After stirring water with camphor, sandalwood and saffron, and preparing a mixture of two draughts of crushed *bakula* flowers, white lotuses grown in the rainy season and fresh garlands of jasmine with some other fragrant flower that is in season, an offering should be made along with the *mantra*. Homage to all *buddhas*, whose teachings are indestructible! The *mantra* is: *he he mahākāruṇika viśvarūpadhāriṇi arghyaṃ pratīcchad pratīcchāpaya samayam anusmara tiṣṭha tiṣṭha maṇḍalamadhye praveśaya praviśa sarvabhūtānukampaka gṛhṇa gṛhṇa hūṁ ambaravicāriṇe svāhā* (*hey hey you of great compassion, bearer of manifold forms regard this offering! receive this offering! remember your vow! abide abide in the center of the maṇḍala! lead into it enter into it! O you who possess compassion for all beings seize seize! O you who traverse the sky! hail!*) The *mudrā* for this is known as "abundance," and it is followed by all *buddhas*.[G2]

The purpose of animating the initiation *maṇḍala* with the forces of the enlightened assembly is to induct the practitioner into this world. By means of the initiation *maṇḍala*, the practitioner is installed in the "circle of the assembly." This assembly, *parṣanmaṇḍala*, is the world transfigured by the compassionate light ray of the Buddha.

4.3.2 The initiation ritual

The first step toward initiation is taken when the potential practitioner approaches the *ācārya* and makes the following supplication: "I desire to enter into, through the agency of the master, the convention of the great *bodhisattva*, the princely, noble Mañjuśrī."[28] This statement marks the two primary aspects of initiation in the *Mmk*. First, it is an entrance into a particular way of life. This way of life is expressed periphrastically here as "the convention of Mañjuśrī."[29] This phrase refers to the *mantracaryā* taught in the *Mmk*. Because the conventions of a life in which a person applies *mantra* rituals as a means of achievement are, by definition, new to the initiate, initiation can be said to generate a change in status. That is, the initiate acquires a new role and new aspects to his identity through the act of adopting the way of life demanded by the *mantracaryā*. Initiation effects a "rebirth" into the family of the Buddha. This is indicated by the father-son metaphor used to describe the relationship between the initiating master and the initiate; for example, the statement that "the appelation 'son' is to be furnished [the newly initiated practitioner] by the master."[30] As this indicates, an additional aspect of initiation is that entrance into the new way of life requires approval by an institutional authority. This approval, in turn, is based on the initiate's capacity to be molded, "by the agency of the master," into a person with specific qualities, abilities, and beliefs. The initiated practitioner is thus a strictly defined institutional type. In this section, I would like to take a closer look at the manner in which the practitioner is initially defined by the *Mmk* community; namely, by means of his participation in the initiation ritual.

There is some ambiguity concerning the stages of participation in this ritual. As Ariane MacDonald says, "[t]he MMK initially mentions five consecrations (*abhiṣeka*), but the details of those are not very clear."[31] She therefore turns to the fifteenth-century Gelukpa scholar, Mkhas grub rje (1385–1438)[32] for clarification. MacDonald herself notes that Mkhas grub rje's interpretation may be plausible in part, but only begins to correspond to the *Mmk* at the final two *abhiṣekas* (67). Mkhas grub rje was, of course, writing a sectarian textbook in which the divergent rituals of many "*kriyātantras*" were absorbed into a single system. Read in light of this fifteenth-century interpretation, the *Mmk* does in fact appear to present many difficulties and inconsistencies. When analyzed on its own terms, however, a historically and textually "plausible"—though by no means transparent—scheme emerges. Thus, what follows is in many regards an attempt at a reconstruction of the stages of the *sādhaka*, and thus of the ideal medieval Indian Buddhist practitioner known as the *sādhaka*. It is based on the description of the ritual found at *Mmk* 2.46.25–52.18. This reconstruction can be diagrammed as follows.

the sādhaka

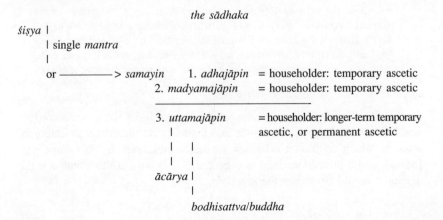

śiṣya |
| single *mantra*
|
or ————> *samayin* 1. *adhajāpin* = householder: temporary ascetic
2. *madyamajāpin* = householder: temporary ascetic
———————————
3. *uttamajāpin* = householder: longer-term temporary ascetic, or permanent ascetic
| |
| |
ācārya |
|
bodhisattva/buddha

The *Mmk* initiation ritual articulates three stages in the career of the *sādhaka*: *śiṣya*, *samayin,* and *ācārya*. Each stage is achieved by a particular consecration. The term *consecration* translates the Sanskrit word *abhiṣeka.* The literal meaning of *abhiṣeka* is simply *to sprinkle, to water*. The term developed a technical meaning as early as the Vedic period. In the archaic royal inauguration ritual, *abhiṣeka* referred specifically to the act of "dedicating" the king to the gods by sprinkling water on his head. The water used in this ritual was, of course, not ordinary water, but water that had itself been "dedicated" by invoking into it the power of the gods. Thus, through the act of *abhiṣeka,* the initiate is believed to be infused with the power of the divinities invoked.[33]

The first step in the Buddhist *abhiṣeka* ritual is thus to fill the jars (*kalaśa*) with the consecrating substance. This is done by combining water with substances, such as gold, silver, gems, rice, and grain. The jars are draped with clean mantles and adorned with fruits and the leaves of mangoes. The master reenters the *maṇḍala* and offers these jars to the forces whose presence variously protect, purify, and consecrate the space of the initiation—the *maṇḍala.* The first, for instance, is offered to Śākyamuni, the second, to all *buddhas*, the seventh, placed at the entrance gate of the outer circle, to all beings. Lighting incense and making the five-crested gesture in imitation of Mañjuśrī, the master then invokes the presence of these beings into the jars. He does this "according to the prescription mentioned previously."[34] In the liturgical section of *Mmk* 2, the invocation of Mañjuśrī is given as the basic pattern of this prescription:

> Here are the *mantras* for invocation: *Oṁ he he kumārarūpisvarūpiṇe sarvabālabhāṣitaprabodhane āyāhi bhagavaṃ āyāhi kumārakrīḍotpaladhāriṇe maṇḍalamadhye tiṣṭha tiṣṭha samayam anusmara apratihataśasana hūṁ mā vilamba ru ru phaṭ svāhā* (*O you whose own form is the form of a prince O awakening spoken by all youth approach O blessed one approach O you who bear the lotus playing as a prince abide abide in the middle of the maṇḍala! remember the vow! O indestructible teaching hūṁ! do not delay! hail!*) This is the *mantra* for invoking the blessed Mañjuśrī, and [for invoking] all beings, all *bodhisattvas*, all solitary *buddhas*, noble hearers, gods, *nāgas, yakṣas, gandarvas, garuḍas, kinnaras, mahoragas, piśācas, rākṣasas, bhūtas.*[G3]

Having thus invoked the presence of the assembly of the *parṣanmaṇḍala* made known at *Mmk* 1, the master and his assistant undertake an elaborate *pūja*, in which additional offerings are made, ablutions and oblations performed, and a protection ritual is executed.[35] It is only at this point that the disciples should be shown the *maṇḍala.*

4.3.2.1 śiṣya

The disciples are "those who have been accepted by the master." The term *śiṣya* (*student, disciple*) denotes the first stage in the career of the practitioner. We are told here, and earlier in the text, of the basic requirements for acquiring this status.[36] The disciple who wishes to be introduced to the *basic* (though not necessarily the advanced) teachings of the *Mmk* must be mentally and physically healthy, virtuous, gracious, and educated. The *śiṣya* may be a monk, nun, layman, or laywoman from any of the four basic social groups. He or she is one who "rides the great vehicle," the Mahāyāna, and has "no desire for any other vehicles." As a devout Buddhist, the *śiṣya* must observe the *upoṣadha,*[37] abstain periodically from all sensual gratifications, make three ablutions daily, observe periodical silence, and have resolved to develop the compassionate mind of the *bodhisattva*. And, finally, like the Buddha himself throughout countless ages, such a practitioner must have proven to the master that he or she is capable of persevering in the practice, expressed as "approaching the seat of enlightenment."

A person who has fulfilled these requirements, according to the judgment of the master, may receive the consecration that permits him or her to a limited practice, namely, the recitation of a single *mantra*[38] sanctioned by the *Mmk* community. This consecration, called the "incantation consecration" (*vidyābhiṣeka*),[39] is effected by sprinkling water from the jar that had been offered to all beings.[40] With this act a person is transformed into one who has entered into "the secret circle of liberation."[41] That is, the *vidyābhiṣeka* constitutes the first stage in the practice of the *mantracaryā.*

There are illuminating parallels between the *Mmk* initiates and those of certain Vaiṣṇava and Śaiva systems of initiation. Although the descriptions and terminology correspond in only one instance, *ācārya*, a look at the Vaiṣṇava and Śaiva terms serves not only to provide some rationale for the reconstructions that I am proposing (in particular those of *samayin* and *samayābhiṣeka*), but also to give the vaguely documented *Mmk* practitioner more definition at each stage. These descriptions make apparent the parallel between the Pañcarātrin and Śaiva Siddhāntin *samayadīkṣās* and the *vidyābhiṣeka* of the *Mmk*. In all three traditions, the consecration marks the initial entrance of the practitioner into the fold of the community, permitting him to serve the master and community, and to engage in the practice of the cult to a limited degree.

Both the Pañcarātra *saṃhitās* and the Śaiva Siddhāntin *āgamas* articulate four general stages in the career of the practitioner and corresponding degrees of initiation (called *dīkṣā* in these traditions):

samayin = *samayadīkṣā*

putraka = *viśeṣadīkṣā*

sādhaka = *nirvāṇadīkṣā*

ācārya = *ācāryābhiṣekā*[42]

In the Pañcarātrin tradition, the *samayin* is the practitioner who has received permission to "draw the *maṇḍala* and worship God and His retinue;" he is "one who honors his *guru*, attends to *yoga*, wears marks of Viṣṇu, [and] keeps holy days," for the first year of the three-year-long initiation period. The *samayin* is, furthermore, "one who has undergone the *japa*-type of *dīkṣā*."[43] In the Śaiva Siddhāntin system, too, the *samayadīkṣā* creates a first-stage practitioner. He is described in that tradition as follows.

> [H]e follows the codes of conduct of a common member (*samayin*) of the Śaiva community: watching after Śiva's garden, sweeping Śiva's house, gathering flowers and other articles suitable for worshiping Śiva, honoring Śiva's devotees [etc.].[44]

The initial stage of practice of the *Mmk śiṣya* also primarily involves service to the master.

> [The master's] hallowed speech is to be
> diligently effected by his disciples *(śiṣya).*
> Possessions are to be given him
> in accordance with his needs.
>
> . . .
>
> Just as the disciple, knowing the *dharma*,
> gives a gift to the master
> glory is achieved
> as is health and long life.
>
> The disciple who honors that teacher (*guru*)
> obtains an excellent destiny.
> His *mantras* are successful
> because he has been thoroughly shown
> the path of the ordinances.
>
> Because of his devotion
> because of his veneration
> because of his respect, too,
> all *buddhas*, indeed,
> those most excellent
> self-produced victors,
> are pleased.

. . .

His eyes obedient and affectionate
the masters, on account of whom
there is instruction,
should make him a disciple
of those who possess glorious bodies.

Where there is mutual respect,
esteem, and continuous affection,
there the *mantra* should be given
by the one who maintains
constant love.

When the master beholds the disciple
or the disciple beholds the teacher
they become attached; both are conjointly
and continuously at ease.[G4]

Because the master diligently protects his son, the child of *dharma*, in this manner, they both acquire contentment and prosperity.[45]

The Śaiva texts record that the practitioner "should stay with the preceptor for at least one year, time enough for the guru to examine carefully the condition of the prospective initiate."[46] This period of observation enables the master to ascertain whether the novice is ready to receive the second, "special initiation" (*viśeṣadīkṣā*), enabling him to practice on his own, perform the oblation, and study texts.[47] Similarly, a *śiṣya* who develops the desire to pursue the practice further may, at some point during this period of service and training, request the master to initiate him further into the cult. If, on close examination, the *śiṣya* is considered worthy, the master gradually grants him the series of initiations that take the practitioner increasingly deeper into the practice.

4.3.2.2 samayin

If the period of service results in a deepened desire to pursue the ritual course of the *Mmk*, the *śiṣya* may be empowered to practice additional rituals. The second *abhiṣeka* described in the text marks this stage in the practitioner's career. The *Mmk's* succinct description reads as follows:

> [Concerning] the consecration in the second *maṇḍala* (i.e., circle): that consecration should be [effected] with the full jar, in the second circle, that was previously offered to all the gods. [The water is sprinkled] just as before on [the initiate's] head, in accordance with the prescriptions. He is [thereby] freed from all fault. He becomes one who is authorized and empowered by all *buddhas* [to perform] all the practices: *mantras*, *mudrās*, the

> *maṇḍala,* and the vow-period towards both ordinary and extraordinary [ends]. He may be given the "master consecration" by all *bodhisattvas.*[G5]

Although the text mentions the *ācāryābhiṣeka* in this passage, I think that this should be understood as referring to the consecration that follows. That is, the subject being consecrated here *may* advance to the level of *ācārya*, or master. This advancement is possible because of the empowerment to engage in advanced practices that is being granted here. Elsewhere, the text refers to the "vow period" and to "the one who has observed the vow." This practitioner is "one who has fulfilled the preliminary practices," that is, who has undergone the period of asceticism (*vratin*) during which he is "engaged always in recitation [of the *mantra*]."[48] All of these synonymous terms define the subject of the above *abhiṣeka*. Since this person is essentially one who may take the vows (*samaya*) which permit him to pursue an intensified practice for a certain length of time (*kālasamaya*), the general term of *samayin* may be applied to him. Similarly, although the consecration which initiates this stage of practice is not identified by name, we may refer to it as the *samayābhiṣeka*.

The second and third stages (*putraka* and *sādhaka*) of the Pañcarātrin and Śaiva Siddhāntin initiation traditions correspond most closely to the *Mmk* practitioner whom I am calling *samayin*. The Pañcarātrin texts define the *putraka* as "one who worships God in the *maṇḍala* with his retinue and can demonstrate this and do his worship unaided."[49] As Richard Davis explains, the practitioner in the Śaiva Siddhāntin system becomes a *putraka* by virtue of his having revealed to the master whom he has been serving an ability and desire to advance in the practice of the cult. Davis cites the *Śaivaparibhāṣā*:[50]

> As he follows his common duties in this way [assisting at the temple, etc.] . . . an ardent desire to worship Śiva, study the *āgamas*, and so on, arises in him. When the preceptor recognizes the ripening indicated by such an ardent desire, he should immediately confer on him *viśeṣadīkṣa*, which enables the pupil to study the *āgamas*, worship Śiva, and so on.

The *Mmk* echoes both the language and sequence of these Vaiṣṇava and Śaiva traditions.

> First, one must take upon oneself intentness towards knowledge, the vow, and moral conduct. First of all, one must obey the precepts and instructions of the master.[G6]
>
> The *sādhaka* . . . should make a request to the *maṇḍala* master [i.e., *guru*] in this manner: "I desire to enter into, through the agency of the master, the vow (*samaya*) of the great *bodhisattva*, the princely, noble Mañjuśrī." This having been said, [he says, "may] the master [become] compassionate, his mind impelled by sympathy for us!" Then, having been carefully examined

> by the *maṇḍala* master, by whom instruction, in accordance with the ordinance, was previously given, as previously described [at *Mmk* 2] the student is introduced [to the practice]. Having conferred the initiation, as previously mentioned [at *Mmk* 2], [the *guru*] should bestow the *mantra*. Duly, by degrees, he should reveal the vow. And, having considered very carefully that the time has arrived, and knowing the mental disposition [of the *sādhaka*] he should reveal the esoteric *mudrās* from the text (*tantra*) as well as the subsequent rituals . . .
>
> Then, the *maṇḍala* master has to bring about the notion "son" (*putraka*). He [the *sādhaka*] should behave like a son, who says "the benefits (*bhoga*) are to be offered to my mother."[G7]

This passage is immediately followed by a brief description of the *samayin* phase of practice: the period during which the practitioner lives under the strict vows (*samaya, vrata*) of a mendicant ascetic in order to develop the power to effect the *mantra* toward specific ends. This corresponds to the *sādhaka/nirvāṇadikṣā* in the Pañcarātrin and Śaiva Siddhāntin traditions. The Pañcarātrin work *Jayākhyasaṃhitā* defines the *sādhaka* as "one who is a recluse, and devotes himself full-time to the worship of Viṣṇu by performing *japa* to his *maṇḍala*-presence."[51] Brunner refers to the Śaiva tradition of the *sādhakavrata*, the "observance of the *sādhaka*" and defines this as "the period of intense effort which precedes the 'realization' of the *mantra* [and which] is marked, in effect, by rigorous discipline—the *vrata* [vow]."[52] The *Mmk* describes this period as follows.

> Taking any among the many *mantras*, the *sādhaka* goes to a lonely place, remaining as previously instructed. Repeatedly, with these *mantras,* he is to make invocations summoning and dismissing deities, and offerings of lamps, fragrances, incense and rice according to the extensive rules spoken in the [initiation] *maṇḍala*. Offering the oblation every half month, he who wears the triple cloths and performs the ablution three times a day should recite the *mantra* there everyday.[G8]

As with the earlier initiation, there appears to be some overlap between the *Mmk samayin* and the *putraka* and *sādhaka* of the Pañcarātrin and Śaiva Siddhāntin traditions. Brunner (414) argues that the older strata of Śaiva Siddhāntin texts indicate that the *nirvāṇadīkṣā* applied to the *putraka* while the *sādhaka* received a consecration known as *sādhakābhiṣeka*. The distinction, later lost in the tradition, she holds, was significant.

> The *nirvāṇadīkṣā,* or liberating initiation, is that which purifies the disciple from all of his defilements; it is destined for him who seeks his own liberation, i.e., the *mumukṣu*. The *sādhaka*, on the other hand, is defined as the one who pursues . . . superior pleasures (he is called *bubhukṣu*).

Richard Davis (46) comments on this distinction further.

> According to the *āgamas*, humans have two basic goals: worldly enjoyment (*bhoga*) and liberation (*mokṣa*). The texts go on to divide members of the Śaiva religious community into two broad categories, according to the goal each hopes to achieve in this lifetime through observance of rituals and proper conduct. The householder (*gṛhastha*) pursues various worldly benefits, such as wealth, offspring, and good crops, and so is described as *bubhukṣu*. Although the householder may also desire liberation, this goal, for him, is remote and secondary. The ascetic or renouncer has repudiated what the householder desires and instead strives to achieve liberation as soon as possible. He is therefore called *mumukṣu*.

The *samayābhiṣeka* described in the *Mmk*, like the *nirvāṇadikṣa* discussed by Brunner, frees the practitioner from "all faults." The practitioner who undergoes this consecration may, like the *putraka* and the *sādhaka* respectively, apply the *mantracaryā* to either worldly benefits or liberation. As we saw at section 1.3.3 on the "index," the *Mmk* makes the *bubhukṣu/mumukṣu* distinction with the terms *laukika* and *lokottara* (ordinary and extraordinary ends); it, too, allows for a full range of applications for its ritual practices. The passage concerning the *samayābhiṣeka* mentions both *laukika* and *lokottara*. The symbolism of the text, too, suggests a wide range of options at the *samayin* stage: the initiate receives the consecration from the jar that was previously offered to all the gods. In relation to the *paṭa*, the phrase "the gods" corresponds to the minor results of the small *paṭa* only (worldly joy, fortunate rebirth, etc.): "the small *paṭa* is for achieving the worldly pleasures (*bhoga*) experienced by the *devas* and *asuras;* that is called 'minor success.'"[53] For many practitioners then, it will be the case that *laukika* ends are the primary intent of the practitioner at this stage, and that *lokottara* is mentioned as an option, like the *ācāryābhiṣeka*, for more ambitious practitioners.

There is a further distinction made in the *Mmk* that indicates the *potentiality* of the *samayābhiṣeka* in the *Mmk*. *Mmk* 27 states that three levels of rituals are taught: superior, intermediate, and lower. The superior level is taken up by the ascetic (*tapasvin*), the second, by the intermediate practitioner (*madhyajāpin*), and the third, by the inferior practitioner (*svalpajāpin*). Any practitioner who takes the *samayābhiṣeka* is empowered to apply the cult of the *Mmk* to his life. He may recite *mantras*, perform oblations, commission the making of a *paṭa*, and so on, toward a broad range of ends. A superior or intermediate practitioner may choose to pursue the practice further. He may wish to extend the period of mendicancy indefinitely in order to effect the *mantra* toward the results ensuing from the *uttamasādhana*. The *samayābhṣeka* allows the practitioner to pursue the *mantracaryā* at any of these levels.

The abundance of terms describing the practitioner during the mendicant phase of his practice shows clearly that the period of renunciation is central to the Buddhist practice of the *Mmk*. Whether the practitioner is in pursuit of worldly gain or ultimate liberation from *saṃsāra*, he must undertake to "effect" the *mantra* (*mantrasiddhi*). Once he has done so, he may engage in rituals appropriate to the extent of his effectuation (*sādhana*). The purpose of this undertaking is thus to acquire power to effect desired ends by means of the *mantracaryā*.

As we saw above, the eighth century Pañcarātrin text *Jayākhyasaṃhitā* describes the *sādhaka* as "one who is a recluse, and devotes himself full-time to the worship of Viṣṇu by performing *japa* to his *maṇḍala* presence."[54] The *Mmk sādhaka* is similarly described as follows: "He is intent on *mantra* recitation, engaged always in practice; because of his discipline of renunciation he is a knower of *mantra*."[55]

During this phase of practice, the *sādhaka* of the *Mmk* is neither a monk nor a layman. He is a renunciate ascetic. His sole occupation is to practice the rituals prescribed in the text. At times, he builds a hut and remains stationary for several days. Otherwise, he practices mendicancy. In following this course, the *sādhaka* is imitating the Buddha. Śākyamuni is presented in the text as "abiding in complete renunciation (*sanyāsa*)."[56] The term *sanyāsa* evokes the ancient model of asceticism that the Buddha, and the *sādhaka*, engaged in. The innovations to this practice recorded in the *Mmk*, are to fuse the model of the *sanyāsin* with those of the *bodhisattva* ("he rejoices in the welfare of all beings"), and the *jāpin* ("he is a knower of *mantra*").

The primary terms that explicitly identify the *sādhaka* as an ascetic are *munīndra,* and *maunin*.[57] Because one of the traditional vows taken by the ascetic is the vow of silence, or of speaking only at appointed times, he is referred to as a "silent one," *maunin*.[58] The *Munisutta* of the *Suttanipāta* defines a *muni* as "one who wanders alone," "one who is accustomed to living in distant places," one who appreciates "homelessness and detachment."[59] The classic textbook of Brahmanical asceticism, the *Yatidharmasamuccaya*, states that "a sage (*muni*) should live alone without fire or house and enter a village to obtain food. He should remain disinterested, not acquisitive, and mentally composed," that is, devoted to meditation.[60] The *muni's* life is thus characterized by wandering, begging, strict diet, and devotion to prescribed rituals or meditative practices.

Like the strict mendicant tradition reflected in the *Yatidharmasamuccaya*, however, the *Mmk* allows for stationary living at certain times.[61] In the *Mmk*, for instance, the periods of both intense *mantra* recitation that precede specific rituals, and the actual performance of those rituals call for temporary residency. At *Mmk* 10, we read, for instance:

> He should dwell for a short time
> according to the *mantra* instructions.
> Then, at other times, he should go—
> [such as] when the moon is in eclipse
> [i.e., at an inauspicious time when no rituals may be performed].
>
> When the proper time has arrived
> he should remain there for a short time, not otherwise.
> And then, at other times,
> he who is capable—the knower of *mantras*—
> should proceed hastily.[G9]

At *Mmk* 11, the ascetic (called both *muni* and *vratin*) builds a hut in a pure place and remains to practice a specific ritual with the *paṭa*.[62] The allowance to remain stationary is made most explicit in the formulaic passages that precede the descriptions of the rituals.

> Having gone to a great forest, he who eats leaves and roots, who subsists on fruits and water, should recite [the *mantra*] three million times. He becomes one who has completed the preliminary practice. Then, [he climbs to the top of a mountain, sets up the large *paṭa*, and proceeds with the ritual, etc.][G10]

In this manner, the *Mmk* practice of *puraścaraṇa* combines the mendicant tradition with that of forest reclusion. The *Yatidharmasamuccaya* defines the forest hermit in the following manner.

> [He is an ascetic who lives in the forest] eating roots and fruits, and practicing austerities. He should bathe at dawn, noon, and dusk . . . and subsist on wild produce. He may also subsist on almsfood, but he should never enter a village.[63]

The *puraścarin* is likewise "one who performs the three ablutions (*trisnāyin*), who wears the three garments (*tricelaparivartin*), who observes the vow of silence (*maunin*), the *sādhaka* who lives on begged alms or subsists on fruit, milk, and grains."[64] The purpose of this ascetic life is to create the purity and discipline of both body and mind necessary to effect the *mantra*. For this reason, the place of practice is of utmost importance. The *Mmk* does not limit that place to a forest. Rather as elsewhere, it provides a range of possibilities. After mentioning some hundred ideal places, the text, at *Mmk* 10, states that if none of those mentioned is possible, the preliminary rituals may simply be performed "in a pure place somewhere."[65] The place must, however, always be isolated.[66] Often this is expressed formulaically as "a lonely place . . . a place of great desolation—isolated, deserted by men, devoid of calamity and fear—[on] the peak of a mountain."[67]

Mmk 10, however, includes a long section on the places that may be inhabited by the *sādhaka* engaged in the *puraścaraṇa*. This section is of interest for several reasons. It provides a vivid image of the practitioner as "one who wanders about as he pleases";[68] and it marks the extent of his geographical range. The boundary of the *sādhaka* extends from the tip of southern India to China, Tibet, Kashmir, Khotan, Nepal, and to the oceans on the east and west. It includes river banks, hills and mountains, cemeteries, *caityas*, forests, and fields. It does not include monasteries or family houses. This section thus presents the *siddhikṣetra* of the *Mmk*: it evokes an image of the idealized "field of realization" being claimed by the *Mmk* community. A practitioner who wishes to use the *mantracaryā* successfully will have to inhabit, for some time, the "meritorious lands" (*puṇyadeśa*)[69] of this field. In this regard, the *siddhikṣetra* parallels both the cosmic *maṇḍala* and the initiation *maṇḍala*. All are spaces reconfigured as the purified sphere of the Buddha's active power—the "field of the Buddha" (*buddhakṣetra*). The *sādhaka* receives the *samayābhiṣeka*, which is "like the royal consecration ritual,"[70] and is thus empowered to wander as freely as a *cakravartin* who has as his retinue the enlightened forces revealed at *Mmk* 1.

The following excerpts from this geographical section of the *Mmk* should give some indication of the sweeping "field of success" delineated in the text.

> At the great ocean,
> in hills abounding in blossoming trees —
> in these places, the Conqueror has said,
> the *mantras* succeed.
>
> In a desolate place, clean, secluded,
> removed from the ways of village life,
> in an impenetrable hill,
> all the royal *mantras* succeed . . .
>
> On the banks of the delightful Bhāgirathī
> or the splendid Yamuna,
> in the bosom of the Narmadā and the Sindhu,
> on the pure banks of the Candrabhāgā;
>
> the rivers Kāverī, Sarasvatī, Sitā (Ganges) —
> these have been called fields of accomplishment
> by the sons of *buddhas*.
>
> The *buddhas* have proclaimed
> the fields and mountains of the north,

Kaśmīra, the region of Tibet (*cīna*),
Nepāla and Kāviśa.

China (*mahācīna*), too, [and Khotan: S. *siddhi*?; T. 149b.3. *li yul*= Khotan]
as absolute fields of accomplishment —
one should practice in the northern region
with its mountains and rivers . . .

On the great mountain, Śrīparvata,
in what is called the southern region,
at glorious Dhānyakaṭaka, at the *caitya*,
on the ground which holds the relic (*dhātu*)
of the Conqueror.

There, *mantras*, in rituals for every purpose,
achieve success quickly.
At Gayā (*vajrāsana*), at the great *caitya*,
the splendid [place]
where the wheel of the teaching [was turned]

the greatest of the sages attained peace;
there, too, perfection manifests.
At Devāvatāra—at the great *caitya* in Sāṅkāśya —
the place of extraordinary occurrences.

In the great city called Kapila,
in the best grove, the eminent Lumbinī,
the royal *mantras* succeed in that place,
praised and extolled by the Conqueror . . .

In these and in other areas —
regions, villages, countries, districts,
cities, capitals,
near the best auspicious rivers;

there, he becomes one
who rejoices in *homa* and *jāpa*,
and who subsists on alms,
settling always
in open spaces and empty dwellings.[G11]

The *sādhaka* may wander at will seeking a place conducive to practice. Eventually, however, he settles in an open space or empty dwelling and lives as "one who subsists on alms and rejoices in performing the oblation and *mantra* recitation." A section of *Mmk* 11 describes this aspect of the *sādhaka's* life.[71] In doing so, it presents a close up view of what was described in the geographical section of *Mmk* 10, just excerpted. Once he has settled in one of the appropriate areas described there, the *sādhaka* commences a life of concentrated ritual activity.

The section of *Mmk* 11 referred to above is reminiscent of chapter six of the *Yatidharmasamuccaya*. This chapter is called *ahorātrakriyā*, "daily practices," in that Brahmanical textbook of mendicancy.[72] The *Mmk* chapter is more cumbersomely titled "the chapter on succeeding in the practice of all rituals by means of performing ablutions, visualization-meditation, and the fire oblation, of observing the vow to recite the *mantra*, of engaging in the training phase of mendicancy—the expedient to success in the rituals."[73] Nonetheless, it is apparent from both the content and style of the section referred to that the *Mmk* is describing the daily duties of a nonmonastic, nonlay renunciant (whether temporarily or permanently so). This similarity further indicates the close connection between the *Mmk sādhaka* and the Brahmanical and early Buddhist mendicant traditions, and underscores the continuation, or perhaps revival, of this tradition in the medieval period.

The *Yatidharmasamuccaya* outlines the renunciant's morning duties as follows.[74]

> Rising in the morning, he should purify himself according to the rules. Then, after he has sipped some water, he should diligently use a toothstick to clean his teeth, except on days of the lunar phases.
>
> After bathing, he should pray silently until the sun comes into view. The *mantra* prescribed at the sunrise begins "Rise up, O Brahmaṇaspati!"

The *Mmk* describes the same activities: body ablutions, practical hygiene, *mantra* recitation, and worship until dawn.

> Rising early in the morning from sleep,
> and bathing in pure water,
> in water devoid of living matter,
> which arises from the great current of a river,
> the *mantra*-knower rubs his limbs
> with ground up cow dung and earth.
>
> After having purified the water
> with the *mantra*,
> made it clean, resplendent,
> he bathes, uttering prayers,[75]
> concentrated in mind;
> he rises [after] not too long.
>
> Then, having risen, he stands on the shore,
> cleanses his hands with earth —
> seven, seven, again seven—twenty-one times.
>
> Having performed in this manner,
> he should thoroughly clean
> his teeth with a toothstick.

Discharging, the teeth cleaned,
he should praise the protector.

Having offered such praise,
he joyfully worships
the master of the world,
praising him repeatedly
with offerings of various hymns of praise.

Let him praise thus with fragrant flowers,
offering half a measure of *mantra* recitation.
Lowering his head in obeisance to the *buddhas*,
he then becomes a disciple.
He should, in their presence,
make a confession of sins.

He worships in the presence
of these masters of the world.
Offering food before the *paṭa*,
he [places it] there, in the middle [of the *paṭa*].

Making a mound of *kuśa* grass that is there,
he arranges it into a seat.
He should recite prayers intently,
using his prayer beads . . .

He uses his most beautiful voice
with all *buddhas* attendant.
Never does he recite in the presence of another
who practices another ritual.
In secret, in a place known to himself alone,
he should recite the *mantra* in a medium voice.[G12]

Using his most beautiful voice, the practitioner recites before the *buddhas*. He must be certain that no practitioner of other rituals is within the vicinity.[76] He recites in this manner until the "first dawn," when the sky turns copper-red.[77]

Both the *Mmk* and the *Yatidharmasamuccaya* prescribe that at this point the practitioner should spend the rest of the morning in reflective activities.

> (*Yatidharmasamuccaya*) He should spend the remainder of the day engaged in controlling the breath, silent prayer, meditation, and divine praise, as well as in reciting epic and *purāṇic* texts that have *vedic* sanction.[78]

(*Mmk*) The remainder of the time [after *mantra* recitation]
is spent engaged in the *sasana*
of the silent one,
in the words of the good law,
such as the *Prajñāpāramita*.

Books enumerating the ten stages [of the *bodhisattva*]
[T. singular, and clearly: or the book known as the *Daśabhūmika*.]
are to be worshipped and recited always.[79]
When the time comes, the eminent conquerors
are to be paid obeisance.[G13]

After this early morning practice, the *sādhaka* goes into a village or town to beg for alms. As the *Yatidharmasamuccaya* states: "[t]hen, to sustain his life, he should always go on his begging round."[80] The practitioner must seek out "righteous" households, preferably, of course, Buddhist ones. For example, he seeks out a home "whose mistress holds correct views, and who is kindly disposed towards the teachings of the Buddha."[81]

This, and the following sections, in both the *Mmk* and the *Yatidharmasamuccaya*, on eating and after-meal rituals are largely unremarkable additional examples of the close connection between the two traditions. What is remarkable about the *Mmk* section on begging, however, is its harsh portrayal of women. The rhetoric here is one of battle and danger. We may understand this tone as reflecting the fact that the *puraścarin* may be a practitioner of slight, worldly ambition, a householder who has only temporarily taken on the vows of a mendicant ascetic. The *Yatidharmasamuccaya*, by contrast, is written with the advanced practitioner exclusively in mind, and thus had less need to warn about the dangers of being thrown off course by sexual desire.

The *Mmk* alms beggar should commence as a well-armed soldier going into a dangerous battle, because, as the *buddhas* have declared, "all women are the root of suffering."[82] Men roam about completely incompetent, deceived by women. Because they immerse themselves in women, men sink into the deep mire, the prison of the ocean of *saṃsāra*. Thus, the foolish man who becomes attached to women never finds success.

The practitioner who is consecrated during the *samayābhiṣeka* goes into battle in order to perfect the power of his *mantra*. The task that he undertakes is presented as arduous and dangerous because it takes him far afield from his usual course of living. The purpose of this undertaking is to develop the traits necessary for success in the practice of the *mantracaryā*. As we have seen throughout this section, this success is dependent on the practitioner's ability to reconstitute himself physically, mentally, and verbally as the *sādhaka* presented in the text. To succeed, he must develop restraint, concentration, and expertise. This is accomplished through service to the master, and, during the *puraścaraṇa*, through constant engagement with the teachings of, and ritual course prescribed by, all *buddhas*. Space, too, is central to the development of the practitioner. From his training, he knows that the universe in which he moves is permeated by the power and compassion of the Buddha's assembly. He knows, too, that his entrance into the initiation *maṇḍala* established him as a consecrated member of this assembly, much as the light of the Buddha transfigured the beings of the cosmic *maṇḍala*. Through his engagement with the ancient code of mendicancy, the practitioner dwells in the worldly spaces in which the Buddha had dwelt, and, it is believed, still dwells—Gayā, Lumbinī, *caityas*, desolate fields and forests—repeating the course of ritual action that led to the Buddha's enlightenment. Finally, the *paṭa* which the *sādhaka* carries with him condenses the power of all of these worlds into the space of the cult object. As presented in the passage on the *uttamasādhana*, its use in the ritual field brings the journey of the *sādhaka* to completion. Once he has fulfilled the course prescribed for the first two levels of initiation, his worship to the *paṭa* is shown, *in the text*, to result in a return to the space of the cult's origination. In this moment, all of the seemingly separate spheres of the Buddha's field of activity—the cosmic *maṇḍala*, the various *siddhikṣetra*, the initiation *maṇḍala*, the place of temporary habitation, the *paṭa*, the *mantra*, and the text itself—coalesce in the mind of the practitioner. Bearing all of this in mind will yield a fruitful rereading of the *uttamasādhana* presentation.

> First, he who has observed the vow, fulfilled the preliminary practices, received the initiation, taken the essential, basic *mantra* from this best of ordinances, or the *upahṛdaya* or some other *mantra*, or having received a single syllable [*mantra*] or another one—according to one's wishes—and who, having gone to a great forest, eats leaves and roots, who subsists on fruits and water, should recite [the *mantra*] three million times. He becomes one who has completed the preliminary practice. Then, having climbed to the top of a mountain and set up the superior cult image facing to the west, he faces east himself, seated on a mound of *kuśa* grass. He should offer one lac of white lotuses and oiled white saffron at the base of the *paṭa* to the blessed Śākyamuni and to all the noble disciples, solitary *buddhas*, *bodhisattvas*, and *buddhas*. And he should burn as much camphor and incense as he can afford. He should worship the *nāgas* and gods with as many lotuses as he can procure. Then, at midnight, during the equinox, when the moon is bright and extraordinarily full, after having created an area for the fire at the base of the *paṭa*, and having lit the lotus-shaped fire with sticks of white sandalwood, combining saffron and camphor he should then make one thousand and eight oblations—creating as much protection as possible. Thereupon, rays of light proceed from the blessed Śākyamuni, and the entire *paṭa* blazes forth as a single shining [object]. Then, when the *sādhaka* has made three quick circumambulations around the *paṭa*, and has paid homage to all *buddhas, bodhisattvas*, solitary *buddhas* and noble disciples, the *paṭa* is to be taken hold of. Just as he grasps the edge of the previously drawn *paṭa*, the *sādhaka* flies up. He proceeds instantly to the Brahmaloka. He stays in the world-realm Kusumāvātī, where the *tathāgata* Saṅkusumitarājendra dwells, exists, abides and teaches the *dharma*. He beholds Mañjuśrī directly. He hears the true teaching. He also sees several thousand *bodhisattvas*, and worships them. He becomes one who playfully enjoys non-aging and im-

> mortality for a thousand great eons. The *paṭa* is also there. He is empowered by all *buddhas* and *bodhisattvas*, and he declares to them his firm resolution [to attain enlightenment] and proceeds to their hundred thousand paradises. [Their] hundred thousand bodies are revealed to him. He becomes possessed of numerous powers and supernatural abilities. The noble Mañjuśrī becomes his virtuous friend. He becomes one for whom the goal of enlightenment is certain.[C2]

What happens here is possible only for the most advanced practitioner. This passage thus presents the highest point and culmination of the *mantracaryā*. The practitioner depicted is an image of the ideal *sādhaka*, one who has becomes an adept and master in his own right. But in order to be empowered with the capacity to serve the community as a master, the practitioner must receive a further consecration, the *ācāryābhiṣeka*.

4.3.2.3 ācārya

The *ācāryābhiṣeka*, "master consecration," consists of three aspersions. Here, too, the text is succinct and direct.

> In the third [circle/square of the initiation] *maṇḍala* [the practitioner] is sprinkled on the head [with water] from the full jar that had previously been offered to the *śrāvakas* and *pratyekabuddhas*, according to the prescriptions. [The initiating master] says: "You are authorized by all *buddhas* and *bodhisattvas* possessing great supernatural powers to teach and draw the *maṇḍala*, recite the *mantras* and texts of ordinary and extraordinary *mantras*, to teach the rituals [employing] hand gestures; [thus] you yourself both practicing and teaching. In this birth and in successive [births; T. for this and the following eight lives], up to the final one, the attainment of buddhahood is certain." . . . [Then] with [water from] the full jars previously offered to the blessed Buddha and the *bodhisattvas*, [the practitioner] should be sprinkled. It is then said [by the master]: "you are authorized by all blessed *buddhas*, great *bodhisattvas*, and *śrāvakas*. Unassailable by all demons, invincible to all humans, may you conquer all *mantras*, and realize all that you desire!"[G14]

The master is presented as the practitioner who has fulfilled the ritual course prescribed in the *Mmk*, and who, as an exemplar of the community, may therefore teach and initiate others into the *mantracaryā*. This function is suggested by the term for master used in the *Mmk*: *ācārya*. The semantic range of the verbal root from which the term is derived, *ā* √*car*, covers three basic meanings: (1) *to come near to, to address*, (2) *to proceed, to behave one's self*, and (3) *to practice, to perform*. The *ācārya* is the person whom a student approaches to learn the rules (*ācāra*) of a particular discipline because he himself has practiced those rules in an exemplary fashion. When the *sādhaka* has successfully completed the training described in the previous two sections, he may wish to receive the consecration empowering him to employ his powers in service to the others.

In the *Mmk* the *ācārya* is described both explicitly and implicitly. At *Mmk* 11 we read of his general attributes as preceptor and community leader.[83] These are ascribed specifically to the *ācārya*. The description here is largely formulaic. Drawing from traditional descriptions of the *ācārya*, it is virtually indistinguishable from those found in the Vaiṣṇava and Śaiva manuals.[84] Perhaps the text presents the *ācārya* in such broad terms in order to make him clearly recognizable to the Indian religious culture at large.

> He who proclaims your [= Mañjuśrī's] royal ordinance is clear, wise, has received the initiation of a master, is experienced in the Buddha's teaching, is good, unambiguous, righteous, a speaker of truth, possesses great power, is knowledgeable of what is correct, firm in friendship, is not too old, not too young, free from desire; he is among those who are favorable towards all kinds of benefit, is celibate, compassionate, without the slightest confusion, and does not speak falsely of the reason for discipline, or of the reason for enjoyment. He who speaks without even the slightest degree of confusion or perplexity, is firm in his promise, takes pity on all beings equally, possesses the virtue of generosity, has completed the preparatory rites, repeatedly recites your secret *mantra*, has acquired knowledge of the preliminary practice, has been systematically initiated into your *maṇḍala*, is knowledgeable of the world, is learned in the rituals; he is very gracious, is industrious, discerning, he is occupied with what is most superior, is fearless, unfrightened, unvacillating, firm in vigor, healthy; where there is sickness and lack of effort towards one's duties, he is born into a great, exalted family. The master is endowed with these characteristics.[G15]

The *ācārya* is presented here as being dignified in his speech, appearance, and behavior, ethically irreproachable and intellectually sovereign. His knowledge encompasses secular matters, the Buddhist teachings, and, in particular, the *mantracaryā* taught in the *Mmk*. The master is tolerant of the wide range of motivations that his students might legitimately possess, but he himself is firmly fixed on the highest goal of the practice. Toward this end he is assiduously engaged in the practice. From the terms *brahmacarin*, *celibate,* and *ekākīcarasaṅgakṛt*,[85] "solitary, having a fondness for wandering," it appears that the ideal *ācārya* is a mendicant ascetic. But the text is not clear about whether or not this is the case exclusively. Another term that is suggestive but inconclusive is *mahoccakulaprabhūta*, "born from a great family." Elsewhere at *Mmk* 11, we read that the *ācārya* is from a "high-born and eminent family" (*mahākuloccaprabhūta*). This might be echoing the Śaiva Siddhāntin notion that only a high-born Brahmin may become an *ācārya*.[86] In any case, the *Mmk ācārya* must possess, by acquisition, if not by birth, every characteristic of a cultured, upper-class member of society.

The *ācārya* of the *Mmk*, however, exceeds these gentlemanly traits. For, as a realized adept of a form of practice that is, according to the *Mmk*, superior to all other forms—Buddhist and non-Buddhist—the *ācārya* represents the extreme limit of human possibility. In order to see the figure of the *ācārya* in this light, we will have to turn to implicit descriptions of him. By this I mean the terms and phrases that reveal the practitioner's transformation through ritual practice. The descriptions of the results attained during the *uttamasādhana* illuminate the practitioner who has completed the course of the *mantracaryā*, and thus, by definition, illuminate the *ācārya*. The language in these passages is transformative, referring to the changes in character, ability, and status undergone as a result of this ritual realization. We read above of the final result of the *uttamasādhana*.

> He is empowered by all *buddhas* and *bodhisattvas*, and he declares to them his firm resolution [to attain enlightenment] and proceeds to their hundred thousand paradises. [Their] hundred thousand bodies are revealed to him. He becomes possessed of numerous powers and supernatural abilities. The noble Mañjuśrī becomes his virtuous friend. He becomes one for whom the goal of enlightenment is certain.[C2]

This description of what occurs within the ritual field of the *uttamasādhana* contains the same elements of that which unfolds within the initiation *maṇḍala*. At the outset of his career, the *sādhaka* expressed to the *ācārya* his resolution to become a *buddha* when he said, "I desire to enter into the secret circle of liberation . . . may I become a *buddha*."[87] Empowered by the water that had been previously consecrated by the *ācārya*, the bodies and fields of the *buddhas* were revealed to the practitioner by means of the initiation *maṇḍala*. And he became the "son" of the *ācārya*. At the culmination of the *uttamasādhana* practice described here, the practitioner encounters the *buddhas* and *bodhisattvas* directly, expresses his resolution to them, and is consecrated by them. The final three statements mark the culminating results of the *Mmk* ritual practice: he becomes possessed of supernatural powers; Mañjuśrī becomes his virtuous friend; and he becomes bound for certain enlightenment.

These parallels reveal the essential characteristic of the *ācārya*: he serves the community as a living *bodhisattva* possessed of great power and ability. But the manner in which the *ācārya* does so is indicated in the text not by the term *bodhisattva*, but by the epithet *vidhyādhara*. Therefore, it will be necessary to look more closely at these two terms as they appear in the *Mmk*.

The use of the term *bodhisattva* in the *Mmk* reflects the early Mahāyāna figure known from the *Prajñāpāramitā* texts. This connection is made explicit when the *Mmk* states that the practitioner arrives at his status as a *bodhisattva*, in part, by "writing, thoroughly contemplating, teaching, reciting, and meditating on the perfection of wisdom."[88] We read, too, that, ideally, he dwells in isolated places.[89] The great innovation of the *Mmk* is, of course, that the classic *bodhisattva*-type has achieved his status through the practice of the *mantracaryā*, rather than strictly meditation. This applies to both the cosmic *bodhisattva* (Mañjuśrī, Avalokiteśvara, Vajrapaṇi) and the human *bodhisattva*, such as the *ācārya*. A section of *Mmk* 1 describes these various aspects of the *ācārya* as *bodhisattva*.[90] A few examples should illustrate this point.

The section contains eight sets of "qualities" (*dharma*) that the *bodhisattva*-practitioner must be endowed with if the *mantras* are to be conducive to success. Each set then gives a corresponding number of such qualities: the first set lists one quality, the second, two, and so on. Every set begins with a phrase similar to the one for the first: "the *mantras* of a *bodhisattva*, a great being, who is endowed with a single quality would be conducive to success; with which one?" The characteristics then follow. The *bodhisattva* becomes successful when he, first of all, fulfills certain classical requirements: "in regard to the investigation which causes the quieting of all phenomena," "in regard to the non-abandonment of the thought of enlightenment, and identification with all beings," "in regard to the protection of the *bodhisattva* vows of moral conduct," "in regard to possessing a mind pervaded by great compassion," "being in a state of perfection concerning great joyousness, great equanimity, great benevolence, and great compassion." These "classical" qualities, however, are merely preliminary to acquiring the status of the *bodhisattva* in the *Mmk*. That is, they enable effective use of the *mantras* at the highest level for oneself and others: "[these] qualities are conducive to the fulfillment of the goals of the *mantracaryā*."

While he was engaged in the training necessary for acquiring this ability to employ the *mantra* universally, the practitioner was called a *mantrin* and *japin*. The *ācārya*, who has realized the *mantra* (*mantrasiddhi*), is called a *vidyādhara*. As Jean Przyluski noted in an early article on the closely related term *vidyārāja* in the *Mmk*, *vidyādhara* has at least two senses in the *Mmk*. He writes that, "it sometimes signifies 'those who possess the *vidyā*, knowledge or magic,' sometimes a class of aerial genies considered to be divine enchanters."[91] As the one who has mastered the *Mmk*, the *ācārya* is a *vidyādhara* (bearer of knowledge) in the several senses of the term. He holds the knowledge contained in the text—the knowledge of both the ritual prescriptions and the cosmic structure underlying those prescriptions. As a *mantrasiddha*, he possesses a profound experiential knowledge of the *man-*

tras. This knowledge gradually creates the extraordinary powers of the *bodhisattva*, the five supernatural perceptions (*abhijñā*), for instance, which in turn open up the *dharmadhātu* to him, allowing him to perceive the *bodhisattvas* directly within the ritual field. Thus, *vidyā* is knowledge acquired intellectually (through instruction, analysis, and study) and experientially (through ritual application). Most important, it is a form of knowledge that gives the bearer both power over, and the power of, the object of that knowledge. As we saw, the "incantations" (*mantra, vidyā, dhāraṇī*) of the *Mmk* contain the essence (*hṛdaya*) of what they refer to. The mastery of the *mantracaryā* is the mastery of this "essence." This mastery is what lies at the heart of the initiating *ācārya's* ability to invoke the presence of enlightened power and consecrate the spaces and subjects of the ritual field.

Because he bears all of this knowledge, the *ācārya*, through "mere repetition [of the *mantra*] accomplishes all deeds: he terrifies all demons, attracts, subjugates, hurts, kills, or whatever is desired by the bearer of knowledge/practitioner of spells (*vidyādhara*), all of that is effected."[92] This statement reveals the complex nature of both the *ācārya* and the form of Buddhism that he represents. As the references to killing and subjugation indicate, the *ācārya* sometimes employs his power on behalf of others by performing oblations and *mantra* recitation for purely nonsoteriological reasons. "All deeds" might include attracting a wife (*Mmk* 3, for instance), curing illnesses with consecrated herbs (*Mmk* 9), and even, in later chapters of the text, reviving a corpse (*Mmk* 26) or soliciting wealth from a beautiful goddess (*Mmk* 52). It is no doubt in reference to such passages that Tucci commented that in the *Mmk* "the Buddha descends to the level of a witch-doctor, revealing *vidyā* by which any miracle, and even crime, can be performed."[93] But through the text's descriptions of the various stages of the practitioner's career, and through its description of the ultimate ritual act of the *uttamasādhana*, we can see that the *Mmk ācārya's* actions—and therefore those of his exemplar, the Buddha—were by no means a "descent." The *ācārya* was a Buddhist master who, like the Buddha himself, recognized the complex, multidimensional nature of human beings and their efforts toward happiness "in the impenetrable wilderness that is *saṃsāra*," and sought only to "act on behalf of their welfare."[94] But, as the text presents him, the *ācārya* is able to do so only because he himself embodies this complexity. As the following passage from the final *uttamasādhana* section of the *Mmk* shows, the *ācārya* perfects and embodies both ordinary and extraordinary powers, fusing together the lowly and the exalted toward a universal "abode of welfare for all beings."[95]

> First, setting up the large *paṭa* facing west, he positions himself facing east. Mixing soil taken from either the top of an anthill or the banks of the

Ganges river and the fragrant *uśīra* root, white sandalwood and saffron with camphor, etc., he should fashion the form of a peacock [out of clay]. Arranging this in front of the *paṭa*, he then forms a circle with the uncut blades of *kuśa* grass grown in a pure area. He takes hold of the front of the *paṭa* with his right hand, and with his left, the peacock. On a night when the moon is full, he offers extensive worship to the *paṭa*. Burning camphor incense, he recites [the *mantra*] until dawn. Then, at sunrise, the clay peacock becomes Mahāmayūrarājan, and the circle blazes. He himself assumes a divine body adorned with divine ornaments, clothing and garlands, a beautiful body, resplendent like the rising sun. Making salutations to all *buddhas* and *bodhisattvas*, he circumambulates the *paṭa*, takes hold of the *paṭa*, sits down in the "peacock" posture, and immediately proceeds to the Brahmaloka. He becomes the sovereign of the *vidyādharas,* possessing a retinue of countless trillions of *vidyādharas*. . . He becomes one who traverses space just like the *vidhyādhara* fairies, enters into the status of the *bodhisattva*, is in possession of the five supernatural perceptions, has achieved the stages [of the *bodhisattva* path]; and with that body proceeds through the phenomenal world for the sake of completely fulfilling the lineage of those who possesses the ten powers, for the sake of beholding Mañjuśrī directly, for the sake of hearing the *dharma* teachings on productive insight, for the sake of continuing the lineage of the Buddha, for the sake of seeking and attaining wisdom and omniscience, for the sake of entering fully into that which pours forth from the cloud of *dharma*, for the sake of soothing pain through the raining of immortal nectar onto the parched afflictions of the world.[G16]

CHAPTER 5

Summary and Conclusion

Useful is the letting-lie-before-us.
So, too, the taking-to-heart.
For not separately from the presence of what is present
can you find out the taking-to-heart.

— Parmenides

In this study of the *Mañjuśrīmūlakalpa,* I have attempted to recover and analyze a form of Buddhist practice that was present in India from the early medieval period. In this regard, this study might be considered as a contribution to our historical understanding of Indian Buddhism. I will return to some of the more concrete results of my analysis in a few pages. First, I would like to consider more specifically what it was that was "recovered" in this study. In doing so, I hope to articulate some important aspects of the *Mañjuśrīmūlakalpa.* Just as important, perhaps, I hope to trace in this process a method of reading and studying Buddhist literature.

Recover

When I began my study of the *Mañjuśrīmūlakalpa*, I viewed recovery of its contents as a task of historical reconstruction. The practice, like the ruins of an ancient city buried in the desert sand, and gloriously described in an equally ancient book, would be unearthed and reassembled. The text would be my guide. It would lead me to the world of the practice. *Recover* can mean this: salvage, rescue, restore. But I think that the authors of the *Mañjuśrīmūlakalpa* would claim that I have made a recovery of another, more significant, sort. If the text has achieved what the community of *Mmk* believers intended it to achieve, my recovery involved *observing once again* something (a specific world) in its proper, original condition. If this is true, the text, far from being the guide to this world, was inseparable from that world itself. The practice that I sought, too, was bound up in these. Practice, world, and text were identical: precisely this practice exists and is effective because the world is precisely how it is; the text, and only *this* text, contains all of the necessary knowledge about each. The city in the sand, *in its original glory*, no longer exists, and probably never existed as gloriously as it is described, apart from the book of its description. But in that moment when an inquisitive reader of the *Mañjuśrīmūlakalpa* enters into the mix, practice, world, and text are simultaneously observed once again, and a recovery occurs. The world behind the rituals, the text claims, is forever present. Our inability to perceive this fact is due to the darkness of our minds. With the proper knowledge, this world, and the practices that are woven into its structure, can be recovered. Such claims of the text notwithstanding, it is fair to ask: observed, present, perceived where—and in what sense?

In Italo Calvino's *Invisible Cities*, Marco Polo describes to Kublai Khan the wondrous city of Leonia. At the conclusion of his tale, he and the emperor reflect on the nature of the image that had just appeared before their minds.

> *Polo*: Perhaps the terraces of the garden [of the city] overlook only the lake of our mind. . .
>
> *Kublai*: . . . and however far our troubled enterprises as [scholars] may take us, we both harbor within ourselves this silent shade, this conversation of pauses, this evening that is always the same.
>
> *Polo*: Unless the opposite hypothesis is correct: that those who strive in [the city] exist only because we two think of them, here, enclosed among these bamboo hedges, motionless since time began . . .
>
> *Kublai*: To tell the truth, I never think of them.
>
> *Polo*: Then they do not exist.
>
> *Kublai*: To me this conjecture does not seem to suit our purposes. Without them we could never remain here swaying, cocooned in our hammocks.
>
> *Polo*: Then the hypothesis must be rejected. So the other hypothesis is true: they exist and we do not.
>
> *Kublai*: We have proved that if we were here, we would not be.
>
> *Polo*: And here, in fact, we are.[1]

In the *Mañjuśrīmūlakalpa*, as in the dialogue of Kublai Khan and Marco Polo, the dualistic categories that impose a sense of certainty on our views of reality are dismantled, as Stephan Beyer has put it, by "the metaphysics of the vision and the dream."[2] That is, unequivocality gives way to metaphor, and the distinctions between the mythic and the literal, as between the imagined and the real, become quite subtle. To force the reader to challenge this distinction is, I suggest, part of the *Mañjuśrīmūlakalpa's* design. The practice, the *mantracaryā* of the text, can only be discovered—in its mythic perfection—in the act of committed, imaginative reading. This is as true for the scholar as for the aspiring practitioner. For both, nothing is perceived or apprehended if not the luster of *bodhisattvas* arrayed throughout the cosmos, the reverberation of *mantras* in the ear, the promise of happiness, and of the recovery of the Buddha's power in the present moment. The *Mañjuśrīmūlakalpa* cannot be read without encountering the possibility of recovery that the text presents. The difference between the scholar and the practitioner arises, perhaps, in their reactions to this possibility. Whereas the practitioner enters more fully into the recovery of the world presented by the text, I chose to remain here analyzing, cocooned in my study.

Analysis

The aim of analysis is to separate something into parts or basic principles in order to determine the nature of the whole. Whereas the understanding of some objects of investigation, say, a poem, may ultimately suffer from severe dissection, the *Mañjuśrīmūlakalpa* is enhanced by it. This is because the text, at virtually every turn, presents some part that stands for the whole, and insists on the equivalence of the two. For instance, the entire cosmos, discussed in chapter 2 of this study, containing countless components, forces, and forms of being, is contained in the simple circle of the initiatory *maṇḍala*, or even in a single seed- or *bījamantra*. So, it would be possible to review the results of my analysis by juxtaposing the many parts that I found with the whole that is postulated. However, I would like to consider some of the results of this study, chapter by chapter, in light of four properties/strategies of the text that served, for me, as the background against which I could begin to see something of the abstract whole being ordered by the concrete parts. These four are darkness, disclosure, transformation, and totality. These are not meant as progressive terms. That is, the text does not move from one to the other—from darkness to disclosure, for example. Rather, each property appears in the text mingled with the others, in varying combinations.

By "property," I mean a quality or characteristic that the text possesses. The *Mañjuśrīmūlakalpa* has the quality of being opaque and dark. This is due, for instance, to the idiosyncratic nature of its Sanskrit vocabulary, grammar, and syntax, and to the gaps in essential information left open by its authors. This same quality, however, is part of its very design—darkness is used in the work as a rhetorical strategy. The *buddhas'* enlightened power is present in the world, yet obscured by the world's impenetrable darkness.

> I [Śākyamuni] have dwelled for a long time in the impenetrable wilderness that is *saṃsāra*.[3]

The invisibility of the *buddhas'* presence in the dense thicket of the world is a result of the moral and mental darkness of the men and women dwelling therein.

> In the future, when the teacher of the world passes away, when the sun lineage of the *tathāgata* disappears . . . when the receptacle of the world becomes darkened . . . When, devoid of good people, beings in the world are deprived of light, they will become lazy, desirous of destruction, faithless, divided, surrounded by bad friends, deceitful, deluded, of fraudulent conduct. Hearing this discourse on the teaching, these will be seized by fear. Those who delight in sloth and indolence will not have faith; those seeking pleasure, rejoicing in false doctrines, will not exert themselves.[4]
>
> . . . it is for this reason that [men and women] wander about aimlessly in the darkness of *saṃsāra*.[5]

Darkness—that is, opaqueness, invisibility, and ignorance—is intrinsic to both the world and the text. This quality is countered, however, by the property/strategy of disclosure.

> Intermixed in the realm of reality, out of compassion for beings, the lord of the world, the maker of light, remains through the form of the *mantra*, The omniscient one, possessing all forms, appears on the surface of the earth.[6]
>
> This is revealed in precisely this ordinance,
> in the extensive discourse on *mantras*.[7]

The text mirrors the world in both its obscurity and its potential for disclosing the "light" that abides before our eyes, and before our minds.

I will now discuss darkness, disclosure, transformation, and totality in relation to the individual chapters. In chapter 1 of this book, I argued that several passages at *Mmk* 1 function collectively as an "index." This index operates on several levels simultaneously. At a fundamental level, it reveals the subject matter of the text, similarly to a table of contents. Each subject covered in the *Mañjuśrīmūlakalpa* falls within one of the following categories: there are general claims; for example, the index points to the fact that the text will treat such topics as ritual, the means of attainment, *mantras*, *mudrās*, the fire oblation; preliminary topics having to do with preparatory rituals, such as the initiation ceremony, the creation of the cult object, prolonged *mantra* recitation; *ordinary attainment*, such as long life, good health, the development of virtues, and certain psychic powers; *extraordinary attain-*

ment of becoming a *bodhisattva* or *buddha*; and, finally, *universality*—the complete fulfillment of every wish of every individual in the past, present, and future, the destruction of all suffering.

Because of the manner in which this content is made known, however, the index' functions exceed those of a table of contents. As we saw, it is Śākyamuni who announces the ritual course prescribed in the text. Moreover, it is claimed that he does so situated at present in a heaven above the earth. Given this context, the index becomes a form of argument by which it is claimed that the ritual course of the text is *the* proper form of Buddhist practice. Śākyamuni is declaring "that upon which all beings depend" for long life, good health, security, fortune, happiness, and enlightenment. The Buddha's statement thus possesses both rhetorical and polemical force: the *mantracaryā* of precisely *this* text inaugurates completion and finality. It marks not only the culmination of Buddhism and of India's religious culture, but of the *universal* effort to codify, in texts called *śāstras, what should be done* in order to lead a good life that is ultimately directed toward liberation. *Śāstras* contain teachings which derive their authority from the fact that they have been received from a primordial source—from a deity, for instance, beyond space and time. Like a *śāstra*, the index of the *Mañjuśrīmūlakalpa* discloses the components of a fulfilled life and founds these on an ultimate authority, the Buddha. In this manner, the disclosure is placed within a totalizing framework.

Given the claims of ritual power in the *Mañjuśrīmūlakalpa*, the question of philosophical justification arises. So, in chapter 1 I also considered the problem of efficacy. It was argued there that the text, in characteristic fashion, *shows* the reader the structure supporting the rituals, rather than constructing an intellectualized argument. The support of the rituals is revealed cursorily in the opening statement of the text:

> Hear, O *devaputras*, about that upon which all beings depend: the inconceivable, wondrous, miraculous transformation of the *bodhisattva*.[8]

The term for " miraculous transformation," *vikurvaṇa*, alludes to the doctrinal axiom of "the ontological equivalence or ultimate convertibility of phenomena and absolute."[9] In realizing the illusory nature of the world, *buddhas* and *bodhisattvas* acquire the power to transform themselves at will, subjecting the forms of the world—all ultimately lacking substantiality—to manipulation. Whereas the doctrine of *bodhisattvavikurvaṇa* is carefully worked out in Buddhist philosophical texts, the strategy of the *Mañjuśrīmūlakalpa* is to disclose the mechanism of transformation by reflecting it. This was shown in the section of chapter 1 devoted to the *mantra*. The numerous passages presented in this section exhibited the double function of disclosure and transformation. That is, the source of power is revealed ("This is Mañjuśrī in the form of the *mantra*," "the *bodhisattva* Mañjuśrī is approached through the form of the *mantra*," etc.), in language that demonstrates that power. Through this strategy, both the language and the images that arise out of that language are intended to effect a transformation in the reader of the passage.

> Then Mañjuśrī [bestowed] the preeminently heroic, all achieving essence (*hṛdaya*) of the sovereign of wrath, Yamāntaka . . . *oṃ āḥ hūṁ*. This is the essence of he whose wrath is great; it is all accomplishing; it is taught by the great being Mañjughoṣa for use in all *maṇḍala* and *mantra* rituals; it destroys all obstacles. Then Mañjuśrī lifted his right hand and placed it on the head of Krodha, and spoke thus: "Obeisance to all *buddhas*! May the blessed *buddhas* pay heed! May the *bodhisattvas,* who are dwelling in whatever world of the ten directions, and who possess unlimited, infinite, supernatural power, be firm in their vow!" Saying that, he circled around the king of wrath, and dismissed him. The instant that the great king of wrath was dispatched to the entire world-realm, beings possessing great supernatural powers immediately restrained all evil-minded beings. He made them enter the Śuddhāvāsa, the great assembly. Making them remain there, becoming the family of those who are engulfed in flaming garlands, he stood at the head, among the evil-beings.[10]

In gaining access to the source of the *mantra's* power, and in "seeing" it demonstrated, the knowledge and, therefore, perspective, of the reader is altered.

The section on *mantras*, furthermore, offers additional evidence of the text's totalizing strategy. Although virtually every major *mantra* prescribed in the *Mañjuśrīmūlakalpa* is known from other Buddhist, Vaiṣṇava, Śaiva, and Śākta literature, these *mantras* are appropriated, synthesized, and individualized in the text. We read, for example, of *mantras* that have been declared by Brahma, in the *Vedas*, by Viṣṇu, and Garūḍa. Each of these, however, was originated by Mañjuśrī, who had merely taken on the forms of these deities as a means of converting people.

> Those extensive ordinances that were proclaimed
> in the Vaiṣṇava *tantra*
> were spoken by Mañjughoṣa
> as but a means for converting people. . .
>
> Just as a mother watchfully plays
> with her children in various ways,
> I (Mañjuśrī) wander among those
> of child-like intelligence in the form of the *mantra*.[11]

It is the mental darkness, the ignorance, of people that prevents them from realizing the true nature of the *mantras* that they recite. The text corrects this misperception by disclosing the source of all *mantras* made available by India's millennia-long religious culture, thereby transforming ignorance into knowledge. This knowledge, in turn, transforms the practitioner-reader's perspective of the relation of the parts to the whole—a conversion, whereby the whole is transfigured.

In order for the transformation of ignorance into knowledge to have a lasting and significant effect on the life of the reader, however, more is required than a passing encounter with this disclosure. The practitioner must learn to use *mantras* much as a child must learn to use language. With the support of Harvey Alper's research on the "social dimension of mantric utterance," I argued in chapter 1 that the power of the *mantracaryā* can be harnessed only through painstakingly acquired technique. That is, realizing the claims of the *Mañjuśrīmūlakalpa* concerning its ritual practice presupposes that the practitioner has acquired (1) knowledge of the nature of the universe, that is, of both its structure and the powers that the community holds to be woven into that structure; (2) specific skills, for instance, how to fashion and use the cult object, how to recite *mantras*, how to perform the oblations, ablutions, *mudrās*, and so on; (3) and training within a socially authorized structure, or "inculturation," by one who has mastered the community's means and realized its ideals. It is only through the acquisition of these skills that the power of the *buddhas* is unlocked. Like ordinary speech, successful *mantric* utterance is founded on the mastery of its grammar, that is, on successfully combining its component parts. The social dimension of *mantric* utterance thus involves a process whereby disclosure of knowledge leads, by degrees, to transformation. The premises of this process are, furthermore, the initial mental darkness of the practitioner and the final totality of the teaching. Chapters 2, 3, and 4 of the book detail this process. I will now turn to a brief discussion of my analysis in these chapters.

Chapter 2 is primarily an analysis of *Mmk* 1. *Mmk* 1 reveals the space from which the teaching of the text originates and unfolds into the world. This place is "the vault of sky above the Śuddhāvāsa ('Pure Abode'), in the pavilion of the assembly of inconceivably, miraculously, wondrously distributed *bodhisattvas*," where the Buddha is said to be presently residing. In this single statement, the *Mañjuśrīmūlakalpa* is positing several related notions known from Mahāyāna *sūtra* and scholastic literature, such as the existence of the sphere of a given *buddha's* activity (*buddhakṣetra*), the continued presence of a *buddha* and his retinue within his field, the ability of these enlightened forces to manipulate and enter the material and sonic forms of the human world, and the accessibility of the enlightened realm to the trained practitioner. In disclosing this realm at the very outset, the *Mañjuśrīmūlakalpa* establishes, as the foundation of its ritual course, the very structure of the cosmos. The teaching is what it is, and its efficacy is ensured, because nothing less than the cosmos—transfigured by the light of the Buddha—is embedded in each of its elements: the successful utterance of a single *mantra* requires the cooperation of the entire universe. The basic function of *Mmk* 1 is to evoke for the reader the proper vision of the cosmos. Chapter 2 thus looks at the manner by which the reader is guided—emotionally, imaginatively, and conceptually—by the text to an understanding of the structure and forces of the previously hidden world behind, and within, the rituals.

In evoking the picture that they do, the words of *Mmk* 1 fashion an image. This image is of the generative event behind the cult of the *Mañjuśrīmūlakalpa*. In this disclosure, the text synchronizes an invisible, ideal, and "mythic" past with the visible and real present of the reader. The image arising out of the words of the text is thus intended to effect a response identical to that of a cult image; it is to be encountered, worshiped, and activated in one's life. *Mmk* 1 thus serves the triple function of alluding to the knowledge—known from other sources—of the structure of the cosmos, creating a picture of that cosmos, and of moving the powers of that otherwise hidden reality into the possession of the practitioner.

While chapter 2 discussed the source of the power behind the rituals, chapter 3 analyzed the manner in which that power is refracted within the immediate ritual field of the practitioner. Thus, chapter 3 is primarily based on *Mmk* 4 and 7, two chapters delineating the construction of the *paṭa*. The *paṭa* is a cult object consisting of an image (of the "array" described at *Mmk* 1) painted on a cotton canvas.

The *paṭa* undergoes three stages of development: from raw cotton to canvas, from empty canvas to painted image, and from painted image to animated cult object. As this final term suggests, the final aim of *paṭa* creation is to produce an instrument of liveliness and efficacy. Through a lengthy process of ritualized production, the *paṭa* is transformed from raw cotton into an object suffused with the power of enlightened forces (*buddhas, bodhisattvas,* celestial and earthly forces). Therefore, like relics, architectural monuments, or consecrated books, the *paṭa* was seen as possessing the same miracle-producing properties that accompany a living Buddha.

The properly trained practitioner was able to employ this potent object within the ritual field, whereby the *paṭa* served as a catalyst of transformation. This transformation is related in the main passage of analysis in my study—that of the *uttamasādhana*. After having performed several preliminary rituals, this passage relates, the practitioner circumambulates the *paṭa*, grabs hold of it, and subsequently becomes possessed of supernatural powers, sees the bodies of *buddhas* and *bodhisattvas* in their paradises, converses with them, and so on. Yet, this is not a description of a mechanical process. The ritual succeeds because numerous conditions had been fulfilled prior to the specific act described in the *uttamasādhana* sequence. These conditions, such as knowledge of the nature of the cosmos, instruction on ritual practice by a qualified teacher, proper construction of the *paṭa*, and so on, are precisely the content of this book. Only when these have been fulfilled, the text claims, does real presence of, and encounter with, enlightened power become possible. The *paṭa*—as well as the words describing the *paṭa*—thus, refracts both the image and the power of the enlightened cosmos described at *Mmk* 1 and analyzed in chapter 2. Both disclose an otherwise hidden reality, transforming darkness (symbolized by the empty canvas) into vision (the colorful image), and spiritual impotency into power.

Chapter 4 takes a closer look at the person who undergoes the training that is held to culminate in the ability to fulfill the ritual course of the text. My approach is to analyze the several attributive expressions ascribed to the practitioner (called *sādhaka*) during the several stages of his rise to becoming a practitioner empowered to practice fully and teach the rituals to others. The primary epithets of the practitioner are, in ascending order, *śiṣya, samayin,* and *ācārya.* Within each of these categories there are numerous others: *mantrin, tricelaparivartin, bodhisattva*, and so on. These terms relate central facts about the practitioner as he is presented in the text: he is one who must be inculturated (*śiṣya*) by an authorized teacher (*ācārya*), who recites *mantras* as his primary practice (*mantrin*), who, for varying periods of time, lives under strict vows (*samayin*) according to the code of the mendicant ascetic (*tricelaparivartin*), who develops great supernatural powers (*vidyādhāra*), who is motivated in his practice by compassion for all living beings (*bodhisattva*), who has perfect understanding of the nature of reality (*buddha*). Because each phase of this process is defined by the particular spaces occupied by the practitioner, I also analyze the passages relating the nature of these spaces. Each phase is formally commenced within the initiatory *maṇḍala.* This is followed by training in specific areas: the *śiṣya* is molded in the home of the teacher; the *samayin* in the solitary places—river banks, mountain caves, forests—that comprise the "field of success" (*siddhikṣetra*), the space within which the rituals are perfected; the *ācārya* in the community of practitioners.

The success of the ritual course prescribed in the *Mañjuśrīmūlakalpa* rests on the practitioner's ability to become the type of person described in the text. What the reader encounters in the text, however, is a normative image of an ideal figure. The *sādhaka* that I have sought to understand is not a historical figure, he is a rhetorical and discursive one. In disclosing to the historical practitioner-reader the personal characteristics and training required of the aspiring *sādhaka*, the text becomes the space for mediating the actual and the ideal. It presents a vision of a transformed person, and serves as a guide to that undertaking.

This book has traced the process through which a ritual act becomes situated in an all-encompassing "ritual universe." Together, the four previous chapters have shown the interlocking conceptual, personal, and ritual aspects that must be realized before success in the *mantracaryā* can be achieved. The components of both—act and universe—are taken from the rich soil of India's religious culture. In this respect, the *Mañjuśrīmūlakalpa* appears to offer scant new data for our understanding of the religious lives of Indian Buddhists in the medieval period. By emphasizing the text itself as a datum of that ritual universe, however, I hope to have thrown some light onto the manner by which generalized cultural forms are transformed into the property of an individual community. Friedhelm Hardy offers a fertile analogy for this process when he says that it is similar to "the improvisatory character of the Indian musical tradition."[12] The diverse components of the numerous performances, discussed in this study, that enable the practitioner to enter fully into the ritual universe created by the text are transformed into a unique creation by the structuring performance of the text itself. Through the process of appropriation, synthesis, improvisation, and experimentation, the *Mañjuśrīmūlakalpa* transforms common elements of Indian religious culture into vehicles of quite particular forms of knowledge and power.

In attending to the ways in which such processes unfold in a text as apparently formulaic as the *Mañjuśrīmūlakalpa*, I hope to signal to students of Buddhist literature the need of a hermeneutical strategy in our field that more fully acknowledges the interplay of the two dimensions of the general and the specific. Long before the *Mañjuśrīmūlakalpa* can be recognized as a Buddhist text, it must be seen as an Indian one. The seeming opaqueness concerning its date, language, tone, structure, rhetoric, and content could be pierced only by the light thrown onto it from the outside. That is, the nature of the *Mañjuśrīmūlakalpa* began to become apparent to me only when placed in relation to Vaiṣṇava and Śaiva ritual manuals. Because it employed the same common devices as these—devices spanning the history of India—the *Mañjuśrīmūlakalpa* is heavily marked by generality. When this general aspect is recognized, the reader begins to gain some insight into the basic thrust of the text. As this study should have made clear, however, this is not to suggest uniformity. The thrust of the general is marked by a simultaneous resistance to this thrust. Herein lies the uniqueness of the community that has adopted the general features of Indian religious culture in order to fashion its specific rituals, literature, and so forth. It is in this tension between the general and the specific that improvisation and experimentation occur. One of the questions that this study leaves open for students of Buddhism is to what extent this relationship between the general and the specific bears on all Buddhist literature.

Many years ago, Jean Przyluksi wrote that the *Mañjuśrīmūlakalpa* is "a sort of encyclopedia that treats of . . . the most varied subjects."[13] Yet, as Ariane MacDonald wrote thirty years later, the text owes its "fortune" to a single chapter, *Mmk* 53. *Mmk* 53 is the chapter on Buddhist history that was used by the Tibetan historians Bu-ston (1290–1364) and Tāranātha (born 1575).[14] It is almost inevitable that, when one encounters the title *Mañjuśrīmūlakalpa* in the index of some secondary book, the reference is to a citation from the work by one of these two historians. It does indeed appear that without chapter fifty-three the fate of the *Mañjuśrīmūlakalpa* would be quite unfortunate. As Przyluski notes, though, the *Mañjuśrīmūlakalpa* is a voluminous text covering many subjects. There is thus a great deal of study awaiting it.

It was with the hope that the fortune of the text would thus improve that I have included a synopsis in the Appendix. The next step in the study of the *Mañjuśrīmūlakalpa* might be to investigate in more detail the contents of chapters 12–55. What does the data there teach us about the practices of astrology, astronomy, iconography, and medicine in medieval India? How does the very presence of such subjects in a Buddhist text alter our understanding of the scope of Buddhism in the daily lives of common people? How does this data further clarify the place of the practitioners of the *Mañjuśrīmūlakalpa* on the continuum between the monastic universities and the antinomian lay tantric cults? Some answers to even broader questions might begin to emerge from this type of detailed research. For example, does the *Mañjuśrīmūlakalpa,* viewed from close range, support the characterizations of the later Indian exegetes concerning the various typologies of *tantras*? That is, to what extent is its later reputation as a very specific type of Buddhism—the type characterized as a *kriyātantra*—justified; and what new insights would emerge in reading medieval Mahāyāna and tantric literature if we stopped assuming the utility of such categories? On a more pragmatic level, our understanding of the date, provenance, and compilation history of the *Mañjuśrīmūlakalpa* would benefit from a close comparison of the Sanskrit text and the several Tibetan and Chinese translations. It would be hoped that such an investigation would be undertaken with a copy of the Sanskrit manuscript (still extant? where?) from which the printed edition was created. In this way, unusual grammatical forms and spelling now exhibited by the text may be shown to be errors of the editor or printer.

In its selection and presentation of its contents, an encyclopedia both presupposes and creates a specific conceptual world. In this study of the *Mañjuśrīmūlakalpa*, I chose to trace certain processes and strategies at work behind this selection and presentation. In the process of doing so, I was able to see faint images of a world foreign to my own conceptual universe. In the very act of seeing, that conceptual universe is expanded and transformed. This is what happens when we read in a concerned, watchful, and deeply respectful manner.

Appendices

Abbreviations and symbols

Mmk = *Āryamañjuśrīmūlakalpa*, edited by T. Gaṇapati Śāstrī, Trivandrum Sanskrit Series: Part I = no. LXX, 1920; Part II = LXXVI, 1922; Part III = LXXXIV, 1925, Trivandrum.

V. = *Mahāyānasūtrasaṅgraha,* edited by P. L. Vaidya, Buddhist Sanskrit Texts, Part II, no. 18, Bihar, 1964. CBH Publications, Trivandrum, 1992.

T. = Tibetan text. Taipei Edition, vol. XVIII *bka' 'gyur, 'phags pa 'jam dpal gyi rtsa ba'i rgyud*, 540 no. 543, 25/175 (1)-96/667.

\\\\\ = missing text.

Appendix A1: Terminus ad quem/a quo

I have argued in this study that the *Mmk* was compiled in the eighth century C.E., at the latest, and that the strongest evidence for this is indirect; namely, the Śaiva and Vaiṣṇava ritual texts record identical cultic patterns. These texts are dated from the seventh to the ninth centuries with some certainty.[1] I believe that I have shown that the *Mmk* shows similar intention, function, style, and structure as these texts. As I said at 1.3.1, dating the *Mmk* to this period is based on the evidence of ascendancy of both the cultic pattern and literary genre of which it is a type. Here, I would like to offer some suggestive data for considering the *terminus ad quem/a quo* of the *Mmk.*

(1) These works are mentioned in the *Mmk* (*Mmk* 2.38.11–14; 11.109.27–110.1; 11.99.10–11) as works to be studied and recited from. Dates are approximate:

1. *Prajñāpāramitās* (1st century C.E.)
2. *Candrapradīpasamādhi* (= *Samādhirājasūtra*, 5th C.E.)

3. *Daśabhūmaka* (1st C.E.)
4. *Suvarṇaprabhāsottamasūtra* (4th C.E.)
5. *Mahāmāyūrī* (4th C.E.)
6. *Ratnaketudhāriṇī* (?)
7. *Gaṇḍavyūha* (1st C.E.)
8. *Maṅgalagāthā* (?)
9. *Svastikagāthā* (?)

(2) Sanskrit: 55 chapters		Tibetan 37		Chinese: 32
1–17	=	1–17	=	1–17
18–23	=	not trans.	=	not trans.
24–34	=	18–28	=	18–28
35–38	=	29–32	=	not trans.
39–40	=	not trans.	=	not trans.
41	=	not trans.	=	T.1276*
42–49	=	not trans.	=	not trans.
50	=	33	=	T. 1215*
51	=	34	=	T. 1216 [A]*
52	=	35	=	T. 1216[B]*
53–54	=	36 a, b	=	not trans.
55	=	not trans.	=	not trans.

*In Chinese canon (Taishō) independent works.
(From Matsunaga 1985:885)

(3) The Sanskrit manuscript from which Śāstri's edition was compiled has "the appearance of being 300 to 400 years old," that is, it may date from approximately the sixteenth century. Theoretically, therefore, the Sanskrit chapters that have no Tibetan or Chinese translations (namely: 18–23, 39, 40, 42–49, and 55), and whose dates can thus not be set, may be dated as late as the date of the manuscript. But short of a major revision of the institutional role played by Buddhism in India after the twelfth century, the introduction of new material at this late date is untenable.

(4) The Chinese translation consists of 28 chapters dated to ca. 980; there are an additional 4 chapters in the canon, dated to the early eighth century, which correspond in part to *Mmk* chapters (although see Matsunaga 1985 for qualifications).[2]

(5) The Tibetan translation consisting of 37 chapters dates to between 1034 and 1044.[3]

(6) *Mmk* 50 = ca. 750 (see Chandra n.d:115).

(7) *Mmk* 41, 51, and 52 = "T'ang dynasty" (618–906) (see Matsunaga 1985:883 and passim). The Taishō apparatus assumes Amoghavajra (8th century: Chandra n.d:114) to be the translator of these three chapters. But for a qualification of this, see Matsunaga 1985:889–893.

(8) *Mmk* 53 is datable to ca. 770, the reign of Gopāla: though Gopāla is mentioned in this "dynastic history" (*rājavyākaraṇaparivarta*), his immediate successors, who were patrons of Buddhism, are not (see Jayaswal 1934).

Appendix A: Colophons and chapter synopses

What follows are abbreviated colophons of the *Mmk*. These are recorded here together with brief synopses in order to give some indicatation of chapter contents. The bold brackets **[]** mark off subsections.

1–17 = Sanskrit, Tibetan, and Chinese versions.

1. *sannipātaparivartaḥ*. Section on the cosmic assembly. 24 pp. Prose.

2. *maṇḍalavidhinirdeśaparivartaḥ*. Instructions on constructing the *maṇḍala* used in the initiation rite; *mantras* employed in various rituals; instructions for the initiation ritual. 28 pp. Prose. Translation: MacDonald 1962, from *Mmk* 2.36.21.

3. *maṇḍalavidhānaparivartaḥ*. Arrangement of a *maṇḍala* used for protecting against illness, etc. 1.5 pp. Prose. Translation: MacDonald 1962.

[4–7 = section on the creation of the *paṭa*.

4. *prathamapaṭavidhānavisaraḥ*. First chapter on the arrangement of the largest and superior (*uttama*) painted cloth cult object. 13 pp. Mixed prose and verse. Translation: Lalou 1930.

5. *dvitīyaḥ paṭavidhānavisaraḥ*. Second chapter on the arrangement of the cult object: the medium (*madhyama*) *paṭa*. 3 pp. Mixed prose and verse. Translation: Lalou 1930.

6. *tṛtīyaḥ kanyasapaṭavidhānaḥ*. Third chapter on the arrangement of the cult object: the small one (*kanyasa*). 1.5 pp. Mixed prose and verse. Translation: Lalou. 1930.

7. *caturthaḥ paṭavidhānapaṭalavisaraḥ*. Fourth chapter on the arrangement of the cult object: a simplified rite for corrupted times. 5 pp. Prose with short verse section. Translation: Lalou 1930.**]**

[**8–10** = section on the rituals leading to superior success.

8. *uttamasādhanaupayikakarmapaṭalavisarāt prathamaḥ*. First chapter in the section on the ritual serving as the means to the highest accomplishment. 2.5 pp. Mixed prose and verse.

9. *dvitīyaḥ°*. Second chapter, etc. Discusses the single syllable (*ekākṣara*) *mantra, kḷhīṃ*; applications of this *mantra*. 3.5 pp. Prose.

10. *uttamapaṭavidhānapaṭalavisaraḥ*. The arrangement of the large *paṭa*; rituals done on a boat; geographical areas conducive to the practice of *mantras* (called *siddhikṣetra*). 8 pp. Mixed prose and verse.]

[**11–12** = rituals employing the medium *paṭa*.

11. *caturthaḥ* [note: second line reads *madhyamaṃ paṭavidhānaṃ madhyamakarma°*) *sādhanaupayikakarmasthānajapaniyamahomadhyānaśaucācārasarvakarmavidhisādhanapaṭalavisaraḥ*. The fourth section, etc.; describes the *ācārya* and *sādhaka*; places where rituals are done; procedure of worship: namely, bathes, praises *buddhas*, etc., in front of *paṭa*, recites *mantras* all night, in the morning enters a village to beg alms; warnings about women and other "dangerous" people, procedure for eating, etc. 25 pp. Mixed prose and verse.

12. *madhyamapaṭavidhānavisarād dvādaśamaḥ akṣasūtravidhipaṭalavisaraḥ*. The prescriptions for making and using prayer beads; selection and consecration of wood, etc. 5 pp. Verse with prose introduction.]

13. *trayodaśamapaṭalavisaraḥ*. States only "chapter thirteen." Prescriptions for performing the fire oblation (*homa*); making the lotus-shaped pit (*agnikuṇḍa*); proper places; preliminary ritual of pacification; types of wood chips or twigs to be burnt; *ābhicāruka* and *raudrakarma* are forbidden; example of procedure. 6 pp. Verse with prose introduction.

14. *cakravartipaṭalavidhānamaṇḍalasādhanaupayikavisaraḥ*. Power of the single syllable (*ekākṣara*) *mantra, bhrūṃ*; *paṭa* of Ratnaketu described; ritual service to *paṭa*, including oblations into *agnikuṇḍa*, etc.; practitioner attains seven *bodhisattvabhūmis*, sees *buddhas* and attains the *pañcābhijñā*; *śāntika* rituals. 16 pp. Verse with prose introduction. Translation: Lalou 1930 (from *Mmk* 14.131: several lines on the *paṭa*).

15. *sarvakarmakriyārthaḥ paṭalavisaraḥ*. (Text reads "chapter 13"; see editor's note at bottom of *Mmk* 15.165. From here on, until *Mmk* 55, the colophon chapter numbers are behind two numbers.) Analysis of dreams; four types of dreams: *śleṣma, pitta, vātika, satya*; the prevalent dream imagery of each type: water, fire, sky; types of person: *uttama, madhyama, adhas*; physiologi-

cal features of each type; relationship between astrology and personal *karma*; significance of particular heavenly signs; praise of *Mmk*. 20.3 pp. Verse with prose introduction and additional brief prose section.

16. *gāthāpaṭalanirdeśavisaraḥ*. Summary of the previous chapter in verse. Concerns obtaining a superior birth, heavenly signs of success. 3 pp. Verse with short prose introduction.

[17–21 = section on astrology/astronomy

17. *karmasvakapratyayapaṭalavisaraḥ*. Ascertaining one's own *karma*. Best path is Mahāyāna; *karma* is determined by signs: "just as a grain is manifested through a sprout of rice, success is manifested through a sign of wealth"; signs and marks are determined by the cause; the relationship between personal *karma* and astrology/astronomy; story of how the Buddha Śālendra attained enlightenment under the *bodhi* tree by reciting a *mantra*; 80,000 recitations of this *mantra* destroys bad omens, dreams, signs, obstacles, etc.; 4 pp. Verse with short prose introduction.

18. *dvitīyo grahanakṣatralakṣaṇakṣetrajyotiṣajñānaparivartapaṭalavisaraḥ*. The second chapter on the astronomical/astrological knowledge of the distinctive characteristics of the fields of planets and stars. On the course, consequences, and activities of agreeable planets on the practices; when to undertake the practices. 8 pp. Verse with short prose introduction.

19. *tṛtīyo jyotiṣajñānapaṭalavisaraḥ*. The third chapter on astrological knowledge; actions of the *krodharāja* Yamāntaka to coerce planets, etc. 13.3 pp. Verse with prose introduction.

20. *caturtho nimittajñānamahotpādapaṭalaparivartaḥ*. The fourth chapter on great omens and the knowledge of signs. On the emblems and signs of marvels; destroying the emergence of perils (*bhaga*); the signs of auspiciousness and inauspiciousness; good and bad places for the practice of particular rituals. 22.3 pp. Verse with short prose introduction.

21. *pañcamaḥ grahotpādaniyamanimittamantrakriyānirdeśaparivarta-paṭalavisaraḥ*. The fifth chapter instructing on *mantra* rituals relating to the reasons for, and controlling of, great planetary omens. 11 pp.]

[22–26 = additional prognostication

22. *sarvabhūtarutajñānanimittaśakunanirdeṣaparivartapaṭalavisaraḥ*. Knowledge of the significance of particular sounds. 23.1 pp. Verse with prose introduction.

23. *śabdajñānagaṇanānāmanirdeśaparivartapaṭalavisaraḥ*. The knowledge of the various sounds of the *alphabet: ma, ta bha*, etc.; various types of recita-

tion and sound: *repha* (guttural), etc.; different sounds adorn the three types of *mantra* (*śāntika, pauṣṭika,* and *ābhicāruka*); 11 pp. Verse with short prose introduction.

24. *nimittajñānajyotiṣapaṭalavisaraḥ.* On astrology and the knowledge of omens; knowing the proper time for doing different rituals; *uttama, madhyama, kanyasa* distinction of practice and result. 20 pp. Verse with short prose introduction.

25. *ekākṣaracakravartyudbhavapaṭalavisaraḥ.* The generation of Cakravartin, one of the ten protective deities known as *uṣṇīṣarāja* (cf. *Mmk* 8.41.7, 10, 11, and *BHSD* 149, *s.v. uṣṇīṣa*). Cakravartin protects the *dharma* during the evil age by means of the single syllable *mantra, bhrūṃ.* Rituals of protection and subjugation in an evil age; the *mantra* as "fleshless" (*nirāmiṣā*) relic, the means by which *buddhas* continue to wander the earth; subjugation ritual. 4.5 pp. Mixed verse and prose.

26. *ekākṣaracakravartikarmavidhipaṭanirdeśapaṭalavisaraḥ.* Prose elaboration on previous verse chapter. Practice for an age when people will be unable to practice to the *paṭa* at length; various rituals using specific items in concert with the *ekākṣara bhrūṃ*; prescriptions for a *vetālasādhana*, a ritual whereby a corpse is reanimated (see, Boord 1993:42f.); rituals for attracting Śiva, Viṣṇu, Brahma, *yakṣīṇīs, nāgīs*; Vajrapāṇi ritual for a full-moon night, etc. 11.5 pp. Prose. Translation: Lalou 1930 (*Mmk* 26.289.9: several lines on the *paṭa*).]

27. *ekākṣaramūlamantrāryamañjuśrīhṛdayakalpapaṭavidhānavisaraḥ.* Rituals with the *ekākṣara mantra, muṁ.* Prescriptions for a *paṭa* of Amitāyus/Amitābha. Description of Amitāyus/Amitābha worship for a degenerate age. 10 pp. Mixed prose and verse. Translation: Lalou 1930 (*Mmk* 27.304.14: several lines on the *paṭa*).

28. *karmavidhānāryamañjuśrīyaparivarttapaṭalavisaraḥ.* Practices for degenerate times. Paints *paṭa*, sets it up at a *caitya* and offers worship of fragrance, flowers, incense, lamps, etc.; recites from the *Bhagavatī Prajñāpāramitā*; oblations, recitation, etc., for summoning Mañjuśrī; 10.2 pp. Prose with some verse at end. Translation: Lalou 1930 (*Mmk* 28.311.10; 315; 318: several lines on the *paṭa*).

29. *mañjuśrīpaṭavidhānaparivartakarmavidhiḥ saptamakapaṭalavisaraḥ.* On Mañjuśrī's "essence" *mantra* (*hṛdaya*), *oṁ vakyeda namaḥ*; ritual at *caitya*; image painted, worshipped, image trembles, oblations, and recitation throughout night, etc.; practitioner becomes invisible, flies through sky; mentions the practitioner as *mahāgṛhapati*; degenerate time throughout. 3 pp. Prose with a few lines of verse.

30. *kṣetrakālavidhiniyamapaṭalavisaraḥ*. Specific places for practicing to particular deities, *buddhas, bodhisattvas*, etc. 4 pp. Verse with short prose introduction.

31. *āviṣṭaceṣṭavidhiparivartapaṭalavisaraḥ*. Signs of an auspicious or inauspicious birth; Uṣṇīṣa and *uṣṇīṣamudrā*; protective ritual; languages and sounds: *l* sound, *r* sound, *d* sound, *gha* sound, *ṣaṭ* sound, etc. 5.1 pp. Verse with short prose introduction.

32. *vidhiniyamakālapaṭalavisaraḥ*. Astrology: auspicious or inauspicious times for practice; no success if rituals are conducted at inauspicious times; when the rules are applied, the *mantras* succeed; *jinakula, padmakula, vajrakula*—the *mantras* of all of these succeed during *kaliyuga*. 3.5 pp. Verse with short prose introduction.

33. *karmakriyāvidhinimittajñānanirdeśapaṭalavisaraḥ*. Knowledge of sound omens; best *mantras* are those spoken by the *buddhas*, second best are those spoken by the *bodhisattvas*, third, *rakṣasas*; examples of sounds made with different parts of the mouth; *mlecchabhāṣa, apabhraṃśa, saṃskṛta*; the marks of *mantras*—numerous examples; various threefold divisions; importance of following the prescriptions of the *mantracaryā*. 10.2 pp. Verse with short prose introduction.

[34–37 = descriptions of individual *mantras* and *mudrās*.

34. *mudrācodanavidhimañjuśrīparipṛcchanirdeśaparivartaḥ paṭalavisaraḥ*. Exaltation of *mudrās*; the importance of keeping them secret: *mudrās* are revealed to those who have faith in the Buddha's teaching, who are adorned with *bodhicitta*, who remain fixed on the Buddha's path, etc.; *mantras* are well-sealed with *mudrās*. 4.5 pp. Verse with short prose introduction.

35. *mudrāvidhipaṭalavisaraḥ*. Lists, names, and describes 108 *mudrās*. 27 pp. Verse with short prose introduction.

36. (Two chapters counted as one; two separate colophons; see editor's note at the top of page 384.) [first colophon:] *dvitīyamudrāvidhipaṭalavisaraḥ*. Addition to *Mmk* 35—*mahāmudrās*, etc. On the application of *mudrās*. 2 pp. Mixed verse and prose.

[36: second colophon:] *mahāmudrāpaṭalavisaraḥ*. Numerous *mudrās* and *mantras;* specific *śāntika, pauṣṭika*, and *rakṣasa* rituals employing these; *ābhicāruka* not permitted. 27.5 pp. Mixed verse and prose.

37. *mantramudrāniyamakarmavidhipaṭalavisaraḥ*. Additional *mudrās* and *mantras*; worship of Samantabhadra; several *kulas* mentioned, for example: *padmakula, dhvajakula, rājakula, maṇikula, yakṣakula, divyakula, tathāgatakula*. 16.5 pp. Prose with some verse interspersed.]

38. *mudrāmaṇḍalatantrasarvakarmavidhi*. Drawing a *maṇḍala* which attracts the members of the various *kulas* mentioned in previous chapter. 4.5 pp. Verse with two line prose introduction.

[**39–40** = section on meditation

39. *mahākalparājapaṭalavisarād uttamasādhanaupayikasarvakarmārtha-sādhanatatveṣu prathamaḥ dhyānapaṭalavisaraḥ*. The *tṛdhā karmapatha/mārga* consists of *dāna, śīla,* and *dhyāna*; contains; a visualization proced-ure; discusses the three paths: *uttama (buddha/lokottara), madhyama (pratyekabuddha/ śīla), adha (śrāvaka/laukika)*, and three types of rituals: *uttama (buddha), madhyama (deva), kanyasa* (*nṛpadvāra* [i.e., "man"]*)*; short sequence of imaginative worship. 6.1 pp. Verse with short prose introduction. Translation: Lalou 1930 (*Mmk* 39.322 [after verse]: several lines on the *paṭa*).

40. *dvitīyasarvalokatattvārthatārakriḍāvidhisādhanaupayikasarvadhyānapaṭa-lavisaraḥ*. Ratnaketu *sādhana*: visualization, worship, etc.; three types of *dhyāna* and corresponding levels of attainment: *uttama/bodhi, madhyama/ śāntika, kanyasa/śrāvakabodhi*; truths of *śunyatā* and *nairātmya*; three types of person: *uttama/rājasa, madhyama/tāmasa, kanyasa/sāttvika*. Amitābha visualization; discusses three types of path as above; 19 pp. Verse with short prose introduction.]

[**41–46** = section on *mudrās*

41. *garuḍapaṭalaparivartaḥ*. Practices (*mantras, mudrās*, and *maṇḍalas)* for attracting, subjugating, and destroying serpents (*nāgas*). 10 pp. Mixed verse and prose. See Lalou 1932 for discussion and partial translation.

42. *sarvakarmasādhanaupayikaḥ*. Esoteric *mudrās* performed and drawn in *maṇḍalas* of deities; rituals employing these. 5 pp. Verse with short prose introduction.

43. *dvitīyaḥ sarvakarmottamasādhanopayikaḥ mahāmudrāpaṭalavisaraḥ*. Praise and instruction on the one great *mudrā*, the best of all: *pañcaśikha*, the *mudrā* depicting Mañjuśrī. 3 pp. Verse with short prose introduction. For a discussion of this *mudrā*, see Lalou 1930: 66ff.

44. *mahāmudrāpaṭalavisaraḥ*. The *pañcaśikhamudrā* is praised; specific instructions on this and other *mudrās*. 13 pp. Verse with short prose introduction.

45. *mudrāpaṭalavisaraḥ*. Numerous *mudrās* explained. 21 pp. Verse with short prose introduction.

46. *mahāmudrāpaṭalavisaraḥ*. 5 *mudrās* praised. 2 pp. Mixed verse and prose.]

[47–49 = *caturbhaginīmaṇḍala*

47/(45). *prathamaḥ caturbhaginīmaṇḍalam anupraveśasamayaguhyatama-paṭalavisaraḥ*. On the *maṇḍala* of the four female deities known as *bhaginīs* (also called *caturkumārī*; cf. *BHSD s.v. kumārī*); *mantras*, etc., associated with these. 14 pp. Mixed verse and prose.

48. *dvitīyasādhanaupayika*°. Continuation of above. 13.3 pp. Mixed verse and prose.

49. *tṛtīyaḥ catuḥkumāryopayikasarvasādhanajapaniyamamudraudhitantraman-trasarvakarmapaṭalavisara*. Five *mahāmudrās* explained in detail. 4 pp. Mixed verse and prose.]

[50–52 = *yamāntakakrodharāja*

50. *yamāntakakrodharājaparivarṇamantramāhātmyaniyamapaṭalavisaraḥ*. Praise of Yamāntaka's powers; protection ritual. 5 pp. Verse with prose introduction.

51. *yamāntakakrodharājābhicārukaniyamaḥ dvitīyaḥ paṭalavisaraḥ*. Yamāntaka's powers in relation to astronomical forces. 7 pp. Verse with short prose introduction.

52. *yamāntakakrodharājāsarvavidhiniyamaḥ tṛtīyaḥ paṭalavisaraḥ*. Numerous specific practices, *mantras*, etc. 19.3 pp. Prose with verse interspersed.]

53. *rājavyakāraṇaparivartaḥ*. A history of Buddhism; imperial history of India up to the death of Gopāla in ca. 772. 78 pp. Verse with short prose introduction. Summary, discussion, and abbreviated translations: Jayaswal 1934.

[54 = conclusion

54 (Note: 50, not 52, in colophon). *anuśosāvigarhaṇaprabhāvapaṭalavisaraḥ*. Praise of the *Mmk*; ten praises to be made known, e.g., the recitation, worship, copying, etc., of books; no greater teaching than that contained in the *Mmk*, which should be worshiped, etc.; how to worship a book, *buddhas*, *bodhisattvas*, etc.; some *mantra* practices for destroying evil forces, preventing death, etc. 10.5 pp. Mixed verse and prose.]

55. *hemasādhanapaṭalavisaraḥ*. Numerous *mantra* practices for attraction, subjugation, and protection. Prescriptions are written in clipped, abbreviated form. 54 pp. Prose.

Appendix B: Indexical Lists

(For readers of the following transliterations I want to repeat what I said in chapter 1 about the language of the *Mmk*: The *Mmk* is written in a form of Sanskrit that deviates regularly from the norms of Pāṇini. In virtually every sentence examples of the following are found: homogeneity of nominative and accusative; use of plural subject with singular verb and vice versa; mixing of passive and active forms; variant and inconsistent spellings. While many of these forms can be found in other *vaipulya* works, as is documented by Edgerton in both volumes of the *Buddhist Hybrid Sanskrit Grammar and Dictionary*, others await further analysis of internal consistency, as well as a comparison of the printed text with the purported single known manuscript of the *Mmk*, in order to determine whether they are viable local forms of written Sanskrit, editor's errors, or printer's errors.)

(Note: *mantras* in the transliteration of the Tibetan text are transliterated exactly as given.)

B1 [*Mmk* 1.1.6–9]

śṛṇvantu devaputrā mañjuśriyasya kumārabhūtasya bodhisattvasya mahāsattvasyācintyādbhutaprātihāryacaryāsamādhiśuddhiviśeṣavimokṣa-maṇḍala-[4]*bodhisattvavikurvaṇaṃ sarvasattvopajīvyam āyurārogyaiśvary-amanorathapāripūrakāṇi mantrapadāni*

[T.175.2–4 (88a)]

lha'i bu dag khyed cag ñon cig / byaṅ chub sems dpa' sems dpa' chen po 'jam dpal gźon nur gyur pa'i cho 'phrul gyi spyod pa bsam gyis mi khyab pa ṅo mtshar rmad du byuṅ ba'i tiṅ ṅe 'dzin gyi bye brag daṅ / rdzu 'phrul daṅ / rnam par thar pa'i dkyil 'khor byaṅ chub sems dpa'i rnam par 'phrul pa daṅ / byaṅ chub sems dpa' thams cad kyi ñe bar 'tsho ba / tshe daṅ nad med pa daṅ dbaṅ phyug daṅ / yid la bsam pa yoṅs su rdzogs par byed pa'i sṅags kyi gźi dag [/]

B2 [*Mmk* 1.1.12–18]

atha śuddhāvāsakāyikā devaputrāḥ sāñjalayo bhūtvā \\\\ [T. *bcom ldan 'das la legs so źes gsol te / byaṅ chub sems dpa' rnams kyi sbyod pa tiṅ ṅe 'dzin gyi*] *viśeṣabhūmipratilābhavajrāsanākramaṇamāradharṣaṇa-dharmacakrapravartanasarvaśrāvakapratyekyabuddhaniryāṇadevam-anuṣyopapattisarvaduḥkhapraśamanadaridravyādhitāḍhyarogo-pakarṣaṇatāṃ sarvalaukikalokottaramantracaryānabhibhavanatāṃ sarvāśāparipūraṇataḥ sarvatathāgatānām avaśyavacanadhāraṇam / tad vadatu bhagavān maitracitto hitacitto 'smākam anukampāmupādāya sarvasattvānāṃ ca //*

[T.175.5 (88a)–176.1 (88b)]
de nas gnas gtsaṅ ma'i ris kyi lha'i bu de dag gyis thal mo sbyar ba btud nas / bcom ldan 'das la legs so źes gsol te / byaṅ chub sems dpa' rnams kyi spyod pa tiṅ ṅe 'dzin gyi khyad par daṅ / sa chen pa thob par bya ba daṅ / rdo rje'i gdan gnon pa daṅ / bdud gdul ba daṅ / chos kyi 'khor lo bskor ba daṅ / ñan thos daṅ raṅ saṅs rgyas thams cad kyi ṅes par 'byuṅ ba daṅ / lha rnams daṅ mi rnams su skye bar bya ba daṅ / sdug bsṅal daṅ / dbul ba daṅ / nad thams cad źi bar byed pa / loṅs spyod kyis phug pa 'dren par byed pa / 'jig rten daṅ 'jig rten las 'das pa'i sṅags kyi spyod pas phoṅs par mi byed pa / re ba thams cad yoṅs su rdzogs par byed pa de bźin gśegs pa thams cad kyi gsuṅ 'bras bu med par byed pa ma yin pa / bcom ldan 'das kyis byams pa'i thugs daṅ / phan pa'i thugs daṅ bdag daṅ sems can thams cad la thugs brtsa ba ñe bar bzuṅ nas bcom ldan 'das de bśad du gsol /

B3 [*Mmk* 1.2.13–15]
sarvamantracaryāsādhanaupayikamaṇḍalavidhānaṃ kalparahasyapaṭa-vidhāna [T. *cho ga źib mo* < °*paṭalavisara*?] *rūpa* [T. *cho ga'i ṅo bo daṅ* < *vidhi-* or *vidhānasvabhāva*] *sarvatathāgatahṛdayaguhyamudrāb-hiṣekaṃ nirdeṣṭuṃ sarvasattvānāṃ sarvāśāṃ paripūrayitum //*

[T.177.2-4 (89a)]
sṅags thams cad kyi spyod pa daṅ / sgrub thabs daṅ / dkyil 'khor daṅ / cho ga daṅ / gsaṅ ba daṅ / cho ga źib mo daṅ / cho ga'i ṅo bo daṅ / de bźin gśegs pa thams cad kyi thugs daṅ / gsaṅ ba daṅ / phyag rgya daṅ / dbaṅ bskur ba bstan pa daṅ / sems can thams cad kyi bsam pa thams cad yoṅs su rdzogs par bya ba'i phyir /

B4 [*Mmk* 1.2.22–27]
mantracaryāmaṇḍalakalparahasyābhiṣekamudrāpaṭavidhāna [T. *phyag rgya'i tshogs* < °*mudrāpaṭalavisara* (literally °*gaṇa*). Cf. two lines later: *rin po che'i tshogs* < *ratnapaṭalavisara*] *homajapaniyamasarvāśā-pāripūrakasarvasattvasaṃtoṣaṇajyotiratnapaṭalavisarātītānāgata-vartamānajñānarājyaiśvaryavyākaraṇamantrāvartanadeśaniṣṭhāvasān-āntardhānakālasamayavisarapaṭala* [T. *tshogs* < *paṭalavisara*] *samastā-śeṣalaukikalokottarasarvabuddhabodhisattvāryaśrāvakapratyekabuddha-bodhisattvabhūmyākramaṇataścaryāniṣṭhaṃ*

[T.179.1-4 (90a)][5]
sṅags kyi spyod pa daṅ / dkyil 'khor daṅ cho ga źib mo daṅ gsaṅ ba daṅ / dbaṅ bskur ba daṅ phyag rgya'i tshogs daṅ cho ga daṅ sbyin sreg daṅ / bzlas pa daṅ brtul źugs bsam pa thams cad yoṅs su rdzogs par byed sems can thams cad dga' bar byed pa / 'od rin po che'i tshogs kyis rab

'byam 'das pa daṅ da ltar byuṅ ba daṅ ma 'oṅs pa'i śes pa rgyal po'i dbaṅ phyug luṅ ston par byed pa / sṅags bzla ba yul gyi mthar 'gro bar byed pa mi snaṅ bar byed pa daṅ / ṅus daṅ dam tshig rab 'byam gyi tshogs thams cad daṅ / 'jig rten pa ma lus pa daṅ / 'jig rten las 'das pa'i saṅs rgyas daṅ / byaṅ chub sems dpa' daṅ 'phags pa ñan thos daṅ raṅ saṅs rgyas kyi ṅes par 'byuṅ ba'i spyod pa mthar thug pa gsuṅs pa daṅ /

B5 [*Mmk* 1.6.13–26]
mahāsattva caryā [T. *sems dpa' chen po'i spyod pa*< *mahāsattva caryā* (genitive relationship)] *sarvabuddhyadhiṣṭhitanirhārasarvabodhisattvārtthasamprāpakasarvamantrapadasarahasyābhiṣekamudrāmaṇḍalakalyabhiṣeka* [> °*kalpābhiṣeka* < T. *cho ga daṅ / dbaṅ bskur ba*] *āyurārogyaiśvaryasarvāśāpāripūrakaḥ sarvasādhanaupayikatantrajñānajñeyakālāntarādhānarājyakṣetra atītānāgatavartamānasaṃkṣepataḥ sarvasattvānāṃ sarvāśāpāripūraka svaguṇodbodhanamantracaryānuvarttitaparasattvaprītikaraṇa antarddhānākāśagamana pādapracārika medhāvīkaraṇa ākarṣaṇa pātālapraveśana ābhicārika sarvakāmāvāptisaṅkula yakṣayakṣiṇī kiṅkarapiśācasarvabhūtākarṣaṇa bālavṛddhataruṇayathāsthita sthāpakasaṃkṣepataḥ sarvakarmakara sarvamanorathaparipūraka abhicāraka śāntikapauṣtikeṣu prakurvāṇaḥ yathā yathā prayujyamānas tathā tathā śrāvyamānabodhisattvapiṭakāvataṃsakaṃ mahākalparatnapaṭalavisaraṃ asmābhiranujñātaḥ sarvabuddhaiś ca bhāṣantaṃ śuddhasattve* \ \ \ \ \ [T: *raṅ gi sṅags spyod pa'i don gyi* (*chos kyi mdzod*)] *ye dharmakośaṃ bahujanahitāya bahujanakāmāya devānāṃ ca manuṣyāṇāṃ ca sarvasattvānuddiśya //*

[T.183.3 (92a)–184.2 (92b)]
sems dpa' chen po'i spyod pa saṅs rgyas thams cad kyis byin gyis brlabs pa bsgrub pas byaṅ chub sems dpa' thams cad kyi don thob par byed pa / sṅags thams cad kyi tshig daṅ gsaṅ ba daṅ bcas pa daṅ / dbaṅ bskur ba daṅ phyag rgya daṅ / dkyil 'khor daṅ cho ga daṅ / dbaṅ bskur ba daṅ tshe daṅ nad med pa daṅ / dbaṅ phyug daṅ bsam pa thams cad yoṅs su rdzogs par byed pa / sgrub pa'i thabs thams cad daṅ ldan pa rgyud śes pa daṅ / śes bya daṅ dus daṅ mi snaṅ ba daṅ / rgyal po'i źiṅ du gyur pa 'das pa daṅ ma oṅs pa daṅ da ltar byuṅ ba śes par byed pa mdor na sems can thams cad kyi bsam pa thams cad yoṅs su rdzogs par byed pa / raṅ gi yon tan daṅ mthun pa'i sṅags kyi spyod pa rjes su 'jug pa / sems can gźan dga' bar byed pa mi snaṅ bar 'gro ba / nam mkha' la 'gro ba / chur mi nub par 'gro ba / yid gźuṅs par byed pa / 'gugs par byed pa / sa 'og tu 'jug pa / mṅon du spyod par byed pa / 'dod pa thams cad thob par byed pa / gnod sbyin daṅ / gnod sbyin mo thams cad daṅ / mṅag gźug pa daṅ śa za daṅ 'byuṅ po thams cad 'gugs par byed pa

/ byis pa daṅ / rgan po daṅ gźon nu gnas nas ci lta ba bźin 'jog par byed pa / mdor na las thams cad byed pa ste / yid la re ba thams cad rdzogs par byed pa / mṅon spyod daṅ rgyas pa daṅ / źi ba'i las dag rab tu byed pa ji lta ji ltar rab tu sbyar ba de lta de ltar byaṅ chub sems dpa'i sde snod phal po che / bskal pa chen po'i rin po che'i le'u rab 'byam 'di ṅas kyaṅ rjes su gnaṅ źiṅ saṅs rgyas thams cad kyis gyuṅ gsuṅs te / sems can dag pa'i raṅ gi sṅags spyod pa'i don gyi chos kyi mdzod / skye bo maṅ po la phan pa daṅ / skye bo maṅ po la bde ba daṅ / lha daṅ mi rnams daṅ / sems can thams cad kyi don du bstan pa'i phyir ro //

Appendix C: *uttamasādhana*

C1 [*Mmk* 8.78.27–8.79.9]

yo idaṃ sūtrendrarājaṃ mañjuśrīmūlakalpāvidyācaryānuṣṭhānakarmasādhanopayikasamavaśaraṇa[6]*-dharmameghaniḥśritaṃ samanupraveṣānuvartakaṃ kariṣyanti dhārayiṣyanti vācayiṣyanti śraddhāsyanti pustakalikhitaṃ kṛtvā pūjayiṣyanti candanacūrṇānulepanadhūpamālyaiḥ chatradhvajapatākaiḥ vividhair vā prakārair vādyaviśeṣair vā nānātūryatāḍāvacaraiḥ / antaśaḥ anumodanāsahagataṃ vā cittasantatir vā pratilapsyante romaharṣaṇaṃ sañjanaṃ vā kariṣyanti vidyāprabhāvaśaktiṃ vā śrutvā saṃhṛṣyante anumodiṣyante caryāṃ vā pratipatsyanti / vyākṛtās te mayā anuttarāyāṃ samyaksambodho sarve te bhaviṣyanti / buddhā bhagavantaḥ / ata eva jināḥ smitaṃ kurvanti nānyathā iti //*

[T.286.1 (143b)–286.4 (143b)]

gaṅ źig mdo sde'i dbaṅ po'i rgyal po 'de 'jam dpal gyi rtsa ba'i cho ga rig pa'i spyod pa rdzas su sgrub pa las sgrub pa'i thabs la yaṅ dag par gźol ba / chos gyi sprin la rten pa la yaṅ dag par 'jug ciṅ rjes su 'braṅ bar byed pa daṅ / 'dzin par 'gyur ba daṅ / klog par 'gyur ba daṅ / dad par 'gyur ba daṅ / glegs bam la 'dri ba byas nas mchod par 'gyur ba daṅ / tsandan gyi phye ma daṅ byug pa daṅ / bdug pa daṅ / pheṅ ba daṅ / gdugs daṅ / rgyal mtshan daṅ / bdan rnam pa sna tshogs pa'am / tshig gi bye brag gis sam / sil sñan rnam pa sna tshogs daṅ / pheg rdob pa dag gam tha na rjes su yi raṅ ba daṅ ldan pa'i sems rgyud la thob pa'am / ba spu ldaṅ bar byed pa'am / rig pa'i mthu thos nas dga' ba skyes pa'am / rjes su yi raṅ dbaṅ 'gyur ba'am / spyod pa thob par 'gyur ba de dag ni ṅas bla na med pa yaṅ dag par rdzogs pa'i byaṅ chub tu saṅs rgyas bcom ldan 'das su 'gyur bar luṅ bstan te / des na rgyal ba da ltar 'dzum pa mdzad kyi gźan du ni ma yin no //

C2 [*Mmk* 8.79.10–28]

adau tāvat dṛṣṭasamayaḥ kṛtapuraścaraṇaḥ labdhābhiṣekaḥ asmin kalparājamūlamantrahṛdayaṃ upahṛdayaṃ vā anyataraṃ vā mantraṃ gṛhītvā ekākṣaraṃ vā anyaṃ vā yathepsitaṃ mahāraṇyaṃ gatvā triśallakṣāṇi jape phalodakāhāraḥ mūlaparṇabhakṣo vā kṛtapuraścaraṇo bhavati // tato parvatā[gra]ṃ [< T. *ri'i rtse mor*] *abhiruhya jyeṣṭaṃ paṭaṃ paścānmukhaṃ pratiṣṭhāpya ātmanā pūrvābhimukho kuśaviṇḍakopaviṣṭaḥ śvetapadmānāṃ śvetakuṅkumābhyaktānāṃ lakṣam ekaṃ bhagavataḥ śākyamuneḥ sarvabuddhabodhisattvapratyekabuddhāryaśrāvakāṇāṃ paṭasyādhas tān nivedayet / karpūradhūpaṃ ca yathāvibhavataḥ dahet / devaputranāgānāṃ ca pūjāṃ kuryāt / yathālabdhaiḥ puṣpaiḥ // tato 'rdharātrakālasamaye śuklapūrṇamāsyāṃ prātihārakapratipūrṇāyāṃ paṭasyāgrataḥ agnikuṇḍaṃ kṛtvā padmākāraṃ śvetacandanakāṣṭhair agniṃ prajvālya kuṅkumakarpūraṃ caikīkṛtya aṣṭasahasrāhutiṃ juhuyāt / yathāvibhavataḥ kṛtarakṣaḥ // tataḥ bhagavataḥ śākyamuneḥ raśmayo niścaranti samantācca paṭaḥ ekajvālībhūto bhavati / tataḥ sādhakena sattvaramāṇarūpena* [<V.56.8 reads *tvaramāṇarūpena* which corresponds to T.287.3 (144a) *riṅs pa'i tshul gyis*] *paṭaṃ triḥ pradakṣiṇīkṛtya sarvabuddhabodhisattvapratyekabuddhāryaśrāvakāṇāṃ praṇamya paṭaṃ grahetavyam // atītenapūrvalikhitasādhakapaṭāntadeśe tato gṛhītamātrotpatati / acchaṭāmātreṇa brahmalokam atikrāmati / kusumāvatīṃ lokadhātuṃ sampratiṣṭhati / yatrāsau bhagavāṃ saṅkusumitrājendras tathāgataḥ tiṣṭhati dhriyate* [*Mmk* 8.80 missing = V.8.56.12-16] *yapāyati dharmaṃ ca deśayati / āryamañjuśrīyaṃ ca sākṣāt paśyati / dharmaṃ śṛṇoti / anekānyapi bodhisattvaśatasahasrā paśyati / tāṃś ca parupāste / mahākalpasahasraṃ ajarāmaralīlī bhavati / paṭas tatraiva tiṣṭhati / sarvabuddhabodhisattvādhiṣṭhito bhavati / teṣāṃ cādhiṣṭānaṃ saṃjānīte kṣetraśatasahasraṃ cākrāmati / kāyaśatasahasraṃ vā darśayati / anekarddhiprabhāvasamudgato bhavati / āryamañjuśriyaś ca kalyāṇimitro bhavati / niyataṃ bodhiparāyaṇo bhavatīti //*

[T.286.4 (143b)–288.1 (146b)]
'dir daṅ por re źig cho ga'i rgyal po 'di la dam tshig mthoṅ ba sṅon du bya ba rnam byas pa daṅ dbaṅ bskur ba thob pa / rtsa ba'i sṅags sam sñiṅ po'am ñe ba'i sñiṅ po 'am / sṅags gaṅ yaṅ ruṅ ba bzuṅ nas yi ge gcig pa'am / gaṅ 'dod pa dgon pa chen por soṅ ste 'bum phrag gsum bzla bar bya'o // 'bras bu daṅ chus 'tsho ba'am / rtsa ba daṅ / lo ma'i bza' ba byas / sṅon du bya ba byas par 'gyur ro // de nas ri'i rtse mor'dzegs nas ras ris chen po'i tshad nub phyogs su mṅon du lta ba bźag pa byas la bdag ñid śar du bltas de / ku śa'i khres la 'dug nas / padma dkar po la tsandan daṅ gur gum gyis btags de / bcom ldan 'das śākya thub pa daṅ / saṅs rgyas daṅ byaṅ chub sems dpa' thams cad daṅ / raṅ saṅs rgyas daṅ ñan thos dag la 'bum phrag gcig ri mo'i ras ris kyi 'og tu dbul bar bya'o // ga pur gyi bdug pa yaṅ ci 'byor pas bdug go // lha'i bu daṅ klu rnams la yaṅ ci rñed pa'i me tog gis mchod par

bya'o // de nas mtshan phyed kyi dus su cho 'phrul gyi zla phyed kyi zla ba ña ba la / ras ris kyi mdun du padma'i rnam pa lta bu'i me thab byas pa la / tsandan dkar po'i śiṅ gis me sbar nas / gur gum daṅ ga pur bsres pas sreg blugs ci 'byor pas stoṅ rtsa brgyad sbyin sreg bya'o / de nas bsruṅ ba bya'o // de nas bcom ldan 'das śākya thub pa las 'od zer byuṅ ste / ras kyi ri mo'i 'khor yug nas gcig tu 'bar 'gyur te / sgrub pa pos gur gum daṅ / tsandan gyis btags pa'i tsandan dkar po'i me tog gis mchod yon dbul lo // de nas sgrub pa pos riṅs pa'i tshul gyis ras ris la lan gsum bskor ba byas te / saṅs rgyas daṅ byaṅ chub sems dpa' thams cad daṅ / raṅ saṅs rgyas thams cad daṅ 'phags pa ñan thos rnams la phyag byas nas / sgrub pa pos bris pa'i ras ris kyi mtha' ma'i phyogs nas 'jigs pa med pas ras ris gzuṅ bar bya'o // de nas zuṅ ba tsam gyis 'phur te / se gol gtogs pa tsam gyis tshaṅs pa'i 'jig rten du phyin par 'gyur te / me tog can gyi 'jig rten gyi khams su rab tu gans par 'gyur te / gaṅ du bcom ldan 'das me tog yaṅ dag par skyes pa'i rgyal po'i dbaṅ po de bźin gśegs pa de bźugs de / 'tsho źiṅ gźes la chos kyaṅ ston to / 'phags pa 'jam dpal yaṅ mṅon du mthoṅ ṅo // chos kyaṅ thos so / byaṅ chub sems dpa' du ma tag kyaṅ mthoṅ źiṅ / de dag la bsñen bkur yaṅ byed de bskal pa chen po stoṅ du rga ba daṅ 'chi ba med ciṅ gnas par 'gyur ro // ras ris kyaṅ de na gnas par 'gyur ro // saṅs rgyas daṅ byaṅ chub sems dpa' thams cad kyis byin gyis brlabs par 'gyur ro / de dag gis byin gyis brlabs par yaṅ dag par źes so // saṅs rgyas kyi źiṅ stoṅ yaṅ 'da' bar byed do // lus stoṅ yaṅ ston par byed do // rdzu 'phrul gyi mthu du ma yaṅ 'byin par byed do // 'phags pa 'jam dpal yaṅ dge ba'i bźes gñen du 'gyur ro // des par byuṅ chub la gźol par 'gyur ro //

C3 [*Mmk* 11.98.8–13]
tato vandeta tāpinam /

vanditvā lokanāthaṃ tu pūjāṃ kuryān manoramām /
vividhaiḥ stotropahārais tu saṃstutya punaḥ punaḥ //

sugandhapūṣpais tathā śāstu ardhaṃ dattvā tu jāpinaḥ /
praṇamya śirasā buddhānāṃ tadā tu śiṣyasambhavāṃ //

teṣāṃ lokanāthānāṃ agrato yāpadeśanā [> *pāpa°* = T. *sdig pa*]/

[*Mmk* 11.99.7–12]
ato vyomne dite bhānoḥ mantrajāpaṃ tadā tyajet /
mantrajāpaṃ tadā tyaktvā visarjyārdhaṃ dadau vratī //

[T.310.3–4 (155b)]
de nas skyob la phyag kyaṅ bya //
'jig rten mgon la phyag 'tshal nas //
mchod pa yid du 'oṅ bar bya //

rnam pa sna tshogs mchod bstod daṅ //
yaṅ dag bstod pa yaṅ yaṅ bya //
dri źim me tog de bźin du //
ston la zlos pas mchod yon dbul //

saṅs rgyas rnams daṅ de'i slob la //
spyi bos rab tu phyag 'tshal lo //
'jig rten mgon po de dag gi //
mdun du sdig pa bśags par bya //

[T.311.3 [156a])
de nas ñi ma phyed śar na //
sṅags bzlas de tshe spaṅ bar bya //
sṅags bzlas de tshe btaṅ ba na //
sdom brtson mchod yon slar gśegs gsol //

Appendix D: *mantras*

D1 [*Mmk* 1.2.20–22; 1.2.27-3.1–9]
atha bhagavān saṅkusumitarājendras tathāgato mañjuśriyaṃ kumārabhūtam etad avocat [/] *api tu kumāra śatasahasragaṅgānadīsikataprakhyais athāgatair arhadbhiḥ saṃyaksambuddhais tvadīyaṃ mantracaryā° . . . bhāṣitavantaḥ bhāṣiṣyante ca* [/] *mayāpyetarhi anumoditum eva* [/] *gaccha tvaṃ mañjuśrīḥ kumārabhūta yasyedānīṃ kālaṃ manyase / śākyamunisamīpaṃ sammukham / iyaṃ dharmaparyāyaṃ śroṣyasi / tvam api bhāṣiṣyase bhavati cātra mantraḥ* [/] *namaḥ sarvatathāgatānām acintyāpratihataśāsanānāṃ oṁ ra ra smara / apratihataśāsanakumārarūpadhāriṇa hūm hūm phaṭ phaṭ svāhā // ayaṃ sa kumāra mañjuśrīḥ mūlamantraḥ / sarveṣāṃ tathāgatānāṃ hṛdayaḥ sarvaiś ca tathāgatair bhāṣitaḥ bhāṣiṣyante / sa tvam apīdānīṃ bhāṣiṣyase / sahāṃ lokadhātuṃ gatvā vistaravibhāgaśaḥ sarvakarmakaram / śākyamuninā tathāgatenābhyanujñātaḥ / paramahṛdayaṃ bhavati cātra oṁ vākye da namaḥ / upahṛdayaṃ cātra vākye hūm //*

[T.178.7 (89b)–179.1 (90a); 179.4–7 (90a)]
de nas bcom ldan 'das me tog yaṅ dag par skyes pa rgyal po'i dbaṅ po de bźin gśegs pas 'jam dpal gźon nur gyur pa la 'di skad ces bka' stsal to // gźan yaṅ gźon nu gaṅ gā'i kluṅ brgya stoṅ gi bye ma sñed kyi de bźin gśegs pa dgra bcom pa yaṅ dag par rdzogs pa'i saṅs rgyas kyis khyod kyi sṅags kyi spyod pa daṅ / . . . gsuṅs pa daṅ / gsuṅ ba daṅ / gsuṅ bar 'gyur ba yin te / de ltar rjes su yi raṅ ba ñid de / 'jam dpal gźon nur gyur pa de'i dus la bab par śes na soṅ śig / śākya thub pa'i spyan sṅar mṅon sum du chos kyi rnam graṅs 'di thos par 'gyur te / khyod

kyaṅ ston par 'gyur ro // 'dir yaṅ gsuṅs pa / namaḥ sarba tathāgatānāṃ atsintyapratihataśāsanāṃ oṁ smara smara apratihataśāsanakumārarūpadhāriṇa oṁ hūm hūm phaṭ phaṭ svāhā / 'di ni 'jam dpal gźon nur gyur pa'i rtsa ba'i sṅags so // de bźin gśegs pa thams cad kyi sñiṅ po ste / de bźin gśegs pa thams cad gyis gsuṅs la / gsuṅ śiṅ gsuṅ bar 'gyur la / khyod kyaṅ mi mjed kyi 'jig rten gyi khams su soṅ nas / dbye ba daṅ rnam par dbye ba rgya cher ston par 'gyur te / de bźin gśegs pa śākya thub pa źes bya bas kyaṅ las thams cad byed pa 'de rjes su gnaṅ bar 'gyur ro // 'dir sñiṅ po mchog tu gyur pa ni / oṁ bāgye daṃ namaḥ / 'dir ñe ba'i sñiṅ po ni bākye hūṁ /

D2 [*Mmk* 4.55.21–26]
namaḥ sarvabuddhabodhisattvānām apratihatamatigati[7]*-praticāriṇām / namaḥ saṃśodhanaduḥkhapraśamanarājendrarājāya tathāgatāyārhate samyaksambuddhāya / tadyathā / oṁ śodhaya śodhaya sarvavighnaghātaka mahākāruṇika kumārarūpadhāriṇe / vikurva vikurva / samayam anusmara / tiṣṭha tiṣṭha hūm hūm phaṭ phaṭ svāhā //*

[T.258.4–5 (129b)]
namaḥ samantabuddhānāṃ bodhisattvāpratihatagatimatipratsāriṇāṃ / namaḥ saṃśodhanaduḥkhapraśamanendrārādzāya / tathāgatāyārhate samyaksambuddhāya / tadyathā / oṁ śodhaya saṃśodhaya / sarbabighnaghātaka mahākāruṇika kumārarūpadhāriṇi / bikurba bikurba samayam anusmara tiṣṭha tiṣṭha hūm hūm phaṭ phaṭ svāhā /

D3 [*Mmk* 2.25.17–18; 2.25.22-26.7]
atha mañjuśrīḥ kumārabhūtaḥ yamāntakasya krodharājasya hṛdayaṃ sarvakarmikaṃ ekavīraṃ . . . oṁ āḥ hūṁ / idaṃ tan mahākrodhasya hṛdayaṃ / sarvakarmikaṃ sarvamaṇḍaleṣu sarvamantracaryāsu ca nidiṣṭaṃ mahāsattvena mañjughoṣeṇa sarvavighnavināśanam / atha mañjuśrīḥ kumārabhūtaḥ dakṣiṇaṃ pāṇim udyamya krodhasya mūrdhni sthāpayāmāsa / evañ cāha / namas te sarvabuddhānām / samanvāharanta [>°*antu*] *buddhā bhagavantaḥ / ye kecid daśadiglokadhātuvyavasthitā anantāparyāntāś ca bodhisattvā maharddhikāḥ samayam adhitiṣṭhanta* [>°*antu*] */ ityevam uktvā taṃ krodharājānaṃ bhrāmayitvā kṣipiti sma / samanantaranikṣipte mahākrodharāje sarvāvantaṃ lokadhātuṃ sattvā kṣaṇamātreṇa ye duṣṭāśayāḥ sattvā maharddhikāḥ tāṃ nigṛhānayati sma / taṃ mahāparṣanmaṇḍalaṃ śuddhāvāsabhavanaṃ praveśayati sma / vyavasthāyāñ ca sthāpayitvā samantajvālāmālākulo bhūtvā duṣṭasattveṣu ca mūrdhni tiṣṭhate sma //*

[T.217.6–7 (109a); 218.2–6]
de nas 'jam dpal gźon nur gyur pas khro bo'i rgyal po gśin rje gśed kyi sñiṅ po la thams cad byed pa daṅ / dpa'bo gcig pa spyan . . . oṁ āḥ hūṁ

/ 'di ni khro bo chen po de'i sñiṅ po ste las thams cad byed pa dkyil 'khor thams cad daṅ sṅags thams cad kyi spyod pa la sems dpa' chen po 'jam pa'i dbyaṅs kyis smras te / bgegs thams cad 'jigs par byed pa'o // de nas 'jam dpal gźon nur gyur pas lag pa g.yas pa bteg ste / khro bo'i sbyi bor gźag pa byas so // 'di skad du yaṅ smras te / saṅs rgyas thams cad la phyag 'tshal lo // saṅs rgyas bcom ldan 'das rnams dgoṅs su gsol / gaṅ su dag phyogs bcu'i 'jig rten gyi khams na rnam par gnas śiṅ mtha' yas mu med ba'i rdzu 'phrul daṅ ldan pa'i byaṅ chub sems dpa' rnams dam tshig la lhag par gnas par gyis śig / de skad ces smras nas / khro bo'i rgyal po la lag pa bskor nas btaṅ bar gyur to // khro bo'i rgyal po chen po btaṅ ma thag tu thams cad daṅ ldan pa'i 'jig rten gyi khams dag tu soṅ nas / skad cig tsam gyis gaṅ dag sdaṅ ba'i bsam pa daṅ ldan pa'i sems cad rdzu 'phrul che bdag tshar bcad ciṅ der bkug par gyur nas / 'khor gyi dkyil 'khor chen po gnas gtsaṅ ma'i gźal med khaṅ de yaṅ dag par bcug ste /

D4 [*Mmk* 2.28.21–22–2.29.1–11]
atha khalu mañjuśrīḥ kumārabhūta vajrapāṇiṃ bodhisattvam āmantrayate sma / imāni guhyakādhipate mantrapadāni sarahasyāni paramaguhyakāni [. . .] *namaḥ sarvabuddhabodhisattvānām apratihataśāsanānāṃ / uṃ kara kara kuru kuru mama kāryam bhañja bhañja sarvavighnāṃ daha daha sarva vajravināyakam mūrdhaṭakajīvitāntakara mahāvikṛtarūpiṇe paca paca sarvaduṣṭāṃ mahāgaṇapatijīvitāntakara bandha bandha sarvagrahāṃ ṣaṇmukha ṣaḍbhuja ṣaṭcaraṇa rudramānaya viṣṇumānaya brahmādyāṃ devānānaya mā vilamba mā vilamba iyal iyal maṇḍalamadhye praveśaya samayam anusmara hūṁ hūṁ hūṁ hūṁ hūṁ hūṁ phaṭ phaṭ svāhā / eṣa saḥ paramaguhyakādhipate paramaguhyaḥ mahāvīryaḥ mañjuśrīḥ ṣaṇmukho nāma mahākrodharājā sarvavighnavināśakaḥ / anena paṭhitamātreṇa daśabhūmipratiṣṭhāpitabodhisattvā vidravante / kiṃ punar duṣṭavighnāḥ / anena paṭhitamātreṇa mahārakṣā kṛtā bhavati / mudrā cātra bhavati mahāśūleti vikhyātā sarvavighnavināśikā /*

[T.222.4–5; 6 (111b)–223.3 (112a)]
de nas 'jam dpal gźon nur gyur phas byaṅ chub sems dpa' phyag na rdo rje la smras pa gsaṅ ba pa'i bdag po sṅags kyi tshig 'di ni gsaṅ ba daṅ bcas śiṅ mchog tu gsaṅ bar bya pa yin te / [. . .] *namaḥ samantabuddhānāṃ / apratihataśāsanānāṃ / oṃ kara kara / kuru kuru / mama kāryam bhañja bhañja / sarbabighna daha daha sarba bajrabināyakaṃ mūrdhagaṭaṃ dzīvitāntakara mahābikṛtarūpathāriṇi / patsa patsa sarbaduṣṭāna / mahāganapatidzībivitāntakara banda banda sarbagrahāna / ṣaṭmukha ṣaṭbhudza / ṣaṭtsaraṇa rudramānaya / biṣṇumānaya brahmādyāṃ debamānaya mā bilaṃba / lahu lahu maṇḍalamadhye prabeśaya / samayam anusmara hūṁ hūṁ hūṁ hūṁ hūṁ hūṁ phaṭ phaṭ / svāhā / gsaṅ ba pa'i bdag po 'di ni 'jam dpal gźon nur gyur pa'i*

mchog tu gsaṅ ba'i sṅags chen po gdoṅ drug pa źes bya ba yin te / khro bo'i rgyal po bgegs thams cad 'jig par byed pa sten / 'di brjod pa tsam gyis sa bcu'i dbaṅ phyug la gnas pa'i byaṅ chub sems dpa' yaṅ 'jigs par byed pa yin na / bgegs ma ruṅs pa lta smos kyaṅ ci dgos 'di brjod pa tsam ñid kyis sruṅ ba chen po byas par 'gyur ro // 'dir yaṅ phyag rgyar 'gyur ba ni / nag po chen po źes bya ba'i / bgegs rnams thams cad 'jig byed pa'o /

D5 [*Mmk* 2.29.11–21]
asyaiva krodharājasya hṛdayaṃ / oṁ hṛīṁḥ jñīḥ vikṛtānana hum / sarvaśatruṃ nāśaya stambhaya phaṭ phaṭ svāhā / anena mantreṇa sarvaśatrūṃ mahāśūlarogeṇa caturthakena vā gṛhṇāpayati / śatatajapena [> *satata°* = T. *rtag tu*] *vā yāvad rocate maitratāṃ vā na pratipadyate / atha karuṇācittaṃ labhate / jāpānte muktir na syāt / mṛyate iti ratnatrayāpakariṇāṃ kartavyaṃ nāśeṣaṃ saumyacittānāṃ* [/] *mudrā mahāśūlaiva prayojanīyā / upahṛdayaṃ cātra bhavati / oṁ hṛīṁḥ kālarūpa hūṃ khaṃ svāhā / mudrā mahāśūlyaiva prayojanīyā / sarvaduṣṭāṃ yam icchati taṃ kārayati / paramahṛdayam / sarvabuddhādhiṣṭhitaṃ ekākṣaraṃ nāma / hūṁ / eṣa sarvakarmakaraḥ / mudrā mahāśūlyaiva prayojanīyā / sarvānarthanivāraṇam / sarvabhūtavaśaṅkaraḥ saṃkṣepataḥ / eṣa krodharāja sarvakarmeṣu prayoktavyaḥ* [/]

[T. 223.3–7 (112a)]
'di ñid kyi khro bo'i rgyal po'i stiṅ po ni / oṁ hṛīṁḥ jñīḥ bikṛtānana hūṁ sarbaśatrūṃ nāśaya stambhaya phaṭ phaṭ svāhā / sṅags 'di brjod pas dgra thams cad zug gzer chen po daṅ / nad chen po daṅ ñin bźi pa'i rims gyis thebs par 'gyur ro // rtag tu dga' ba med pa daṅ / byams pa med pa daṅ / sñiṅ rje'i sems thob par mi 'gyur te / bzlas pa zin gyi bar du grol bar mi 'gyur źiṅ 'chi bar 'gyur ro // dkon mchog gsum la gnod pa byed pa dag la bya'i / źi ba'i sems yod pa gźan dag la ni ma yin no // phyag rgya ni rtse gsum chen po źes bya ba sbyar bar bya'o // 'dir ñe ba'i sñiṅ por 'gyur ba ni / oṁ hri kākarūpa huṁ khaṃ svāhā / phyag rgya ni rtse gsum chen po źes bya ba ñid sbyar bar bya'o // ma ruṅs pa thams cad la gaṅ 'dod pa de byed par 'gyur ro // sñiṅ po'i mchog saṅs rgyas thams cad kyis byin gyis brlabs pa'i yi ge gcig źes bya'o // hūṁ / 'di ni las thams cad byed pa'o / phyag rgya yaṅ rtse gsum chen po źes bya bar sbyar bar bya'o // phuṅ khrol thams cad zlog par byed pa / 'byuṅ po thams cad dbaṅ du byed pa ste / mdor na khro bo'i rgyal po 'di ni las thams cad la sbyar bar bya'o //

D6 [*Mmk* 2.26.13–27.3]
namaḥ samantabuddhānāṃ / oṁ ra ra smara apratihataśāsanakumārarūpadhāriṇa hūṁ hūṁ phaṭ phaṭ svāhā / ayaṃ samāryāḥ [> *sa mārṣāḥ*: T. *grogs po dag 'di ni*] *madīyamūlamantraḥ / āryamañjuśriyaṃ nāma*

mudrā pañcaśikhā mahāmudreti vikhyātā taṃ prayojaye asmin mūlamantre sarvakarmikaṃ bhavati hṛdayaṃ / buddho sarvakarmakaraṃ śivaṃ / oṁ dhānyada namaḥ / mudrā cātra bhavati triśikheti vikhyātā sarvabhogābhivarddhanī / upahṛdayaṃ cātra bhavati / bāhye hūṁ / mudrā cātra bhavati triśikheti vikhyātā sarvasattvākarṣaṇī / paramahṛdayaṃ cātra bhavati / muṃ / mudrā bhavati cātra mayūrāsaneti vikhyātā sarvasattvavaśaṅkarī / sarvabuddhānāṃ hṛdayam / aparam api mahāvīraṃ nāma aṣṭākṣaraṃ paramaśreyasaṃ mahāpavitraṃ tribhavavartmīyacchedaṃ [T. *chos* > *dharma* for *vartmīya*] *sarvadugati-nivāraṇaṃ sarvaśāntikaraṃ sarvakarmakaraṃ kṣemaṃ nivāraṇa-prāpaṇaṃ buddham iva saṃmukhadarśanopasthitam / svayam eva mañjuśrīr ayaṃ bodhisattvaḥ sarvasattvānām arthāya paramahṛdayaṃ mantrarūpeṇopasthitaḥ sarvāśāpāripūrakaṃ yatra smaritamātreṇa pañcānantaryāṇi pariśodhayati / kaḥ pūnarvādo jāyeta / katamaṃ ca tat / oṁ āḥ dhīra hūṁ svacara / eṣa saḥ mārṣā yūyam evāhaṃ aṣṭākṣaraṃ mahāvīraṃ paramaguhyahṛdayaṃ buddhatvam iva pratyayasthitam* [> *pratyupa*°: T. *rab tu ñe bar gnas pa*] / *sarvakāryeṣu saṃkṣepato mahāgu* \ \ \ \ \ *antaniṣṭhādakṣamiti* [> T. *yon tan gyi mtha' rgya chen po brjod par ni bskal pa bye ba khri phrag brgya stoṅ du mar yaṅ mi num te*] / *mudrā cātra bhavati mahāvīreti vikhyātā sarvāśāpāripūrakī* /

[T.219.1 (110a)–220.2 (110b)]
namaḥ sarbabuddhānāṃ / oṁ ra ra smara / apratihataśāsana/ kumārarūpadhāriṇe hūṁ hūṁ phaṭ phaṭ svāhā / grogs po dag 'di ni rtsa ba'i sṅags yin te 'phags pa 'jam dpal źes bya ba yin no // phyag rgya ni gtsug phud lda pa źes grags te de la rab tu sbyar bar bya'o // rtsa ba'i sṅags 'di ni las thams cad pa źes bya'o // sñiṅ po'i sṅags 'di ni las thams cad byed ciṅ śes pa yin de / oṁ bākyedaṃ namaḥ / 'dir phyag rgyar 'gyur ba ni gtsug phud gsum źes bya ba yin te / loṅs spyod thams cad mṅon par 'phel bar byed pa'o // dir ñe ba'i sñiṅ por 'gyur ba ni / bahkye hūṁ / 'dir phyag rgyar 'gyur ba ni gtsug phud gsum pa źes grags pa yin te / sems can thams cad 'gugs par byed pa yin no / 'dir sñiṅ po mchog tu 'gyur ba ni maṃ / 'dir phyag rgyar 'gyur ba ni rma bya'i gdan źes bya bar bstan yin te / sems can thams cad dbaṅ du byed pa'o / gźan yaṅ phyag rgya thams cad kyi sñiṅ po dpa' po chen po źes bya ba yi ge brgyad yod de / dpal mchog tu byed pa / dag byed chen po srid pa gsum gyi chos ñe bar gcod par byed pa / ṅan 'gro thams cad zlog par byed pa / źi ba thams cad byed pa / las thams cad byed pa / mya ṅan las 'das pa'i bde ba thob par byed pa / saṅs rgyas mṅon sum du mthoṅ ba bźin du ñe bar gnas pa / byaṅ chub sems dpa' 'jam dpal gźon nur gyur pa ñid bźin du ñe bar gnas pa / sems can thams cad gyi don gyi phyir / mchog tu gsaṅ ba'i ṅo bos ñe bar gnas pa re ba thams cad yaṅs su rdzogs par byed pa / gaṅ du dran pa tsam gyis mtshams med pa lṅa yaṅ

yoṅs su sbyoṅ bar byed na bzlas pas lta sm[r]os khyad ci dgos / de yaṅ gaṅ źe na / oṁ āḥ bīra hūṁ / khe tsa ra / grogs po dag 'di ni yi ge brgyad po dpa' bo chen po źes bya ba / gsaṅ pa'i sñiṅ po'i bdag ñid yin te / saṅs rgyas ñid bźin du rab tu ñe bar gnas pa yin no // mdor na bya thams cad la yon tan gyi mtha' rgya chen po brjod par ni bskal pa bye ba khri phrag brgya stoṅ du mar yaṅ mi nus te / 'dir phyag rgya yaṅ stobs po che źes par rnam par grags pa / re ba thams cad yoṅs su rdzogs pa'o //

D7 [*Mmk* 2.27.3–9]
āhvānanamantrā cātra bhavati / oṁ he he kumārarūpisvarūpiṇe sarvabālabhāṣitaprabodhane āyāhi bhagavaṃ āyāhi / kumārakrīḍotpaladhāriṇe maṇḍalamadhye tiṣṭha tiṣṭha / samayam anusmara / apratihataśāsana hūṁ / mā vilamba ru ru phaṭ svāhā / eṣa bhagavaṃ mañjuśriyaḥ āhvānanamantrā / sarvasattvānāṃ sarvabodhisattvānāṃ sarvapratyekabuddhāryaśrāvakadevanāgayakṣagandharva[*asura* = T. *lha ma yin*]*garuḍakinnaramahoragapiśācarākṣasasarvabhūtānāṃ* [/]

[T.220.1–4 (110b)]
spyan draṅ ba'i sṅags ni / oṁ he he kumārabisvarūpiṇe / sarbabālabhāṣitaprabodhane / eyāhi bhagabaṃ / eyāhi kumāra / krīḍanutpaladhāriṇe maṇḍalamadhye tiṣṭha tiṣṭha samayam anusmara / apratihataśāsana hūṁ / mā bilamba kuru phaṭ svāhā / 'di ni bcom ldan 'das 'jam dpal gyi spyan draṅ ba'i sṅags so // saṅs rgyas thams cad daṅ / byaṅ chub sems dpa' thams cad daṅ / raṅ saṅs rgyas thams cad daṅ / 'phags pa ñan thos daṅ / lha daṅ / klu daṅ / gnod sbyin daṅ / dri za daṅ / lha ma yin daṅ / nam mkha' ldiṅ daṅ / mi 'am cid daṅ / lto 'phye chen po daṅ / śa za daṅ / srin po daṅ / 'byuṅ po thams cad kyi 'aṅ yin no //

D8 [*Mmk* 2.27.10–26]
saptābhimantritaṃ candanodakaṃ kṛtvā / caturdiśamityūdhvam adhastiryaksarvataḥ kṣipet / sarvabuddhabodhisattvāḥ mañjuśriyaḥ svayaṃ tasya parivāraḥ sarvalaukikalokottarāś ca mantrāḥ sarve ca bhūtagaṇāḥ sarvasattvāś ca āgatā bhaveyuḥ / namaḥ sarvabuddhānāṃ apratihataśāsanānām / oṁ dhu dhura dhura dhūpavāsini dhūpārciṣi hūṁ tiṣṭha samayam anusmara svāhā / dhūpamantraḥ / candanaṃ karpūraṃ kuṅkumaṃ caikīkṛtya dhūpaṃ dāpayet tataḥ / āgatānāṃ tathāgatānāṃ sarvabodhisattvānāṃ ca dhūpāpyāyitamanasaḥ ākṛṣṭā bhavanti / bhavati cātra mudrā yasya māleti vikhyātā sarvasattvākarṣaṇī śivā / āhvānanamantrāyāś ca ayam eva mudrā padmamālā śubhā / āgatānāṃ ca sarvabuddhabodhisattvānāṃ sarvasattvānāṃ cāgatānāṃ arghyo deyaḥ / karpūracandanakuṅkumair udakamāloḍyajātīkusumana-

vamālikavārṣikapunnāganāgavavakulapiṇḍitagarābhyāṃ eteṣāmanyatamena puṣpeṇa yathārttukena vā sugandhapuṣpeṇa miśīkṛtya anena mantreṇa arghyo deyaḥ / namaḥ sarvabuddhānāṃ apratihataśāsanānāṃ tadyathā / he he mahākāruṇika viśvarūpadhāriṇi arghyaṃ pratīcchad pratīcchāpaya samayam anusmara tiṣṭha tiṣṭha maṇḍalamadhye praveśaya praviśa sarvabhūtānukampaka gṛhṇa gṛhṇa hūṁ ambaravicāriṇe svāhā / mudrā cātrapūrṇeti vikhyātā sarvabuddhānuvartinī /

[T.220.4 (110b)–221.4 (111a)]
tsandan gyi chur gyas te / lan bdun bsṅags nas / phogs pa'i daṅ / steṅ daṅ / 'og daṅ / thams cad du gtor na saṅs rgyas daṅ / byaṅ chub sems dpa' daṅ / 'jam dpal gźon nur gyur pa raṅ ñed 'khor daṅ bcas pa thams cad daṅ // 'jig rten daṅ 'jig rten las 'das pa thams cad daṅ / sṅags daṅ de bźin du 'byuṅ po'i tshogs daṅ sems can thams cad 'gugs par 'gyur ro // namaḥ sarbabuddhānāṃ / apratihataśāsanānāṃ / oṁ dhu dhura dhura dhūpabāsini / dhūmarartsiśi hūṁ tiṣṭha samayam anusmara svāhā / bdug pa'i sṅags so // tsandan daṅ / ga pur daṅ / gur gum gcig tu byas te / bdug pas bdugs na de bźin gśegs pa rnams daṅ / byaṅ chub sems dpa' thams cad daṅ / sems can thams cad bdug pas tshim źiṅ dgyes nas bźugs par 'gyur ro // 'dir yaṅ phyag rgyar 'gyur ba ni // padma'i phreṅ bźes grags pa // thams cad 'gugs byed źi ba yin // spyan draṅ ba yi sṅags la yaṅ // padma'i phreṅ ba bzaṅ po źes // bya ba'i phyag rgya 'di ñid do // saṅs rgyas daṅ byaṅ chub sems dpa' thams cad daṅ / sems can thams cad byon pa la mchod yon dbul bar bya ste / ga pur daṅ tsandan daṅ gur gum chu daṅ sbyar nas me tog ku su daṅ mālika daṅ / dbyar gyi me tog daṅ me tog punnāga daṅ me tog ba kula daṅ / me tog piṇḍita garu 'di dag gaṅ yaṅ ruṅ ba'i me tog gam / dus ci lta ba'i me tog dri źim po bcug ste / sṅags 'dis mchod yon dbul bar bya'o // namaḥ sarbabuddhānāṃ / apratihataśāsanānāṃ / tadyathā / he he mahākāruṇika / biśwarūpadhāraṇi / arghyaṃ pratītstshapaya / samayam anusmara / tiṣṭha tiṣṭha / maṇḍalamadhye prabeśaya prabeśaya / sarvabhūtānukaṁpaka gṛhṇa gṛhṇa hūṁ / oṁbarabitsāriṇe svāhā / 'dir yaṅ phyag rgya ni gaṅ bźes bya bar grags pa sems can thams cad daṅ rjes su mthun źiṅ brtan pa'o //

D9 [*Mmk* 2.27.27–2.28.20]
dhruvā gandhamantrā cātra bhavati / namaḥ sarvabuddhānāṃ namaḥ samantagandhāvabhāsaśriyāya tathāgatāya / tadyathā / gandhe gandhe gandhāḍhye gandhamanorame pratīcche pratīccheyaṃ [> based on T. = *pratītstshamaṃ*] *gandham samantānusāriṇe svāhā / bhavati cātra mudrā pallavā nāma sarvāśāparipūrikā / puṣpamantrā cātra bhavati / namaḥ sarvabuddhānām apratihataśāsānām / namaḥ saṅkusumitarājasya tathāgatasya / tadyathā / kusume kusume kusumāḍhye kusumapuravāsini kusumāvati svāhā / tenaiva dhūpamantreṇa pūrvoktenaiva dhūpena dhūpayet /*

sarvabuddhāṃ namaskṛtya acintyādbhutarūpiṇām /
balimantraṃ pravakṣyāmi samyaksambuddhabhāṣitām //

namaḥ sarvabuddhabodhisattvānām apratihataśāsānāṃ tadyathā / he he bhagavaṃ mahāsattva buddhāvalokita mā vilamba idaṃ baliṃ gṛhṇāpaya gṛhna hūṁ hūṁ sarvaviśva ra ra ṭa ṭa phaṭ svāhā / nivedyaṃ cānena dāpayet baliṃ / ca sarvabhautikam / bhavati cātra mudrā śāktiḥ sarvaduṣṭanivāriṇī / namaḥ sarvabuddhānām apratihataśāsānāṃ sarvatamo'ndhakāravidhvaṁsināṃ namaḥ samantajyotigandhāvabhāsa-śriyāya tathāgatāya / tadyathā / he he bhagavaṃ jyotiraśmiśatasahasra-pratimaṇḍitaśarīra virkurva vikurva mahābodhisattvasamantajvālod-yotitamūrti khurda khurda avalokaya avalokaya sarvasattvānāṃ svāhā / pradīpamantrā / pradīpaṃ cānena dāpayet / mudrā vikāsinī nāma sarvasattvāvalokinī / namaḥ samantabuddhānāma pratihataśāsānāṃ / tadyathā / jvala jvala jvālaya jvālaya / hūṁ / vibodhaka harikṛṣṇapiṅgala svāhā / agnikārikā mantrā / bhavati cātra mudrā sampuṭa nāma lokaviśrutā / sarvasattvaprabhodyotanī bhāṣitā munivaraiḥ pūrvaṃ bodhisattvasya dhīmataḥ /

[T.221.4 (111a)–222.4 (111b)]
'dir yaṅ dri'i sṅags su 'gyur ba ni / namaḥ samantabuddhānāṃ / samantagandhābabhāsaśriye / tathāgatāya / tadyathā / gandhe gandhe gandhāḍhyāte/ gandhamanorathe pratītstsha pratītstshamaṃ gandham samantānutsāriṇi svāhā / 'dir phyag rgyar 'gyur ba ni lo ma źes bya ba re ba thams cad yoṅs su rdzogs par byed pa'o // 'dir me tog gi sṅags su 'gyur ba ni / namaḥ samantabuddhānāṃ / apratihataśāsānām / namaḥ saṅkusumitarādzasya / tathāgatasya / tadyathā / kusume kusume kusumāḍhye / kusumapurabāsini / kusumabati svāhā / bdug pa'i sṅags 'di ñid daṅ goṅ du bstan pa'i bdug pas bdug par bya'o //

sku ni rmad byuṅ bsam mi khyab //
saṅs rgyas thams cad phyag 'tshal te //
rdzogs saṅs rgyas kyis gsuṅs pa yi //
gtor ma'i sṅags ni bśad par bya //

namaḥ sarbabuddhānāṃ / apratihataśāsānāṃ / tadyathā / he he bhagabān / mahāsatwa sarbāvalokita imaṃ baliṃ gṛhṇāpaya gṛhnāpaya hūṁ hūṁ / sarbabiświa ra ra ṭa ṭa phaṭ svāhā / 'dis ni bśos dbul par bya ste / 'byuṅ po thams cad kyi gtor ma yaṅ bya'o // 'dir yaṅ phyag rgyar 'gyur ba ni / mduṅ źes bya ba ma ruṅs pa / thams cad zlog par byed pa'o / namaḥ samantabuddhānāṃ / apratihataśāsānāṃ / sarbatamo'ndhakārabid-hvansanāṃ / namaḥ samantadzyotigandhābabhāsaśriye / tathāgatāya / tadyathā / he he bhagavāṃ zyotirasmiśatasahasrapratimaṇḍitaśarīra birkurba bikurba mahābodhisatwasamantadzvālodyotitamūrti khurda khurda / abalokaya / abalokayamāna / laṃ sarba / satwānāṃ / tsa swāhā / mar me'i sṅags te 'dis ma me dbul bar bya'o // kha bye ba źes bya ba'i phyag rgya ni // sems can kun gyis mthoṅ ba'o // namaḥ samantabuddhānāṃ / apratihataśāsānāṃ / tadyathā / dzwala dzwala / dzwālaya dzwālaya / hūṁ bibhodaka harikṛṣṇapiṅgala swāhā / me'i bya ba byed pa'i sṅags so // 'dir yaṅ phyag rgyar 'gyur ba ni // sems can kun la 'od gsal byed / kha sbyar źes byar 'jig rten grags / byaṅ chub sems dpa' blo ldan gyir / thub pa mchog gis sṅon bśad pa'o //

D10 [*Mmk* 2.29.22–29]

visarjanamantrā bhavanti / namaḥ sarvabuddhānām apratihata-śāsanānām / tadyathā / jaya jaya sujaya mahākāruṇika viśvarūpiṇe gaccha gaccha svabhavanaṃ sarvabuddhāṃś ca visarjaya / saparivārāṃ svabhavanaṃ cānupraveśaya / samayam anusmara / sarvārthāś ca me siddhyantu mantrapadāḥ manorathaṃ ca me paripūraya [°*ntu* = T.] *svāhā / ayaṃ visarjanamantrāḥ sarvakarmeṣu prayoktavyaḥ / mudrā bhadrapīṭheti vikhyātā / āsanaṃ cānena dāpayet / manasā saptajaptena visarjanaṃ sarvebhyaḥ laukikalokottarebhyo maṇḍalebhyaḥ mantrebhyaś caiva mantrasiddhiḥ / samayajapakālaniyameṣu ca prayoktavyeti //*

[T.223.7 (112a)–224.3 (112b)]

'dir gśegs su gsol ba'i sṅags su 'gyur ba ni / namaḥ sarbabuddhānāṃ / apratihataśāsanānāṃ / tadyathā / dzaya dzaya sudzaya / mahākāruṇika biśwarūpiṇi gatstsha gatstsha sarbabuddhāśca / bisardzdzaya saparīvārāṃ swabhabanaṃ tsaprabeśaya samayam anusmara sarbārthāśtsa me siddhyantu mantrapadāḥ manorathaṃ tsa / me paripūrayantu svāhā / 'di ni gśegs su gsol ba'i sṅags te / las thams cad la sbyar bar bya'o // phyag rgya ni bzaṅ po'i gdan źes bya byin te / 'dis gdan la yaṅ sbyar bar bya'o // yid kyis bzlas pa bdun byas te gśegs su gsol lo // 'jig rten daṅ 'jig rten las 'das pa thams cad kyi dkyil 'khor daṅ sṅags daṅ sṅags grub pa dag daṅ / dam tshig daṅ / bzlas pa daṅ / dus daṅ ṅes par sdom pa dag la yaṅ sbyar bar bya'o //

D11 [*Mmk* 2.30.3–7; 2.30.23-26; 2.31.20–23]

namaḥ sarvabuddhānām apratihataśāsānām / oṁ riṭi svāhā // mañjuśriyasyedam anucarī keśinī nāma vidyā sarvakarmikā / mahāmudrāyā pañcaśikhāyā yojyasarvaviṣakarmasu / namaḥ samanta-buddhānām apratihataśāsānām / oṁ niṭi / upakeśinī nāma vidyeyaṃ sarvakarmikā mudrayā vikāsinyā ca yojayet / sarvagrahakarmeṣu/

namaḥ samantabuddhānām acintyādbhūtarūpiṇām [/]
oṁ nu re [T. = *tāre*] *svāhā /*
vidyā tārāvatī nāma praśastā sarvakarmasu /
mudrayā śaktiyaṣṭayā tu yojitā vighnaghātinī //

namaḥ sarvabuddhānām apratihatagata [T. *śākti*]*pracāriṇām* [/]
tadyathā / oṁ śrīḥ /
eṣā vidyā mahālakṣmī lokanāthais tu deśitā /
mudrā sampuṭayā yuktā mahārājyapradāyikā //

[T.224.4 (112b); 225.2 (113a); 225.7 (113a)–226.1 (113b)]
namaḥ samantabuddhānāṃ / apratihatagātāṇām [> *śāsānām* ?] */ oṁ riṭi ni swāhā / 'di ni 'jam dpal gyi rjes su 'braṅ ba skra can ma źes bya ba'i rig pa / las thams cad byed pa / phyag rgya chen po gtsug phud lda źes bya bdug gi las thams cad la sbyar bar bya'o //*

namaḥ samantabuddhānāṃ / atsintyādbhūtarūpīṇāṃ /
oṁ tāre swāhā /
rig pa phug ron źes bya ba // las rnams kun la rab du bsṅags //
phyag rgya mduṅ daṅ ldan pa yis // bgegs ni 'joms par byed pa yin //

namaḥ samantabuddhānāṃ / apratihataśāktipratsarīṇāṃ /
tadyathā / oṁ śrīḥ /
rig pa 'di ni dpal chen mo // 'jig rten mgon gyis bstan pa ste /
phyag rgya kha sbyar sbyar byas na / rgyal srid chen po sbyin byed pa'o //

D12 [*Mmk* 2.32.18–2.33.18]
bhāṣitā bodhisattvena mañjughoṣeṇa nāyinā [T. *skyob pa* < *tāyinā*] /
ṣaḍvikārā mahī kṛtsnā pracacāla samantataḥ //
hitārthaṃ sarvasattvānāṃ duṣṭasattvanivāraṇam /
maheśvarasya [T. *mi bzad* < *sahā°*] *sūto ghoro vaineyārtham ihāgataḥ //*
skandam aṅgārakaś caiva grahacihnaiḥ sucihnitaḥ /
mañjubhāṣiṇī tato bhāṣe karuṇāviṣṭena [T. *brlan pa* < *°āvṛṣṭi*] *cetasā //8*
mahātmā bodhisattvo 'yaṃ bālānāṃ hitakāriṇaḥ /
sattvacaryā yataḥ prokto viceruḥ sarvato jagat //
mudrāśaktiyaṣṭyānusaṃyukto sa mahātmanaḥ /
āvartayati brahmādyāṃ kiṃ punar mānuṣaṃ phalam //
kaumārabhittamakhilaṃ kalyamasya samāsataḥ /
kārttikeyamañjuśrīḥ mantro 'yaṃ samudāhṛtaḥ //
sattvānugrahakāmyarthaṃ bodhisattva ihāgataḥ /
tryakṣaraṃ nāma hṛdayaṃ mantrasyāsya udāhṛtam //
sarvasattvahitārthāya bhogākarṣaṇa tatparaḥ [T. *mchog* < *°parama*]/
mudrayā śaktiyaṣṭyā tu vinyastaḥ sarvakarmikaḥ //

oṁ hūṁ jaḥ /
eṣa mantraḥ samāsena kurān mānuṣakaṃ phalam /

namaḥ samantabuddhānāṃ samantodyotitamūrtinām [/]
vikṛtagraha hūṃ phaṭ svāhā //
upahṛdayaṃ cāsya saṃyukto mudrā śaktinā tathā /

āvartayati bhūtāni sagrahāṃ mātārāṃ tathā //
sarvamudritamudreṣu vinyastā saphalā bhavet /
vitrāsayati bhūtānāṃ duṣṭāviṣṭavimocanī //
eṣa mañjuśriyasya kumārabhūtasya kārttikeyamañjuśrī nāma kumāraḥ anucaraḥ sarvakarmikaḥ japamātreṇaiva sarvakarmāṇi karoti sarvabhūtāni trāsayati ākarṣayati vaśamānayati śoṣayati ghātayati yathepsitaṃ vā vidyādharasya tat sarvaṃ sampādayati /

[T. 226.5 (113b)–227.6 (114a)]
skyob pa byaṅ chub sems dpa' ni // 'jam pa'i dbyaṅs gyis bśad pa na //
sa rnams ma lus rnam drug tu // kun nas yoṅs su rab tu g.yos //
sems can kun gyi don phyir daṅ // ma ruṅs sems can zlog pa'i phyir //
mi bzad dbaṅ phyug bu'i gzugs su // gdul ba'i don du 'dir ston te //
skem byed daṅ ni mig dmar gyi // phyag mtshan gyis ni mtshon pa ste //
sñiṅ rjes thugs ni brlan pa yis // 'jam pa'i ṅag gyis gsuṅ pa yin //
sems dpa'i naṅ bdag ñid che // byis pa rnams la phan byed gaṅ //
sems can spyod phyir brtson pa ni // 'gro ba kun la rnam par spyod //
phyag rgya mduṅ daṅ ldan pa yis // bdag ñid chen pos sbyar na ni //
tshaṅs pa sogs pa'aṅ 'gyugs byed na // mi rnams ni smos ci dgos //
gźon nu'i sems su mtha' dag ni // bsdus nas yoṅs su bśad par bya //
smin drug bu daṅ 'jam dpal gyi // sṅags su 'di ni yaṅ dag bstan //
sems can rjes su gzuṅ ba'i phyir // byaṅ chub sems dpar'di ston to //
yig gsum źes bya'i sñiṅ po ni // 'di yi sṅags su brjod pa yin //
sems can kun la phan pa'i phir // loṅs spyod 'dren pa'i mchog de yin //
phyag rgya mduṅ daṅ ldan pa yin // bkod na las kun byed pa yin //

oṁ hūṁ dzzaḥ //
sṅags 'di mdo ru bsṅu byas na // mi rnams kyi ni don byed do //

namaḥ samantabuddhānāṃ / samantodyotitamūrtināṃ //
oṁ bikṛtagraha hūṃ phaṭ swāhā //
'di yaṅ ñe ba'i sñiṅ po ste // de bźin phyag rgya mduṅ ldan pas //
'byuṅ po thams cad 'gugs byed ciṅ // de bźin gza' daṅ ma mor bcas //
phyag rgya kun gyis phyag rgya la // bkod na 'bras bur bcas par 'gyur //
'byuṅ po rnams ni daṅ ṅas byed ciṅ // ma ruṅs 'jug pa zlog par byed //

'jam dpal gźon nur gyur pa 'di'i gdoṅ drug gi bu źes bya ba'i 'jam dpal gźon nu'i rjes su 'braṅ ba ste / las thams cad byed pa ste / bzlas pa tsam kho nas las thams cad byed par 'gyur ro // 'byuṅ po thams cad daṅ ṅes par byed pa daṅ / skrag par byed pa daṅ / 'gugs par byed pa daṅ / dbaṅ du byed pa daṅ skem par byed pa daṅ / 'jig par byed pa daṅ rig pa 'dzin pa ji ltar 'dod pa de thams cad sgrub par byed pa'o //

D13 [*Mmk* 2.33.18–2.34.5]
namaḥ samantabuddhānām apratihataśāsānām / tadyathā / oṁ brahma subrahma bramavarcase śāntiṃ kuru svāhā //

eṣa mantro mahābrahmā bodhisattvena bhāṣitaḥ /
śāntiṃ prajagmurbhūtāni tatkṣaṇād eva śītalā //

mudrā pañcaśikhāyuktā kṣipraṃ svastyayanaṃ bhavet /
ābhicārukeṣu sarveṣu athavo cedapaṭhyate [T. *srid sruṅ gi ni rig byed < atharvaveda] [/]*
eṣa saṃkṣepata ukto kalpamasya samāsataḥ [//]

namaḥ samantabuddhānām apratihataśāsanānām [/][9]
tadyathā / oṁ garūḍavāhana cakrapāṇi caturbhuja hūṁ hūṁ samayam anusmara /
bodhisattvo jñāpayati svāhā //

ājñapto mañjughoṣeṇa kṣipram arthakaraḥ śivaḥ /
vidrāpayati bhūtāni viṣṇurupeṇa dehinām //

mudrā triśikhe yuktaḥ kṣipramarthakaraḥ sthiraḥ /
ya eva vaiṣṇave tantre kathitāḥ kalpavistarāḥ /
upāyavaineyasattvānāṃ mañjughoṣeṇa bhāṣitāḥ //

[T.227.6 (114a)–228.3 (114b)]
namaḥ samantabuddhānāṃ / apratihataśāsānāṃ / tadyathā / oṁ brahma bramaratsasa śāntiṃ kuru svāhā /

sṅags 'di tshaṅs pa chen po ste // byaṅ chub sems dpas bśad pa yin //
'byuṅ pos źi gyur rab tu thob // skad cig ñid la bas li bar gyur //
phyag rgyag tsug phud lda sbyar na // myur du dge legs thob par 'gyur //
mṅon spyod dag ni thams cad la // srid sruṅ gi ni rig byed 'dod //
'di ni mdor bsdu bstan pa ste // 'di yi cho ga bsdus pa yin //

namaḥ samantabuddhānāṃ / apratihataśāsānāṃ / tadyathā / oṁ garūḍabāhana tsakrapāṇi / tsaturbhudza hūṁ hūṁ samayam anusmara / bhodhisattwo dzñāpayati swāhā /

'jam pa'i dbyaṅs kyis bka' stsal pa // źi ba'i don ni myur byed yin //
'byuṅ po rnams ni rnam 'jig ciṅ // khyab 'jug gzugs kyi lus can yin //
phyag rgya gtsug phud gsum sbyar na // las rnams kun byed brtan pa yin //
gaṅ dag khyab 'jug rgyud la ni // bya ba rgya cher bstan pa dag //
thabs kyis gdul bya'i sems can la // 'jam pa'i dbyaṅs kyis bśad pa yin //

D14 [*Mmk* 2.35.5–10]
yathā hi dhātrī bahudhā bālānāṃ lālati yatnataḥ /
tathā bāliśabuddhīnāṃ mantrarūpī carāmyaham //
daśabalaiḥ kathitaṃ pūrve adhunā ca mayoditam /
sakalaṃ mantratantrārthaṃ kumāro 'pyāham mahādyutiḥ //
jinavaraiś ca ye gītā gītā daśabalātmajaiḥ /
mañjusvareṇa te acintyādbutarūpiṇām //

[T.229.3–4 (115a)]
ji ltar ma mo maṅ po ni / 'bad pas byis pa rnams sruṅ ba //
de bźin byis pa'i blo can la / sṅags kyi tshul gyis ṅa yis bśad //
sṅon ni stobs bcu ldan pas bstan / da ni ṅa yis bstan pa yin //
sṅags rgyud don ni ma lus pa / 'od chen gźon nus bstan pa yin //
rgyal ba mchog gis gaṅ gsuṅs daṅ / stobs bcu ldan pa'i sras gsuṅs daṅ //
rmad byuṅ bsam mi khyab tshul gyis / 'jam dbyaṅs kyis gsuṅs de dag go //

D15 [*Mmk* 11.93.14–15]
ādau tāvad vidyāvrataśīlacaryāsamādānaṃ prathamata eva samādadet / prathamaṃ tāva nmaṇḍalācāryopadeśanasamayam anupraviśet /

[*Mmk* 11.93.26–11.94.6; 11.94.10–11]
sādhakaś ca . . . maṇḍalācāryam abhyarthya prārthayet / icchāmyācāryeṇa mahābodhisattvasya kumārabhūtasyāryamañjuśriyasya samayam anupraviṣṭum / tad vadatvācāryo 'smākam anukampārthaṃ hitacitto dayāvāṃ / tatas tena maṇḍalācāryeṇa pūrvanirdiṣṭena vidhinā śiṣyāṃ yathāpūrvaṃ parīkṣya praveśayet / pūrvavad abhiṣekaṃ dattvā mantraṃ dadyāt / yathāvat kramaśo samayaṃ darśayet / rahasyatantramudrāmanukarmāṇi karmāṇi ca prabhūtakālenaiva suparīkṣya āśayaṃ jñātvā darśayet /. . . [11.94.10–11] *tatas tena maṇḍalācāryeṇa putrasaṃjñā upasthāpayitavyā / putravat pratipattavyam / mātuś ca bhogā upasaṃhartavyā iti //*

[T.304.7 (152b)–305.1 (153a)]
daṅ por re źig rig pa daṅ brtul źugs daṅ / tshul khrims kyi yi dam [*yi dam > dam bca' = samādāna, samaya*?] *daṅ po ñid du blaṅ bar byas la / daṅ po re źig dkyil 'khor gyi slob dpon gyis bstan pa'i dam tshig khyod kyi cho ga'i rgyal por bstan ciṅ sṅar bśad pa / la rjes su 'jug par bya'o //*

[T.305.6 (153a)–306.2 (153b); 306.3 (153b)]
sgrub pa po yaṅ de daṅ / . . . slob dpon daṅ ldan cig byaṅ chub sems dpa' chen po 'phags pa 'jam dpal gźon nur gyur pa'i dam tshig la rjes su 'jug par 'tshal na / slob dpon gyis bdag la thugs brtse ba'i slad du / phan pa'i thugs daṅ brtse ba'i thugs kyis de bśad du gsol / de nas dkyil 'khor gyi slob dpon des sṅar bstan pa'i cho gas slob ma la sṅa ma ci lta bu bźin du brtags nas rab tu gźug par bya ste / sṅar ci ltar dbaṅ bskur ba bźin du phyis kyaṅ sbyin par bya'o // go rims ci lta ba bźin du dam tshig bstan te / gsaṅ ba'i phyag rgya daṅ rgyud daṅ sṅags daṅ las gyaṅ ṅus riṅ po ñid nas ṅes par brtags te / bsam pa śes nas bstan par bya ste / . . . [306.3 (153b)] *de nas dkyil 'khor gyi slob dpon des bu'i 'du śes ñe bar gźag par bya ste / bu bźin du bsgrub par bya źiṅ ma bźin du yaṅ loṅs spyod kyis ñe bar bsdu bar bya'o //*

D16 [*Mmk* 11.96.3-4]
puṣkalaṃ gatiṃ āpnoti śiṣyo pūjyas tu taṃ guruṃ / mantrāstasya ca sidhyanti vidhimārgopadarśanāt //

[T.308.2–3 (154b)]
slob mas bla ma de mchog na // dag pa'i 'gro ba thob par 'gyur // lam ni sna tshogs ñer bstan pas // de la sṅags ni 'grub par 'gyur //

Appendix E: Chapter Two

E1 [*Mmk* 1.24.24–25]
mahāyānamantracaryānirdeśyamahākalpāt mañjuśrīkumārabūtabodhisattvavikurvaṇapaṭalavisarāt mūlakalpāt prathamaḥ sannipātaparivartaḥ

[T.216.6–7 (108b)]
theg chen po sṅags kyi spyod pa bstan pa'i cho ga źib mo chen po las / byaṅ chub sems dpa' 'jam dpal gźon nur gyur pa'i rnam par 'phrul pa'i le'u rab 'byam rtsa ba'i cho ga źib mo las 'dus pa'i le 'u ste daṅ po'o //

E2 [*Mmk* 1.4.1–13.]
āgatya copari gaganatalamahāmaṇiratnapratiṣṭhite śuddhāvāsadevanikāye pratyaṣṭhāt / sarvaṃ ca taṃ śuddhāvāsabhavanaṃ mahatā raśmyavabhāsenāvabhāsya jyotiratnapratimaṇḍanoddyotanīṃ nāma samāpadyate sma / samanantarasamāpannasya mañjuśriyaḥ kumārabhūtasyānekaratnapravibhaktakūṭāgāraratnacchatrānekayojanaśatasahasravistīrṇadivyadṛśyamahāpaṭṭakalāpopaśobhitaviracitadivyapuṣpadhvajapatākamālākularatnakiṅkiṇījālopanaddhamadhurasarvanirghoṣavaivartikatvabodhisattvapratiṣṭhāpanadivyaṃ ca gandhamālyavilepanasrakcūrṇapravarṣaṃ cābhinirmame bhagavataḥ śākyamuneḥ pūjākarmaṇe tamāścaryādbhūtaprātihāryaṃ bodhisattvavikurvaṇaṃ dṛṣṭvā // atha te śuddhāvāsakāyikā devaputrā saṃhṛṣṭaromakūpajātā bhavanaṃ prakampamānaṃ dṛṣṭvā āhosvit kiṃ ṛddheḥ parihīyāma iti saṃtvaramāṇarūpāḥ uccaiḥ krośitum ārabdhāḥ evaṃ cāhuḥ paritrāyasva bhagavan paritrāyasva śākyamune //

[T.178.4–6 (89b) > 180.1–4 (90b)][10]
sten gi nam mkha'i dkyil na nor bu rin po che rab tu gnas pa'i gnas gtsaṅ ma'i ris kyi lha rnams gnas su 'dug ste / gnas gtsaṅ ma'i gnas de thams cad 'od chen po'i snaṅ bas gsal bar byas te / 'od kyi rin po che sa rab tu brgyan ciṅ gsal ba źes bya ba'i tiṅ ṅe 'dzin la sñoms par źugs so // 'jam dpal gźon nur gyur pa sñoms par źugs ma thag tu rin po che rnam pa tha dad pa du ma'i khaṅ pa brtsegs pa daṅ / rin po che'i gdugs daṅ dpag tshad brgya stoṅ phrag du ma rgya che ba'i lha'i gos daṅ / dar maṅ po'i tshogs kyis ñe bar mdzes par byas pa'i [skip to end of

180.1 (90b)] *lha'i me tog rnam par bkod pa daṅ / rgyal mtshan daṅ ba dan daṅ phreṅ ba'i tshogs daṅ / rin po che'i dril bu'i dra bas 'brel pa sñan pa'i sgra sgrogs pa / phyir mi ldog pa'i byaṅ chub sems dpa'i sa thob par byed pa / lha dri daṅ byug pa daṅ phreṅ pa daṅ phye ma'i char 'bab par mṅon par sprul to / de nas gnas gtsaṅ ma'i ris kyi lha'i bu rnams kyis byaṅ chub sems dpa'i ṅo mtshar rmad du byuṅ ba'i cho 'phrul gyi rnam par 'phrul pa mthoṅ nas / ba spu ldaṅ źiṅ gnas g.yo ba mthoṅ nas sñiṅ 'dar źiṅ daṅ ṅas de / ci bdag cag gi 'byor pa ñams par ma gyur tam źes phan tshun du riṅs par 'gro źiṅ skad mthon pos smra ba rtsam par byed de / 'di skad du bcom ldan 'das yoṅs su bskyab tu gsol / śākya thub pa yoṅs su bskyab tu gsol źes gsol to //*

E3 [*Mmk* 1.1.1–1.2.2]
namaḥ sarvabuddhabodhisattvebhyaḥ /
evaṃ mayā śrutam / ekasmin samaye bhagavāṃ śuddhāvāsopari gaganatalapratiṣṭite acintyāścaryādbhutapravibhaktabodhisattvasaṃnipāta maṇḍalamāle viharati sma / tatra bhagavāṃ śuddhāvāsakāyikān devaputrān āmantrayte sma / śṛṇvantu devaputrā mañjuśriyasya kumārabhūtasya bodhisattvasya mahāsattvasyācintyādbhutaprātihāryacaryāsamādhiśuddhiviśeṣavimokṣamaṇḍalabodhisattvavikurvaṇaṃ sarvasattvopajīvyamāyurā rogyaiśvaryamanorathapāripūrakāṇi mantrapadāni sarvasattvānāṃ hitāya bhāṣiṣye / taṃ śṛṇu sādhu ca suṣṭhu ca manasi kuru bhāṣiṣye 'haṃ te /
[*Mmk* 1.1.10] *atha śuddhāvāsakāyikā devaputrāḥ sāñjalayo bhūtvā* \\\\ [T. *bcom ldan 'das la legs so źes gsol te / byaṅ chub sems dpa' rnams kyi spyod pa tiṅ ṅe 'dzin gyi*] *viśeṣabhūmipratilābhavajrāsanākramaṇamāradharṣaṇadharmacakrapravartanasarvaśrāvakapratekyabuddhaniryāṇadevamanuṣyopapattisarvaduḥkhapraśamanadaridravyādhitāḍhyarogopakarṣaṇatāṃ sarvalaukikalokottaramantracaryān abhibhavanatāṃ sarvāśāparipūraṇataḥ sarvatathāgatānām avaśyavacanadhāraṇam / tad vadatu bhagavān maitracitto hitacitto 'smākam anukampām upādāya sarvasattvānāṃ ca //*
[*Mmk* 1.1.17] *atha bhagavān śākyamuniḥ sarvāvantaṃ śuddhāvāsabhavanaṃ buddhacakṣuṣāvalokya viśuddhaviṣayajyotir vikaraṇavidhvaṃsinīṃ nāma samādhiṃ samāpadyate sma / samanantarasamāpannasya bhagavata* \\\\ [T. *mdzod spu nas*] *saṅkusumitabodhisattvasañcodanī nāma raśmi* \\\\ [T. *'od bye ba khrag khrig phrag ba rgya stoṅ dum'i 'khor gyis bcom ldan 'das la lan gsum bskor ba byas nas / stoṅ gsum gyi stoṅ chen po'i 'jig rten gyi khams su soṅ nas / byaṅ śar gyi phogs su brgya stoṅ gi gaṅ gā'i kluṅ gi 'jig rten gyi khams 'das nas / me tog daṅ ldan pa źes bya ba'i 'jig rten gyi khams su rjes su źugs te / gaṅ na me tog kun du skyes pa'i rgyal po'i dbaṅ po źes bya ba'i de*

bźin gśegs pa bźugs par ro / der yaṅ 'jam dpal gźon nur gyur pa sṅon gyi smon (> spu na) lam gyi dbaṅ gis byaṅ chub sems dpa' sems dpa' chen po'i spyod pa daṅ ldan pa rnams daṅ lhan cig gnas par gyur to // 'jam dpal gźon nur gyur pas] *sitaraśmyavabhāsaṃ dṛṣṭvā īṣat prahasitavadano bhūtvā taṃ bodhisattvagam āmantrayate sma / iyaṃ bho jinapūtrāḥ asmākaṃ raśmisañcodanī / ihāyāta / sajjībhavantu bhagavantaḥ //*

[T.175.1–5 (88a)]
saṅs rgyas daṅ byaṅ chub sems dpa' thams cad la phyag 'tshal lo // 'di skad bdag gis thos pa dus gcig na / bcom ldan 'das gnas gtsaṅ ma'i steṅ gi nam mkha'i dkyil na / byaṅ chub sems dpa' 'dus pa'i 'khor gyi tshogs so so tha dad pa bsam gyis mi khyab pa ṅo mtshar rmad du byuṅ ba / so sor rab tu gnas pa daṅ thabs cig tu bźugs te / de nas bcom ldan 'das kyis gnas gtsaṅ ma'i ris kyi lha'i bu rnams la bka' stsal pa / lha'i bu dag khyed cag ñon cig // byaṅ chub sems dpa' sems dpa' chen po 'jam dpal gźon nur gyur pa'i cho 'phrul gyi spyod pa bsam gyis mi khyab pa ṅo mtshar rmad du byuṅ ba'i tiṅ ṅe 'dzin gyi bye brag daṅ / rdzu 'phrul daṅ / rnam par thar pa'i dkyil 'khor byaṅ chub sems dpa'i rnam par 'phrul pa daṅ / byaṅ chub sems dpa' thams cad kyi ñe bar 'tsho ba / tshe daṅ nad med pa daṅ dbaṅ phyug daṅ / yid la bsam pa yoṅs su rdzogs par byed pa'i sṅags kyi gźi dag sems can rnams la phan pa'i phyir bśad par bya ste / de śin du legs par ñon la yid la zuṅ śig daṅ / ṅas bśad par bya'o //

[T.175.5 (88a)–176.1 (88b)] *de nas gnas gtsaṅ ma'i ris kyi lha'i bu de dag gyis thal mo sbyar ba btud nas / bcom ldan 'das la legs so źes gsol te / byaṅ chub sems dpa' rnams kyi spyod pa tiṅ ṅe 'dzin gyi khyad par daṅ / sa chen pa thob par bya ba daṅ / rdo rje'i gdan gnon pa daṅ / bdud gdul ba daṅ / chos kyi 'khor lo bskor ba daṅ / ñan thos daṅ raṅ saṅs rgyas thams cad kyi ṅes par 'byuṅ ba daṅ / lha rnams daṅ mi rnams su skye bar bya ba daṅ / sdug bsṅal daṅ / dbul ba daṅ / nad thams cad źi bar byed pa / loṅs spyod kyis phug pa 'dren par byed pa / 'jig rten daṅ 'jig rten las 'das pa'i sṅags kyi spyod pas phoṅs par mi byed pa / re ba thams cad yoṅs su rdzogs par byed pa de bźin gśegs pa tham cad kyi gsuṅ 'bras bu med par byed pa ma yin pa / bcom ldan 'das kyis byams pa'i thugs daṅ / phan pa'i thugs daṅ bdag daṅ sems can thams cad la thugs brtse ba ñe bar bzuṅ nas bcom ldan 'das de bśad du gsol /*

[T.176.1 (88b)–177.4 (89a)] *de nas bcom ldan 'das śākya thub pas thams cad daṅ ldan pa'i 'khor rnams daṅ gnas gtsaṅ ma'i gnas la saṅs rgyas kyi spyan gyis gzigs nas / dag pa'i yul la 'od rnam par spros te / yul rnam par 'jigs pa źes bya ba'i tiṅ ṅe 'dzin la sñoms par źugs so // bcom ldan 'das sñoms par źugs ma thag tu mdzod spu nas me tog kun tu skyes pa śes bya pa daṅ / byaṅ chub sems dpa' yaṅ dag par bskul ba źes bya ba'i 'od phyuṅ ste / 'od bye ba khrag khrig phrag ba rgya stoṅ du ma'i 'khor gyis bcom ldan 'das la lan gsum bskor ba byas nas / stoṅ gsum gyi stoṅ chen po'i 'jig rten gyi khams su soṅ nas / byaṅ śar gyi phogs su brgya stoṅ gi gaṅ gā'i kluṅ gi 'jig rten gyi khams 'das nas / me tog daṅ ldan pa źes bya ba'i 'jig rten gyi khams su rjes su źugs te / gaṅ na me tog kun du skyes pa'i rgyal po'i dbaṅ po źes bya ba'i de bźin gśegs pa bźugs par ro // der yaṅ 'jam dpal gźon nur gyur pa sṅon gyi smon* [> *spu na*] *lam gyi dbaṅ gis byaṅ chub sems dpa' sems dpa' chen po'i spyod pa daṅ ldan pa rnams daṅ lhan cig gnas par gyur to // 'jam dpal gźon nur gyur pas 'od zer gyi snaṅ pa de mthoṅ nas / bźin cuṅ zad 'dzum daṅ ldan par gyur nas byaṅ chub sems dpa'i tshogs de dag la smras pa / rgyal ba'i sras dag 'od 'di ni ṅa la yaṅ dag par bskul ba'i phyir 'oṅs pa yin gyis / khyed cag gyeṅ ba med par gyis śig ces smras so //*

E4 [*Mmk* 33.346.17–20; 33.346.24–33.347.2; 33.347.11–14]
saṃsāragahane kāntāre cirakālaṃ uṣito hyaham /
yathā vaineyasattvānāṃ tathā tatra karomyaham //
yathā yathā ca sattvā vai hitaṃ karma samādadheḥ /
tathā tathā karomyeṣāṃ hitārthaṃ karma śubhālayam //

. . .

taṃ tathaiva karomyeṣāṃ vicitrāṃ rūpasampadām //
ahaṃ tathā veṣadhārī syā vicitrāṅgaṃ nijānijām /
hitāśayena sattvānāṃ vicitraṃ rūpa nirmime //
maheśvaraḥ śakrabrahmādyāṃ viṣṇurdhanadanirṛtām /
vicitrāṃ graharūpāstu nirmime 'haṃ tathā purā //

. . .

kṣemo 'haṃ nirjaraṃ śāntaṃ aśokaṃ vimalaṃ śivaṃ /
prāpto 'haṃ nirvṛtiṃ śāntiṃ mukto 'haṃ janmabandhanā //
adhunā pravartitaś cakraḥ bhūtakoṭisamāśrita /
darśayām eṣa kalpah vai mantravādaṃ savistaraṃ //

[T.481.4–5 (241a); 481.6–482.1 (241b); 482.3–4]
bdag gis su ni bśad pa yin //
'khor ba'i dgon pa'i tshaṅ tshiṅ du // bdag ni yun riṅ dus su gnas //
ji ltar gdul bya'i sems can la // de ltar bdag gis de bźin byas //
ji lta ji ltar sems can rnams // phan pa'i las ni len pa dge //
phan don las kyis dge ba'i gźi // de lta de ltar 'di dag byas //

. . .

'di la de bźin byas ba yin // sna tshogs 'gro ba'i skye gnas su //
bdag gis de bźin cha byad byas //
phan pa'i bsam pas sems can la // sna tshogs gzugs ni bdag gis sprul //
dbaṅ phyug brgya byin tshaṅs pa sogs // khyab 'jug nor sbyin bden bral daṅ //
sna tshogs gza' yi gzugs sogs kyaṅ // de tshe sṅon ni ṅa yis sprul //

. . .

bde ba nad med yaṅ dag źi // dri med mya ṅan med źi ba //
ṅas thob mya ṅan 'das źi ba // skye ba'i 'chiṅ las ṅa rab grol //
yaṅ na 'khor lo rab bskor źiṅ // yaṅ dag mtha' la brten nas ni //
sṅags kyi tshig ni rgya chen daṅ // cho ga 'di ni ṅa yis bstan //

E5 [*Mmk* 1.4.22–1.5.7]
namaste muktāyājanya namaste purṣottama /
namaste puruṣaśreṣṭha sarvacaryārthasādhakaḥ //
namaste puruṣasiṃha sarvānarthanivāraka /
namaste astu mahāvīra sarvadurgavināśaka //
namaste puruṣapuṇḍarīkapuṇyagandhamanantaka /
namaste puruṣapadma tribhavapaṅkaviśodhaka //
namaste muktāya sarvaduḥkhavimocaka /
namaste śāntāya sarvādāntasudāntaka //
namaste siddhāya sarvamantracaryārthasādhaka /
namaste maṅgalāya sarvamaṅgalamaṅgala //
namaste buddhāya sarvadharmāvabodhane /
namaste tathāgatāya sarvadharmatathāgata /
niḥprapañcākārasamanupraviṣṭadeśika //
namaste sarvajñāya sarvajña jñeyavastusaṃskṛtāsaṃskṛta-triyānamārganirvāṇapratiṣṭhāpanapratiṣṭhitāya iti //

[T.180.7 (90b)–181.3 (91a)]
skyes bu bskyed pa khyod phyag 'tshal // skyes mchog khyod la phyag 'tshal lo //
skyes bu gtso bo khyod phyag 'tshal // spyod pa thams cad don sgrub pa //
skyes bu seṅ ge khyod phyag 'tshal // phuṅ khrol thams cad zlog byed pa //
dba' bo chen po khyod phyag 'tshal // ṅan 'gro thams cad 'jig byed pa //
skyes bu pad dkar khyod phyag 'tshal // kun nas bsod nams dri ldan pa //
skyes bu padma khyod phyag 'tshal // srid gsum' 'dam ni rnam dag byed //
rnam grol khyod la phyag 'tshal lo // sdug bsṅal ma lus rnam grol byed //
źi gyur khyod la phyag 'tshal lo // thams cad ldan pa legs 'dul byed //
thams cad grub pa khyod phyag 'tshal // sṅags kyi spyod pa'i don sgrub byed //
bkra śis khyod la phyag 'tshal lo // bkra śis kun gyi bkra śis pa//

saṅs rgyas kun la khyod phyag 'tshal // chos kun rnam par rtogs mdzad pa //
chos thams cad kyi de bźin ñid spros pa med pa'i ṅo bo la yaṅ dag par rjes su źugs śiṅ ston par byed pa'i de bźin gśegs pa khyod la phyag 'tshal lo //
śes pa daṅ śes bya'i dṅos po thams cad daṅ // 'dus byas daṅ 'dus ma byas daṅ //
theg pa gsum gyi lam daṅ // mya ṅan las 'das pa'i lam la 'jog par byed pa daṅ // gnas par byed pa tham cad mkhyen pa khyod la phyag 'tshal lo źes //

E6 [*Mmk* 1.2.3-13; 1.2.16-1.3.2]
athakhalu mañjuśrīḥ kumārabhūto bodhisattvo mahāsattva utphullanayano 'nimiṣanayano yenāsau raśmyavabhāsaḥ tenābhimukhas tastau // atho sā raśmiḥ mañcodanī kusumāvatī lokadhātuṃ mahatāvabhāsenāvabhāsya bhagavataḥ saṅkusumitarājendrasya tathāgatasya triḥ pradakṣiṇīkṛtya mañjuśriyasya bodhisattvasya mahāsattvasya mūrdhanyantardhīyate sma // atha mañjuśrīḥ kumārabhūta utthāyāsanād bhagavantaṃ saṅkusumitarājendraṃ tathāgataṃ triḥ pradakṣiṇīkṛtya śirasā praṇamya dakṣiṇaṃ jānumaṇḍalaṃ pṛthivyāṃ pratiṣṭhāpya bhagavantaṃ saṅkusumitarājendram etad avocat // samanvāhṛtāsya bhagavatā śākyamuninā tathāgatenārhatā samyaksambuddhena / gacchāmo vayaṃ bhagavannito sahāṃ lokadhātuṃ bhagavantaṃ śākyamuniṃ draṣṭuṃ vanditum upāsituṃ . . . evam ukte bhagavān saṅkusumitarājendras tathāgato mañjuśriyaṃ kumārabhūtam etad avocat / gaccha tvaṃ mañjuśrīḥ kumāra yasyedānīṃ kālaṃ manyase / api tvasmad vacanena bhagavān śākyamunir alpābādhatāmalpātaṅkatāṃ laghutthānatāṃ sanyāsavihāratāṃ praṣṭavyaḥ / atha bhagavān saṅkusumitarājendras tathāgato mañjuśriyaṃ kumārabhūtam etad avocat / api tu kumāra śatasahasragaṅgānadīsikataprakhyais tathāgatair arhadbhiḥ samyaksambuddhais tvadīyaṃ mantracaryā . . . bhāṣitavantaḥ ca bhāṣiṣyante ca mayāpyetarhi / anumoditum eva gaccha tvaṃ mañjuśīḥ kumārabhūta yasyedānī kālaṃ manyase / śākyamunisamīpaṃ sammukham / iyaṃ dharmaparyāyaṃ śroṣyasi / tvam api bhāṣiṣyase /

[T.176.6 (88b)–177.2 (89a); 177.4 [text out of place; skips to 178.6 (89b)–179.1 (90a); 179.4–5]
de nas byaṅ chub sems dpa' sems dpa' chen po 'jam dpal gźon nur gyur pa mig mi 'dzums śiṅ kha bye bas / 'od gaṅ na ba de logs su mṅon du bltas nas 'dug go // de nas bskul ba'i 'od des me tog daṅ ldan pa źes bya ba'i 'jig rten gyi khams snaṅ ba chen pos snaṅ bar byas te / me tog kun du skyes pa rgyal po'i dbaṅ po de źin gśegs pa la lan gsum ba skor byas te / byaṅ chub sems dpa' sems dpa' chen po 'jam dpal gźon nur

gyur pa'i spyi bor nub par gyur to // de nas 'jam dpal gźon nur gyur pa stan las laṅs te / bcom ldan 'das me tog kun du yaṅ dag par skyes pa rgyal po'i dbaṅ po de bźin gśegs pa la lan gsum bskor ba byas te / spyi bos phyag 'tshal nas / pus mo gyas pa'i [lha ṅa sa btsug te (? S. = *jānumaṇḍalaṃ pṛthivyāṃ pratiṣṭhāpya*)] */ bcom ldan 'das me tog kun du skyes pa rgyal po'i dbaṅ po la 'di skad ces gsol to // bcom ldan 'das śākya thub pa źes bya ba de bźin gśegs pa dgra bcom pa yaṅ dag par rdzogs pa'i saṅs rgyas kyis bdag la dgoṅs te / bcom ldan 'das bdag ni bcom ldan 'das śākya thub pa la blta ba daṅ phyag bya ba daṅ bsñen bkur bya ba daṅ / . . . mi mjed kyi 'jig rten gyi khams 'di nas mchi bar 'tshal lo / de skad ces bcom ldan 'das me tog gun du skyes pa rgyal po'i dbaṅ po de bźin gśegs pa la gsol pa daṅ /* [178.6 (89b)] *'jam dpal gźon nur gyur pa la 'di skad ces bka' stsal to // 'jam dpal gźon nur gyur pa de'i ṅus la bab par śes na soṅ śig / 'on kyaṅ ṅa'i bkas bcom ldan 'das śākya thub pa la gnod pa ñuṅ ṅam / ñam ṅa ba chuṅ ṅam / bskyod pa yaṅ ṅam / bde ba la reg par gnas sam źes źu bar bya'o // de nas bcom ldan 'das me tog yaṅ dag par skyes pa rgyal po'i dbaṅ po de bźin gśegs pas 'jam dpal gźon nur gyur pa la 'di skad ces bka' stsal to // gźan yaṅ gźon nu gaṅgā'i kluṅ brgya stoṅ gi bye ma sñed kyi de bźin gśegs pa dgra bcom pa yaṅ dag par dzogs pa'i saṅs rgyas kyis khyod kyi sṅags kyi spyod pa daṅ / . . . gsuṅs pa daṅ / gsuṅs par 'gyur ba yin te / de ltar rjes su yi raṅ ba ñid de / 'jam dpal gźon nur gyur pa de'i ṅus la bab par śes na soṅ śig / śākya thub pa'i spyan sṅar mṅon sum du chos kyi rnam graṅs 'di thos pa 'gyur de / khyod kyaṅ ston par 'gyur ro //*

Appendix F: Chapter Three

F1 [*Mmk* 8.79.10–28]

adau tāvat dṛṣṭasamayaḥ kṛtapuraścaraṇaḥ labdhābhiṣekaḥ asmin kalparājamūlamantrahṛdayaṃ upahṛdayaṃ vā anyataraṃ vā mantraṃ gṛhītvā ekākṣaraṃ vā anyaṃ vā yathepsitaṃ mahāraṇyaṃ gatvā triśallakṣāṇi jape phalodakāhāraḥ mūlaparṇabhakṣo vā kṛtapuraścaraṇo bhavati // tato parvatā[gra]ṃ [< T. *ri'i rtse mor*] *abhiruhya jyeṣṭaṃ paṭaṃ paścāntmukhaṃ pratiṣṭhāpya ātmanā pūrvābhimukho kuśaviṇḍakopaviṣṭaḥ śvetapadmānāṃ śvetakuṅkumābhyaktānāṃ lakṣam ekaṃ bhagavataḥ śākyamuneḥ sarvabuddhabodhisattvapratyekabuddhārya-śrāvakāṇāṃ paṭasyādhas tān nivedayet / karpūradhūpaṃ ca yathāvibhavataḥ dahet / devaputranāgānāṃ ca pūjāṃ kuryāt / yathālabdhaiḥ puṣpaiḥ // tato 'rdharātrakālasamaye śuklapūrṇamāsyāṃ prātihārakapratipūrṇāyāṃ paṭasyāgrataḥ agnikuṇḍaṃ kṛtvā padmākāraṃ śvetacandanakāṣṭhair agniṃ prajvālya kuṅkumakarpūraṃ caikīkṛtya aṣṭasahasrāhutiṃ juhuyāt*

/ yathāvibhavataḥ kṛtarakṣaḥ // tataḥ bhagavataḥ śākyamuneḥ raśmayo niścaranti samantācca paṭaḥ ekajvālībhūto bhavati / tataḥ sādhakena sattvaramāṇarūpena [<V.56.8 reads *tvaramāṇarūpena* which corresponds to T.287.3 (144a) *riṅs pa'i tshul gyis*] *paṭaṃ triḥ pradakṣiṇīkṛtya sarvabuddhabodhisattvapratyekabuddhāryaśrāvakāṇāṃ praṇamya paṭaṃ grahetavyam // atītenapūrvalikhitasādhakapaṭāntadeśe tato gṛhītamātrotpatati / acchaṭāmātreṇa brahmalokam atikrāmati / kusumāvatīṃ lokadhātuṃ sampratiṣṭhati / yatrāsau bhagavāṃ saṅkusumitrājendras tathāgataḥ tiṣṭhati dhriyate* [*Mmk* 8.80 missing = V.8.56.12–16] *yapāyati dharmaṃ ca deśayati / āryamañjuśrīyaṃ ca sākṣāt paśyati / dharmaṃ śṛṇoti / anekānyapi bodhisattvaśatasahasrā paśyati / tāṃś ca parupāste / mahākalpasahasraṃ ajarāmaralīlī bhavati / paṭas tatraiva tiṣṭhati / sarvabuddhabodhisattvādhiṣṭhito bhavati / teṣāṃ cādhiṣṭānaṃ saṃjānīte kṣetraśatasahasraṃ cākrāmati / kāyaśatasahasraṃ vā darśayati / anekaṛddhiprabhāvasamudgato bhavati / āryamañjuśriyaś ca kalyāṇimitro bhavati / niyataṃ bodhiparāyaṇo bhavatīti //*

[T.286.4 (143b)–288.1 (146b)]
'dir daṅ por re źig cho ga'i rgyal po 'di la dam tshig mthoṅ ba sṅon du bya ba rnam byas pa daṅ dbaṅ bskur ba thob pa / rtsa ba'i sṅags sam sñiṅ po 'am ñe ba'i sñiṅ po 'am / sṅags gaṅ yaṅ ruṅ ba bzuṅ nas yi ge gcig pa 'am / gaṅ 'dod pa dgon pa chen por soṅ ste 'bum phrag gsum bzla bar bya'o // 'bras bu daṅ chus 'tsho ba'am / rtsa ba daṅ / lo ma'i bza' ba byas / sṅon du bya ba byas par 'gyur ro // de nas ri'i rtse mor 'dzegs nas ras ris chen po'i tshad nub phyogs su mṅon du lta ba bźag pa byas la bdag ñid śar du bltas de / ku śa'i khres la 'dug nas / padma dkar po la tsandan daṅ gur gum gyis btags de / bcom ldan 'das śākya thub pa daṅ / saṅs rgyas daṅ byaṅ chub sems dpa' thams cad daṅ / raṅ saṅs rgyas daṅ ñan thos dag la 'bum phrag gcig ri mo'i ras ris kyi 'og tu dbul bar bya'o // ga pur gyi bdug pa yaṅ ci 'byor pas bdug go // lha'i bu daṅ klu rnams la yaṅ ci rñed pa'i me tog gis mchod par bya'o // de nas mtshan phyed kyi dus su cho 'phrul gyi zla phyed kyi zla ba ña ba la / ras ris kyi mdun du padma'i rnam pa lta bu'i me thab byas pa la / tsandan dkar po'i śiṅ gis me sbar nas / gur gum daṅ ga pur bsres pas sreg blugs ci 'byor pas stoṅ rtsa brgyad sbyin sreg bya'o // de nas bsruṅ ba bya'o // de nas bcom ldan 'das śākya thub pa las 'od zer byuṅ ste / ras kyi ri mo'i 'khor yug nas gcig tu 'bar 'gyur te / sgrub pa pos gur gum daṅ / tsandan gyis btags pa'i tsandan dkar po'i me tog gis mchod yon dbul lo // de nas sgrub pa pos riṅs pa'i tshul gyis ras ris la lan gsum bskor ba byas te / saṅs rgyas daṅ byaṅ chub sems dpa' thams cad daṅ / raṅ saṅs rgyas thams cad daṅ 'phags pa ñan thos rnams la phyag byas nas / sgrub pa pos bris pa'i ras ris kyi mtha' ma'i phyogs nas 'jigs pa med pas ras ris gzuṅ bar bya'o / de nas zuṅ ba tsam gyis

'phur te / se gol gtogs pa tsam gyis tshaṅs pa'i 'jig rten du phyin par 'gyur te / me tog can gyi 'jig rten gyi khams su rab tu gaṅs par 'gyur te / gaṅ du bcom ldan 'das me tog yaṅ dag par skyes pa'i rgyal po'i dbaṅ po de bźin gśegs pa de bźugs de / 'tsho źiṅ gźes la chos kyaṅ ston to // 'phags pa 'jam dpal yaṅ mṅon du mthoṅ ṅo // chos kyaṅ thos so // byaṅ chub sems dpa' du ma tag kyaṅ mthoṅ źiṅ / de dag la bsñen bkur yaṅ byed de bskal pa chen po stoṅ du rga ba daṅ 'chi ba med ciṅ gnas par 'gyur ro // ras ris kyaṅ de na gnas par 'gyur ro // saṅs rgyas daṅ byaṅ chub sems dpa' thams cad kyis byin gyis brlabs par 'gyur ro // de dag gis byin gyis brlabs par yaṅ dag par źes so // saṅs rgyas kyi źiṅ stoṅ yaṅ 'da' bar byed do / lus stoṅ yaṅ ston par byed do // rdzu 'phrul gyi mthu du ma yaṅ 'byin par byed do // 'phags pa 'jam dpal yaṅ dge ba'i bźes gñen du 'gyur ro // des par byaṅ chub la gźol par 'gyur ro //

F2 [*Mmk* 25.285.22–23, 25 and 25.286.1–10]
eṣa bhagavāṃ sarvajñaḥ buddhairmantrarūpena vyavasthitaḥ /
mahākaruṇikaḥ śāstā viceruḥ sarvadehināṃ //

. . .

karuṇādha [T. *sñiṅ rje* < *karuṇāya*] *samāgamya sthito 'yameṣamakṣaraḥ //*
sa dharmadhātuṃ niḥsṛtya sthito 'yaṃ viśvarūpiṇaḥ /
yathā hi buddhānāṃ śarīrā pravṛttā dhātavo jane //
sāmiṣā lokapūjyāste nirāmiṣāḥ ṣu [> *nirāmiṣāstu*] *viśeṣataḥ /*
saddharmadhātavaḥ proktā nirāmiṣā lokahetavaḥ //
sāmiṣā kalevare proktā jinendrāṇāṃ maharddikā /
vividhā dhātavaḥ proktāḥ municandrā nirāśravāḥ //
sāmiṣā nirāmiṣāś caiva prasṛtā lokahetavaḥ /
dharmadhātuṃ sanmiśraṃ sattvānāṃ karuṇāvaśāt //
tiṣṭhate mantrarūpeṇa lokanāthaṃ prabaṅkara /
sa viśvarūpī sarvajñaḥ dṛśyate ha mahītale //

[T.408.1, 2-4 (204b)]
bcom ldan 'di ni thams cad mkhyen // saṅs rgyas sṅags gzugs rnam par gnas //
ston pa thugs rje che daṅ ldan // sems can kun la rnam par spyod //

. . .

sñiṅ rje dbaṅ la brten nas ni // 'di ni yi ge gcig tu gnas //
chos kyi dbyiṅs la brten nas ni // 'di ni sna tshogs gzugs la gnas //
ji ltar saṅs rgyas sku rnams ni // skye bo rnams la sku gduṅ gyur //
'jig rten gyis mchod zaṅ ziṅ bcas // zaṅ ziṅ med pa 'aṅ khyad par du //
dam chos sku gduṅ dag tu bstan // 'jig rten zaṅ ziṅ med pa'i rgyu //
sku ni zaṅ ziṅ bcas par gsuṅs // thub pa'i zla ba zag pa med //

zaṅ ziṅ bcas daṅ zaṅ ziṅ med // 'jig rten rgyur ni gsuṅs pa yin //
chos kyi dbyiṅs la brten nas ni // thugs rje'i dbaṅ gis sems can la //
'jig rten mgon po 'od byed pa // sṅags kyi tshul gyis bźugs pa yin //
sna tshogs gzugs can thams cad mkhyen // sa steṅ 'di la snaṅ ba yino //

F3 [*Mmk* 4.55.1–11]
atha khalu mañjuśrīḥ sarvāvantaṃ śuddhāvāsabhavanam avalokaya punar api tan mahāparṣanmaṇḍalasannipātam avalokya śākyamuneś caraṇayor nipatya prahasitavadano bhūtva bhagavantam etad avocat / / tat sādhu bhagavāṃ sarvasattvānāṃ hitāya mantracaryāsādhana-vidhānanirhāraniṣyandadharmameghapravarṣaṇayathepsitaphalaniṣ-pādanapaṭalavisaraḥ paṭavidhānaṃ anuttarapuṇyaprasavaḥ samyaksam-bodhibījam abhinirvartakaṃ sarvajñajñānāśeṣābhinirvartakaṃ saṃkṣepataḥ sarvāśāpāripūrakaṃ sarvamantraphalasamyaksamprayuktaḥ saphalīkaraṇa avandhyasādhitasādhakaṃ sarvabodhisattvacaryāpāri-pūrakaṃ mahābodhisattvasannāhasannaddhaḥ sarvamārabala abhibhavanaparāpṛṣṭhīkaraṇaṃ tat vadatu bhagavān asmākam anukampām upādāya sarvasattvānāṃ ca //

[T.257.4 (129a)–258.1 (129b)]
de nas 'jam dpal gźon nur gyur pas thams cad daṅ ldan pa'i gnas gtsaṅ ma la gzigs nas / gźan yaṅ 'khor gyi dkyil 'khor chen po der 'dus pa la yaṅ gzigs te / bcom ldan 'das śākya thub pa'i źabs gñis la btus nas źal 'dzum pa daṅ ldan pas bcom ldan 'das la 'di skad ces gsol to // bcom ldan 'das sems can thams cad la phan pa'i phyir sṅags kyi spyod pa'i cho ga'i sgrub pa'i rgyu mthun pa / chos kyi char ci ltar 'dod pa'i 'bras bu sgrub pa'i cho ga rab 'byam las ras kyi ri mo'i cho ga bsod nams bla na med pa skyed pa yaṅ dag par rdzogs pa'i byaṅ chub kyi sa bon mṅon par sgrub par byed pa / mdor na bsam pa thams cad yoṅs su rdzogs par byed pa sṅags thams cad kyi 'bras bul rab tu sbyor źiṅ 'bras bu daṅ bcas par byed pa / don med pa ma yin pa grub ciṅ sgrub par byed pa / byaṅ chub sems dpa' thams cad kyi spyod pa yoṅs su rdzogs par byed pa / byaṅ chub sems dpa' chen po'i go cha bgos pa / bdud thams cad gyi stobs zil gyis mnan ciṅ rgyab kyis phyogs par byed pa bdag daṅ sems can thams cad la thugs brtse phyir de legs par bśad du gsol /

F4 [*Mmk* 4.55.14–18]
sādhu sādhu mañjuśrīḥ yastvaṃ bahujanahitāya pratipanno lokānu-kampāyai yastvaṃ tathāgatam etam arthaṃ paripṛṣṭhavyaṃ manyase / tacchṛṇu sādhu ca suṣṭhu ca manasi kuru bhāṣiṣyehaṃ te tvadīyaṃ paṭavidhānavisarasarvasattva [T. *sṅags thams cad* = *sarvasattva* > *sarvamantra*] *caryāsādhanam anupraveṣamanupūrvakaḥ vakṣye 'haṃ pūrvanirdiṣṭaṃ sarvatathāgataiḥ / aham apyedānīṃ bhāṣiṣye //*

[T.258.1–3 (129b)]
'jam dpal gźon nur gyur pa khyod skye bo maṅ po la phan pa'i phyir źugs pa daṅ / 'jig rten la sñiṅ brtse ba'i phyir gaṅ khyod de bźin gśegs pa la don 'di 'dri bar sems pa ni legs so // de śin du legs par ñon la yid la zuṅ śig daṅ / ṅas bśad par bya'o // khyod kyi ras ris kyi cho ga rab 'byam sṅags thams cad sgrub par byed pa la rab tu 'jug pa mthar gyis ṅas bśad par bya'o // sṅon yaṅ de bźin gśegs pa thams cad kyis bstan te da ltar yaṅ ṅas bśad par bya'o //

F5 [*Mmk* 7.73.7–18]
anāgate 'dhvani nirvṛte lokagurau astamite tathāgatādityaṃ vaṃśe riñcite sarvabuddhakṣetre sarvabuddhabodhisattvāryaśrāvakapratyekabuddhaiḥ andhakārībhūte lokabhājane vicchinne āryamārge sarvavidyāmantroṣadhimaṇiratnopagate [T. *med pa = apagate < upagate*] *sādhujanaparihīṇe nirāloke sattvadhātau sattvā bhaviṣyanti kusīdā naṣṭaspṛhatayā aśrāddāḥ khaṇḍakā akalyāṇamitraparigṛhītā śaṭhā māyāvino dhūrtacaritāḥ / te imaṃ dharmaparyāyaṃ śrutvā ca saṃtrāsam āpatsyante / ālasyakausīdyābhiratā na śraddhāsyanti kāmagaveṣiṇo na patīṣyanti* [= T. *yid ches par*. V.51.12 emends *patīṣyanti* > *yatiṣyanti*, and Lalou: 51, note 2 mentions the more common form, *pratyeṣyanti*] *mithyādṛṣṭiratāḥ / te bahu apuṇyaṃ prasaviṣyanti saddharmapratikṣepakāḥ avīciparāyaṇāḥ ghorād ghorataraṃ gatāḥ / teṣāṃ duḥkhitānāmarthāya avaśānāṃ vaśamānetā vaśyānāmabhayapradāyā upāyakauśalyasaṅgrakayā mantrapaṭavidhānaṃ bhāṣatu bhagavāṃ / yasyedānīṃ kālaṃ manyase //*

[T.279.1–6 (140a)]
ma 'oṅs pa'i dus na 'jig rten gyi bla ma 'das pa na / de bźin gśegs pa'i ñi ma'i rigs nub pa daṅ / saṅs rgyas kyi śiṅ thams cad spaṅs pa daṅ / saṅs rgyas daṅ byaṅ chub sems dpa' thams cad daṅ / 'phags pa ñan thos daṅ raṅ saṅs rgyas rnams kyis mun par gyur pa daṅ / snod kyi 'jig rten rnam par 'jig pa daṅ 'phags pa'i lam daṅ / rig pa thams cad daṅ sṅags daṅ sman daṅ / nor bu rin po che med pa daṅ / skye bo dam pa rnams kyis 'jig rten na yoṅs su ma zin pa daṅ / sems can gyi khams thams cad 'byung bar 'gyur te / le lo can daṅ dran pa ñams pa daṅ / ma dad pa daṅ mi ruṅ pa daṅ mi dge ba'i bśes gñen gyis yoṅs su zin pa daṅ g.yo sgyu daṅ ldan pa daṅ / slu ba spyod pa de dag chos kyi rnam graṅs 'di thos nas skrag par 'gyur te / le lo la mṅon par 'dod ciṅ dad par mi 'gyur la / 'dod pa tshol źiṅ yid ches par mi 'gyur ro // log pa'i lta ba skye źiṅ bsod nams ma yin pa 'phel bar 'gyur ro // mtshams med par gźol źiṅ śin tu mi bzad pa'i yaṅ śin tu mi bźad pa 'thob pa sdug bsṅal ba de dag gi don daṅ dbaṅ med par dbaṅ du bya ba'i don daṅ / dbaṅ du gyur pa la mi 'jigs pa sbyin pa'i phyir daṅ / thabs mkhas pas bsdu ba'i sbyor ba

/ sṅags kyi ras kyi ri mo'i cho ga gaṅ de'i dus la bab par mkhyen na bcom ldan 'das kyis bśad du gsol /

F6 [*Mmk* 7.73.19–7.74.17]
atha bhagavāṃ cchākyamuniḥ mañjuśriyaṃ kumārabhūtaṃ sādhukāram adāt / sādhu sādhu mañjuśrī yastvaṃ tathāgatam arthaṃ paripraṣṭavyaṃ manyase / asti mañjuśrī tvadīyaṃ paramaṃ guhyatamaṃ vidyāvrata-sādhanacaryāpaṭalapaṭavidhānavisaraṃ paramahṛdayānām arthaṃ paramaṃ guhyatamaṃ mahārthaṃ nidhānabhūtaṃ sarvamantrāṇāṃ ṣaḍete ṣaḍākṣaraparamahṛdayāḥ avikalpato tasmiṃ kālo siddhiṃ gacchanti / teṣāṃ sattvānāṃ damanāya upāyakauśalyasambhārasamantra-praveśanatāya niyataṃ sambodhiprāpaṇatāyā ṣaṭsaptatibuddha-koṭibhiḥ pūrvabhāṣitam aham apyetarhi idānīṃ bhāṣiṣye / anāgata-janatāpekṣāya taṃ śṛṇu sādhu ca suṣṭhu ca manasi kuru / bhāṣiṣye 'ham te / katamaṃ ca tat / atha khalu bhagavāṃ śākyamunir mantraṃ bhāṣate / oṁ vākyārthe jaya / oṁ vākyaśeṣe sva / oṁ vākyeyanayaḥ / oṁ vākyaniṣṭheyaḥ / oṁ vākyeyanamaḥ / oṁ vākyedanamaḥ / ityete mañjuśrī tvadīya ṣaḍmantrāḥ ṣaḍakṣarāḥ mahāprabhāvāḥ tulyasamavīryāḥ paramahṛdayāḥ paramāsiddhāḥ buddham ivotpannāḥ sarvasattvānām arthāya sarvabuddhaiḥ samprabhāṣitāḥ samayagrastāḥ [T. *dam tshig ñams*] *sampracalitāḥ sarvakarmikāḥ bodhimārgānudeśakāḥ tathāgatakule mantrapravarāḥ uttamamadhyametaratṛdhāsamprayuktāḥ suśobhanaṃ karmaphalavipākapradāḥ śāsanāntardhānakālasamayasiddhiṃ yāsyanti / samavaśaraṇaṃ saddharmanetrā* [> *netrī*] *rakṣārthaṃ ye sādhayiṣyanti teṣāṃ mūlyaprayogeṇaiva mahārājyamahābhogaiśvaryārthaṃ te sādhayiṣyanti / teṣāṃ kṣiprataraṃ tasmiṃ kāle tasmiṃ samaye siddhiṃ yāsyanti / antato jijñāsanahetor api sādhanīyā hyete paramahṛdayāḥ saṃkṣepataḥ yathā yathā prayujyante tathā tathā siddhiṃ yāsyanti samāsataḥ / eṣāṃ paṭavidhānaṃ bhavati tasmiṃ kāle tasmiṃ samaye mahābhairave pañcakaṣāye sattvā alpapuṇyā bhaviṣyanti / alpeśākhyāḥ alpajīvinaḥ alpabhogāḥ mandavīryā na śakyanti ativistarataraṃ paṭavidhānādīni karāṇi prārabhantum / teṣām arthāya bhāṣiṣye saṃkṣiptataram //*

[T.279.6 (140a)–281.1 (141a)]
de nas bcom ldan 'das śākya thub pas 'jam dpal gźon nur gyur pa la legs so źes bya ba byin te / 'jam dpal gźon nur gyur pa de bźin gśegs pa la don 'di 'dri bar sems pa legs so legs so // 'jam dpal khyod kyi mchog tu gsaṅ ba rig pa'i brtul źugs spyod pa'i le lu ras ris kyi cho ga rab 'byam yod de / sñiṅ po mchog rnams kyi don mchog tu gsaṅ ba dam pa don chen po sṅags thams cad kyi cho gar gyur pa drug po 'di dag yi ge drug gi sñiṅ po'i mchog / the tshom med pa de'i tshe 'grub par 'gyur te / sems can de dag gdul ba'i phyir daṅ / thabs la mkhas pa la

yaṅ dag par rab tu źugs pa'i phyir daṅ / ṅes par yaṅ dag pa'i byaṅ chub thob pa'i phyir / saṅs rgyas bye ba phrag bdun cu rtsa drug gis sṅar gsuṅs śiṅ da ltar yaṅ ṅas bśad de / ma oṅs pa'i skye bo'i tshogs la phan pa'i phyir legs par ñon la yid zuṅ śig daṅ / ṅas bśad par bya'o // de gaṅ źe na / de nas bcom ldan 'das śākya thub pas sṅags gsuṅs pa / oṁ bākye artha dzaya / oṁ bākye śeṣa sva / oṁ bākye baṃ dzaya / oṁ bākyaniṣṭheyaḥ / oṁ bākyeya namaḥ / oṁ bākyedaṃ namaḥ / de ltar 'di dag 'jam dpal gźon nur gyur pa khyod kyi sṅags drug daṅ yi ge drug pa mthu chen po daṅ stobs mñam pa / sñiṅ po dam pa mchog tu grub pa / saṅs rgyas bźin du 'byuṅ ba sems can thams cad kyi don gyi phir / saṅs rgyas thams cad kyis rab tu gsuṅs pa / dam tshig ñams pa daṅ dam tshig g.yos [S. *samaya*° (*dam tshig*) read for *sampracalitāḥ*?] *pa rnams kyi las thams cad byed pa / byaṅ chub kyi lam rjes su ston pa / de bźin gśegs pa'i rigs la sṅags kyi mchog tu gyur pa / mchog daṅ 'briṅ daṅ tha ma gsum la rab tu sbyor ba / legs par sbyaṅs pa'i las kyi 'bras bu'i rnam par smin pa sbyin pa / bstan pa nub pa'i dus su yaṅ dṅos grub thob par 'gyur ro // las kyi tshul daṅ bcas pa la yaṅ dag par gźol ba la / skad cig gis don bsgrub par 'gyur ba de dag myur du śin tu myur bar de'i tshe daṅ de'i dus su 'grub par 'gyur ro // ñam sad pa'i phyir yaṅ sñiṅ po dam pa 'di dag bsgrub par bya ste / mdor na ji lta ji ltar rab tu sbyar ba de lta de ltar 'grub par 'gyur ro // des na ras ris kyi cho ga 'di bya ba yin te / de'i tshe de'i dus na 'jigs pa chen po daṅ / sñigs ma la sems can bsod nams chuṅ ba 'byuṅ bar 'gyur te / grags pa chuṅ ba daṅ / tshe thuṅ ba daṅ loṅs spyod chuṅ ba daṅ / chos spyod pa chuṅ bas śin tu rgya che ba'i ras ris kyi cho ga'i sgrub pa la sogs pa rtsom par mi nus te / de dag gi phyir śin tu mdor bstan par bya'o //*

F7 [*Mmk* 4.55.19–21]
ādau tāvacchucau pṛthivīpradeśe rajovigate picuṃ gṛhya samayapraviṣṭaiḥ tatpicuṃ saṃśodhayitavyam / saṃśodhya ca anena mantrena maṇḍalācāryenābhimantritavyam aṣṭaśatavārāṃ /

[T.258.3–4 (129b)
daṅ por re źig sa'i phyogs gtsaṅ ba rdul med pa las ras bal yaṅ dag par blaṅs la / dam tshig la źugs pa'i sems can rnams kyis ras bal de yaṅ dag par byas te / yaṅ sṅags 'dis dkyil 'khor gyis brgya rtsa brgyad tu bsṅags par bya'o //

F8 [*Mmk* 4.55.21–26]
namaḥ sarvabuddhabodhisattvānām apratihatamatigatipraticāriṇām / namaḥ saṃśodhanaduḥkhapraśamanarājendrarājāya tathāgatārhate samyaksambuddhāya / tadyathā / oṁ śodhaya śodhaya sarvavighnaghātaka mahākāruṇika kumārarūpadhāriṇe / vikurva vikurva / samayam anusmara / tiṣṭha tiṣṭha hūm hūm phaṭ phaṭ svāhā //

[T.258.4–5 (129b)]
namaḥ samantabuddhānāṃ /bodhisatvāpratihatagatimatipratitsāriṇām / namaḥ saṃśodhanaduḥkhapraśamanendrarādzāya / tathāgatāya ārhate samyaksaṃbuddhāya / tadyathā / oṁ śodhaya saṃśodhaya / sarbabighnaghātaka mahākāruṇika kumārarūpadhāriṇi / bikurba bikurba / samayam anusmara tiṣṭha tiṣṭha hūm hūm phaṭ phaṭ swāhā /

F9 [*Mmk* 4.56.1–4]
tataḥ avitatha [> *avidita* < T. *mi śes pa*]*grāmyadharma*[11] *kumārībrāhmaṇa-kulakṣatriyakulaprasūtaṃ vaiśyakule prasūtaṃ nātikṛṣṇavarṇayonivarṇa-varjitāṃ avikalaṃ sarvāṅgaśobhanāṃ mātāpitṛanuṣkṛtāṃ upoṣadha-parigṛhītāṃ utpāditabodhicittāṃ karūṇikāṃ avadātavarṇāṃ anyavarṇavivarjitāṃ saṃkṣepataḥ strīlakṣaṇasupraśastacihnāṃ* [/]

[T.258.5–7 (129b)]
de nas groṅ gyi chos mi śes pa'i gźon nu ma / bram ze'i rigs daṅ rgyal rigs su skyes pa daṅ / rje'u'i rigs su skyes pa daṅ rigs ṅan pa'i skyes gnas yoṅs su spaṅs pa / dbaṅ po ma tshaṅ ba med pa / yan lag thams cad mdzes pa pha daṅ mas rjes su gnaṅ ba / gso sbyoṅ byas pa / byaṅ chub tu sems bsked pa / sñiṅ rje daṅ ldan pa / bźin dkar ba / kha dog gźan rnam par spaṅs ba / mdor na bud med kyi mtshan ñid rab tu źi ba'i mtshan ñid kyis mtshan pa /

F10 [*Mmk* 4.56.6–14]
śucau pradeśe pūrvanirdiṣṭāṃ kumārīṃ snāpayitvā śucivastraprāvṛtena sunivastāṃ kṛtvā anenaiva mantrena mahāmūdropetarakṣāṃ kṛtvā śvetacandanakuṅkumaṃ niṣprāṇakenodakenāloḍya tatpibantāṃ [T. *ras bal de* > *tatpicuṃ*] *ca kanyāṃ tenaiva mantrena saṃśodhanenābhyukṣayet / caturdiśaṃ ca kṣipet ūrdhvamadhaś ca vidikṣu śvetacandanakuṅkuma-karpūraṃ caikīkṛtya pūrvaṃ dāpayet / svayaṃ vā dadyāt / sādhakācārye vā / tadedaṃ vācā bhāṣitavyaṃ trīn vārāṃ adhitiṣṭhantu buddhā bhagavanto idaṃ paṭasūtraṃ daśabhūmipratiṣṭhitāś ca mahābodhisattvāḥ / tataste buddhā bhagavanto samanvāharanti mahābodhisattvāś ca /*

[T.258.7 (129b)–259.3 (130a)]
phyogs su sdar bstan pa'i gźon nu ma khrus byas śiṅ gos gtsaṅ ma bgos te / gos kyis legs par bkab pa byas pa la sdags 'di phyag rgya chen po daṅ ldan pas bsruṅ bar ste / tsandan dkar po daṅ / gur gum srog chags med pa'i chu daṅ sbyar bas ras bal de daṅ bu mo de sṅags de ñid kyis yaṅ dag par sbyaṅ te gtor la / tsandan dkar po daṅ / gur gum gyi chus steṅ daṅ og daṅ phyogs bźir yaṅ gtor bar bya'o // tsandan dkar po daṅ gur gum daṅ ga bur gcig tu byas ba'i bdug pas bdug par bya ste / raṅ ñid kyis sbyin pa'am / sgrub pa'i grogs mchog gyi slob dpon gyis sbyin

par bya' o // sańs rgyas bcom ldan 'das dań sa bcu' i dbań phyug la gnas ba' i byań chub sems dpa' chen po rnams / ras kyi dog pa 'di la lhag par gnas par mdzod cig ces lan gsum brjod par bya' o // de nas sańs rgyas bcom ldan 'das dań byań chub sems dpa' chen po rnams dgońs su gsol źes byas nas /

F11 [*Mmk* 4.56.16–18]

tat sādhakena jñātavyam / saphalaṃ me etat karma adhiṣṭhitaṃ me buddhair bhaghavadbhir mahābodhisattvaiś ca me / tat paṭasūtraṃ sujīvitaṃ meha janmani avandhyā me mantrasiddhiḥ /

[T.259.4–5 (130a)]

las 'di ni 'bras bu dań bcam ba yin no źes sgrub pa pos śes par bya' o // sańs rgyas bcom ldan 'das dań byań chub sems dpa' chen po rnams kyis bdag gi ras skud 'di la byin gyis brlabs te / bdag gi skye ba dam pa ni legs par 'tsho ba yin te / bdag gyi sńags sgrub pa 'bras bu med par mi 'gyur ro //

F12 [*Mmk* 4.57.12–13]

tataḥ prabhṛti yat kiñcit pāpaṃ karma purākṛtaṃ /
naśyate tatkṣaṇād eva sūtrārthaṃ ca na cetane //

[T.260.6 (130b)]

ci ltar nus pa bźin du bya // de nas brtsams te gań cuń zad //
sdig pa sńar ni byas pa dag // dog par sems kyis dmigs pa na //

F13 [*Mmk* 4.57.14–19]

saṅgṛyam idaṃ sūtraṃ śucau bhāṇḍe niveśayet /
na hi tantugato kṛtvā [> nihitaṃ tu tato kṛtvā < T. de nas bźag pa byas nas] dhūpayet karpūradhūpanaiḥ //
aprāṇyaṅgasamutthaṃ vā kuṅkumacandanādibhiḥ /
architaṃ sugandhapuṣpair mallikacampakādibhiḥ //
śucau pradeśe saṃsthāpya kṛtarakṣāpidhānitaṃ /
mantravit sarvakarmajño kṛtajāpaḥ susamāhitaḥ //

[T.260.6 (130b)–261.1 (131a)]

dog pa 'di dag yań dag blańs // gtsań ma' i snod du gźug par bya //
de nas bźag pa byas nas de // ga bur gyi ni bdug pas bdug //
srog cags yan lag byuń ba 'am // gur gum tsandan la sogs dań //
me tog ma le tsam pa ka // dri źim sogs pas yońs su bsgo //
bsruń ba' i cho ga byas nas ni // gtsań ma' i phyogs su yań dag bźag //
sńags rig las kun śes pa yin // śin du mñam gźag bzlas pa bya //

F14 [*Mmk* 4.57.21–29]
avyaṅgamakṛśaṃ caiva śukladharmasadāratam //
avyādhyartam avṛddhaṃ ca kāsaśvāsa [keśaśveta <*T. skra dga]vinirmuktam / kāsaśvāsa-[keśaśveta* <T. *skra dga]vinirmuktaṃ aṣaṇḍaṃ yonisatyajam //*
anavadyamakubjaṃ caivāpaṅgupativarjitam /
samastalakṣaṇopetaṃ praśastaṃ cārudarśanam //
śubhabuddhisamācāraṃ laukikīṃ vṛttimāśritam /
siddhikāmo 'tra taṃ yāced uttame paṭavāyane //
praśastā śubhavarṇe vā buddhimanto suśikṣitaḥ /
atotkṛṣṭatamaiḥ śreṣṭhaiḥ paṭavāyanaśreyasaiḥ //

[T.261.1–3 (131a)]
raṅ dbaṅ yan lag ma ñams daṅ // dgar po'i chos la rtag tu daṅ //
rgan min nad kyis gduṅs pa min // lud pa dbugs mi bde ba spaṅs //
ma niṅ smad pa ma yin daṅ // 'phyi bo ma yin skra dgar spaṅs //
gun gyis bgur ba'i mtshan ñid ldan // rab bsṅags blta na sdugs pa daṅ //
blo daṅ yaṅ dag spyod pa dge // 'jig rten pa yi tshul la brten //
dṅos grub 'dod pas de la ni // ras bzaṅ btags pa'i ched du bskul //
grogs po rigs bzaṅ rab bsṅags źiṅ // blo ldan bzo ni mkhas ba daṅ //

F15 [*Mmk* 4.58.7–9]
kṣiprasiddhikaro hyeṣa paṭaśreṣṭho niruttaraḥ /
sarvakarmakaro pūjyo divyamānuṣyasaukhyadaḥ /
śreyasaḥ sarvabhūtānāṃ samyaksaṃbuddhabhāṣitam //

[T.261.5–6 (131a)]
'di ni myur du 'grub byed pa'i // ras ni bzaṅ po bla na med //
las gun byed ciṅ mchod pa ste // lha daṅ mi yi bde ba sbyin //
'byuṅ po gun gyi dbal 'gyur źes // yaṅ dag rdzogs saṅs rgyas kyis gsuṅs //

F16 [*Mmk* 4.58.11–14]
suśubhe nakṣatre prātihārakapakṣe śukle 'hani śubhagrahanirīkṣite anye vā śuklapakṣe sukusumitasahakāramañjarīvaratarupuṣpāḍhyavasantasamaye kratuvare tasmin kāle tasmin samaye pūrvāhṇodite savitari . . . /

[T.261.6–7 (131a)]
rgyu skar bzaṅ po 'am / tsho 'phrul gyi zla ba phyed dam ñin źag dge ba 'am gza' dge ba bltas te gso sbyoṅ sbyin / yaṅ na ṅus kyi mchog dpyid kyi ṅus kyi zla ba yar gyi do la śiṅ amra'i me tog skyes śiṅ śiṅ gi mchog rnams kyi yal ga daṅ me tog rgyas pa de'i ṅus mtsham su / sṅa dro ñi ma 'char ba la . . . /

F17 [*Mmk* 4.58.19–21]
śucau pṛthivīpradeśe apagatakolāhale vigatajanapade viviktāsane prasanne gupte puṣpārcite //

[T.262.2 (131b)]
gtsaṅ ma'i sa phyogs su ca co med ciṅ skye bo daṅ bral ba dben pa'i gnas su bkab [> *bkrab*] *pa daṅ gsaṅ bar me tog gis mchod do* /

F18 [*Mmk* 6.71.27–6.72.11]
yat kṛtaṃ kāritaṃ cāpi pāpaṃ karma sudāruṇam /
kalpakoṭisahasrāṇi darśanāt paṭamucyate //
paṭaṃ tu dṛṣṭhamātraṃ vai tatkṣaṇādeva mucyate/
buddhakoṭīsahasrāṇi satkuryād yo hi buddhimāṃ //
kanyasaṃ tu paṭaṃ dṛṣṭvā kalāṃ nāyāti ṣoḍhaśīm /
yat puṇyaṃ sarvabuddhānāṃ pūjā kṛtvā tu tāpinām[12] //
tat puṇyaṃ prāpnuyād vidvān kanyase paṭadarśane /
śobhanāni ca karmāṇi bhogahetor ihācaret //
yāvanti kecana mantrā brahmendrarṣibhāṣitāḥ /
vainateyena tu proktāḥ varuṇādityakuberayoḥ //
dhanādyaiḥ rākṣasaiḥ sarvair dānavendrair mahoragaiḥ /
somavāyuyamādyaiś ca bhāṣitā hariharādibhiḥ //
sarve mantra ihānītāḥ sidhyante paṭamagrataḥ /

[T.277.7 (139a)–278.3 (139b)]
phran tshegs las rnam dag la śes //
bskal pa bye bar mi bzad las // *ras ris mthoṅ ba tsam gyis grol* //
ras ris mthoṅ ba tsam gyis ni // *skad cig de la grol bar 'gyur* //
saṅs rgyas bye ba stoṅ phrag ni // *mthoṅ ba tsam gyis grol 'gyur te* //
ras ris mthoṅ ba tsam gyis kyaṅ // *de yi mod la grol bar 'gyur* //
saṅs rgyas bye ba stoṅ phrag la // *blo daṅ ldan pas bsñen bkur bas* //
ras ris tha ma mthoṅ ba ni // *bcu drug char yaṅ mi phod do* //
saṅs rgyas skyob pa kun la ni // *mchod byas bsod nams gaṅ yin pa* //
mkhas pas bsod nams gaṅ thob de // *ras ris mtha' ma mthoṅ ba'i yin* //
dge ba dag gi las rnams la // *'oṅs spyod phyir yaṅ 'dir spyad do* //
sṅags rnams gaṅ dag ci yod pa // *tshaṅs dbaṅ draṅ sroṅ gis bśad daṅ* //
nam mkha' ldiṅ gyis gaṅ bśad daṅ // *chu lha ñi ma lus ṅan daṅ* //
nor sbyin sogs daṅ srin po daṅ // *lha min dbaṅ po lto 'phye daṅ* //
zla ba rluṅ daṅ gśin rje sogs // *khyab 'jug lha chen sogs bśad pa* //

F19 [*Mmk* 4.59.11–13]
vidhibhraṣṭā na sidhyeyuḥ śakrasyāpi śacīpateḥ //
sidhyante kṣipram evaṃ tu sarvakarmā na yatnataḥ /
vidhinā ca samāyuktā ityasyāpi tṛjanminaḥ [T. *mi yi skye ba tha ma*] //

[T.262.7 (131b)–263.1 (132a)]
brgya byin bde sogs bdag po la 'aṅ // cho ga ñams na 'grub mi 'gyur //
cho ga yaṅ dag ldan na ni // mi yi skye ba tha ma la 'aṅ //
las rnams tham cad 'bad med par // myur ba ñid du 'grub par byed //

F20 [*Mmk* 4.60.2–6]
śaucācārasaṃpanno śilpino nityadhiṣṭhitaḥ //
dūrādāvastathā [> dūrādāvasathāt < T. *gnas nas thag riṅ*[13]*] gatvā*
kuṭi [> gūtha > T. *bśaṅ*[14]*]prasrāvam utsṛjet /*
sacelas tu tataḥ snātvā anyavāsānnivāsya ca //
śuklāmbaradharaḥ sragmī [> sragvī < T. *phreṅ ba ldan par*[15]*]*
upaspṛśya punaḥ punaḥ /
śvetacandanaliptāṅgo hastau uddhṛṣya śilpinaḥ //
bhūyo vayeta yatnena ślakṣṇaṃ sandhotaṃ [> sandhitaṃ < T. *dri*
med par[16]*] sadā //*

[T.263.5–6 (132a)]
gtsaṅ sbra'i spyad pa phun sum tshogs // bzo bo rtag tu byin brlabs ldan //
gnas nas thag riṅ soṅ nas ni // bśaṅ daṅ gci ba yoṅs su dor //
de nas gos bcas khrus byas te // gos gźan dag kyaṅ bgo bya źiṅ //
gos dkar phreṅ ba ldan par 'chaṅ // yaṅ daṅ yaṅ du ñe reg bya //
lus ni tsandan dkar pos byugs // bzo bos lag pa gñis kyaṅ byugs //
legs 'jam rtag tu dri med par // 'bad pas gyaṅ ni tha ga bya //

F21 [*Mmk* 4.60.21–4.61.11]
mañjuśriyo mahāvīraḥ mantrarūpeṇa bhāṣitaḥ /
atītair bahubhir mantrair [> °buddhair< T. *saṅs rgyas*[17]*]*
mayāpyetarhi punaḥ punaḥ //
*sa eva sarvamantrāṇāṃ viceruḥ [*T. *rnam par spyod*[18]*] mantrarūpiṇaḥ /*
mahāvīryo mahātejāḥ sarvamantrārthasādhakaḥ //
karoti trividhākārāṃ [> vividhā° < T. *rnam pa sna tshogs*[19]*]*
vicitrā trāṇahetavaḥ /
jambūdvīpagatāḥ sattvāḥ mūḍācāracetanāḥ //
aśrāddhaviparītās tu mithyācārasalolupāḥ /
na sādhayanti mantāṇi sarvadravyāṇi vai punaḥ //
ata eva bhramante te saṃsārāndhārcārake /
yastu śuddhamanaso nityaṃ śrāddho kotukamaṅgale sadā //
autsukaḥ sarvamantreṣu nityaṃ grahaṇadhāraṇe /
siddhikāmā mahātmāno mahotsāhā mahojasāḥ //
teṣāṃ siddhyantyayatnena mantrā ye jinabhāṣitāḥ /
aśrāddhānāṃ tu jantūnāṃ śuklo dharmeṇa rohate //
bījamūṣare kṣiptaṃ aṅkuro 'phalo yathā /

śrāddhāmūlaṃ sadā dharme uktaṃ sarvārthadarśibhiḥ [/]
mantrasiddhiḥ sadā proktā teṣāṃ dharmārthaśīlinām //

[T.264.2–7 (132b)]
dpa' bo chen po 'jam dpal gyis // sṅags kyi bzlas pa gsuṅs pa daṅ //
'das pa'i saṅs rgyas maṅ po daṅ // ṅas kyaṅ da ltar gsuṅs pa yin //
de ñid sṅags ni thams cad kyi // sṅags kyi ṅo pos rnam par spyod //
brtson 'grus che źiṅ gzi brjid che // sṅags kyi don gun sgrub byed pa //
cha byad rnam pa sna tshogs byed // skyob pa rnam pa sna tshogs rgyu //
'dzam gliṅ gnas pa'i sems can rnams // rmoṅs pa spyod ciṅ sems pa med //
ma dad phyin ci log par byed // log spyod śin tu brkam chags kyis //
rdzas rnams ma lus pa dag daṅ // sṅags rnams kyis kyaṅ 'grub mi byed //
'k hor ba'i mun pa'i btson rar [> brtson raṅ] ni // de ñid kyis ni 'khor bar 'gyur //
gaṅ yaṅ rtag tu yi dag ciṅ // dad ldan bkra śis dag la dga' //
sṅags rnams kun la spro pa daṅ // rtag tu 'dzin daṅ 'chaṅ ba daṅ //
bdag ñid chen po dṅos grub 'dod // spro ba che źiṅ gzi brjid che //
rgyal pos gsuṅs pa'i sṅags dag ni // 'bad pa med par 'grub par 'gyur //
dad pa med pa'i skye bo la // dkar po'i chos rnams mi skye ste //
sa bon tshwa sgor btab pa la // myu gu skye ba med pa bźin //
dad pa'i rtsa ba rtag tu chos // chos don gzigs pas gsuṅs pa ste //
chos don spyod pa de dag la // sṅags rnams rtag tu 'grub par gsuṅs //

F22 [*Mmk* 7.74.27–7.75.1]
oṁ he he bhagavaṃ bahurūpadhara divyacakṣuṣe avalokya avalokya māṃ samayam anusmara kumārarūpadhāriṇe mahābodhisattva kiṃ cirāyasi hūṁ hūṁ phaṭ phaṭ svāhā /

[T.281.4–5 (141a)]
oṁ he he bhagaban bahurūpadhara dibyatsakṣuṣe / abalokya / abalokya / māṃ samayam anusmara kumārarūpadhāriṇe / mahābodhisatwa kiñtsirāyasi hūṁ sphaṭe sphaṭe swāhā /

F23 [*Mmk* 4.61.20–22]
pūrvābhimukhaḥ kuśapiṇḍakpaviṣṭaḥ svasthabuddhiḥ sarvabuddha-bodhisattvagatacittaḥ sūkṣmavartipratigṛhītapāṇiranāyāsacittiḥ taṃ paṭam ālikhet //

[T.265.3 (133a)]
śar du mṅon par phyogs pas ku śa'i khres la 'dug ste blo legs par gnas pa daṅ / saṅs rgyas daṅ byaṅ chub sems dpa' la dmigs pa'i sems kyis

pir phra mo lag par blaṅs nas / 'khrug pa med pa'i sems kyis ras de la bri bar bya'o //

Appendix G: Chapter Three

G1 [*Mmk* 2.28.21–22–2.29.1–11]
atha khalu mañjuśrīḥ kumārabhūta vajrapāṇiṃ bodhisattvam āmantrayate sma / imāni guhyakādhipate mantrapadāni sarahasyāni paramaguhyakāni [. . .]*namaḥ sarvabuddhabodhisattvānām apratihataśāsanānāṃ / uṃ kara kara kuru kuru mama kāryam bhañja bhañja sarvavighnāṃ daha daha sarva vajravināyakam mūrdhaṭakajīvitāntakara mahāvikṛtarūpiṇe paca paca sarvaduṣṭāṃ mahāgaṇapatijīvitāntakara bandha bandha sarvagrahāṃ ṣaṇmukha ṣaḍbhuja ṣaṭcaraṇa rudramānaya viṣṇumānaya brahmādyāṃ devānānaya mā vilamba mā vilamba iyal iyal maṇḍalamadhye praveśaya samayam anusmara hūṁ hūṁ hūṁ hūṁ hūṁ hūṁ phaṭ phaṭ svāhā / eṣa saḥ paramaguhyakādhipate paramaguhyaḥ mahāvīryaḥ mañjuśrīḥ ṣaṇmukho nāma mahākrodharājā sarvavighnavināśakaḥ / anena paṭhitamātreṇa daśabhūmipratiṣṭhāpitabodhisattvā vidravante / kiṃ punar duṣṭavighnāḥ / anena paṭhitamātreṇa mahārakṣā kṛtā bhavati / mudrā cātra bhavati mahāśūleti vikhyātā sarvavighnavināśikā /*

[T.222.4–5; 6 (111b)–223.3 (112a)]
de nas 'jam dpal gźon nur gyur pas byaṅ chub sems dpa' phyag na rdo rje la smras pa gsaṅ ba pa'i bdag po sṅags kyi tshig 'di ni gsaṅ ba daṅ bcas śiṅ mchog tu gsaṅ bar bya pa yin te / [. . .] *namaḥ samantabuddhānāṃ / apratihataśāsanānāṃ / oṃ kara kara / kuru kuru / mama kāryam bhañja bhañja / sarbabighna daha daha sarba bajrabināyakaṃ mūrdhagaṭaṃ dzīvitāntakara mahābikṛtarūpathāriṇi / patsa patsa sarbaduṣṭāna / mahāganapatidzībivitāntakara banda banda sarbagrahāna / ṣaṭmukha ṣaṭbhudza / ṣaṭtsaraṇa rudramānaya / biṣṇumānaya brahmādyāṃ debamānaya mā bilaṃba / lahu lahu maṇḍalamadhye prabeśaya / samayamanusmara hūṁ hūṁ hūṁ hūṁ hūṁ hūṁ phaṭ phaṭ / svāhā / gsaṅ ba pa'i bdag po 'di ni 'jam dpal gźon nur gyur pa'i mchog tu gsaṅ ba'i sṅags chen po gdoṅ drug pa źes bya ba yin te / khro bo'i rgyal po bgegs thams cad 'jig par byed pa ste / 'di brjod pa tsam gyis sa bcu'i dbaṅ phyug la gnas pa'i byaṅ chub sems dpa' yaṅ 'jigs par byed pa yin na / bgegs ma ruṅs pa lta smos kyaṅ ci dgos 'di brjod pa tsam ñid kyis sruṅ ba chen po byas par 'gyur ro / 'dir yaṅ phyag rgyar 'gyur ba ni / nag po chen po źes bya ba'i / bgegs rnams thams cad 'jig byed pa'o //*

G2 [*Mmk* 2.27.10–26]
saptābhimantritaṃ candanodakaṃ kṛtvā / caturdiśam ityūdhvamadhastiryaksarvataḥ kṣipet / sarvabuddhabodhisattvāḥ mañjuśriyaḥ svayaṃ

tasya parivāraḥ sarvalaukikalokottarāś ca mantrāḥ sarve ca bhūtagaṇāḥ sarvasattvāś ca āgatā bhaveyuḥ / namaḥ sarvabuddhānām apratihataśāsanānām / oṁ dhu dhura dhura dhūpavāsini dhūpārciṣi hūṁ tiṣṭha samayam anusmara svāhā / dhūpamantraḥ / candanaṃ karpūraṃ kuṅkumaṃ caikīkṛtya dhūpaṃ dāpayet tataḥ / āgatānāṃ tathāgatānāṃ sarvabodhisattvānāṃ ca dhūpāpyāyitamanasaḥ ākṛṣṭā bhavanti / bhavati cātra mudrā yasya māleti vikhyātā sarvasattvākarṣaṇī śivā / āhvānanamantrāyāś ca ayam eva mudrā padmamālā śubhā / āgatānāṃ ca sarvabuddhabodhisattvānāṃ sarvasattvānāṃ cāgatānāṃ arghyo deyaḥ / karpūracandanakuṅkumair udakamāloḍyajātīkusumanavamālikavārṣikapunnāganāgavavakulapiṇḍitagarābhyāṃ eteṣāmanyatamena puṣpeṇa yathārttukena vā sugandhapuṣpeṇa miśīkṛtya anena mantreṇa arghyo deyaḥ / namaḥ sarvabuddhānāṃ apratihataśāsanānāṃ tadyathā / he he mahākāruṇika viśvarūpadhāriṇi arghyaṃ pratīcchad pratīcchāpaya samayam anusmara tiṣṭha tiṣṭha maṇḍalamadhye praveśaya praviśa sarvabhūtānukampaka gṛhṇa gṛhṇa hūṁ ambaravicāriṇe svāhā / mudrā cātra pūrṇeti vikyātā sarvabuddhānuvartinī /

[T.220.4 (110b)–221.4 (111a)]
tsandan gyi chur gyas te / lan bdun bsṅags nas / phogs ba'i daṅ / steṅ daṅ / 'og daṅ / thams cad du gtor na saṅs rgyas daṅ / byaṅ chub sems dpa' daṅ / 'jam dpal gźon nur gyur pa raṅ ñed 'khor daṅ bcas pa thams cad daṅ / 'jig rten daṅ 'jig rten las 'das pa thams cad daṅ / sṅags daṅ de bźin du 'byuṅ po'i tshogs daṅ sems can thams cad 'gugs par 'gyur ro // namaḥ sarbabuddhānāṃ / apratihataśāsanānāṃ / oṁ dhu dhura dhura dhūpabāsini / dhūmarartsiśi hūṁ tiṣṭha samayam anusmara svāhā / bdug pa'i sṅags so // tsandan daṅ / ga pur daṅ / gur gum gcig tu byas te / bdug pas bdugs na de bźin gśegs pa rnams daṅ / byaṅ chub sems dpa' thams cad daṅ / sems can thams cad bdug pas tshim źiṅ dgyes nas bźugs par 'gyur ro // 'dir yaṅ phyag rgyar 'gyur ba ni // padma'i phreṅ bźes grags pa // thams cad 'gugs byed źi ba yin / spyan draṅ ba yi sṅags la yaṅ // padma'i phreṅ ba bzaṅ po źes / bya ba'i phyag rgya 'di ñid do // saṅs rgyas daṅ byaṅ chub sems dpa' thams cad daṅ / sems can thams cad byon pa la mchod yon dbul bar bya ste / ga bur daṅ tsandan daṅ gur gum chu daṅ sbyar nas me tog ku su daṅ mālika daṅ / dbyar gyi me tog daṅ me tog punnāga daṅ me tog ba kula daṅ / me tog piṇḍita garu 'di dag gaṅ yaṅ ruṅ ba'i me tog gam / dus ci lta ba'i me tog dri źim po bcug ste / sṅags 'dis mchod yon dbul bar bya'o / namaḥ sarbabuddhānāṃ // apratihataśāsanānāṃ / tadyathā / he he mahākāruṇika / biśwarūpadhāraṇi / arghyaṃ pratītstshapaya / samayam anusmara / tiṣṭha tiṣṭha / maṇḍalamadhye prabeśaya prabeśaya / sarvabhūtānukaṁpaka gṛhṇa gṛhṇa hūṁ / oṁbarabitsāriṇe svāhā / 'dir yaṅ phyag rgya ni gaṅ bźes bya bar grags pa sems can thams cad daṅ rjes su mthun źiṅ brtan pa'o //

G3 [*Mmk* 2.27.3–9]
āhvānanamantrā cātra bhavati / oṁ he he kumārarūpisvarūpiṇe sarvabālabhāṣitaprabodhane āyāhi bhagavaṃ āyāhi / kumārakrīḍotpaladhāriṇe maṇḍalamadhye tiṣṭha tiṣṭha / samayam anusmara / apratihataśāsana hūṁ / mā vilamba ru ru phaṭ svāhā / eṣa bhagavaṃ mañjuśriyaḥ āhvānanamantrā / sarvasattvānāṃ sarvabodhisattvānāṃ sarvapratyekabuddhāryaśrāvakadevanāgayakṣagandharvagaruḍakinnaramahoragapiśācarākṣasasarvabhūtānāṃ [/]

[T.220.2–4 (110b)]
spyan draṅ ba'i sṅags ni / oṁ he he kumārabisvarūpiṇe / sarbabālabhāṣitaprabodhane / eyāhi bhagabaṃ / eyāhi kumāra / krīḍanutpaladhāriṇe maṇḍalamadhye tiṣṭha tiṣṭha samayamanusmara / apratihataśāsana hūṁ / mā bilamba kuru phaṭ svāhā / 'di ni bcom ldan 'das 'jam dpal gyi spyan draṅ ba'i sṅags so // saṅs rgyas thams cad daṅ / byaṅ chub sems dpa' thams cad daṅ / raṅ saṅs rgyas thams cad daṅ / 'phags pa ñan thos daṅ / lha daṅ / klu daṅ / gnod sbyin daṅ / dri za daṅ / lha ma yin daṅ / nam mkha' ldiṅ daṅ / mi 'am ci daṅ / lto 'phye chen po daṅ / śa za daṅ / srin po daṅ / 'byuṅ po thams cad kyi 'aṅ yin no //

G4 [*Mmk* 11.95.24–25; 11.96.1–6; 11.96.15–20]
alaṅghyaṃ tasya vacanaṃ śiṣyaiḥ kartavya yatnataḥ /
bhoghāstasya dātavyāḥ yathāvibhavasambhavāḥ //

. . .

tathaiva śiṣyo dharmajño ācāryāya dade dhanam /
prāpnuyād yaśaḥ siddhiṃ āyurārogyam eva tu //
puṣkalaṃ gatimāpnoti śiṣyo pūjyastu taṃ guruṃ /
mantrāstasya ca sidhyanti vidhimārgopadarśanāt //
sevanād bhajanād teṣāṃ mānanā pūjanādapi /
tuṣyante sarvabuddhās tu tathaiva jinavarātmajāḥ //

. . .

snehānuvartinī cakṣuḥ supratiṣṭhitadehināṃ /
tam eva kurācchiṣyatvaṃ ācāryā śiṣyahetavaḥ //
anyonyānuvartinī yatra snehasantatimāninī /
snigdhasantānānudharā tu mantraṃ dadyāt tu tatra vai //
ācāryo śiṣyaṃ evaṃ tu śiṣyo vā gurudarśane /
utsukau bhavataḥ nityā sādhvasayogataḥ ubau //

[T.308.1–7 (154b)]
de yi bka' ni mi 'gom par // slob mas 'bad nas bya ba yin //
ci ltar 'byor pa yod pa bźin // loṅs spyod de la sbyin par bya // . . .

. . .

slob ma chos rig de bźin du // slob dpon phyir ni ṅor sbyin na //
tshe daṅ nad med de bźin du // grags pa thob par 'gyur ba yin //
slob mas bla ma de mchog na // dag pa'i 'gro ba thob par 'gyur //
lam ni sna tshogs ñer bstan pas // de la sṅags ni 'grub par 'gyur //
de la bsten daṅ bsñen bkur byas // ri mo byas daṅ mchod pas ni /[20]
saṅs rgyas rnams daṅ de bźin du // rgyal ba'i sras rnams mñes par 'gyur //

. . .

mig ni gaṅ la yod gyur pa // de ni slob ma ñid bya ste //
slob dpon rgyur yaṅ bya ba yin // gaṅ du phan tshun rgyud la ni //
brtse ba'i phreṅ ba yod pa daṅ // brtse ba'i rgyud ni 'dzin pa la //
de la sṅags ni sbyin par bya // slob dpon la ni slob ma'am //
bla mas slob ma mthoṅ ba'aṅ ruṅ // rtag tu spro bar 'gyur ba la //
gñi gal ni grub pa gnas // de dag la ni rtag tu yaṅ //

G5 [*Mmk* 2.51.3–8]
dvitīyamaṇḍalābhiṣekaṃ dvitīyamaṇḍale sarvadevānāṃ yat pratipāditakaṃ pūrṇakalaśaṃ tenābhyaṣiṅcet / mūrdhani yathaiva vā pūrvakaṃ tenaiva vidhinā mucyate sarvakilviṣāt / anujñātaś ca bhavati sarvabuddhair sarvalaukikalokottarasamayamaṇḍalaṃ sarvamantramudrāsādhaneṣu ca avyaṣṭo[21] *bhavati / sarvabodhisattvair iti ācāryābhiṣekaṃ dadyāt //*

[T.252.6 (126b)–253.1 (127a)]
dkyil 'khor gñis pa la dbaṅ bskur ba ni gñis pa'i dkyil 'khor du lha thams cad la bstabs pa'i sṅar gyi bum pa des dbaṅ bskur bar bya'o // spyi bo la sṅar gyi cho ga ci lta ba de ñid kyis byas na sdig pa'i rñog pa thams cad las grol bar 'gyur de / saṅs rgyas bcom ldan 'das thams cad gyis gnaṅ źiṅ / saṅs rgyas daṅ byaṅ chub sems dpa' thams cad kyis 'jig rten daṅ 'jig rten [253.1 (127a)] *las'das pa thams cad kyi dam tshig daṅ / dkyil 'khor daṅ sṅags daṅ phyag rgya thams cad sgrub pa la byin gyis brlabs par 'gyur źiṅ / slob dpon du dbaṅ bskur ba sbyin no //*

G6 [*Mmk* 11.93.14–15]
ādau tāvad vidyāvrataśīlacaryāsamādānaṃ prathamata eva samādadet / prathamaṃ tāvanmaṇḍalācāryopadeśanasamayam anupraviśet /

[T.304.7 (152b)–305.1 (153a)]
daṅ por re źig rig pa daṅ brtul źugs daṅ / tshul khrims kyi yi dam [*yi dam > dam bca' = samādāna?*] *daṅ po ñid du blaṅ bar byas la / daṅ po re źig dkyil 'khor gyi slob dpon gyis bstan pa'i dam tshig khyod kyi cho ga'i rgyal por bstan ciṅ sṅar bśad pa / la rjes su 'jug par bya'o //*

G7 [*Mmk* 11.93.26–11.94.6; 11.94.10–11]
sādhakaś ca . . . maṇḍalācāryam abhyarthya prārthayet / icchāmyācāryeṇa mahābodhisattvasya kumārabhūtasyāryamañjuśriyasya samayam anupraviṣṭum / tad vadatvācāryo 'smākam anukampārthaṃ hitacitto dayāvāṃ / tatas tena maṇḍalācāryeṇa pūrvanirdiṣṭena vidhinā śiṣyāṃ yathāpūrvaṃ parīkṣya praveśayet / pūrvavad abhiṣekaṃ dattvā mantraṃ dadyāt / yathāvat kramaśo samayaṃ darśayet / rahasyatantramudrām anukarmāṇi karmāṇi ca prabhūtakālenaiva suparīkṣya āśayaṃ jñātvā darśayet /. . . [11.94.10–11] *tatas tena maṇḍalācāryeṇa putrasaṃjñā upasthāpayitavyā / putravat pratipattavyam / mātuś ca bhogā upasaṃhartavyā iti //*

[T.305.6 (153a)–306.2 (153b); 306.3 (153b)]
sgrub pa po yaṅ de daṅ / . . . slob dpon daṅ ldan cig byaṅ chub sems dpa' chen po 'phags pa 'jam dpal gźon nur gyur pa'i dam tshig la rjes su 'jug par 'tshal na / slob dpon gyis bdag la thugs brtse ba'i slad du / phan pa'i thugs daṅ brtse ba'i thugs kyis de bśad du gsol / de nas dkyil 'khor gyi slob dpon des sṅar bstan pa'i cho gas slob ma la sda ma ci lta bu bźin du brtags nas rab tu gźug par bya ste / sṅar ci ltar dbaṅ bskur ba bźin du phyis kyaṅ sbyin par bya'o // go rims ci lta ba bźin du dam tshig bstan te / gsaṅ ba'i phyag rgya daṅ rgyud daṅ sṅags daṅ las gyaṅ ṅus riṅ po ñid nas ṅes par brtags te / bsam pa śes nas bstan par bya ste / . . . [306.3 (153b)] *de nas dkyil 'khor gyi slob dpon des bu'i 'du śes ñe bar gźag par bya ste / bu bźin du bsgrub par bya źiṅ ma bźin du yaṅ loṅs spyod kyis ñe bar bsdu bar bya'o //*

G8 [*Mmk* 11.94.12–16]
tatas tena sādhakena anyatamaṃ mantraṃ gṛhītvā ekāntaṃ gatvā pūrvanirdiṣṭe sthāne peyālaṃ taireva mantraiḥ āhvānavisarjanapradīpagandhadhūpabalinibedyaṃ maṇḍaloktena vidhinā vistareṇa karttavyaṃ / āhuya ardhamāsanaṃ dattvā trisandhyā trisnāyī tricailaparivartī jāpaṃ kuryāt pratyahaṃ tatra [/]

[T.306.3–5 (153b)]
de nas sgrub pa po des sṅags gaṅ yaṅ ruṅ ba bzuṅ ste / gcig pu dben par soṅ nas sṅar bstan pa goṅ ma bźin du rgya cher sbyar de / de dag ñid kyis sṅags dag gis ni spyan draṅ gśegs su gsol ba daṅ / mar me daṅ dri daṅ bdug pa daṅ gtor ma daṅ lha bśos dkyis 'khor la gsuṅs pa ñid kyi tsho gas rgya cher bya ste / spyan draṅs nas gdan daṅ mchod yon phul la / dus mtshams gsum ṅu khrus lan gsum bya źiṅ / gos lan gsum brje źiṅ ñin re bźin du bzlas ba bya'o //

G9 [*Mmk* 10.90.3–6]
kin tu mantāpadeśena kiñcit kālaṃ vaseta vai /
anyatra vā tato gacche samaye somagrahe travat [ābhavet] //
samayaprāpto (°o >°e; T: *dus te)*
vasatatra kiñcit kālaṃ tu nānyathā /
anyatra vā tato kṣipraṃ gacche śaktā tu mantravit //

[T.299.6 (150a)]
'on kyaṅ sṅags ni bstan pa yin // cuṅ zad dus ni bstan pa'o //
dam tshig tshogs pa'i rgyu ldan na // de las gźan du 'ṅ 'gro bya ste //
der ni dam tshig thob bsten pa // cuṅ zad dus te gźan du min //
de nas gźan du 'aṅ myur du ni // sṅags rig pas ni ci nus 'gro //

G10 [*Mmk* 8.79.12-14]
mahāraṇyaṃ gatvā triśallakṣāṇi jape phalodakāhāraḥ mūlaparṇabhakṣo vā kṛtapuraścaraṇo bhavati // tato . . . /

[T.286.5 (143b)–288.1 (146b)]
gaṅ 'dod pa dgon pa chen por soṅ ste 'bum phrag gsum bzla bar bya'o // 'bras bu daṅ cus 'tsho ba'am / rtsa ba daṅ / lo ma'i bza' ba byas / sṅon du bya ba byas par 'gyur ro //

G11 [*Mmk* 10.87.15–10.88.26 (some verses omitted)]
mahāsamudre tathā śaile vṛkṣāḍhye puṣpasambhave /
ete deśeṣu siddhyante mantrā vai jinabhāṣitā [//]
viviktadeśe śucau prānte grāmyadharmavivarjite [/]
siddhyante mantrarāṭ sarve tathaiva girigahvare [//]

. . .

bhagīrathītaṭe ramye yamune caiva suśobhane /
sindhunarmadavakṣe ca candrabhāge śucau taṭe //
kāverī sarasvatī caiva sitā devamahānadī /
siddhikṣetrāṇyetāni ukktā daśabalātmajaiḥ //
daśabalaiḥ kathitāḥ kṣetrāḥ uttarāpathaparvatāḥ /
kaśmīre cīnadeśe ca nepāle kāviśe tathā //
mahācīne tu vai siddhi siddhikṣetrāṇyaśeṣataḥ /
uttarāṃ diśim āśritya parvatāḥ saritāś ca ye //

. . .

śrīparvate mahāśaile dakṣiṇāpathasaṃjñike /
śrīdhānyakaṭake caitya jinadhātudhare bhuvi //
siddhiyante tatra mantrā vai kṣipraḥ sarvārthakarmasu /

vajrāsane mahācaitye dharmacakre tu śobhane //
śāntiṃ gataḥ muniḥ śresto tatrāpi siddhi dṛśyate /
devāvatāre mahācaitye saṅkaśye mahāprātihārike //
kapilāhvaye mahānagare vare vane lumbini puṅgave /
siddhyante mantrarāṭ tatra praśastajinavarṇite //
gṛdhrakūṭe tathā śaile sadā sītavane bhuvi /
kusumāhvaye puradhare ramye tathā kāśīpurī sadā //

. . .

ete cānye ca deśā vai grāmajanapadakarvaṭā /
pattanā puravarā śreṣṭā puṇyā vā saritāśityā //
tatra bhikṣānuvartī ca japahomarato bhavet /
lapane[22] *cābhyavakāśe ca śūnyam āyatane sadā //*

[T.297.6 (149a)–299.2 (150a)]
de bźin rgya mtsho chen po daṅ // ri ni śiṅ ldan me dog yod //
'di dag gi ni phyogs dag du // sṅags grub par ni rgyal bas gsuṅs //
gtsaṅ źiṅ bas mtha' dben phyogs su // grod gi chos ni rnam par spaṅs //

. . .

chu bo gaṅgā'i 'gram daṅ ni // de bźin legs mdzes yamuna //
sindu narmadā naṅ daṅ // zla ba'i cha ni gtsaṅ ṅogs daṅ //
de bźin kābi sarasvata // chu bo chen po sīta rnams //
'di dag grub pa'i źiṅ du ni // stobs bcu ldan sras rnams kyis bśad //
stobs bcu ldan pas bśad pa'i źiṅ // byaṅ phyogs yod pa'i ri dag daṅ //
kha ce daṅ ni rgya yul daṅ // bal po de bźin maṅ yul daṅ //
rgya yul chen daṅ li yul dag // de dag ma lus grub pa'i źiṅ //
byaṅ phyogs la ni gnas pa daṅ //[23] *ri daṅ chu bo dag la yaṅ //*

. . .

dpal gyi ri bo'i ri chen ni // lho yi phyogs na yaṅ dag gnas //
dpal ldan 'bras phuṅ mchod rten ni // rgyal ba'i riṅ bsrel gnas pa'i sa //
thams cad don gyi gnas dag la // der ni sṅags rnams myur du 'grub //
mchod rten chen po rdo rje gdan // chos kyi 'khor lo rab bskor daṅ //
thub mchog źi bar rab gśegs pa // der yaṅ grub par rab tu snaṅ //
lha las babs pa'i mchod rten daṅ // naikaśa daṅ cho 'phrul bstan //
groṅ mchog ser skya źes bya daṅ // nags tshal lum bi ni ra [?] *'khruṅs la //*

. . .

de daṅ gźan yaṅ yul dag daṅ // groṅ daṅ ljoṅs daṅ ri bor daṅ //
gnas daṅ groṅ mchog gtso bo ni // bsod nams gnas la rab brten nas //
de na ni sloṅ mos rdzes 'tsho źiṅ // bzlas daṅ sbyin sreg dga' ba daṅ //
gnas khaṅ bla kab med pa daṅ // rtag tu khyim ni stoṅ pa la //

G12 [*Mmk* 11.97.25–11.98.18]

prātarutthāya śayanāt snātvā caiva śuce jale //
niḥprāṇake jale caiva sarin mahāsarodbhave /
uddhṛṣya gātraṃ mantrajño mṛdgomayacūrṇitaiḥ //
mantrapūtaṃ tato kṛtvā jalaṃ caikṣaṃ sanirmalam /
snāyīta japī yuktātmā nātikālaṃ vilaṅghayet //
tatotthāya taṭe sthitvā hastau prakṣālya mṛttikaiḥ /
sapta sapta punaḥ sapta vārānyekaviṃśati //
upaviśya tatas tatra dantakāṣṭhaṃ samācaret /
visarjayitvā dantadhāvanaṃ tato vandeta tāyinam //
vanditvā lokanāthaṃ tu pūjāṃ kuryān manoramām /
vividhaiḥ stotropahārais tu saṃstutya punaḥ punaḥ //
sugandhapuṣpais tathā śāstu ardhaṃ dattvā tu jāpinaḥ /
praṇamya śirasā buddhānāṃ tadā tu śiṣyasambhavanāṃ //
teṣāṃ lokanāthānāṃ agrato yāpadeśanā [āpāpa°< T. *sdig pa]/*
nividya cāśano tatra paṭasyāgrata madhyame //
kuśaviṇḍakṛtaḥ tatsthaḥ niṣaṇṇopasamāhitaḥ /
japaṃ kuryāt prayatnena akṣasūtreṇa tena tu //
yathālabdhaṃ tu mantraṃ vai nānyamantraṃ tadā japet /
atihīnaṃ ca varjīta at[y]utkṛṣṭa eva vā //

[T.310.1–5 (155b)]

tho raṅs mal nas laṅs nas ni // mtsho chen las byuṅ chu bo las //
byuṅ chu srog chags skyon med pa'i // bzaṅ pos khrus ni rab tu bya //
sṅags śes pas ni lus dril bya // sṅags kyis de bźin dag byas pa'i //
dri med gtsaṅ sbrar byas pa'i chus // sṅags ldan bdag ñid grus bya źiṅ //
ha caṅ riṅ bar 'dug mi bya // de nas laṅs nas chu ṅogs 'dug //
sa dag gyis kyaṅ lag gñis bkru // bdun daṅ bdun daṅ yaṅ bdun ni
ñi śu rtsa gcig bar du'o // de bźin du yaṅ ñe reg bya //
so śiṅ dag kyaṅ yaṅ dag byed // so śiṅ rnam par bor nam ni //
'jig rten mgon la phyag 'tshal nas // mchod pa yid du oṅ bar bya //
rnam pa sna tshogs mchod bstod daṅ // yaṅ dag bstod pa yaṅ yaṅ bya //
dri źim me tog de bźin du // ston la zlos pas mchod yon dbul //
saṅs rgyas rnams daṅ de'i slob la // sbyi bos rab tu phyag 'tshal lo //
'jig rten mgon po de dag gi // mdun du sdig pa bśags par bya //
ras ris bar ma'i mdun du ni // bdag ñid dag kyaṅ dbul bar bya //
kuśa'i khres ni byas pa der // legs par mñam gźag 'dug nas ni //
des ni phreṅ ba thogs nas // 'bad pas bzlas pa bya ba yin //

G13 [*Mmk* 11.99.9–12]

śeṣakālaṃ tadādyukto kuśale 'smin śāsane munau /
sadharmavācanādīni prajñāpāramitādayaḥ //
pustakā daśabhūmākhyāḥ pūjyā vācyāstu vai sadā /
kālam āgamya tasmā vai praṇamya jinapuṅgavāṃ //

[T.311.3–4 (156a)]
de tshe btaṅ ba'i lhag dus la // thub pa'i stan la dge ba bya //
dam chos bklag la sogs pa ni // śes rab pha rol phyin la sogs //
glegs bam sa bcu źes bya pa // mchod daṅ bklag pa rtag tu bya //
de nas dus la bab gyur na //[24] *thub pa mchog la phyag 'tshal nas //*

G14 [*Mmk* 2.51.9–19]
tṛtīyamaṇḍale sarvaśrāvakapratyekabuddhebhyaḥ pūrṇakalaśaṃ niryātitkaṃ tenaiva vidhinā mūrdhanyabhiṣecayet / vaktavyaṃ anujñātastvaṃ sarvabuddhaiḥ bodhisattvaiś ca maharddhikaiḥ sarvalaukikalokottarāṇāṃ mantrāṇāṃ likhanapaṭhanamaṇḍalopadeśamantratantramudrācaryānirdeśaṃ svayaṃ caritum nirdeśtuṃ vā / ihaiva janmani paramparāsu ca yāvat paścimakaṃ niyataṃ buddhatvaṃ prāptavyam iti // . . . bhagavato buddhaniryātitakapūrṇakalaśena bodhisattvaniryāti / tena ca pūrṇakalaśena tathaivābhyaṣicyat / evaṃ ca vaktavyam anujñātastvaṃ sarvabuddhair bhagavadbhir mahābodhisattvaiś ca śrāvakaiḥ

adhṛṣyaḥ sarvabhūtānāmajitaḥ sarvadehinām /
vijayatvaṃ sarvamantrāṇāṃ sādhayestvaṃ yathepstaḥ //

[T.253.1–5 (127a)]
dkyil 'khor gsum pa la ni raṅ saṅs rgyas thams cad daṅ / ñan thos thams cad la phul ba'i bum pa gaṅ ba de ñed kyi cho gas spyi bo nas dbaṅ bskur bar bya'o // saṅs rgyas daṅ byaṅ chub sems dpa' rdzu 'phrul chen po daṅ ldan pa thams cad kyis 'jig rten daṅ 'jig rten las 'das ba thams cad kyi sṅags rgyud dag 'don pa daṅ / dkyil 'khor bri ba daṅ ston pa phyag rgya daṅ spyod ston pa daṅ raṅ ñid spyod ciṅ ston par khyod la rjes su gnaṅ źiṅ brjod par bya ba yaṅ tshe 'di ñid la yin la / phyi nas skye ba brgyud pa dag la ni saṅs rgyas ñid thob par 'gyur ba yin no // . . . saṅs rgyas bcom ldan 'das la sṅar phul ba'i bum pa daṅ / byaṅ chub sems dpa' la phul ba'i bum pa gaṅ bas kyaṅ de bźin du dbaṅ bskur ro // saṅs rgyas bcom ldan 'das thams cad daṅ / byaṅ chub sems dpa' chen po daṅ / ñan thos rnams kyis kyaṅ de bźin du brjod par bya źi pa khyod la rjes su gnaṅ ba yin no // 'byuṅ po thams cad kyis rab tu thub par dka' źiṅ lus can thams cad kyis mi pham pa daṅ sṅags pa thams cad las khyod rgyal ba daṅ ci ltar 'dod pa sgrubs śig pa'o //

G15 [*Mmk* 11.93.15–25]
tvadīyam kalparājoktaṃ vyaktaṃ meghāvinaṃ labdhvācāryābhiṣekatvaṃ śāsanābhijñaṃ kuśalaṃ vyaktaṃ dhārmikaṃ satyavādinaṃ mahotsāhaṃ kṛtajñaṃ dṛḍhasauhṛdaṃ nātivṛddhaṃ nātibālaṃ niḥspṛhaṃ sarvalābhasatkāreṣu brahmacāriṇaṃ kāruṇikaṃ na lobhamātreṇa bhogahetor

vā anunayahetor vā na mṛṣāṃ vadate kaḥ punar vādo svalpamātreṇaiva lobhamohaprakāraiḥ dṛdhapratijñā samata sarvabūteṣu dayāvāṃ dānaśīlaḥ kṛtapuraścaraṇaḥ tvadīya guhyamantrānujāpī pūrvasevakṛtavidyaḥ tvadīya maṇḍalasamanupūrvapraviṣṭaḥ lokajñaḥ vidhijñaḥ samanugrāhakaḥ kāryāvāṃ vicakṣaṇaḥ śreyasapravṛttaḥ abhiru acchambhinamamaṅkubhūtaḥ dṛdhavīryaḥ avyādhitaḥ yena vyādhinā akarmaśīlī mahoccakulaprabhūtaś ceti / ebhir guṇair yukto maṇḍalācāryo bhavati //

[T.304.7 (152b)–305.6 (153a)]
khyod kyi cho ga'i rgyal por bstan ciṅ sṅar bśad pa la rjes su 'jug par bya'o / blo gsal ba yid gźuṅs pa daṅ ldan pa / slob dpon du dbaṅ bskur ba khyod kyis bstan pa'i cho ga śes pa / dge ba gsal ba'i chos daṅ ldan pa / bden par smra ba sbro pa chen po daṅ ldan pa byas pa gzo ba / yid gźuṅs pa daṅ ldan pa / 'dris brten pa ha caṅ mi rgan ha caṅ mi gźon pa rñed pa daṅ / bkur sti la chags pa med pa tshaṅs par spyod pa / sñiṅ rje daṅ ldan pa rñed pa tsam mam / 'oṅs spyod kyi rgyu tsam mam / rjes su chags pa'i rgyur yaṅ rdzun mi smran cuṅ zad tsam mam / chags pa 'am rmoṅs pa tsam gyis rnam par ldan smos kyaṅ ci dgos / dam bcas pa brtan pa daṅ sems can thams cad la sems mñam pa daṅ / sñiṅ rje daṅ ldan pa daṅ tshul khrims daṅ ldan pa daṅ / sṅon du spyad pa byas pa daṅ khyod kyi gsaṅ ba'i sṅags rjes su zlos pa daṅ sṅa ma ñid du rig pa goms par byas pa daṅ / khyod kyi dkyil 'khor la mthar gyis yaṅ dag par źugs pa daṅ / 'jig rten śes pa daṅ cho ga śes pa daṅ yaṅ dag par rjes su 'dzin par byed pa daṅ / 'bras bu daṅ ldan źiṅ mkhas pa daṅ legs pa la rab tu źugs pa daṅ gzugs mdzes pa daṅ 'dod pa med pa daṅ / chags pa med pa daṅ dpa' ba daṅ brtson 'grus brtan pa daṅ nad med pa ste / nad gaṅ gyis las mi nus pa'i daṅ tshul can gyi nad med pa daṅ rigs mthon por skye ba'o // yon tan de dag daṅ ldan na ni dkyil 'khor gyi slob dpon du 'gyur la /

G16 [*Mmk* 10.90.27–10.91.7; 10.92.16–21]
ādau tāvaj jyeṣṭhaṃ paṭaṃ paścān mukhaṃ pratiṣṭhāpya ātmanaś ca pūrvābhimukhaṃ pratiṣṭhāpya valmīkāgramṛttikāṃ vā gaṅgānadīkūlamṛttikāṃ vā gṛhya uśīraśvetacandanakuṅkumaṃ vā karpūrādibhir vyatimiśrayitvyā mayūrākāraṃ kuryāt / taṃ paṭasyāgrataḥ sthāpayitvā acchinnāgaiḥ kuśaiḥ śucideśasamubhdavaiḥ cakrākāraṃ kṛtvā paṭasyāgrataḥ dakṣiṇahastena gṛhītvā vāmahastena mayūraṃ śuklapūrṇamāsyāṃ rātrau mahatīṃ pūjāṃ kṛtvā karpūradhūpaṃ dahatā tāvaj japet yāvat prabhāta iti // tataḥ sūryodayakālasamaye tan mṛnmayaṃ mayūraḥ mahāmayūrarājā bhavati / ātmanaś ca divyadehī divyamālyāmbarābharṇavibhūṣitaḥ uditādityasaṅkāśaḥ kāmarūpī / sarvabuddhabodhisattvānāṃ praṇamya paṭaṃ pradakṣiṇīkṛtya paṭaṃ

gṛhītvā tasmin mayūrāsane niṣaṇṇaḥ murhūtena brahmalokamatikrāmati / anekavidyādharakoṭīnayutaśatasahasraparivāritaḥ vidyādharacakravartī bhavati / . . . vidyādharatvam ākāśāgamanaṃ bodhisattvam anupraveśaṃ pañcābhijñatāṃ bhūtam anuprāpaṇatāṃ anenaiva dehene lokadhātusaṅkramaṇatāṃ daśabalavaṃśaparipūritāyai āryamañjuśriyaṃ sākṣāt darśanatāyai avandhyadarśanadharmadeśanaśravaṇatāyai buddhavaṃśānupacchedanatāyai sarvajājñānānukramaṇasamanuprāpaṇatāyai dharmameghavisṛtasamanupraveśanatāyai kleśānucchoṣaṇāmṛtavṛṣṭidhāribhiḥ praśamanatāyai [/]

[T.300.3 (150b)–301.1 (151a); 303.3–5 (152a)]
daṅ por re źig ras ris chen po nub tu bltas pas bźag ste / bdag ñid śar du bltas la / grog mkhar gyis 'am / gaṅ gā'i kluṅ gi ṅogs na yod pa'i sa blaṅs de / rtsa uśi ra daṅ tsandan dkar po daṅ daṅ gur gum daṅ gar pur la sogs pas bsre ba bya ste / rma bya'i gzugs byas la ras ris de'i mdun du bźag go // ku śa'i rtse mo ma ñams pa sa phyogs gtsaṅ mar skyes pa 'khor lo'i gzungs su byas te / ras ris kyi mdun du lag pa g.yas pas bzuṅ źiṅ / lag pa g.yon pas rma bya bzuṅ la / yar ṅo'i zla ba'i mtshan mor ras ris la mchod pa chen po byas de / ka pur daṅ tsandan gyi dud pa bsregs la / nam laṅs kyi bar du bzlas pa byas na / de nas ñi ma śar ba'i dus su lha'i raṅ bźin gyi rma bya ni rma bya chen po'i rgyal mor 'gyur ro // 'khor lo ni kun du 'bar bar 'gyur śiṅ / bdag ñid kyaṅ lha'i lus su 'gyur ro // de nas lha'i phreṅ ba daṅ gos daṅ rgyan gyis brgyan par 'gyur ro // ñi ma śar ba daṅ 'dra ba' 'dod pa'i gzugs mdzes par 'gyur ro // saṅs rgyas daṅ byaṅ chub sems dpa' la phyag byas nas / ras ris la g.yos phyogs su bskor ba byas la / ras ris blaṅs de rma bya'i stan / de la 'dug na yud tsam gyis tshaṅ pa'i 'jig rten gnon par 'gyur ro // rigs pa 'dzin pa bye ba khri phrag brgya stoṅ gyi 'kor du ma daṅ ldan pa'i rigs pa 'dzin pa'i 'khor los sgyur bar 'gyur ro // . . . rig pa 'dzin pa ñid du nam mkha' la 'gro ba daṅ / byaṅ chub sems dpa'' rjes su źugs pa daṅ mṅon par śes pa lṅa ñid daṅ sa daṅ sṅags thobs pa ñid daṅ lus 'di ñid kyis 'jig rten gyi khams dag tu 'gro ba ñid daṅ stobs bcu'i rgyud yoṅs su rdzogs par bya ba'i phyir daṅ / 'phags pa 'jam dpal mṅon sum du mthoṅ ba ñid kyi phyir daṅ 'bras bu yod par mthoṅ ba'i chos ston mñan pa'i phyir daṅ / saṅs rgyas kyi gduṅ rgyud mig cad pa'i phyir daṅ / thams cad mkhyen pa'i ye śes mthar gyis rjes su thob pa ñid kyi phyir daṅ / chos kyi sprin las byaṅ ba'i sṅags bzaṅ po la 'jug pa ñid kyi phyir daṅ / ñon moṅs pa bskam pa daṅ bdud rtsi'i char gyis ñon moṅs pa źi bar bya ba'i phyir daṅ /

Notes

Preface

1. For examples, see Makransky 1997; Griffiths 1994; Dunne 1996; and Eckel 1992.

Chapter 1

1. See Davis 1991:ix–xii, where the idea of a specifically "ontologically organized and constituted [ritual] world" is introduced.

2. Hardy 1994:141–142.

3. For this term, see Davidson 1995.

4. Hardy 1994:143.

5. Hereafter referred to as *Mmk*. The chapters of the text are referred to as *Mmk* 1, *Mmk* 2, etc.

6. This section owes much to an e-mail exchange with Ronald Grimes.

7. Hacker 1961:483–484.

8. Matsunaga 1985:886.

9. In Przyluski 1923.

10. See MacDonald 1962:17.

11. For a detailed summary of Przyluski's argument, see MacDonald 1962:3ff; for a briefer one, see Matsunaga 1985:887–888.

12. See Matsunaga 1985:886.

13. See Smith 1980 and Gonda 1977.

14. MacDonald 1962:2, note 2.

15. Jayaswal 1934:3.

16. Gonda 1977a:467.

17. Ibid.

18. Davis 1991:9.

19. Ibid:10.

20. *BHSD, s.v. vaitulya.*

21. *Kathāvatthu* 17.6, cited in Dutt (n.d.):8.

22. Chandra n.d:11.

23. Lamotte 1962:66.

24. See Renou 1953:366 (#2003).

25. See MacDonald 1962:8. For the *Bodhisattvapiṭaka*, see Pagel 1995.

26. The translation of the term *avataṃsaka* has both a literal and a figurative, allusive aspect. Literally, it means "ornament." In this case, the entire term may be rendered "the extensive Mahāyāna *sūtra*, which is an ornament of the *bodhisattva* canon." However, the existence, by at least the fourth century, of a text known as the *Buddhāvataṃsakasūtra* suggests the possibility of an intentional allusion on the part of the authors of the *Mmk* colophons. The *Buddhāvataṃsakasūtra* was, and for certain Buddhist communities still is, "a scripture of great importance in various cultural areas of the world" (Nakamura 1989:194). In this sense, the term *avataṃsaka* can be construed as indicating a type of text, namely, one resembling, in scope and spirit, the massive *Bodhisattvapiṭaka*. (See Nakamura 1989:194ff.)

27. *bodhisattvapiṭakāvataṃsakād mahāyānavaipulyasūtrād āryamañjuśrīmūlakalpān navamapaṭalavisarād dvitīyaḥ uttamasādhanaupayikakarmapaṭalavisaraḥ parisamāpta iti.*

28. See Appendix A for a full listing of chapter colophons and synopses of chapter contents.

29. The details of this are given in chapter 2.

30. *Mmk* 8.784–785.

31. The page is missing from Śastri's edition, which I am consulting. I have referred to Vaidya's reprint: 8.56.18: *aṣṭama uttamasādhanaupayikakarmapaṭalavisarāt prathamaḥ.*

32. *Mmk* 9.84.18–19.

33. *Mmk* 10.92.29–30.

34. *Mmk* 10.75.1–2.

35. *Mmk* 10.92.14–16.

36. *Mmk* 4.59.4–5.

37. *Mmk* 4.59.22.

38. *Mmk* 4.59.5–6.

39. *Mmk* 4.59.5–6.

40. *Mmk* 6.72.12–13.

41. *Mmk* 7.72.4–5.

42. For example: *Mmk* 1.1.13–14, 1.2.25–26, 2.23.6–7, and 10, 2.27.11–12, 9.81.8, 11.95.9.

43. *Mmk* 2.25.10.

44. *Mmk* 1.1.14–15.

45. *Mmk* 1.2.25–26

46. *Mmk* 8.78.4.

47. For an analysis of the type of claim being made in the passage, see below, 3.2.1.

48. At *Mmk* 1.3.8–9 the *hṛdaya mantra* and *upahṛdaya mantra* are given respectively as *oṁ vākyeda namaḥ* and *vākye hūm*. The *hṛdaya mantra* appears again at *Mmk* 29.322.7–16 as Mañjuśrī's "incomparable," and so on, six-syllable *mantra*. There, it is employed in a *caitya* ritual.

49. This is discussed at length in chapter 4.

50. For a detailed description and discussion of the vow and the initiation see below 4.1.3.

51. Gupta 1989:239–40.

52. *Mmk* 10.90.19–20.

53. *Mmk* 10.91.22–25.

54. See Watanabe 1912:41–50.

55. See Crosby and Skilton 1996:9–13.

56. *Mmk* 11.98.14.

57. *Mmk* 9.83.8–10.

58. *Mmk* 1.1.1. This is followed by, *evaṃ mayā śrutaṃ*, marking the beginning of the text.

59. *Mmk* 55.721.23–24.

60. See, for example, *Lakṣmītantra* 18, summarized in Smith 1975:353.

61. *Mmk* 1.3.21–24.

62. *Mmk* 1.12.20; *Mmk* 1.10.14–15.

63. *PED s.v. vikubbana*.

64. *Mahāvyupatti* 767, cited in *BHSD s.v. vikurvaṇa.*

65. *Mmk* 2.26.24–25.

66. *Mmk* 2.26.25. "The five acts entailing immediate retribution" (*pañcānantarya)*: killing one's own mother or father, killing an *arhant*, causing dissension in the monastic order, deliberately causing a *buddha's* blood to flow; see *BHSD*:95.

67. *Mmk* 1.1.20.

68. Gómez 1977:225.

69. Ibid.

70. This text is also known as *Candrapradīpasamādhi* (see Warder 1991 [1970]: 395), by which it is referred at *Mmk* 2.38.12.

71. Gómez 1977:225–226.

72. *Mmk* 2.38.12.

73. The vow is sometimes referred to as *pranidhāna* in the *Mmk*; for example, at *Mmk* 22.230.6 and 34.354.5, where a short vow is given.

74. *Gaṇḍavyūha* 433.7–18 and 436.3–4: *ṛddhibalena samantajavena jñānabalena samantamukhena / caryabalena samantaguṇena maitrabalena samantagatena // puṇyabalena samantaśubhena jñānabalena asaṅgagatena / prajñ[o]pāyasamādhibalena bodhibalaṃ samudānayamānaḥ // karmabalaṃ pariśodhayamānaḥ kleṣabalaṃ parimardayamānaḥ // mārabalaṃ abalaṃkaramāṇaḥ pūrayi bhadracarībala sarvān / / . . . tāṃś ca ahaṃ paripūrya aśeṣān sattvahitaṃ kari yāvata loke //*

75. *Mmk* 2.25.10.

76. *Mmk* 2.25.11.

77. *Mmk* 2.25.17.

78. See Smith:1980 *s.v. mudrā*; Davis 1991:32f; Gonda 1977:73. Discussed in detail in chapter 2.

79. *Mmk* 34.351.8 and 35.355.10.

80. *Mmk* 34.350.16. See Appendix A for a synopsis of these chapters.

81. See, for example, *Mmk* 2.26.8–35.10, where numerous *mantras* and *vidyās* are given with their corresponding *mudrās*. The correspondences are made fairly explicit there.

82. *Mmk* 34.351.20–21.

83. Beyer 1973:146. See *Mmk* 35.355.24ff. for obvious examples of this category of *mudrā*. Gestures given there include *utphala, svastika, dhvaja, chatra, ghaṭa, mālā, śūla, kumbha*, and *Mmk* 2.27.10ff. for similar correspondences.

84. Beyer 1973:146.

85. See, for instance, *Mmk* 34.350.10–21, a section on the requirements of the practitioner who receives instructions on the use of the *mudrā*: he must be adorned with *bodhicitta*, follow the *buddhas'* path interminably, and so forth.

86. *Mmk* 34.351.9 and 22.

87. *Mmk* 2.30.4, 7, 25, 31.11, and 22, respectively.

88. See, for example, *Mmk* 1.10.14–15.

89. *Mmk* 2.34.6–13 and 14–26, respectively.

90. Alper 1989b:258. All citations of Alper henceforth are from ibid. 249–294 unless otherwise noted.

91. See footnote 48, chapter 1.

92. *Mmk* 2.35.5–6.

93. *Mmk* 11.96.24.

94. See, for example, Alper:1989c:330 for bibliographical references.

95. *Mmk* 32.336.19.*t*.

96. *Mmk* 33.342.8, 7.77.4, 11.101.9.

Chapter 2

1. See Griffiths 1994:127–128 for an explanation of this translation. His translation takes into account the meanings of *bhoga* as both "food" and "pleasure." He writes there, in part: "the object of the communal enjoyment of the *sambhogakāya* and its audience is paradigmatically the dharma, the doctrine whose flavor is unsurpassed. This doctrine is consumed at a communal meal, and in the act of consumption unparalleled salvific benefit are produced."

2. Gómez 1996:52.

3. Beyer 1977:340.

4. Ibid.

5. Iser 1980:111. Iser's comments here are in reference to the work of Jane Austen.

6. Respectively: August Karl Reischauer, W. Kirfel, D. Suzuki, P. Mus, and Richard Robinson; quoted in Kloetzli 1983:7.

7. Ibid.

8. 1957 edition, vol. 6:502.

9. Munitz 1986:59.

10. Tambiah 1985:87, and Davis 1991, passim.

11. See Kloetzli 1983:15.

12. Hallisey 1995:302. Further page numbers are in the main text in parentheses.

13. Gombrich 1975:134.

14. Gómez 1996:35

15. Ibid.

16. Kloetzli's phrase, 1983:76.

17. Hallisey 1995:304.

18. Macdonald 1962:31.

19. Ibid:30.

20. See Przyluski 1923.

21. See MacDonald 1962:3ff., and above, 1.3.1.

22. Davis 1991:9.

23. Ibid.

24. Smith 1975, vol. I, passim.

25. Davis 1991:10.

26. At *Mmk* 7.74.13–16, for example: "At this time, in this era of great terror when there exist the five impurities, beings of meager merit will come into existence. Of low origin, short life-span, poor and weak, they will not be able to undertake the creation of the cult image, and so on, which is quite extensive." This theme occurs throughout the work; see below, section 3.2.3.

27. *Mmk* 11.93.1–2 is a typical example: "Then, once again, blessed Śākyamuni, looking down at the palace of the Śuddhāvāsa heaven, spoke to the princely Mañjuśrī."

28. Jauss 1982:88.

29. *Mmk* 1.24.19–22.

30. See Gonda 1977:130.

31. For example, *Mmk* 4.55.2 and 1.1.3 respectively.

32. Snellgrove 1987:199.

33. Peter Gaeffke in *The Encyclopedia of Religion* (M. Eliade, ed.), *s.v. maṇḍala*:153.

34. Davis 1991:42 and 47.

35. For the use of this term see Griffiths 1994:xvii.

36. Griffiths 1994:27–28. He defines a *śāstra* as "an ordered set of descriptive and injunctive sentences, together with arguments to ground and defend them, taken to give systematic authoritative expression to Buddhist doctrine, either as a whole or within some specified area of of human inquiry" (30).

37. *Mmk* 33.346.23.

38. Griffiths 1994 passim, but chapter 7 in particular.

39. Davis 1991:112, 113, 126, 138, 139, 140.

40. See Griffiths 1994:84.

41. Ibid.:12.

42. Ibid.:15.

43. *Mmk* 1.15.19–20.

44. Kato 1975:254.

45. *Mahāvastu* I.122,3: *tathāgato 'ran samyaksaṁbuddhas tisthati dhriyati yāpayati dharmaṁ ca deśayati bahujanahitāya bahujanasukhāya lokānukampāyai mahato janakāyasyārthāya hitāya sukhāya devānāṁ ca manuṣyāṇāṁ ca*. Quoted in Lamotte 1962:396. The *Mmk* refers to the *Suvarṇaprabhasottamasūtra* at *Mmk* 2.38.13 and *Mmk* 11.109.28.

46. *Mmk* 10.88.3, 9.84.11, and 33.347.3. See Dal 1932:19–39, 106ff. and Griffiths 1994:66–75 for full descriptions.

47. *Mmk* 39.435.5, for example.

48. See Iyengar 1993:32–34 for identical *yogic* "powers" (*vibhūti*) in Patañjali's *Yogasūtras*.

49. Griffiths 1994:182.

50. Dal 1932:114.

51. *Mmk* 1.1.21–2.2.

52. *Mmk* 1.4.22, 23, 24; 1.5.5; 25.286.9; 23.257.2.

53. *Suvarṇaprabhasottama* 9.12: *na buddhaḥ parinirvāti na dharmaḥ parihīyate / sattvānāṃ paripākāya parinirvāṇaṃ nirdarśayet // acintyo bhagavānbuddho nityakāyastathāgataḥ / deśeti vividhānvyūhānsattvānāṃ hitakāraṇāt.*

54. *Mmk* 1.5.12.

55. *Mmk* 1.24.24.

56. *Mmk* 1.6.23–24.

57. He sits "below the Lion throne" (*Mmk* 2.41.20). This is discussed in detail in chapter 4, below.

58. *Mmk* 1.1.2.

59. Mus 1928:235 (89), quoted in MacDonald 1962:27.

60. MacDonald 1962:31.

61. *Mmk* 1.4..26 reads *puruṣa puṇḍarīkapuṇyagandhamanantaka*. I follow V.1.3.20: *puruṣapuṇḍarīka puṇyagandhamanantaka*.

62. *Mmk* 1.4.27.

63. *Mmk* 4.59.17.

64. This paragraph summarizes *Mmk* 1.2.5–4.9.

Chapter 3

1. Agrawala 1969:114–115.

2. van Gulik 1959:163–164. See also Mair 1988.

3. Hardy 1994:141–142.

4. Kapstein 1995: 243.

5. Ibid.: 244.

6. Belting 1990:9.

7. François Chenet, quoted in Faure 1996:14.

8. Kapstein 1995:245. Further page numbers are in the main text in parentheses.

9. See also *Mmk* 4.60.

10. See footnote 48, chapter 1.

11. Tucci 1949:216.

12. Smith 1987:110 and 108.

13. Quoted in Davis 1991:163.

14. For instance, *Mmk* 11.110.27f. and *Mmk* 11.99.10.

15. Quoted in Gómez 1977:225–226.

16. Lalou 1930:6–7.

17. Ibid.:7.

18. This is stated explicitly at, for instance, *Mmk* 1.15.19–20.

19. Kapstein 1995:255.

20. *Mmk* 25.285.19.

21. Lalou 1930:51, footnote 5 translates from the Chinese: "Listen! I will proclaim that to you! I possess the six-syllable *mantra* called 'wondrous essence'; that receptacle (*nidhāna*) of great *artha*, good, excellent, and so forth, the most mysterious of all *mantras*, that is success for all beings."

22. Ibid. 52, footnote 1 translates the Chinese: "That *mantra* was previously revealed by 76 *koṭis* os Buddhas. Now, for you and for all living beings until the end of the world, I will proclaim this to you in brief."

23. See Kapstein 1995:247, note 13.

24. *Mmk* 2.37.5.

25. *Mmk* 11.97.26ff.

26. *Mmk* 11.93.14f.

27. *Mmk* 11.101.8.

28. The summary at the end of chapter 2 is a good illustration of this point.

29. Schopen 1978:162.

30. *Mmk* 1.6.23f.

31. At *Mmk* 11.99.11–12.

32. Gómez 1977:256.

33. *Mmk* 33.342.1–2.

34. *Mmk* 33.341.8–9.

35. *Mmk* 7.74.18–22.

36. See Lalou 1930:19, footnote 3.

37. *Mmk* 2.46.26.

38. Tsuda 1974:325.

39. Hardy 1994:156.

40. See Kvaerne 1977.

41. *Mmk* 4.56.5.

42. See Basham 1959:492.

43. *Mmk* 11.94.16–17. Cf. Olivelle 1977:176.72, and footnote.

44. Inden 1985:38.

45. See, for instance, *Mmk* 15.158.1ff.

46. *Mmk* 4.56.6.

47. A particularly powerful protective *mantra* is taught at *Mmk* 9.81.3–20: "The purpose of [the *mantra*] is the protection of the *sādhaka*; [listen to this] most sublime of mysteries, the essence of the most sublime of mysteries, the great lord of spells spoken by all *tathāgatas*. In uttering [this spell] all *mantras* are uttered. Alas, O multitude of gods, this is not to be surpassed, this lord of spells! By means of this lord of spells even the princely Mañjuśrī is attracted, subjugated, becomes acquiescent—how much more does that utterance [subjugate] all other *bodhisattvas* as well as both mundane and supernatural *mantras*? This [spell], which is uniquely potent, possessing the power of great potency, causes the destruction of all obstacles. Precisely this one is declared the foremost of all *mantras*. Precisely this one is declared the syllable among single-syllable [*mantras*]. Which is that single syllable that realizes all goals, is the doer of all work, cuts asunder all *mantras*, destroys all the sins of evil-doers, is the obstruction of all *mantras*, creates auspiciousness, is far above all mundane and supernatural *mantras*, completely fulfills all wishes as the imperishable essence of all *tathāgatas*? Which is that [syllable]? It is *kḷlhīṃ*. Precisely this, O honorable ones, is the most sublime mystery, the all-achiever, indeed the single syllable that is the lord of spells. It is that which is unsurpassable among all beings. It is that which is unassailable by all demons [T. 289]. It is the auspiciousness of all *buddhas*. It is the effectiveness of all *mantras*. It is the master of all worlds, the lord of (*sarvavitteśānām* [line 13] = hap. for *sarvavidviṣṭānām* [line 14] ?). It is loving kindness itself for all who are hated. [T. it creates affection in all beings and is itself loving kindness (*maitrī*) toward all who are despised.] It is compassionate towards all living beings. It is destructive toward all obstacles. [*Mmk* 9.82.27–83.14] There is protection for oneself with a single utterance [of the spell], protection for a companion with two utterances, protection of a house with three utterances, protection of a village with four utterances, protection for who has gone within the power of Yāma with five utterances. Protection for an army is created with as many as one thousand utterances [of the spell]."

48. As Lalou, ibid., footnote 2 points out, this is probably the same *mantra* used for the initial purification of the cotton above: [*Mmk* 4.55.21–26] *oṁ śodhaya śodhaya sarvavighnaghātaka mahākāruṇika kumārarūpadhāriṇe / vikurva vikurva / samayam anusmara / tiṣṭha tiṣṭha hūm hūm phaṭ phaṭ svāhā // (Oṁ purify purify! O destroyer of all obstacles O you of great compassion O bearer of youthful form! perform a miraclulous transformation perform a miraclulous transformation! remember your vow! be present be present! hūm hūm phaṭ phaṭ hail!*).

49. It should be mentioned here that the term *mahāmudrā* has a different connotation in the *Mmk* from that of the antinomian *tantras*. In the *Hevajratantra*, for example, it refers to the female partner in the rites involving *maithuna* (ritualized sexual intercourse), as well as to the principle of absolute truth represented by that female. In the *Mmk*, *mahāmudrā* is a synonym for the principle *mudrā* of Mañjuśrī, the *pañcaśikhāmudrā* (five-pointed hand gesture). This equation is made at *Mmk* 2: "When the fundamental *mantra* is used in conjunction with the hand gesture known

as 'five-crested,' then that becomes the doer of all deeds, the essence, indeed, [it becomes] the noble Mañjuśrī" (*Mmk* 2.26.15-17: *āryamañjuśrīyaṃ nāma mudrā pañcaśikhā mahāmudreti vikhyātā taṃ prayojaye asmin mūlamantre sarvakarmikaṃ bhavati hṛdayaṃ*). At *Mmk* 35.358.24–359.8 there is a detailed description of the *pañcaśikhāmudrā*. See also *Mmk* 44, called *mahāmudrāpaṭalavisaraḥ*, where the *pañcaśikhā* gesture is praised. Lalou 1930:66–70 discusses the headgear of "Pañcaśīkhā-Mañjuśrī." Compare what she says there with the statement at *Mmk* 35.359.3 that the *pañcaśikhā mudrā* is the head of the *bodhisattva*, that is, the *pañcacīra*. The term *mahāmudrā* is also used more generally in the *Mmk* to denote a particularly powerful gesture. At *Mmk* 36, for instance, the gesture called *saṃpātana* is given as the "great protective *mudrā*." See *Mmk* 36.388.17f., where the eight *mahāmudrās* are listed.

50. *Mmk* 4.56.14–17.

51. *Mmk* 11.94. 27, 95.13 and 95.17, respectively.

52. See colophons to *Mmk* 19 and 20, respectively.

53. *The Encyclopaedia Britannica* 1957 edition, vol. 2, p. 679, *s.v. augurs.*

54. Gonda 1989:265.

55. See Smith 1980, vol. II: *s.v. śakuna.*

56. See Appendix for synopsis.

57. *Mmk* 4.56.16.

58. Inden 1985:38 and 39.

59. *Mmk* 17.170.15–18.

60. Sanskrit has lacuna where Tibetan reads "man, woman, boy or girl, or any other person," see Lalou 1930:20.

61. *Mmk* 4.56.18–25.

62. *Mmk* 4.56.26–29.

63. *PED s.v. pañcanantarikakammani* states that these may be either of two sets of five or six "crimes." The first is: matricide, parricide, killing an *arhat*, causing a schism in a Buddhist community, wounding a Buddha, following another teacher (*s.v. abhithana*). The second list is: murder, theft, impurity, lying, intemperance (concerning the five moral precepts—refraining from: taking life, taking what is not given, adultery, lying, indolence arising from the use of intoxicants).

64. *Mmk* 4.57.1–3. At *Mmk* 17.172.5–6 there is a *mantra* for destroying negative omens (*durnimitta*, 17.172.10). The *buddha* Śālendra attained enlightenment by means of this *mantra* (171.19–20). Numerous repetition creates auspiciousness (172.8–9).

65. See Gonda 1980:114ff.

66. Kapstein 1995:249.

67. *Mmk* 4.57.10–11.

68. See Lalou 1930:22 footnote 6 for reconstruction.

69. *Mmk* 11.93.17f.

70. *Mmk* 4.58.3 and 5.

71. The *poṣadha* is still observed on the full moon day of each month. Normatively, a lay practitioner who chooses to honor this day is required to observe eight moral precepts; namely, refraining from the following: taking life, taking what is not given, adultery, lying, slander, rude speech, frivolous conversation, and covetousness.

72. *Mmk* 4.58.14–17.

73. *Mmk* 58.22.26.

74. A *hasta* is "a measure of length from the elbow to the tip of the middle finger," approximating 18 inches (MW. *s.v. hasta*). A cubit is also measured "from the elbow to the middle finger," and also approximates 18 inches (*Webster's New Twentieth Century Dictionary*, 2nd ed., New York 1979, *s.v. cubit*).

75. An *angustha* equals a thumb's breadth; it is "usually regarded as equal to an *angula*," which equals a finger's breadth. Twelve *angulas* equals a *vitasti*, which is "defined either as a long span between the extended thumb and little finger, or as the distance between the wrist and the tip of the fingers, and said to equal 12 Angulas or about 9 inches" (MW). The text elaborates on the *sugatavitasti*: "A *vitasti* of the blessed Buddha means here the size of one *hasta* of a man in Madyadeśa; this is called 'a *vitasti* of the Sugata'" (*Mmk* 4.59.1f.).

76. This is made explicit at, for example, *Mmk* 4.59.22: "Mañjuśrī . . . particularly declares success for those beings who are constantly proceeding towards enlightenment."

77. *Mmk* 4.59.4–7.

78. *Mmk* 15.161.26. *Mmk* 15 deals with the physical, spiritual, mental, astrological, astronomical, and *karmic* attributes (*lakṣaṇa*) of these types.

79. See, for example, *Mmk* 33.242.18–20

80. *Mmk* 32.337.20–21. See also *Mmk* 37.424.18–426.10 for a list of eight *kūlas* and their corresponding *mantras* and deities. MacDonald 1960:41–76 discusses the issue of *kulas* in some depth, referring both to the *Mmk* and the later Tibetan commentarial work of Mkhas grub rje (1385–1438).

81. *Mmk* 40.449.23ff.

82. *Mmk* 41.438.25–41.439.6.

83. *Mmk* 1.10.15,16,26 and 11.2–3.

84. *Mmk* 1.11.15–16 and 25–28.

85. *Mmk* 1.11.8, for instance.

86. *Mmk* 6.71.25.

87. *Mmk* 6.72.12–13.

88. *Mmk* 6.72.13.

89. *Mmk* 4.59.17.

90. *Mmk* 4.60.12: "He removes the thread [i.e., completes the weaving] on a very auspicious day, when the moon is waxing." Cf. Beyer 1973:460 for a similar Tibetan idea attached to the painting of a *thangka*.

91. *Mmk* 4.60.1.

92. *Mmk* 4.60.15.

93. *Mmk* 4.60.17.

94. The Chinese translation is more explicit: "When people are without faith it is not possible to plant the seed of enlightenment in them. They are like a piece of salt: the harvest of a hundred grains does not bear fruit:" Lalou 1930:29, note 3.

95. *Mmk* 7.74.22–24.

96. *Mmk* 7.74.25.

97. *Mmk* 7.74.25–26.

98. *Mmk* 7.74.26–27.

99. *Mmk* 7.75.2–3.

100. *Mmk* 7.75.4–7.

101. It is interesting to note that, according to Kapstein (1995:251), the final six-syllable *mantra*, *oṁ vākyedanamaḥ,* is still employed in Tibet "particularly by those wishing to gain the boon of Mañjuśrī's wisdom as an aid to study."

102. *Mmk* 7.75.9.

103. *Mmk* 4.61.16.

104. Lalou 1930. For detailed descriptions of *thangka* production in present-day Tibetan cultural regions, see Jackson 1984. For actual images, see Huntington 1990.

105. Kapstein 1995: 243.

Chapter 4

1. See, for example, Pranke 1995; Yamasaki 1988:185–190; Gellner 1992:258–266; and Beyer 1973:36–38.

2. See Ray 1994:251ff.

3. *Mmk* 10.87.17.

4. *Mmk* 2.49.28.

5. *Mmk* 10.88.2.

6. *Mmk* 2.54.16, colophon: *maṇḍalavidhānaparivarta.*

7. MacDonald:1962. She begins her treatment twelve pages into the chapter, at *Mmk* 2.36.24, where Mañjuśrī begins his discourse on the "construction of the *maṇḍala*" (*maṇḍalavidhāna*). It is clear from the opening paragraph, however, that the long section on *mantras* and *vidyās* preceding that is a sort of liturgical compendium to the ritualized construction of the *maṇḍala. Mmk* 2 opens with Mañjuśrī's entering into a *samādhi* called *contemplating the entrance of all beings into the vow* (*sarvasattvasamayānupraveśāvalokinīṃ* [*Mmk* 2.25.2; the text reads *maya* for *samaya* here, but six lines later reads *samaya*]). Snellgrove 1987:192–198 and 225–235 translates and discusses respectively the following sections of *Mmk* 2: *Mmk* 2.39.10–16; 40.2–41.13; 41.20–42.3 (these are the sections describing the figures to be traced with the colored powder); and 47.20–27; 48.24–49.21; 50.5–51.24 (these sections deal with the initiation ritual).

8. *Mmk* 2.36.25–27.

9. *Mmk* 2.36.27–28.

10. This section is at *Mmk* 2.36.28–37.2.

11. *Mmk* 2.37.2–3.

12. *Mmk* 2.37.6–9.

13. *Mmk* 2.37.11–12.

14. *Mmk* 2.37.10–14.

15. *Mmk* 2.37.22. MacDonald 1962:101, note 1 observes that the Tibetan translates *kīla* as *phur ba*, dagger. The dagger is an emblem of the *krodhrāja,* Yamāntaka, who is invoked in the following sequence for protection. On the *kīla* see Boord 1993.

16. *Mmk* 2.25.17–18; 2.22–26.7.

17. See *Mmk* 1.22.1–13.

18. *Mmk* 2.37.25–2.38.2. For *bahirnādhaḥ* see MacDonald 1962:101, footnote 10. The assistant is mentioned at *Mmk* 2.38.4.

19. *Mmk* 2.38.4–9.

20. *Mmk* 2.38.9–17.

21. Mentioned at *Mmk* 2.39.1.

22. *Mmk* 2.38.17–28.

23. The construction of this pit, called *agnikuṇḍa*, is described in detail at *Mmk* 13.

24. This *mantra*, mentioned at *Mmk* 7.73.19–74.17, is *oṁ vākyārthe jaya oṁ vākyaśeṣe sva oṁ vākyeyanayaḥ oṁ vākyaniṣṭheyaḥ oṁ vākyeyanamaḥ oṁ vākyedanamaḥ*.

25. *Mmk* 2.39.2–29.

26. Kapstein 1995: 244.

27. *Mmk* 2.39.11–12: "Then the master brings to mind the *buddhas* and *bodhisattvas*, lighting incense [while invoking] the incense *mantra*, as previously described," etc.

28. *Mmk* 11.93.27–11.94.1.

29. I am using *convention* here to translate the Sanskrit word *samaya*. Because this word is almost unanimously translated as *vow, oath* in both the primary (Tibetan, for example) and secondary literature, some elaboration is necessary. *Samaya* is derived from *sam* √*i*. Its literal meaning is thus *to come together*. As with the English phrase *come together*, *samaya* has the idiomatic sense of *agreement, compact, stipulation*. This idiomatic sense often carries with it the implication of pledged action: to make a compact to do (or not to do) something. Thus, *samaya* has the additional sense of both *practice, rule, established custom*, and *pledge, promise, vow, oath*. The Tibetan translation, *binding oath, solemn promise* (*dam tshig*; T.305.7 [153a]), reflects the later (*circa* 10th century) tendency to emphasize the verbal component of *samaya*. If we look at texts closer in time to the *Mmk*, however, it appears prudent to place the emphasis on the action implied by *samaya* (see, for example, Smith 1975:495 [*conduct*] and 1980:117 [*popular custom*]; Gonda 1977:91 [*conventions*], and Hoens 1979:72 [*conduct*]). Furthermore, if we consider the importance of the *parṣanmaṇḍala* in the cult of the *Mmk*, the notion of *coming together, assembly* contained in the term *samaya* must be taken account of. Therefore, I follow Gonda in translating *samaya* as *convention*. *Convention* carries all of the meanings of *samaya*: (1) *conference, assembly;* (2) *practice, tradition, usage; and* (3) *agreement, pact*. It is often a matter of conjecture which of these senses should be emphasized, or if, as here, all senses are being put into play.

30. *Mmk* 11.94.10.

31. MacDonald 1962:65. (Additional page references are given in parentheses in the main text.) For her translation of the section of *Mmk* 2 dealing with the initiation ritual, see pp. 127–143. This is summarized and discussed—in light of the later Tibetan tradition—at pp. 62–76. See also Snellgrove 1987:225–235 for a translation and discussion of several passages concerning the ritual.

32. See Lessing and Wayman 1968.

33. The use of the ancient term *abhiṣeka* in the *Mmk* is somewhat interesting in itself. The term current in the eight century for the initiation ritual was *dikṣa* (see, for example, Smith 1980:42, Davis 1991:89ff, Gonda 1977:70, and Hoens 1979:71ff.). By retaining *abhiṣeka*, the Buddhists not only differentiated their initiation ceremony

from the Vaiṣṇava and Śaiva sects, but they did so in a manner that evoked authority (the *Vedas*) that was prior to those sects. Similarly, the use of the term *abhiṣeka* in conjunction with other symbols of royalty (e.g., the Buddha as *cakravartin*, Mañjuśrī as his "prince," the *maṇḍalācārya* as royal minister, etc.) evoked social dominance and secular mastery as well as the highest "spiritual" achievement.

34. All citations in this paragraph are from *Mmk* 2.47.20–48.3.

35. *Mmk* 2.48.25–2.49.4.

36. *Mmk* 2.49.5–9, and *Mmk* 2.46.25–2.47.4.

37. *Mmk* 2.47.2 reads *upoṣava*; but see *Mmk* 2.49.5 and 7.75.12, for example, which read *upoṣadhika*. The *upoṣadha* is an intensified period of practice, involving recitation of the *pratimokṣa* for monks and observance of the eight moral precepts for the laity. It is held on the full moon, new moon, first and last quarter moon days.

38. Called a *vidyāmūlamantra* at *Mmk* 2.50.21.

39. *Mmk* 2.51.3.

40. This is described at *Mmk* 2.49.16–2.51.3.

41. *Mmk* 2.50.12.

42. For the Pañcarātra *saṃhitās* see Smith 1975:122, for the *Śaivā āgamas*, Brunner 1975:416.

43. Smith 1980:117.

44. Davis 1991:91.

45. *Mmk* 11.96.23–24

46. Davis 1991:92.

47. Ibid.

48. *Mmk* 1.2.25, 8.79.10, 10.89.5, and 3 respectively.

49. Smith 1980:61.

50. Davis 1991:91.

51. Smith 1980:118.

52. Brunner 1975:423.

53. *Mmk* 4.59.6–7.

54. Smith 1989:118.

55. *Mmk* 10.89.3–4.

56. *Mmk* 1.2.19.

57. For instance, at *Mmk* 9.83.6, 10.85.24, 11.97.11, 11.101.9.

58. See Olivelle 1995:79.

59. *Suttanipāta*: verses 213, 220, 207.

60. See Olivelle 1995:126, 147; for *muni*, 312, verse 1.

61. Another possible interpretation is that the text presents two options for the *puraścaraṇa* period: one for an itinerant practitioner, and one for a stationary one. It is noteworthy that both this dual option and the impreciseness of the text on the matter has a parallel in the Śaiva Siddhāntin text *Mṛgendrāgama*. See p. 381, verse 75ff. Brunner (1985:488) comments on these verses: "Two kinds of *sādhakas* are distinguished at the outset: those who are itinerant, travelling from one 'place of success' (*siddhikṣetra*) to another 'place of success,' and those who stay in the same place for the whole of their *sādhana*. . . . The text however is not very clear and it is probably incomplete. We cannot be sure at which point it stops discussing *sādhakas* in general and starts discussing the itinerant ones."

62. *Mmk* 11.113.17–20, and 11.106.20–25.

63. Olivelle 1995:31; the Sanskrit text is given at 197.2–4.

64. *Mmk* 9.83.5–6: *bhikṣabhaikṣāhārasādhakayāvakapayo phalāhāro vā*. For the relationship of these terms to the ascetic code (*dhutaguṇa*) of ancient Buddhism, see Ray 1994: 296–299, 308–314. For *tricelaparivartin* see the synonymous term *s.v. traicīvarika* in *BHSD*. Ray quotes the following concerning the three robes: "How does one undertake (the austerity of) 'three robes'? One immediately gives up extra robes. Knowing the fault of keeping (extra robes) and seeing the benefits of the observance of 'three robes,' (one undertakes thus): 'I refuse extra robes from today and observe (the austerity of) 'three robes.' " Thus one is to have only three robes—the shoulder cloak, the upper garment, and the waist cloth—and refuse a fourth robe. The benefits of this practice are that one is free of the hoarding of what is unnecessary and thus free to wander at will, "as a bird on the wing that does not yearn for what it leaves behind." Ray argues that it is precisely these three—"begging of food, apparel, and habitation"—which form the basic structure of the normative Buddhist ascetic code (316).

65. *Mmk* 10.90.18–20.

66. *Mmk* 11.94.12, for instance.

67. *Mmk* 9.83.29–9.84.2.

68. *Mmk* 11.110.10; 11.113.16.

69. *Mmk* 10.88.7.

70. *Mmk* 2.49.28.

71. *Mmk* 11.97.25–(roughly) 11.117.21.

72. See Olivelle 1995:viii.

73. *sādhanaupayika-karmasthāna-japa-niyama-homa-dhyāna-śaucācāra-sarva-karmavidhi-sādhana-paṭalavisaraḥ.*

74. Olivelle 1995:89; Sanskrit:261.9–12.

75. *Mmk* 11.110.6–8, dealing with the afternoon duties, gives a *mantra* to be recited during bathing: *oṁ sarvaduṣṭāṃ stambaya hūṁ indīvaradhāriṇe kumārakrīḍarūpadhāriṇe banda banda samayam anusmara sphaṭ sphaṭ svāhā* (*obstruct all defilements O you who hold the blue lotus O you who playfully bears the form of a prince! bind bind! remember your vow! hail!*)

76. *Mmk* 11.98.23–24.

77. *Mmk* 11.99.4–5.

78. Olivelle 1995:97; Sanskrit: 271.11–12.

79. Books mentioned at *Mmk* 11.109.27 for this purpose are: *Prajñāpāramitā, Candrapradīpasamādhi, Daśabhūmaka, Suvarṇaprabhāsottama, Mahāmāyurī,* and *Ratnaketudhāraṇī.*

80. Olivelle 1995:99, and 273.14.

81. *Mmk* 11.99.17–20.

82. This section is from *Mmk* 11.99.21–11.101.27.

83. In a prose section at *Mmk* 11.93.25, and in a verse section at *Mmk* 11.94.21–97.4.

84. See, for example, *Lakṣmītantra* XXI, verses 30–36 (Gupta 1972), *Jayākhyasaṃhitā* XVII, verses 46–62.

85. *Mmk* 11.95.14. The term *brahmacarin* is repeated here, too.

86. See Davis 1991:69f.

87. *Mmk* 2.50.12–13.

88. *Mmk* 1.23.15.

89. See Ray 1994:255ff. Ray argues that the *Aṣṭasāhasrikāprajñāpāramitā* presents a twofold *bodhisattva* ideal. The first type may be a layperson. The second type, however, is the higher ideal; he is a solitary forest renunciant.

90. *Mmk* 1.22.21–1.24.8.

91. Przyluski 1923:306.

92. *Mmk* 2.33.16–18.

93. Tucci 1949:216.

94. *Mmk* 33.346.17,20.

95. *Mmk* 33.346.26.

Chapter 5

1. Calvino 1972:117–118.

2. Beyer 1977:340.

3. See chapter 2, 2.4.

4. See chapter 3, 3.2.3.

5. Ibid.

6. See chapter 3, 3.2.2.

7. See chapter 3, 3.2.3.

8. *Mmk* 1.1.6–9.

9. Gómez 1977:225.

10. *Mmk* 2.25.17–18; 2.22–26.7.

11. *Mmk* 2.35.5–10.

12. Hardy 1994:143.

13. Przyluski 1923:301.

14. Cf. Imaeda 1981.

Appendixes

1. See Smith 1980 and Gonda 1977.

2. See Przyluski 1923:302, and Hobogirin:106, 283.

3. See MacDonald 1962:17.

4. The *paṭa* should be understood in place of *maṇḍala*. Later tradition used these terms interchangeably, and modern usage has reduced both to the term *maṇḍala*. The two are mixed up at *Mmk* 4.59.18–19. While the use of ground *maṇḍalas* are taught in the *Mmk* (e.g., at *Mmk* 3 [for magical manipulation toward various "mundane" ends; *Mmk* 2 [for the initiation ceremony]; and *Mmk* 11 [for eating rituals]), a *maṇḍala* is never used in the *Mmk* for "superior liberation." As far as I can determine, this is always the function of the *paṭa*.

5. The Tibetan text is out of order here. It should be read as follows: at 177.4.3 (89a) (*de skad ces . . . gsol pa daṅ*) skip to 178.6.2 (89b) (*'jam dpal gźon nur gyur pa la* [= middle of sentence 2]; continue to 180.1.3 (90a) (*byaṅ chub kyi . . . źugs so*). Including 177.4.2 (89a), this corresponds to *Mmk* 1.2.16–3.12. Read T.177.4.4 (89a) to 178.6.2 (89b) (*dar maṅ po'o . . . byas pa'i* [middle of sentence 2]), then skip to 180.1.4 (90b)ff: this is the continuation of *Mmk* 1.3.12ff. I would like to acknowledge John Dunne for bringing this to my attention.

6. Sanskrit *samavaśaraṇa* is not clear. It might make sense to translate as "refuge and vow" (°*va* > *ya*); but T. has *gźol ba*, "to be fixed." On the basis of this: *samavaśaraṇa* > *samavasthā* ?

7. In my translation of this, I follow the Sanskrit reading *matigati* against the Tibetan *gatimati* (258.4 [129b]). Lalou 1930:18, footnote 8, mentions that the Chinese, too, has *gatimati*. Kapstein 1995:247, footnote 16, translates *matigati.*

8. Inexplicably, the Sanskrit gives feminine *mañjubhāṣinī*. I translate the more consistent masculine form that the Tibetan gives.

9. The *daṇḍas* here are following V.2.23f.

10. As already mentioned, the Tibetan text is out of order here. As above, it should be read as follows: at 177.4.3 (89a) (*de skad ces . . . gsol pa daṅ*) skip to 178.6.2 (89b) (*'jam dpal gźon nur gyur pa la* [= middle of sentence 2]; continue to 180.1.3 (90a) (*byaṅ chub kyi . . . źugs so*). Including 177.4.2 (89a), this corresponds to *Mmk* 1.2.16–3.12. Read T.177.4.4 (89a) to 178.6.2 (89b) (*dar maṅ po'o . . . byas pa'i* [middle of sentence 2]), then skip to 180.1.4 (90b)ff: this is the continuation of *Mmk* 1.3.12ff.

11. As Lalou 1930:19, footnote 1 points out, the phrase *aviditagrāmyadharma* occurs at *Mmk* 2.47.9. There, too, it concerns a young girl (*kumārī*).

12. See Lalou 1930:16, note 2 for some references to this term in Buddhist literature. T. = *skyob pa*, helper, protector.

13. Lalou 1930:27, note 4.

14. Ibid., note 5.

15. Ibid., note 6.

16. Ibid., note 7.

17. Lalou 1930:29, note 1.

18. Lalou 1930:29, note 1 points out that *viceruḥ* is translated as *caryā* in the Chinese, and *vicaryā* in the Tibetan. The same form appears at *Mmk* 25.285.23 in a similar—and, grammatically, equally unclear—passage: *eṣa bhagavāṃ sarvajñaḥ buddhair mantrarūpeṇa vyavasthitaḥ / mahākāruṇikaḥ śāstā viceruḥ sarvadehinām //* "This [i.e., the *mantra bhrūm*] is the blessed omniscient one, who compassionately exists, with [all] *buddhas*, through the form of the *mantra*. Exalted, they wandered among those of various embodiments."

19. Lalou 1930:27, note 7.

20. T. *ri mo* translates S. *mānaḥ*, both of which can mean *likeness, drawing*. S. *mānanā, respecting, honoring*, is more consistent with the sense of the verse.

21. I follow T. here, which reads *empowered* (*byin gyis brlabs par 'gyur*). Edgerton (*BHSD*) suggests *abhyasto* (*practised, exercised*) for *avyaṣṭo*. See MacDonald 1962:141, footnote 2.

22. S. *lapane* > *layane*: T.150a.2: *gnas khaṅ,* settling.

23. T.298.3–4 (148b) has an extra, misplaced, verse here (*nas daṅ grol spyod pa daṅ*).

24. T.311.4 (156a) has an extra *pāda* here (*raṅ sṅags sṅags kyi mgon po daṅ*).

Bibliography

Abbreviations

BEFEO	*Bulletin de l'École française d'Extrême Orient*
BHSD	*Buddhist Hybrid Sanskrit Grammar and Dictionary*, by F. Edgerton
BHSG	*Buddhist Hybrid Sanskrit Grammar and Dictionary*, by F. Edgerton
HR	*History of Religions*
JA	*Journal asiatique*
JRAS	*Journal of the Royal Asiatic Society*
MW	*A Sanskrit-English Dictionary,* by M. Monier-Williams
PED	*Pali English Dictionary*, by T. W. Rhys Davids and W. Stede
WZKS	*Wiener Zeitschrift für die Kunde Südasiens*
ZDMG	*Zeitschrift der deutschen morgenländischen Gesellschaft*

Agrawala, Vasudeva, S. 1969. *The Deeds of Harsha (Being a Cultural Study of Bana's Harshacharita)*. Varanasi.

Alper, Harvey, P. (ed.). 1989. *Understanding Mantras.* New York.

Alper, Harvey. 1989b. "The Cosmos as Śiva's Language-Game: 'Mantra' According to Kṣemendra's *Śivasūtravimarśinī*." In Alper 1989: 240–294.

Alper, Harvey. 1989c. "A Working Bibliography for the study of Mantras." In Alper 1989:327–443.

Basham, A. L. 1959. *The Wonder that was India.* New York.

Bauddha Tantra Kosa (Part 1). 1990. Varanasi.

Belting, Hans. 1990. *Bild und Kult.* Munich.

Beyer, Stephan. 1973. *The Cult of Tārā.* Berkeley.

———. 1977. "Notes on the Vision Quest in Early Mahāyāna." In Lancaster 1977:329–340.

Boord, Martin. 1993. *The Cult of the Deity Vajrakīla* (Buddhica Britannica, vol. IV). Tring.

Brooks, Douglas Renfrew. 1990. *The Secret of the Three Cities.* Chicago.

———. 1992. *Auspicious Wisdom: The Texts and Traditions of Śrīvidyā Śākta Tantrism in South India*. Albany.

Brunner, Hélène. 1975. "Le *sādhaka*, personnage oublié du Śivaisme du sud." *JA* 263:411–443.

———. 1985. *Mṛgendrāgama: section des rites et section du comportement*. (Publications de l'institut français d'indologie, no. 69). Pondichery.

Burnouf, E. 1876. *Introduction a l'histoire du buddhisme indien*. Paris.

Calvino, Italo. 1972. *Invisible Cities*. New York.

Carmen, John B. and Marglin, Frédérique A. (eds.) 1985. *Purity and Auspiciousness in Indian Society*. Leiden.

Chandra, Lokesh. n.d. *Cultural Horizons of India*, vol. 3, New Delhi.

Collison, Robert. 1964. *Encyclopaedias: Their History Throughout the Ages*. New York.

Crosby, Kate and Skilton, Andrew. 1996. *The Bodhicaryāvatāra*. Oxford, New York.

Davidson, Ronald. 1995. "Atiśa's *A Lamp for the Path to Awakening*." In *Buddhism in Practice* (Donald Lopez, ed.). Princeton:290–301.

Davis, Richard. 1991. *Ritual in an Oscillating Universe*. Princeton.

Dunne, John. 1996. "Thoughtless Buddha, Passionate Buddha," *Journal of the American Academy of Religions*, LXIV/3, pp. 525–556.

Eckel, M. David. 1992. *To See the Buddha: A Philosopher's Quest for the Meaning of Emptiness*, Princeton.

Edgerton, Franklin. 1985 A. (1953) *Buddhist Hybrid Sanskrit Grammar and Dictionary*. Vol. I, Grammar. Madras.

———. 1985 B. (1953) *Buddhist Hybrid Sanskrit Grammar and Dictionary*. Vol. II, Dictionary. Madras.

Eimer, Helmut. 1993. "The Classification of the Buddhist Tantras According to the *Vajrajñanasamuccaya*," *WZKS* Supplementband:221–228.

Emmerick, R. E. 1970. *The Sūtra of Golden Light: being a translation of the Suvarṇaprabhāsottamasūtra*. London.

Faure, Bernard. 1996. *Visions of Power*. Princeton.

Gaṇḍavyūhasūtra (P. L. Vaidya, ed.). 1960. Mithila Institute of Post-graduate Studies and Research in Sanskrit Learning (Bauddha Samskṛta Pratyavali 5). Darbhanga, India.

Gellner, David N. 1992. *Monk, Householder, and Tantric Priest*. Cambridge.

George, Christopher. S. 1974. *The Caṇḍramahāroṣaṇa Tantra*. (American Oriental Series, vol. 56.) New Haven

Gombrich, Richard. 1975. "Ancient Indian Cosmology," in Carmen Blacker (ed.), *Ancient Cosmologies*. London:110–142.

Gómez, Luis O. 1977. "The Bodhisattva as Wonder-Worker." In Lancaster 1977:221–261.

———. 1996. *Land of Bliss: The Paradise of the Buddha of Measureless Light*. Honolulu.

Gonda, Jan. 1977a. *The Ritual Sutras*. (A History of Indian Literature, vol. I, fasc. 2.) Wiesbaden.

———. 1977b. *Medieval Religious Literature in Sanskrit*. (A History of Indian Literature, vol. II, fasc.1.) Wiesbaden.

———. 1980. *Vedic Ritual. The Non-Solemn Rites*. (Handbuch der Orientalistik. zweiter Abteilung: Indien; vierter Band: Religionen; erster Abschnitt: Vedic Ritual.) Leiden/Köln.

Griffiths, Paul J. 1994. *On Being Buddha: The Classical Doctrine of Buddhahood*. Albany.

Guenter, Herbert. 1971. *Life and Teachings of Naropa*. New York.

Gupta, Sanjukta, Hoens, Dirk Jan, Goudriaan, Teun. 1979. *Hindu Tantrism*. (Handbuch der Orientalistik, part II, India, vol. IV, Religions.) Leiden/Köln.

Gupta, Sanjukta (trans.). 1972. *Lakṣmī Tantra. A Pāñcarātra Text*. (Orientalia Rheno-Traiectina, vol. XV.) Leiden.

Gupta, Sanjukta. 1989. "The Pañcarātra Attitude to Mantra." In Alper 1989:224–248.

Gupta, Shashibhusan. 1969. *Obscure Religious Cults*. Calcutta.

Hacker, Paul. 1961. "Zur Methode der geschichtlichen Erforschung der anonymen Sanskritliteratur des Hinduismus." *ZDMG* 111/2:483–492.

Hallisey, Charles. 1995. "The Advice to Layman Tundila." In Lopez 1995:302–313.

Hardy, Friedhelm. 1994. *The Religious Culture of India: Power, Freedom and Love*. Cambridge.

Hock, Nancy. 1987. "Buddhist Ideology and the Sculpture of Ratnagiri, Seventh Through Thirteenth Centuries." Dissertation: Berkeley.

Hoens, Dirk Jan. 1979. "Tantric Transmission." In Gupta 1979:71–89.

Huntington, Susan and John. 1990. *Leaves from the Bodhi Tree: The Art of Pala India and Its International Legacy*. Dayton.

Imaeda, Yoshiro. 1981. "Un Extrait Tibétain du *Mañjuśrīmūlakalpa* dans les Manuscripts de Touen-Houang." In *Nouvelles Contributions de Touen-Houang*, Michel Soymié (ed.). Geneva:303–320.

Inden, Ronald. 1985. "Kings and Omens." In Carmen and Marglin 1985:30–37.

Iser, Wolfgang. 1980. "Interaction Between Text and Reader." In *The Reader in the Text: Essays on Audience and Interpretation*, Susan R. Suleiman and Inge Crosman (eds.). Princeton.

Iyengar, B.K.S. 1993. *Light on the Yoga Sūtras of Patañjali*. London.

Jackson, David. 1996. *A History of Tibetan Painting: The Great Tibetan Painters and their Traditions*. (Österreichische Akademie der Wissenschaften, Philosophisch-historische Klasse, Denkschriften, Vol. 242.) Vienna.

Jackson, David and Janice. 1984. *Tibetan Thangka Painting: Methods and Materials*. London.

Jauss, Hans Robert. 1982. *Toward an Aesthetic of Reception*. Minneapolis.

Jayākhysaṃhitā. Edited by E. Krishnamacharya. 1931. (Gaekwad's Oriental Series, no. 54.) Baroda.

Jayaswal, K. P. and Rāhula Saṅkṛityāyana. 1934. *An Imperial History of India in a Sanskrit Text*. Lahore.

Jhavery, Mohanlal, Bhagwandas. 1944. *Comparative and Critical Study of Mantraśāstra*. (Sri Jain Kala Sahitya Samsodhak Series, no. 1.) Ahmedabad.

Joshi, Lal Mani. 1967. *Studies in the Buddhistic Culture of India (During the 7th and 8th Centuries)*. Delhi.

Kapstein, Matthew. 1995. "Weaving the World: The Ritual Art of the *Pata* in Pala Buddhism and its legacy in Tibet." *HR*, vol. 34, no. 3 (February):241–262.

Katō, Bunnō (et al.). 1975. *The Three-fold Lotus Sutra*. Tokyo.

Kirfel, W. 1920. *Die Kosmographie der Inder*. Bonn.

Kloetzli, Randy. 1983. *Buddhist Cosmology*. New Delhi.

Kvaerne, Per. 1977. *An Anthology of Buddhist Tantric Songs: A study of the Caryāgiti*. Oslo.

Lalou, M. 1930. *Iconographie des Étoffes Peintes (Paṭa) dans le Mañjuśrīmūlakalpa*. Paris.

———. 1932. "Un traité de magie bouddhique." *Études d'Orientalisme, publiées par le Musée Guimet a la mémoire de Raymonde Linossier*. Paris: 303–322.

Lamotte, Etienne. 1962. *L'Enseignement de Vimalakīrti (Vimalakīrtinirdeśa)*. (Publications de l'institut orientaliste de Louvain 35.) Louvain.

Lancaster Lewis (ed.). 1977. *Prajñāpāramitā and Related Systems: Studies in Honor of Edward Conze*. (Berkeley Buddhist Studies Series 1.) Berkeley.

La Vallee Poussin, Louis de. 1910 "Cosmogony and Cosmology (Buddhist)." In *Encyclopedia of Religion and Ethics*:129–138.

Lessing, Ferdinand D. and Wayman, Alex (trans.). 1968. *Mkhas grub rje's Fundamaentals of the Buddhist Tantras*. The Hague.

Lopez, Donald S. 1995. *Buddhism in Practice*. Princeton.

Mair, Victor. 1988. *Painting and Performance. Chinese Picture Recitation and Its Indian Genesis*. Honolulu.

Majumdar, A. K. (gen. ed.). 1984. *The Age of the Imperial Kanauj*. (The History and Culture of the Indian People, vol. IV.) Bombay.

Makransky, John. 1997. *Buddhahood Embodied: Sources of Controversy in India and Tibet*, Albany.

Mahāyānasūtrasaṅgraha (P. L. Vaidya, ed.). 1964. Buddhist Sanskrit Texts Part II, no. 18, Bihar.

Malandra, Geri H. 1993. *Unfolding a Maṇḍala: the Buddhist cave temples at Ellora*. New York.

de Mallmann, Marie-Thérèse. 1964. *Étude iconographique sur Mañjuśrī*. Paris

Mañjuśrīmūlakalpa (T. Gaṇapati Śāstrī, ed. [as *Āryamañjuśrīmūlakalpa*]) Trivandrum Sanskrit Series: Part I = no. LXX, 1920; Part II = LXXVI, 1922; Part III = LXXXIV, 1925. Trivandrum.

Matsunaga, Yūkei. 1985. "On the Date of the *Mañjuśrīmūlakalpa*." In *Tantric and Taoist Studies in Honour of R. A. Stein*, Michel Strickmann (ed.), vol. 3, in vol. 22 of *Mélanges Chinois et Bouddhiques*. Brussels:882–894.

MacDonald, Ariane. 1962. *Le Maṇḍala du Mañjuśrīmūlakalpa*. Paris.

Meisezahl, R. O. 1980. *Geist und Ikonographie des Vajrayāna-Buddhismus. Hommage a Marie-Thérese de Mallmann*. (Beiträge zur Zentralasienforschung, vol. 2.) Sankt Augustin.

Munitz, Milton K. 1986. *Cosmic Understanding*. Princeton.

Mus, Paul. 1928. "Le Buddha Paré." In *BEFEO* vol. 28, 1–2:152–278.

———. 1935. *Barabudur*. Volume I. Hanoi.

Nakamura, Hajime. 1989. *Indian Buddhism: A Survey with Bibliographical Notes*. Delhi

Obermiller, E. 1935. "Buston's History of Buddhism and the *Mañjuśrīmūlakalpa*." *JRAS* (1935, part 2): 299–306.

O'Flaherty, Wendy. 1975. *Hindu Myths*. London and New York.

Olivelle, Patrick. 1995. *Rules and Regulations of Brahmanical Asceticism*. Albany.

Payne, Richard Karl. 1990. *The Tantric Ritual of Japan. Feeding the Gods: The Shingon Fire Ritual*. (Śata-Piṭaka Series, vol. 365.) Delhi.

Padoux, André. 1990. *Vāc*. New York.

Pagel, Ulrich. 1995. *The Bodhisattvapiṭaka. Its Doctrine, Practices, and Their Position in Mahāyāna Literature*. (Buddhica Britannica, no. 5.) Tring, U.K.

Pranke, Patrick. 1995. "Becoming a Buddhist Wizard." In Lopez 1995:343–358.

Pryzluski, Jean. 1923. "Les Vidyārāja, contribution a l'histoire de la magie dans les sectes Mahāyānistes." *BEFEO*, XXIII:301–318.

Ray, Reginald. 1994. *Buddhist Saints of India. A Study in Buddhist Values and Orientations*. New York, Oxford.

Renou, Louis and Filliozat, Jean. 1953. *L'inde classique: manuel des études indiennes*. Paris.

Ruegg, David Seyfort. 1964. "Sur les rapports entre le Bouddhism et le 'substrat religieux' Indien et Tibétan." *JA*, vol. 152: 77–95.

Rhys Davids, T. W. and Stede, William. 1986 (1921) *The Pāli Text Society's Pali English Dictionary*. London.

Sanderson, Alexis. 1988. "Meaning in Tantric Ritual." In *Essais sur le Ritual III*. (A.-M. Blondeau and K. Schipper, eds.). Paris.

Schopen, Gregory. 1978. "The *Baiṣajyaguru-Sūtra* and the Buddhism of Gilgit." Dissertation: Australian National University.

Smith, H. Danial. 1975. *A Descriptive Bibliography of the Printed Texts of the Pañcarātrāgama, vol. I*. (Gaekwad's Oriental Series, no. 158.) Baroda.

———. 1980. *A Descriptive Bibliography of the Printed Texts of the Pañcarātrāgama, vol. II: an annotated index to selected topics*. (Gaekwad's Oriental Series, no. 168.) Baroda.

Smith, Jonathan Z. 1982. *Imagining Religion*. Chicago.

———. 1987. *To Take Place*. Chicago.

Snellgrove, David L. 1987. *Indo-Tibetan Buddhism*. London.

Suttanipāta. Translated by H. Saddhatissa 1985. London.

Suvarṇaprabhasottamasūtra (S. Bagchi, ed.). 1967. Mithila Institute of Post-graduate Studies and Research in Sanskrit Learning (Bauddha Samskṛta Pratyavali 8). Darbhanga, India.

Tambiah, Stanley. 1985. *Culture, Thought and Action*. Cambridge, Mass.

Tsuda, Shinichi. 1974. *The Saṃvarodayatantra*. Tokyo.

Tucci, Guiseppe. 1949. *Tibetan Painted Scrolls*. Rome.

de la Vallée Poussin, Louis. 1898. *Bouddhisme: études et matériaux*. London.

van Gulik, R. H. 1959. *Chinese Pictorial Art as Viewed by the Connoisseur*. Rome.

Warder, A. K. 1991 (1970). *Indian Buddhism*. Delhi.

Watanabe, Kaikioku. 1912. *Die Bhadracarī. Eine Probe buddhistisch-religiöser Lyrik*. Leipzig.

Monier-Williams, Monier. 1986 (1899) *A Sanskrit-English Dictionary*. Varanasi.

Index

A

ābhicāruka (and variants *ābhicāraka, ābhicārika*), 121, 123, 174, 176, 177, 179. *See also* malediction.
abhijñā. *See ṛddhi*; supernatural power.
abhiṣeka, 2, 4, 12, 130, 243 n. 33
  definition of, 138
  as rebirth, 137
  ritual, 130, 131–138, 173
  secrecy of, 132–133
  types of, 139, 141, 143–145, 147, 153. *See also maṇḍala.*

ācārya, 12, 109, 111, 129, 130, 137, 138, 174
  as *bodhisattva*, 155–156
  as "father," 137, 143
  characteristics of, 154–155
  definition of, 153
  as human exemplar, 155
  initiation of, 153–154
  as initiation master (*maṇḍalācārya*), 130, 131, 133–134
  and Mañjuśrī, 132, 138
  power of, 157–158
adhiṣṭhāna, 64, 83, 96
Advice to the layman Tuṇḍila, 60
Akaniṣṭha, 2, 73, 79
ākarṣana. *See* attraction.
Alper, Harvey, 50, 54, 165
Amitābha/Amitāyus, 122, 176
anuttarapūjā. *See pūjā.*
astrology/astronomy (*jyotiṣajñāna*), 99–100, 114–115, 131, 175, 176, 177, 179
Asaṅga, 13
Atharvaveda, 48, 128
attraction (rituals of: *ākarṣaṇa*), 16, 19, 20, 22, 70, 179
augury, 116–117, 125, 175–176, 177
auspiciousness, 48, 99, 110, 112, 114, 115, 116–117, 119, 120, 125, 135, 175, 177
Avalokiteśvara, 156
avataṃsaka, 230 n. 26

B

Belting, Hans, 89–90
Beyer, Stephan, 41, 58, 160
Bild und Kult, 89
bhaginī, 179
Bodhisattvabhūmi, 13
Bodhicaryāvatāra, 29
bodhisattvapiṭaka, 13, 230 n. 25
bodhisattva vow, 27, 28, 36, 156. *See also* Mañjuśrī: convention or vow; *samaya.*
bodhisattvavikurvaṇa. *See vikurvaṇa.*
bhaginī, 6
bhikṣāhāra, 129
Boord, Martin, 176
Brunner, Hélène, 143
Buddha/*buddha*
  accessibility of, x, 1, 2, 28, 32–33, 73, 74–76, 77, 78, 91, 95, 96, 102, 105, 107, 109, 110, 112, 117, 131, 155, 161, 162, 165

N

P